COASTING CAPTAIN

Schooner City of Baltimore.

COASTING CAPTAIN

Journals of

CAPTAIN LEONARD S. TAWES

*Relating His Career in Atlantic
Coastwise Sailing Craft
from 1868 to 1922*

EDITED FOR THE MUSEUM BY

ROBERT H. BURGESS

The Mariners Museum

NEWPORT NEWS, VIRGINIA

1967

First Printing, 1967
Second Printing, 1968

MUSEUM PUBLICATION NO. 28

❖

Library of Congress Catalog No. 67-17219

Copyright 1967 by The Mariners Museum, Newport News, Virginia

PRINTED IN U.S.A. BY WHITTET & SHEPPERSON, RICHMOND, VIRGINIA

Foreword

Captain Leonard S. Tawes was my grandfather. He was a slender man of wiry build, somewhat above medium height, with skin permanently bronzed by the sun of the tropics, and deep-set blue-gray eyes.

He retired from the sea at the age of fifty-three but there was nothing passive about his retirement. He despised idleness and remained busy throughout his life. "Captain Len," as he was familiarly known in our town of Crisfield, Maryland, never quite left the sea behind him. At that time Crisfield was the center of the oyster industry so he and a partner went into the oyster business. They had private oyster beds in Pocomoke Sound near the Maryland-Virginia line and, to protect their beds from oyster pirates, they had a shanty built on piling. They hired a regular watchman and grandfather was pleased to take on the job of relief watchman. Although Pocomoke Sound was a poor substitute for the Atlantic Ocean, it was deep water and the shanty site was almost out of sight of land. I am sure that grandfather enjoyed all the time he spent there.

The shanty looked like a one room Noah's Ark with an open porch all around. It was covered with black tar paper and there was a terra cotta chimney jutting out of the roof. Inside there was an iron cookstove, a table, two chairs, and a cupboard for dishes and pans, and two bunks. Grandfather referred to it as "snug," which carried the connotation that it was rather wonderful. It was here on winter nights, when the wind sent the water of the Sound splashing against the piling of the shanty, that grandfather began to write his journals. With the light from an oil lantern, pencils that he sharpened with his pocket knife, and a composition book, he began to recount his long life with the sea.

For years my grandfather's friends had urged him to write the stories that he told when he met with them on bad days at The Crisfield Hardware Store. They would gather around the pot-bellied stove sitting in rocking chairs, with latecomers perched on nail kegs while grandfather told his tales of Atlantic storms and of strange ports like Cayenne and Rio Grande do Sul that these bay captains would never see. The decision to write the journals was not made here, however, but came as a result of a visit from his first grandchild in 1925.

My cousin, Mary Anne, lived with her parents in Cambridge, Maryland. Their visits to us were infrequent because her father, Dr. P. H. Tawes, was a busy country doctor and stayed close to his practice. During a spring vacation Mary Anne came to visit us and grandfather took her for a trip to his shanty. They made the journey in his fourteen-foot motor launch that he had named the *Corn Cob*. It was during this visit that grandfather realized that Mary Anne was interested in, and wanted to hear more, about his travels. He knew, too, that the following year she would be entering college and that there would never be the time to tell the stories she wanted to hear. It was for her that the journals were written.

I have always lived in my grandfather's house and for the first fifteen years of my life grandfather was here too, until his death in 1932. My mother, grandmother, grandfather and myself made up our family. Grandfather was the only father I ever knew. While he was admittedly disappointed that I was not a boy he had certain standards for rearing girls, too. So many women spend their lives being afraid of things! To him this was foolishness.

We always sat in rocking chairs on our front porch during thunderstorms. This was when grandfather would tell me of storms at sea until the limbs of our old pecan tree would become for me the spars of a ship and I could know a storm in all of its awesomeness and beauty. I looked forward to a summer storm in the way that most children look forward to a movie.

Then there were our hunting expeditions. For some unknown reason women seemed to be afraid of mice so this fear too must be dispelled. When I was very young grandfather and I would go out to the old corn house to hunt for mouse beds. We were usually accompanied on these expeditions by our "Tom Cat" who made away with our discoveries.

On nights when grandfather and I would be walking home from church service, or from paying calls to friends, he would teach me the names of the stars and how to locate them. Or we would practice naming the sails of a ship—I always had trouble with jibs. I remember how I disliked New Year's Day because this was the one day of the year I could not accompany him. He would start out shortly after breakfast to pay his New Year calls. Dressed in his Sunday best he would walk through the front gate and up the road to make his rounds of New Year greetings for luck. I, being of the unlucky sex, had to be left at home.

Visits from grandfather's brother, John, who had sailed with him as mate on his three-masted schooner, *City of Baltimore,* and had also sailed in the China trade between San Francisco and Hong Kong, were highlights of my childhood. The two old sailors would sit for hours talking of their voyages. Then, there were visits from Uncle John's two sons, Vernon and Montford, who had made the change from sailing vessels to steamships. Both had served in World War I. Vernon was then captain of a merchant ship plying between New York and Genoa, Italy. Later he was a pilot on the Panama Canal and Director of the Port of Cristobal. He had begun his sea career before the mast on the coffee barkentine *Josephine.* He is now retired and living in Ft. Lauderdale, Florida.

Uncle John's older son, Montford, had been captain of a mine layer in the North Sea during World War I. When I remember his visits he was first officer on the *S. S. Leviathan.*

It was during one of Montford's visits that grandfather expressed a wish to make a crossing to Europe. All of his experience had been coastwise and to South America. He was fascinated by Montford's description of his ship, the *Levia-than,* one of the largest ships that had ever been built. Of course it would never have occurred to grandfather to travel as a passenger on a vessel. What he wanted was a job.

Montford took the problem to Captain Herbert Hartley, master of the liner, and soon a telegram arrived offering grandfather a billet as "sailmaker" for the *Leviathan.* So grandfather signed on for three voyages to mend deck chairs and awnings. I am sure that no sailmaker ever was granted such status. He had the run of the ship and spent more time in the pilot house than elsewhere. The year was 1923; I found it written on the fly leaf of a copy of Wood's *Natural History* that grandfather brought me from London.

When grandfather left home for his job on the *Leviathan* he had carefully packed his quadrant and taken it along. On his second voyage one of the big ship's modern navigational instruments failed, and grandfather was indeed proud that he had been able to figure, as well as any of the officers, the great ship's exact position. Grandfather was astounded by the ease of the life of the modern sailor compared to that which he had known, but he was concerned about their dependency on mechanical devices.

In the late twenties, with his ocean voyages all behind him and the oyster business sold, grandfather again picked up the thread of his still unfinished journals. This time his study was the summer kitchen. The summer kitchen was at the back of our house and connected with it by a passageway. In summer it was a busy place for all the cooking was done there in order to keep the rest of the house cool. In winter it was cold and deserted.

Grandfather took it over in the winter and it became a wonderful, comfortable place. He kept a fire in the coal burning cook-stove and there was always a granite ware coffee pot on the back of the stove for his innumerable cups of coffee.

There was a gas jet above his work table that continued to sing like an out-of-season cicada. On the table were his usual composition books plus a stack of the carefully written logs of the *City of Baltimore*. These were his reference books if his memory failed on an exact date. For three winters he worked. He would disappear into his study after supper and he would still be at work when the rest of the family went to bed. The summer kitchen was completely his domain except for the cat that slept quietly in a chair, and for my nightly intrusions. When my lessons were finished I could visit in the summer kitchen for half an hour. These visits were very special. Grandfather would tell me what voyage he was writing about and as he stopped his work for coffee he would share with me some special treat; sometimes it would be hardtack and a piece of mousetrap-cheese, or smoked herring warmed in the oven, or sardines which we had to share with the cat.

Grandfather had a dignified humility that one seldom meets. He felt that he had been thrust out into the world very early in life and that given the same set of circumstances most persons would have had to work as hard and be deprived of as much if they were to survive. There were two points of pride, however, that he did feel set him somewhat apart from other men. One was in his skill as a navigator. This was no doubt his most difficult achievement. He had little formal education and to master this skill with the mathematical expertness involved was a remarkable achievement. Recognition of his ability in this area was made when he was called upon to teach navigation to merchant seamen in World War I. In the last year of the war he also served as Resident Inspector at the M. M. Davis Shipbuilding Company, Solomon's Island, Maryland, inspecting the work on government contracts of that company.

I remember clearly the second point of pride. During the summer of 1928 grandfather spent long hours studying the navigational handbooks published by the Government Printing Office. One day he announced that he had to make a business trip to Baltimore and he left that evening on the steamer. He always looked forward to these trips on bay steamers, for these captains were his friends. Three days later he was back, a proud and happy man. He had renewed his Masters' licenses, all three of them: Master, Sailing Vessels; Master, Steamships; and Master, Inland Waterways. He was seventy-five years old at the time and the examiner was frank to say that it was the first time he had issued the three licenses to the same man in the same day. Grandfather made a sturdy oak frame for his three licenses and hung them in his room. They still hang there.

In the fall of 1931 grandfather's health began to fail. The journals were finished and he spent more time reading his newspapers and working on his business affairs. In the spring of 1932 a diagnosis of terminal illness was made. Slowly he seemed to fade, never complaining but each day growing a little weaker. He died of pneumonia on December 6, 1932, in his Crisfield home and was buried in Crisfield Cemetery.

Elizabeth W. Hall
Crisfield, Maryland

Introduction

It is doubtful if it ever occurred to Captain Tawes, when he was writing his journals, that they would be read publicly. As his granddaughter, Miss Elizabeth W. Hall, wrote in the Foreword, they were written for her cousin in particular, and the immediate family. To him, the story he wanted to tell was just a part of his workaday world. Being so close to the picture he probably wasn't aware that he had anything too unusual to relate. But apparently he did want members of his family to know something about his seagoing career.

Unconsciously, however, he was documenting a phase of American shipping about which relatively little has been recorded. This is the trade of the American coasting schooner which plied the east coast and carried the bulk of the cargoes before the intervention of the steamer.

It is felt that these journals are unique in that they portray a vivid account of the operation of a schooner from the economical and navigational viewpoint. They not only present a valuable insight of the coasting trade but also that of the Chesapeake Bay area. To the knowledge of The Mariners Museum nothing like these have been published. It is very likely they may be the only account of the entire career of an American schooner captain.

Much has been written about square-riggers, their hardships, and world-wide wanderings. Some of the difficult circumstances described by Captain Tawes rival those encountered on deep-water passages of the larger sailing ships to which so much romance has been attached. Many of the volumes about the square-riggers deal only with a single voyage. Captain Tawes faithfully records just about every passage he ever made under sail from 1868 to 1922.

When Captain Tawes started to work on his journals he relied solely on his memory. Later on, when he reached the section concerning the schooner *City of Baltimore* which he skippered for 20 years, 5 months, and 9 days, he referred to that vessel's logs which he had preserved. However, these were used merely to check a date or passage or to bring some event to mind. Then he would reach back in his memory and elaborate upon that event. When the journals were edited for this publication the log books were borrowed to double check on dates and passages. The journals agreed with the logs.

On one occasion, when he raced the *City of Baltimore* against the *City of Jacksonville,* from Jacksonville to Baltimore, he wrote in his journals that the Baltimore newspapers ran a headline that he had beaten his opponent. To verify this your editor referred to several months of the *Baltimore American* for 1887 at the Enoch Pratt Library, Baltimore. In the issue of March 24 there was a 6-inch long column headed *Captain Tawes Wins Again.* This is reproduced in the text.

Perhaps Captain Tawes would have objected to the title of this volume, implying that he was a *Coasting Captain.* According to a modern maritime dictionary the American coasting trade in its legal sense indicates a trade between only United States ports and/or those of its possessions. It is called intercoastal when between ports separated by foreign waters or territory. Captain Tawes engaged in both of these. He sailed to the West Indies, Caribbean and Gulf ports, and South America which would eliminate him from the strict category of being a coasting captain.

Many a deep-water sailor looked upon a coaster with some disdain. But coasting had its perplexities in the form of fogs in heavily traveled waters, shoals, frequent storms, and aggravating experiences with pilots and tugboatmen. Some of Captain Tawes' most trying times took place along the coast. Most of his sea time was spent in coasting schooners. He never crossed the Atlantic except in the role of sailmaker on the liner *Leviathan.* He never even saw the Pacific Ocean. So, in his

Introduction

"glorious immortality where it is one bright summer always and storms never come," it is hoped he will look favorably upon the title.

Captain Tawes was a frugal man in the operation of his schooners. He always tried to save money for his owners by evading pilotage and towage. The accounts of his experiences with pilots and tugboatmen make amusing reading and offer an interesting contrast to the present day operation of these maritime services. In his effort to save a dollar he took chances on occasion but he and his vessels always came through unscathed and with that much more to show on the credit side of the ledger.

I would have liked to have known Captain Tawes personally. Through his writings he emerges as a plain, kindly, fair man. He did not expect his men to do what he would not consider doing himself. He seemed to have been the type of person one could admire and hold in great respect.

I did know first-hand his last command, the four-masted schooner *Purnell T. White*. With her excessive sheer and graceful lines, she impressed me when I was but a youngster. I considered her the loveliest of the coasting schooners sailing out of Baltimore in my day. Following her through her abandonment in a Baltimore ship graveyard in 1935, I salvaged her port quarterboard. As I edited these journals this carving hung above my desk and helped me relive Captain Tawes' experiences on this schooner. Her eagle figurehead reposes in the den of my home. Memories of that fine vessel and her captain, whom I learned to hold in great admiration as I pored over his journals, have been ever present.

When Miss Hall first brought these journals to my attention I started reading them and found it difficult to set them aside. Here I found a rare first-hand account of coasting schooners of the latter part of the 19th century. However, it was difficult to read them in their original form. There were no sentences as separated by punctuation. Capitalization and periods were used inadvertently. There were no paragraphs.

The journals consist of 758 pages written in pencil in 11 blue-lined note books. When The Mariners Museum decided to publish these it was felt that they should be refined to a certain degree to facilitate reading. The museum trustees, however, specified that none of the flavor of Captain Tawes' writing be tampered with. In his own way he captured a feeling that would have been lost if his work had been transposed or altered. To clarify the text, yet make no pretense at trying to make the story scholarly, a paucity of punctuation and paragraphs was added. Misspelling was left as it appeared in the journals except in instances where Captain Tawes' version would have been distracting to the reader. In the cases of errors in the names of ships, firms, persons, and places, where they could be verified, they were corrected.

The original journals are in the possession of Captain Tawes' granddaughter, Mrs. Herman H. Hoene of Baltimore, for whom they were written. Miss Hall owns the 14 log books kept by Captain Tawes on the *City of Baltimore*. Also in her possession is the W. P. Stubbs painting of that schooner used as a frontispiece in this volume. These descendants of Captain Tawes have been most cooperative in allowing The Mariners Museum the use of this material and permitting it to be published and more widely circulated.

ROBERT H. BURGESS
Curator of Exhibits
The Mariners Museum
Newport News, Virginia

Contents

Illustrations

COASTING CAPTAIN

I

1853–1873

Born in Accomack County, Virginia, October 2, 1853, I was looked upon sickly and weakly while my two brothers and my sister were healthy and hardy. My father and mother kept a county store and had two small farms they tended. My mother died with pneumonia when I was just seven years old. That was the worst blow of my life for everything went bad with us then and many years after. My mother's dying request was that my sister should be boarded at my Aunt Ann's. She was then seven years old. My father kept us together for three years. He also kept his little store but being a bad manager all of his resources were gone. That is when we were all put out to different homes. I went to live with an old doctor to open gates for him.

In those days in Virginia fence laws were in vogue. Nights when I was not out with him I used to cut up wood and bring it in, prepare kindling to make fires of mornings, and do chores around the house. They were good to me but boy-like I only stayed one year. I wanted to get near the neighborhood where I was raised and to see the people that I knew. I made the mistake to leave old Doctor Kellam and go back to live with my father. This time I fared badly. I had to try to cook what little I got to eat which I did not know how to do. Finally, I was hired to a foreman to work at $15 per year which was not sufficient to buy my clothes. The next year I got $25 per and worked day in and day out all the year round. I never had a cent to buy candy and cakes and no time for amusements. The Civil War had just closed, or about so, and people in the south were hard pressed from the effects of it. Everybody had to live close to meet their honest debts which made my chances worse than they would have been.

In the fall of 1868 I left the farm and went dredging as cook on a pungy boat at $6 per month. I was then 15 years old. I dredged all winter and suffered much misery. I had only two little cotton shirts and they were getting so black and dirty I thought I must wash them. I got some rosin soap and drew up some salt water to wash them. I did not know that you could not wash with salt water. I soaped my two shirts and tried to wash them and to my astonishment my shirts were worse than ever. Well, well, I certainly was missing home and mother then. I here advise all children who have a mother to be good and kind to her and make her labor as light as they can because you will never have but one mother. She will never be replaced when gone.

Well, the captain of this dredge boat pungy took me home with him. His good wife washed my shirts and otherwise cleaned me up. She knit me a pair of mittins and made me 2 pairs of underpants which were the first I ever had though 15 years of age. Children of 4 have underpants and overcoats too. I was 22 years of age before I ever had an overcoat.

After the dredging season was over we ran fish on the Potomac River from Freestone Point to Washington. In June of 1869, the fish run being over, I went to a farm of my aunt and uncle, near Crisfield. Then I got nice regular living and was not overworked. They were well fixed people and lived nicely. I helped on this farm the balance of the year of 1869.

My uncle had built for his son a schooner called the *Lizzie Bell* which was launched early in 1870. I went with their son George as cook. We made a trip or two with oysters to Baltimore. After this we loaded Irish potatoes on the seaside and went to New York. When we went in the foot of Vesey Street our consignee, a Mr. Waddy, asked me to go up to Dey Street one day to his office and get some billheads. On my way up through Washington Market I saw my first pineapples. They certainly smelled appetizing to me. I asked a man what they were. He told me and then said, "Did you never see one before? You must be from the country, are you?" "Yes," I replied, "I was never in New York before." So I bought one and paid 15¢ for it. I peeled it and began going along eating it and at the same time looking for Dey Street. Pretty soon two rough boys approached me and asked what I was looking for. I told them. They said, "Come with us. We will show you." They led me to an empty front stall in Washington Market where no one was. I saw I was in a trap. They then said, "You belong on that boat down there don't you?" I said, "Yes." They said, "How much money have you got?" I said, "None." They then grabbed hold of me and took my $1.50 and in the melee I lost my pineapple. Thus was my beginning with pineapples. I went immediately on board with my shirt torn. Shirts were scarce with me in those days, too. I told Mr. Waddy I could not find his office and he had to send someone else.

After this I made 3 more voyages to New York; one with watermelons from King's Creek, now Cape Charles, Virginia, and in the fall I went twice from Metomkin Inlet, on the seaside, with sweet potatoes. It was now late in October, 1870. Then I left the *Lizzie Bell* and shipped on a Jersey schooner, the *E. S. Brady*, as cook at $15 per month. This was a big raise from $6, the wages I was getting in the *Lizzie Bell*.

My new captain, Henry Loper, was from Elizabethport, New Jersey. He was afterwards drowned in the Mississippi

River. He came near being drowned while I was with him. Beating down the Maurice River one chilly afternoon, while tacking, he was pulling the mainsail over and by some misfortune he lost hold on the main sheet and went backward overboard and we never saw him go over. We were tending the fore sheet and jib sheet, but fortunately we were towing the yawl astern. He caught the yawl, got in her, and climbed on board before any of us missed him. He said, "You are a hell of nice set aren't you? Would let a man drown and not attempt to save his life." I sailed with him until Christmas. We were frozen in at Millville, New Jersey. Here I was paid off. I had been with him 2 months and 9 days and had not drawn a cent of my wages, so he paid me $34.50.

Then the next thing was for me to get back to Crisfied and I did not know how to travel. I had never traveled on a train or a steamboat in my life, but I was shown the railroad station. Then I bought a ticket to Camden, New Jersey. On my way I met a man I had met before on a vessel in Little Egg Harbor, New Jersey, while in there for a harbor. I was very glad to meet him for I would never have been able to have found my way from Camden, New Jersey, to Broad Street station without his assistance. My first idea was to go to Crisfield from Philadelphia but after falling in with this man I felt so much more protected that I changed my mind and came to Baltimore with him.

There is one instance I will always remember with much gratitude as long as I live. When I went to buy my ticket I asked the price. The agent told me. I nervously put the money down but somehow in doing so I must have asked him if he could not make the fare less. He said, "Give me the ticket back," and he wrote on it "Poor boy only" and gave me half my money back. That certainly was a big favor to me. I then rode in the same car with this man that I met at Little Egg Harbor to Baltimore.

Arriving at Baltimore I went along at the head of the Basin and then I met old Captain Bill Nelson in the schooner *Abraham P. Upshur*. Captain Bill took me in and I stayed on board with him all night. After breakfast I went to an old Jew named Greentree on Pratt Street. Here I bought the first whole suit of clothes of my life. Never before got more than one piece at the time. I had to take his word about the fitting, for I was no judge in those days about clothes fitting. After this purchase I then proceeded along the docks to find a boat going to Crisfield. Down to the city block I came across a pungy called the *Melissa and Wesley*, commanded by a Captain Pierson, going down to Fairmount. He gave me a passage down and after I helped him to dredge two days in Tangier Sound he put me on a sloop going in to Crisfield. I then went to my Aunt Leah Sterling. She was one of the best old women in the world. She always gave me a home with her whenever I returned from anywhere.

Now 1871 is getting along. I went on board the *Lizzie Bell* again as cook dredging. After the dredging season was over I shipped in a pungy called the *Emma A. Walsh*. I did not stay here long because I did not like the captain, especially after he went up at a place called Worton Creek. There we found a lot of wood corded up on the shore. He, a colored man, and myself took a lighter that was on the shore and nearly loaded that pungy before morning. When I got back to Baltimore I quit him because I was afraid I might get in jail though I was only a boy. Arriving in Baltimore I shipped in a pungy belonging to Smith Island. Her name was the *Romeo*. Captain Lou Evans and myself brought the pungy down to Smith Island. I stayed that summer and helped to paint the house and worked their lot and garden for what I got to eat. But these people were very kind to me. I dredged with them the next winter.

Spring of 1872 was now fast advancing. The oyster season was drawing to a close and I did not want to be idle another summer as I was the last one. In Baltimore, at the head of or along Bowley's Wharf, as it was called in those days, there was a bark loading flour for Rio de Janeiro. I stood there and looked at the flour being hoisted and had a longing to go. I felt how I would love to go in her. I asked the captain for a berth. He asked me several questions as to my ability and if I could steer. I told him I could not keep her perfectly on her course. Sometimes she would get a ¼ of a point off her course. Then he asked me if I knew the compass. I told him I did so he shipped me at $15 per month.

After we finished loading we left Bowley's Wharf on Monday morning, the 8th day of April, 1872. Was there ever as green a boy as I; raw material if there ever was. When the sailors came on board with their chests of clothing, oils, and sea boots it scared me to see my little kit. When the sailors began to take out their tin pot, a pot that would hold very nearly a quart of coffee or tea, a tin to eat out of, and a spoon that they could eat soup with, I did not know what to think. I asked them what they were going to do with them. They said, "To eat out of. Have you none?" I said, "No." "Well," they said, "you had better to quick and get you an outfit. The tow boat will be here soon and you will fare bad if you have nothing to eat out of." I ran up the street and bought me a tin, pan, a spoon, knife, fork, and tin pot. You see I labored under the impression that I slept forward in the forecastle but ate in the cabbin with the captain. That was a big disappointment to me when I came to realize the truth of it.

Well, we towed down to Curtis Creek; that was about as far as any vessel towed in those days. Here we anchored, the wind being ahead. Now we began to make all preparations for sea. We caulked the hatches, lashed the water casks for there were 8 or 10 of these on deck, and we lashed the spare spars. We had about 4 of these on deck so if we carried off any of the masts we could rig up another and keep going on our voyage. My job was to stow away the wood down the hold on top of the flour. It seemed to me that there was a big lot of it too but I did not know we were going on a voyage of more than 5,000 miles. If I had I do believe I should have backed out.

Well, we worked Monday all day, then Tuesday all day getting the bark ready, such as greasing the mast which fell to me to do. Then we put on chafing gear and God knows what all. Such work as I was never used to. Tuesday night it was squally and rainy, much thunder and lightening. I was keeping anchor watch and the light blew out. I had to go up the rigging and get it down. Oh, my I was scared when I was ordered to go up and bring it down out of the rigging. I was so scared of lightening and thunder but I have heard thunder and seen it lighten so many million times since that I would think nothing of a little job like that now.

The next morning being Wednesday, April the 10th, the wind had come out from the northwest and being a fair wind we proceeded to get under way early. We hove our anchor short to the bow and then so many orders were given, one after another, such as I had never heard before this being the first square-rigger I was ever on board. It was loose the fore topsail and set it, loose the jibs and hoist them up. Now break out the anchor and the way we payed off and began running down the Patapsco River. The sailors were flying around first aloft loosing sails and alow to set. I was running around following and doing what I could but this was new business to me. In a short time we had the main topsail on her. The topgallant sails and even the royals were set. Before we got down to the Seven Foot Knoll we were fully underway and had the anchor on the bow.

I forget when we did eat breakfast but by the time we got down to Sandy Point the wind hit us so suddenly hard that the bark heeled over so low that 5 or 6 of her deck seams were under water. The captain, Robert Clark by name and a good man he was too, yelled out with a quick and commanding voice, "Let her come up to the wind." When she came up in the wind the blocks, tacks, and sheets began to flap and make so much noise that I dived under the bulwark to keep from being killed. At the same time the captain ordered the royals clewed up and furled. I was scared I would be ordered aloft to furl the royals as I was supposed to be the royal boy. But while I was still concealed under the weather bulwarks two able seamen sprang quickly aloft to furl the fore and main royals and to my surprise and astonishment just as they reached the topgallant yards both of their hats blew off simultaneously and the last seen of these two hats they were racing like 2 cannon balls for Kent Island on the Eastern Shore. I never heard whether they ever landed at Kent Island or not. We then took in our topgallant sails and went down the bay under topsails. All light sails were furled away.

The next morning, Thursday, we were at Cape Henry and put off our pilot and the apprentice on the pilot boat and proceeded to sea. When we were from the sight of the land the mate reported to the captain that there was a bark away off on the lee bow with his flag up and wanted to speak to us. He said he believed it was Holland by his ensign which proved to be correct when we were close enough to see his flag well. We ran down on him and he asked us how Cape Henry bore. Our captain told him and I presume he got in alright.

Everything seemed to move along nicely on the bark until Sunday the 14th of April, except that I was seasick and could not eat much. It began to breeze up and we had to take in our royals in the afternoon. An able seaman was sent aloft with me to show me how to furl a royal. My, while up there I seemed to be a long way up above the water. I always had to furl the royals after this in my watch on the deck. That night the wind began to blow harder for we were now approaching the stormy region of the Gulf Stream. The topgallant sails were ordered taken in and furled. I was ordered aloft to help furl the fore topgallant sail. Oh, it was dark and the rain falling fast. The two sailors, Tom and Jim, had preceeded me. I went up the fore rigging and when I got to the foretop I thought I could never get above it there was so much rigging. Some of it standing and a lot of running rigging such as clew lines, bunt lines, and leech lines. The standing rigging was all nice and tight but running rigging was all slack and I had to be careful not to take hold of the running rigging or I would fall to the deck and be killed. Finally, I selected the topmast rigging and pulled myself over in the foretop and began to ascend the topmast rigging. This took me to the topgallant yard.

These sailors were very rough and said, "What are you up here for?" I said, "To help furl the topgallant sail." One said, "Lay out that yard and pass the gasket." I said, "No, I will stay in here at the mast and help." They said, "G.D. you, you are no good in here at the mast." To tell the truth I was afraid to go out the yard. I was afraid of falling off the yard. But Jim Ferguson said to them, "Give him a clip and knock him off. Nobody will know what has become of him." And they wouldn't for the bark was so heeled over I would have fallen into the sea instead of on deck. Besides it was so dark I would not have been seen.

The wind kept increasing fast and when I got back to the deck the main topgallant sail had been taken in and furled. The port watch had been called, the fore and main topsails had been lowered, reef tackles hauled out ready for reefing, and the mainsail clewed up. The second mate and crew were ordered aloft to reef the main topsail and, of course, I had to follow. I got aloft with the rest of them. The sailors said,

"You lay out on the end of the yard." The 2nd mate immediately remarked, "Get out there yourselves. You want this boy to fall." I stayed in the bunt near the 2nd mate, rapped my legs around in the topmast rigging, and the 2nd mate gave orders to haul out at the windward end of the yard. When the seaman said it was out to the windward he sang out to man on the lee yardarm to haul out. He felt the band on the topsail and when the band was tight enough he sang out, "Tight band, avast hauling and pass the earrings and tie the reef points." I remember well that I tied one reef point after the topsail was reefed.

The mate sang out from the deck to the 2nd mate to furl the mainsail before coming below. The mate could not see me on the main yard and he hailed the 2nd mate and asked him, "Where is that boy?" The 2nd mate said, "Sir, I think you had better let him go below before he falls." "Alright," said the mate, "come below and go to lay up the ropes." When I got below I was so weak from seasickness that every little sea that hit me on deck would knock me down. This kind Norwegian I will never forget and if I were to meet him too in needy circumstances I would contribute liberally to his relief. But this was 53 years ago and he must have been gathered home to his Father long before this.

This storm turned out to be a very bad one from the southeast. The next day it shifted to the northwest and we ran before it for 8 days under reefed main topsail, foresail, and fore staysail. All other sails being furled away. Of nights when I would be on the lookout alone up forward I was so green that I think, now suppose the captain does not know where he is and he runs up on some desolate island, how quick this barque would go to pieces and we would all be drowned. And again I used to think as the seas were so high that in running down from the top of the waves suppose she strikes the bottom of the ocean, how quick she would break to pieces and drown all of us. I had no idea the ocean was 2 miles deep. When my trick to the wheel came after the 3rd or 4th day of the gale, and the sea had got so high, the captain would say, "You keep her right before the wind, boy, for if you let her broach to on this port quarter the sea will come over and carry you overboard off the starboard quarter. And if you let her broach to on the starboard quarter you will go out over the port quarter."

On the 8th day of the gale the wind dropped quite suddenly. I was at the wheel. It was 4 o'clock in the morning. The barque slacked her speed, a heavy sea ran over the poop deck, covered me all over, and carried away the steps from the poop deck and did some other minor damage. The captain came out, roused all hands on deck, and made more sail to make a run from the sea which was yet very high. We were now getting along to the eastward. Our easting must have been pretty near up and we began steering more to the south and the weather began looking fine.

It was not long before we took the northeast trade wind which usually means fine weather. We got preventer backstays and set them taut so that we could carry on heavy if the trades should blow fresh. Then everybody had to work hard taking the old sails out of the locker and repairing them and putting them in good shape to carry us across the Line to Rio. When they were in good repair we sent down our good sails and bent on the old ones. Then we overhauled the new sails and put them away to bend again when we should come in on our American coast where storms usually prevail. This being all done we began splicing rigging, overhauling foot ropes on the yards and jib boom, and doing hundreds of other jobs.

I remember one day that I was passing the ball around the mizzin backstay while Jim Ferguson was serving it where it goes in the outrigger. There was not much room up there anyway and in passing the ball of spunyarn, and trying to hold on from falling, Jim let the end of the serving board catch in the front of my pants and tore all the buttons off. He cursed me and told me no Eastern Shoreman was any good. This mortified me ever so much as I had such few clothing and this man trying to strip me of the few I had. This fellow kept imposing on me until one night, when near of Cape St. Roque, we tacked ship. After tacking ship I was coiling the braces. Up he came along and said, "That is no way to coil braces." I was coiling them in the right handed way that I thought was correct. I said to him, "There is a mate and a 2nd mate here to look after me; they are paid for it and you are not." He turned the braces over and coiled them in a nice way so that in tacking they would not foul. He knew more about it than I did so when we went below in the forecastle he cursed me up more than I cared to bear and I said, "Jim, you are down on me for something and I think you had better come up on this deck and give me a good licking and you will be satisfied." So I jumped on deck. I did not care whether I lived any longer or died I was so mad. So I took a belaying pin out of the pin rail and if he had come on deck I intended to knock him senseless. After this Jim was friendly to me the remainder of the voyage.

I got along very well after this but we had 21 days of head wind as we fell to the leeward of Cape St. Roque and had a hard time getting by. We stood and made Pernambuco and then I saw my first catamaran. A catamaran is built of cottonwood logs bolted together, maybe seven or 8 logs. The ends are sharpened and seats put on them held up on legs like a chair. There is no such thing as filling as the logs are not dug out. The sea runs over these logs. They carry a sail and cruise many miles at sea for fishing purposes. Our steward, being a Spaniard, the captain got him to hail over and ask him if he had any fish to sell. The fellow said he had none. We stood off to sea again from the land and I never saw land again until we made Cape Frio 70 miles from Rio. The captain began to get jolly then. He would crack jokes with me while at the wheel and say, "When you get home again, Len, you will have to get somebody to throw water up side of the house so you can sleep."

The next day we made Raza Island Light and went into Rio Harbor 56 days from Cape Henry. Here were many interesting things for me to see. The great high Sugar Loaf Mountain was on the port hand going in. Under a fort were 7 coconut trees standing; the first coconut trees I ever saw.

After our visit from the custom house official and board of health we were given a permit to land. I pulled the bow oar which was the custom in those days for boys to do, rowing the captain ashore. While he was gone up town to enter his ship at the custom house I stayed at the boat and there was a Baltimore barque, the *Traveler,* Captain Penfield, discharging flour. Here I learned my first word in a foreign language. They had a long, wide platform. The colored man at the gangway would put 5 barrels on the platform and let them roll on shore and sing out, "Cinco talyo." After doing this a few times I was sure it meant 5 and tally. After discharging our cargo we lay at this pier 3 weeks. I noticed workmen worked ever day and I wondered when their Sunday came. But in Catholic customs they have no Sunday and we are fast coming to the same custom I regret to say.

After staying here 3 weeks I began to feel good getting fresh provisions and fruits. Here I used to go to market with our Spanish steward. I saw grapefruit. I asked the steward what kind of oranges they were. He told me they were not oranges but they were the unforbidden fruit, and, singular to say, after seeing them in the market of the different tropical countries and ports I visited for 35 years, I never used them until I sold my vessel and quit going to sea. I learned to eat them at home in Crisfield. Singular that steward caused me to loose the pleasure of enjoying grapefruit all those 35 years but I made it up in oranges, pineapples, bananas, and mangoes.

Finally, we got orders to haul to a warehouse and we began loading coffee. After taking on a full load we proceeded toward our home. After being at sea about 48 days we crossed the bows of a small 2-masted schooner named *George Washington* of Boothbay, Maine, from New York bound to Baracoa, Cuba. Our captain asked him what his longitude was. He said 74° 10′ west. About 3 or 4 o'clock the next morning we made Cape Henry ahead. About 9 o'clock in morning we stood in well over to the Middle Ground. When the pilot boarded us he said to Captain Clark, "Why did you stand over so close to the Middle Ground?" The captain said, "I have got 5 fathoms of water under her." The pilot said, "Oh, yes, and if you stood 25 fathoms further you would have neither fathoms." We were now 49 days at sea from Rio and our Yankee land looked good to me after being from it about 4 months and 20 days. It was now the latter part of August and the colored waters of the Chesapeake and the green shores on each side of it never looked better to me.

The next day we arrived in Baltimore and as soon as I could I went around to the head of the Basin to see what Eastern Shoremen I could find. Then the pungies were laying loaded with watermelons and cantilopes, peaches, etc. I went on board of Sev Evans who was there with a load and I got a good fill with all the good fruits. After a few days I shipped in the brig *John Pierce,* Captain Murray, with a cargo of coal bound to Boston. My brother John came up from Crisfield and he was anxious to go and the captain took him, though a small boy.

We left Baltimore and got to Hampton Roads and then the captain hung around for 30 days when other vessels would get under way and go to sea. This old skipper would get under way, go as far as Cape Henry, and say that the wind was out of the northeast and the weather not settled yet. Then he would turn back and go into Hampton Roads again. I remember vessels being in there with us and going out with the fleet, go to Boston or Portland, discharge their cargo, come to Baltimore, load, come to Hampton Roads and catch us there, making a round voyage while we were in the Roads. At last, after about 30 days had expired, we summed up a great resolution and got as far as Delaware Breakwater. Here we spent 35 days making bluffo going out with the fleet of vessels. We would get as far as Cape May and the captain would say, "This wind is northeast outside; this weather is not settled yet." We visited everybody around Hampton Roads on both sides; rowed up to Hampton while we were there quite a few times and filled our water casks. We were doing the same thing in the Delaware Breakwater. After 35 days another captain by the name of Townsend from Newport, Rhode Island, where the brig belonged, came down the Breakwater and took charge of her. Captain Murray and his wife and daughter went ashore and I have never heard from them since.

Captain Townsend got the brig under way as soon as possible and we started for Boston. But, unfortunately, we got in a heavy northeast gale of wind which lasted 2 or 3 days. We suffered some damages by loosing our main boom and sails blown away. So the captain put her into Newport just 2 months and 13 days from Baltimore. The brig never went to Boston. Her cargo was sold at Fall River and she went there and discharged. John and I were paid off in Newport. Then we shipped in a small schooner that was engaged in running oysters from the Chesapeake to Providence, Rhode Island. It was cold and hard work this as John and I were put together to dump oyster tubs and keep the oysters shoveled up.

Our first trip was to Deal Island. The next we came to Baltimore and loaded corn for Providence. We had quite a cold heavy norther off the coast and had to beat the ice off her rigging and shovel it off the deck. So the captain went into the Breakwater. We laid here and got frozen in. We could walk from one vessel to another. John and I would walk to other vessels and lug coal in hamper baskets from them to our ship. Then we would go to wood-loaded vessels and bring wood on our back to our ship. There were many vessels in there loaded with coal and wood. In fact, I guess most everything as sail ships in those days carried most all the commerce. There were very few steamers. This was Christmas week of 1872. At last the ice began to run and the vessels were fouling one another, breaking out their jib-booms and main booms, and some were draging to the beach. Some did drag ashore. Two drug down on us so we began to heave up our anchors. We had to heave them home. But we could not on account of the two schooners across our bow. This was an awful hard job but we were all draging for the beach. At last, at about one o'clock in the morning, we got our anchors to the bow and we immediately got under way and went to sea. I do not know how the other two vessels made out but I am sure if their anchors did not take up they went ashore on the beach and were lost.

Well, we got to Providence, unloaded our corn, and went to the James River and loaded oysters for Providence again. At Providence this time I left this schooner, *Matchless* by name, commanded by Captain Fred Harding of Cape Cod. His brother Saul Harding was mate. I came to the Chesapeake on the schooner *Amelia F. Cobb*. From her I came to Crisfield.

I left John on the *Matchless*. She was a mackeral fisher. John stayed with Captain Harding and fished for a year and drifted away and sailed a long time in oil ships running oil up the Baltic and to Germany, and the Mediterannean to Austria. After a few years at this he shipped in the barque *Tillie Baker*. On her he met with an accident in Bordeaux, France, and fell down her hold and broke his arm. He had to be left there and was sent to the hospital in England. After he got well he came across to the United States and fell in with barque *Tillie Baker* again. He joined her and went to Australia, thence to Hong Kong, China, then Iloilo, Philippine Islands and loaded sugar for Boston.

Now for myself, I arrived in Crisfield and dredged the remainder of the oyster season. I stayed with my Aunt Leah the most of the summer. Then I shipped from Philadelphia to Boston in the schooner *S. B. Wheeler*. Then I coasted in the winter in different vessels. I was in one schooner called the *Maria Lunt*. We went to New Bedford with a load of coal. Then the captain laid her up for the winter. We had a sailor on her by name John B. Farren. I thought he was a nice fellow but he served me a mighty dirty trick after I had saved his life. He was coming on board one dark night; he was drunk and laying helplessly across the railroad track very close to the schooner. I found him just in time to get him off before the coal cars came along which would have crushed him to death. The next day while I was attending the guy on the coal tubs he stole my watch and my money and went to Boston. I tried to catch him by wire but did not succeed. After the schooner was discharged Captain Kent paid me what little was due me, some 6 or 8 dollars, and closed up the vessel and went home. I was now in pretty bad circumstances, very little money, shipping bad, and no place to go.

It was now 1873 and the panic was on and jobs were hard to find. Finally, I fell in with an Irish boy living on a little schooner. He interceded for me so the captain and owner let me live on board the schooner with John, the Irish boy. Finally, I got a job to work of nights unloading coal vessels. I rolled the great big hand cart away up on a platform and dumped the coal down a shoot. For this I got 25¢ per hour. The cold northwest winds would pretty near freeze me up there. John brought me a bite to eat one night and my lips were so benumbed with cold I could not talk plain or eat what he brought me. Finally, John shipped in a United States cutter and went away.

II

1874–1878

ON the 12th day of January, 1874, I shipped in a schooner called the *Gamma* of Machiasport, Maine, Captain Horace Guptill. We went from New Bedford to Orient, Long Island, and loaded guano for Port Royal, South Carolina. From there we went to Jacksonville, Florida, and loaded lumber for New York. Coming out over the bar at Jacksonville we pounded heavy on the bar which made her leak badly so we put into Fernandina. The pilot, by the name Captain Sharp, put us on the beach on a high water and at low water the mate looked around her bottom and found some butts started. He caulked them and we pulled off in the channel. The next water her leak was stopped and we proceeded on our voyage to New York.

I suffered very much with the cold going to New York in March for my wardrobe was very scant. Arriving in New York I was paid off and I shipped in a schooner called the *Lillian M. Warren* bound to the West Indies after a load of pineapples. I made two voyages to the West Indies and back in her. Then I shipped in a schooner, Captain Henry Lake. I went to Boston and back to Newark, New Jersey. In New York I met Sev Evans and Jim Frank Tawes there then with a load of watermelons. As soon as I saw them I felt like getting back to Crisfield and I came down with them. I went to my old aunt again. It appeared I was always at home here.

That fall I went dredging again. I dredged until Christmas when I heard my oldest brother, Patrick Henry, had bought 1/8 interest in the brig *Water Witch*. I was very anxious to get with him for I was having a pretty hard time to make a living. I went to Baltimore. It was Christmas night and very long but as soon as the steamer landed I went down town to look for the brig though yet very dark as day had not broken. I found the brig at Wilner and Buck's drydock. I went on board and called him and I was mighty glad to see him too. I joined her before the mast. She loaded flour up in Smith's Dock for Rio de Janeiro. We left Baltimore on the afternoon of December 31st, 1874, going down the bay with the wind east. The night was dark and cloudy. I was in the 2nd mate's watch. We were on the port tack and the weather real cold. I saw a tow coming up the bay showing a green light. The 2nd mate said to me, "Keep her off." I thought it was wrong so I asked him again, "Did you say keep her off?" He said, "Yes, keep her off." The tow boat let go of her hauser and ran clear of us but we ran into the ship *Gray Eagle,* the ship she was towing. We broke out our jib boom and bowsprit with some other minor damages. We also broke the other ship's anchor and damaged her port bow. It cost us $600 to pay the ship's damage. We anchored right off Sharps Island.

The next day we took a tow boat and towed back to Baltimore for repairs. We lay close to the ship *Gray Eagle* while repairing. The *Gray Eagle* was discharging her cargo of coffee. She was such a sharp-built ship that she would not stand up light after the coffee was all out. The tow boat went alongside to move her and when they let the lines go from the wharf she turned right over on top of the tow boat and mashed her to the bottom. Her masts reached over on the other side of the dock and broke all three of her topgallant masts off.

We sailed on Saturday, the 9th day of January, 1875. That afternoon the wind was blowing heavy from the northwest and freezing to beat the band. The owner, or agent, was so scared we would be froze in Baltimore and not get away. We went down the bay that night. I thought I would freeze to death. The next morning we went in Hampton Roads and put the pilot off. We then immediately went to sea. The weather was so cold and freezing I never got any sleep until I was across the Gulf Stream. In those days ships had no stoves in the forecastles to keep sailors warm. The laws of today compel ships to carry stoves in their forecastles for the comfort of their crews, I am glad to say. As far as I can remember we were 56 days from Cape Henry to Rio. We discharged our cargo of flour and loaded a full load of coffee in ten days and started home.

On our passage home the brig sprang a leak. It did not amount to much, as I thought. My brother tried to cut the ceiling for it was aft under the lazerette. He could not succeed so he laid the brig to, tied a rope to himself, and went overboard and caulked the seam and stopped the leak. Sometimes the brig would roll down and carry him under 10 or 12 feet and then she would roll up and he would get his breath and would caulk a few licks. Then she would mash him under again and so on and so on until he stopped her leak. But it was a dear stop to him for in a few days he was taken sick and was never well again.

On her next voyage to Rio, after discharging flour, we came up to Pernambuco and loaded sugar for New York. On his way to New York, on the 3rd day of November, 1876, he died and was buried at sea. I never had my feelings hurt so bad in my life as when he was pushed over the side. When he died we made a box and lined it inside with tarred canvas and lined it outside with tarred canvas and we put him under the long boat on the main hatch. I was in hopes of getting the body home as we were about 900 miles southeast of Cape Henry at the time. But due to weather conditions we were unable to do so. It was moderate weather when we put him over. We put a lot of chain at the foot of the coffin and nailed him up tightly. When we put him over the coffin stood on end and to this day I can see that coffin on its end as we sailed away from it, a sight I shall never forget.

Having gone through all this ordeal, the next day the weather began to get ugly and stormy and we had awful gales of wind. The sea was so bad that it washed all our bulwarks off. Our sails were being blown away one by one. We were now blown around in the different parts of the Gulf Stream for 5 weeks. Our water and provisions were gone and our boat smashed. Our oil was all gone and when we came in the cabbin below it was dark as a dungeon and lonesome. We would have to feel our way to our berths at night if we had an opportunity to get a little rest. We caught a big shark one day, which was a God-send to us, and we lived on him 3 days and tried his liver out which we used in our binnacle to give us light to steer by. The winds kept to the points of northeast and northwest which were adverse to us. So we concluded to try to find Bermuda.

I remember on Sunday morning, it was in my watch on deck, that John, a Norwegian, came to me and said, "Mr. Tawes, there is an abandoned schooner about two points from the starboard bow. She can be seen from aloft." We went to the fore topsail yard and there sure enough was a schooner, jibs down, and her reefed foresail and mainsail partly slacked down. She was laying there and rolling idly. I said, "John, what is the use of us running down on her? We have no boat to go on board of her." With this he said, "I know that but run just as close to her as you can safely and I will jump overboard and swim to her. If she has a boat I will scrape up what provisions I can find, get a little water, and come on board our ship." But as we got in a mile of her some men came on deck and we saw she was not abandoned. So we changed our course for Bermuda. This schooner was from Shediac, New Brunswick, loaded with potatoes and onions bound to Bermuda. She was laying there to get observations when the weather cleared up to obtain his position. This was on Sunday morning. Tuesday, another heavy gale come on and this schooner got on the southwest reef of Bermuda and was lost. The crew, I believe, were saved. We afterwards got his mainmast and put it on our brig. We paid $500 for that mast.

We were suffering very much for water. The sailors would suck sugar, the kind of cargo we had in, which seemed to considerably quench their thirst. But it would not do me so. It was the custom of the steward to use the water in a cask down to about 6 or 8 inches. Then the water would become dreggy and he would open another cask. It was the custom in those days for the mate to assign what cask to open and the same would be noted in the log book and the date thereof and there would be no more account taken of this dreggy water. But after being so many days at sea, sails all blown away excepting our fore topgallant sail, royal, and flying jib, provisions, water, wood, and oil became quite a serious object. We began to go back to these old dreggy casks for water which seemed so precious to us even though they were in much worse condition than when we gave them up. Now they were not only dreggy but had become almost salt. The bungs were left out and lots of the salt sea spray had fallen into them.

I felt myself fast failing for the want of food and water. Fortunately, one day I was searching in the between deck for something which I cannot now remember. I came across one of the empty water casks which had turned half over from the heavy rolling and pitching of the ship. No one could reasonably think this cask could have turned on its chocks for it was under the upper deck where the sea had never touched it. Yet it had rolled half over. By this happening the salt water from the upper deck had never leaked in and could not leak into the bung of this cask. I went on deck and got me a big dipper. I went into the between decks, drew some water from this dreggy discarded cask, and found the water nice and fresh and sweet to me. But you, reader, when you are used to cool water from the springs, with ice in it if necessary, would not have agreed with me. I suppose many people will blame me for not telling that I had found 2 or 3 gallons of good fresh water. It may be mean of me but I told no one about this little find of fresh water which saved my life.

After being tossed and rolled hither and thither from the 7th day of November, to the 14th day of December, we sighted the island of Bermuda which we had been looking for for five weeks. A boat came out from the island and brought a pilot. This boat went ashore and reported our predicament to the English Government. The wind being there from the northwest and a heavy sea on we had to go down around the south of the island to try to get into St. Georges, a port on the east side. When we hauled her up on the wind we were so short of sails we began to drift off to the southeast away from the island. But the English Government, always a friend to the distressed, sent a man-of-war out after us and towed us into St. Georges, where we came to anchor on the 15th day of December, 1876, 61 days from Pernambuco.

We lay here seven weeks repairing bulwarks and getting a full new suit of sails. On the 2nd day of February, 1877, we sailed for New York. We were 16 days getting to New York. We experienced some more very heavy gales before getting to New York.

I wish to say that in my seven weeks in Bermuda I made many agreeable acquaintances. I would certainly love to go there again. I suppose I would see very few of the people there now I knew then as, no doubt, the scythe of time has been busy there as well as in our home land.

After discharging our cargo of sugar we sailed for Baltimore. On arrival there the brig was sold and I never went into her again. Many years after, this brig, the *Water Witch* by name, was lost in the Crooked Island Passage and she was no more. I then came home. Oh, I had no home but I came to Crisfield and there, and in Accomack, spent about a month.

I then went to Baltimore and shipped 2nd mate of the brig *Agnes Barton*. I was on board of this brig one year. It was the hardest year of my life. We went from Baltimore to Santiago, Cuba. We had a good passage out, 14 days, which was good for May as in May the prevailing wind is from southward which was adverse. I will never forget our night in the Crooked Island Passage. It was the squalliest time I ever saw. We were under very short sail; the wind was real shifty. It was first on one side, then the other. The most vivid and blinding lightening I ever saw. We had a hoisting winch of heavy iron just to the fore side of the mainmast. In these shifts of wind I had to attend to shifting the main staysail sheet from one side of the deck to the other as the winds would shift with heavy falls of rain. Captain Knight would say to me, "Tawes, shift the main staysail sheet over to starboard." Then he would say, "Stand away from that mast and winch." The electricity was so severe we expected the lightening to strike the mainmast every minute. This staysail hooked in an eye bolt driven in the deck on each side. We had a long tail rope to slack the staysail over with when the sheet block was hooked. I shifted the staysail over about a dozen times that night expecting to be killed every time I did it. At last Captain Knight got tired of it and ran back out the passage to the open sea and got out of the squalls. I was real glad too that he did. I suppose the heat on the land of the islands was the cause of these electric storms but, strange to say, I have been down through this passage all of 20 times as master of vessels and never experienced anything like it after.

[27]

Coasting Captain

After discharging our cargo of coal it was on a St. John's Day or St. Peter's Day, I forget which, we sailed for Trinidad, south side of Cuba, to load sugar for Boston. The Cubans were having a feast which they generally do on every Saint's day, Catholic religion being the dominant denomination in Cuba. Going down the river or bay that night with very light land breezes we could hear their music from the shore and see the fireworks. After we got to sea we got a nice fresh east wind and we soon ran down to Trinidad, loaded about 600 hogsheads of sugar, and sailed for Boston. The first war between Cuba and Spain was then going on and we took a Cuban on as a passenger. He was a well educated man and spoke English fluently. I think he was escaping the clutches of the Spaniards. This man, Captain Knight, was a seaman all the way from his headworks to his end and a hard, hard master I want to tell you. He kept good order and good discipline and was a safe captain to go with. He kept the brig like a yacht. Every Saturday afternoon in port or at sea all the brass had to be rubbed clean and as bright as gold. This particular brig had lots of brass on the after side of the yards to keep the chafe off the topmast and topgallant back stays. We had a redheaded Dutchman named Lynn. Mr. Wilson, the mate, told him to take the brick dust and oil and go aloft and clean the brass work on the yards. The redhead says, "Who the hell ever heard of brass being rubbed on the yards at sea?" Captain Knight was walking the poop aft and heard him. He flew up like powder just lighted and began to run forward. He said, "What's that you say you g.d., redheaded s.o.b.?" It was a good thing he was partly up the rigging or I am sure there would have been a fight. Captain Knight says, "Mr. Wilson, don't you let that man come down from aloft to eat or to drink until he cleans all the brass on them yards, nice and bright." Mr. Wilson said, "He shall not come down, sir." It always took two men to clean the brass on these yards in the afternoon

[28]

but Lynn was through by seven o'clock and came down and ate a cold supper as we usually had supper at half after five. Lynn never complained anymore about what he had to do. He had now learned it was better on this ship to do his work willingly and without a murmur. Otherwise his work increased and his condition was made unhappy.

We now proceeded on our voyage, as far as I can remember, without anything unusual happening until we were now approaching the South Shoal Lightship. The weather had been foggy and rainy for two or 3 days. The only thing we had seen were numerous schools of whales spouting in every direction. In those days it was the custom among mariners in the offshore trade, when we saw a ship of any nation, as a matter of courtesy and convenience, to hoist her national ensign and approach each other with ship's longitude worked to her position. When in speaking distance, or nearly so, we exchanged longitudes which sometimes served each other a good purpose. If there should be much difference in the longitudes we would ask each other when did you see the land the last time. Or the proper form would be, "Ship ahoy, where are you from? Where are you bound? How many days are you out?" Many times, if a ship was from some port south of the equator bound north and in the variable winds, and would be bound to some port across the equator, we would ask him where he lost the northeast trade winds. In that same lattitude and longitude we would expect to pick them up and then have two or three weeks good sailing with wind one way and very fine weather.

Well, to get back on my course or subject again, it was early in the morning when we sighted an English bark. Captain Knight ordered our American flag hoisted to the main peak, got his longitude worked up, and wrote it in big figures on the spare table leaf. He had me to stand in the most conspicuous place where it could be plainly seen by the English captain.

This bark was running along before the wind with yards all squared. He never set his ensign at all which in those days was a breach of courtesy. We kept off just under his stern and there we could plainly read his name and hailing port. The name of this barque I have long forgotton but he hailed from Liverpool. This was the first time we had learned his nationality. As soon as we saw his nationality Captain Knight says to him, "Had I seen your stern before I would not have bothered to set my ensign and worked up my longitude." The Englishman says, "Oh, if it be any accomodation to you I will haul my jibs down and back the main yards for you." Captain Knight says, "Go on, I want nothing to do with you; I will get to Boston after a while." And we did too that following night.

I learned something which served me a good purpose for many years. In fact, as long I went to sea. We had a very old sailor before the mast and he changed the course on me. It was like this: Captain Knight would not run for Cape Cod that night but took in the light sails and headed her off shore. He gave me a course to steer and went below. We had been running on a certain course for Cape Cod, say for about 10 days. I gave this old fellow the course to steer and then set down on the chicken coop. The passenger began entertaining me with his Cuban war stories. Then I began to notice the wind was changing, as I thought. Then I began to check the yards in little by little also trimming the staysails. I kept at this until after a little while I had the yards all square and was running before the wind straight for Cape Cod. Captain Knight was below asleep. By and by I walked aft, looked in the binicle, and lo and behold this old crank had only kept her off and put her on the same course we had been running on for the past 10 days. Well, I was scared to death. I was afraid Captain Knight would come on deck and witness the whole affair. I believe he would have thrown me overboard had he come on deck and caught me in this affair. I cursed at the old sailor in a whisper, told him to bring her back on her course, and began bracing the yards up on the wind again. Captain Knight never found this out. If he had I should have been forever ruined in the maritime circle and could never have gotten another officer's position. But as I have before said it served me a good purpose for always after this, when the sails began not to stand, I would always look in the binical to see if the wheelsman had her on her course before I would begin to trim the sails to the wind. Finally, we got observations, obtained our position, made Cape Cod Lighthouse, got a pilot, and proceeded to Boston where we had to take the pilot on board. I was slacking up the starboard fore brace. It was blowing fresh. The brace got away from me and the yards flew around so fast the brace came near throwing me overboard.

After discharging our cargo of sugar, we loaded ice for Havana, Cuba. We were 22 days getting to Havana. It was now September, 1877, and we had it very squally and disagreeable around the Bahamas. We were threatened with one of those West India hurrycanes which I was glad to escape. It seemed that Captain Knight was well known by the different light-keepers around the Isaacs and the Double Headed Shot Cays for both of these light-keepers boarded us and got some provisions. The light-keeper at the Great Isaacs went with us as far as the Bimini Islands and there went ashore with some of the pilots. We took one of these pilots to steer us along the edge of the Gulf Stream and keep us out of the strong head current, and yet not run us ashore. He went with us as far down as Watch Cay and there he left us. We were safe from the current of the Gulf Stream.

Sailing vessels drawing over 12 feet of water cannot cross the Bahama Banks but are compelled to go around the Isaacs and sail close to the Great Bahama Banks. If they should be so unfortunate as to get into the strong current of the Gulf

Stream, and the wind die out, they would be carried back to the north of Abaco. Then they would be compelled to get to the eastward, out of the Stream, and come down through the Northeast and Northwest Providence Channel around the Great Isaacs again and loose 15 or more days of time. This route applies to all vessels bound to Havana, Matanzas, and all the ports in the Gulf of Mexico. Fortunately, we were not carried back by the Gulf Stream. Our captain knew these waters well from Watch Key.

We ran across to Double Headed Shot Cay. It was in the night. We ran along close to a chain of rocks to keep out of the current. Captain Knight sat in a chair on the poop deck and piloted her safely by. I thought if I only knew as much as he did at that time. I have done the same thing several times since then in my schooner, the *City of Baltimore,* and thought nothing of it. In fact one Christmas Day the wind came fresh from ahead and before I would tack her in the Stream I ran her across the Salt Bank picking my way through the rocks.

To resume our voyage we got safely by the Double Headed Shot Cay and ere long we arrived safely in Havana. We were now out of one trouble and into another. We were now safe in a port from the hurrycanes and the rocks but here in a port infested with yellow fever with hundreds of cases being reported daily. We moored our ship stern in and bow out with our anchors out away ahead. No one is allowed to lay alongside of the wharf in Havana. All cargo is discharged over the stern or on a platform running out from the wharf alongside of the ship to abreast of the hatches. We rigged a shoot and hoisted our ice out high enough so that it would run on a down grade of its propulsion to the dock or ice house. In six or eight days our ice was out. We then went into the stream and lay at anchor. We began now to repair all our sails and set the rigging tight and everything possible to get the ship in order for the home passage.

Then occurred an incident of my life I shall always remember. While at anchor here there came in the Portland brig *Torrent,* Captain Neal. I knew Captain Neal well. We were in Bermuda together in distress about a year before this. I felt very much like seeing Captain Neal again. So one evening after we got through work and got supper I washed myself up and went on board of her. I met the second mate at the gangway. He asked me on board. I asked him where Captain Neal was. He told me he was on shore, that he thought he would soon be on board. Our captain was on shore too, as it happened. So I sat on deck a while. He suggested for me to come below and see the mate. He was sick. I went below. The stateroom was ordinarily small and the berth he was laying in was under the poop deck. It was hot and he filled it. I spoke to him and began to converse with him. It was getting a little dark and having no lamp lit I could not see him good. I tried to talk to him but he merely mumbled out something. Really, the man was not rational.

I stayed in this little stateroom, about 5 by 6 feet, at least two hours until Captain Neal came on board, which was 9 o'clock. He seemed glad to see me and I him, being so well acquainted. After a nice little chat about this and that pertaining of course to seafaring and different ports, etc., finally he pulled out an old square face containing some mighty good Holland and asked me to take a drink, which I did without persuasion. I am glad I did for I always thought it saved my life which I will explain later. I got down in the boat feeling pretty good and sculled on board, turned in, and had a good, good sleep. The second day after this Captain Knight came on board and while at the supper table he said to the mate and I that Captain Neal's mate was very sick with yellow fever. It had cost him a doubloon to get two Spanish doctors to go on board to see him. Well, just imagine my feelings. Not 48 hours ago I sat breathing his breath and it turned out to be a case of yellow fever. Well I never told anyone I was on board of the *Torrent*.

The next afternoon I saw a boat and some Cubans come on board with a black coffin and bring him out on deck and put his corpse in the black box, lower him overside in a boat, and carry him ashore. This was the worst feeling I ever had in my life. If any judge were to say to me in 10 days you shall be hung by the neck until you are dead I could not feel worse than I did then. Every morning after this when I turned out I would look at my tongue to see if it was coated as every day I was expecting to be stricken down with yellow fever. There were so many cases then in Havana. There were a great many unkempt Spanish soldiers there which were dying like sheep for this was a time when the first Spanish-Cuban war was going on.

This war had now been waging eight years. It did not last long after this. It was now October 1877. The poor Cubans lost out this time. But in 1895, in the month of March, the Cubans broke out again in another rebellion. I was in Guantanamo loading sugar for New York when this occurred. I knew nothing about any rebellion on hand. The captain of the port came down to the ship at 6 o'clock PM and says to me, "Do not let any of your men come on shore tonight and don't you." I said, "Why is this?" He said, "You may be shot if you do, any of you." He did not tell me a rebellion had broken out and that the Cubans were marching on to Caimanera, the place where we were loading. The Spaniards were out to repel them which I suppose they did as no Cubans came into Caimanera. I afterwards heard the Spaniards let their wounded lay on the battle field or under shady trees all the next day in order to bring their wounded in the city to the hospital at night so that the Cuban citizens could not see them for the effect it may have had on the Cubans to encourage the rebellion.

Well, to continue my story, while in Havana we lay at anchor in the harbor for 35 days. First, one of our men then another were taken with yellow fever until we had 3 of our able-bodied seamen in the hospital. I was expecting every morning my turn would come. I could not expect otherwise having been in that little stateroom on the brig *Torrent* about 3 hours breathing the breath of a man dying with yellow fever. I always thought it was the drink of Holland gin Captain Neal treated me to that killed the germs I took from this mate. So I bought me a bottle of good Holland gin and took a drink every morning the first thing when I turned out. And I never took the yellow fever this time.

It began to look somewhat lonesome now on our brig, the *Agnes Barton*. Out of 8 in crew all told there were now 3 gone and they were the working men at that. There were only 3 working men left to wash the decks of mornings, the mate, myself, and our seaman. Finally, our captain chartered to load molasses for New York.

In those days it took a long time to load molasses. The charterer would send off 10 empty casks to begin with all coopered up in good shape for filling. Then he would send off a large tub that would be capable of holding close to 160 gallons of molasses. A large round hole would be cut in the bottom at least a foot in diameter. Then a long leather hose 50 or 60 feet long was made tapering so that the small end would fit in the bung hole of a cask. We would put this tub over the main hatch and block it up even with the ship's rail as the higher we could get the tub up the faster the molasses would run. This being done, we would put out two long planks, about 3″ x 12″, 30 feet long. They would go all the way across the ship's deck from one side to the other, just far enough apart to make a nice track for the hogsheads to run on. We would then stow the ten empty casks down there and dunnage them between the bilge and chime hoops taking fine care that the bilge of the casks did not touch the ship's ceiling anywhere. If the bilge of the casks should happen to touch, the weight of the next casks on top would straiten out the staves in the casks below and all the molasses would leak out at the heads of the casks below. We would always stow them bung up so that we could run them full. Hence the motto being, "Up and bilge free."

Now the ten empty casks are stowed ready for filling. There will then be a lighter alongside with 30 or 40 full casks. The hoisting gear is all rigged and four men get to this winch that I was so scared of from lightening in the Crooked Island Passage six months previous. They hoist up a cask of molasses containing about 160 or 175 gallons, or nearly a ton in weight. We land this on this platform of long planks. We land it bung up, take out this bung, roll it over bung down, and let the molasses run in this large tub. And through this hose the molasses runs in the empty cask below. It takes one man to attend to running the molasses in the empty casks below. When it is filled up to 9 inches from the top the man below nippers the small end of the hose and puts it in another cask. The empty cask above is now let down off the platform on deck and a gang of coopers will take charge of it and cooper it up in nice shape, put on new hoops if needed, and stop every little wormhole in the staves of the cask for oak staves often have little worm holes in them. This empty cask now being in order it is struck down the hold and stowed empty as the other 10 were, ready for filling. The two men do all this stowing and attend to the hose in running them full. In case the tub would fill up, to keep it from running over we have a bung or stopper with a handle 3 feet long which by reaching under the cask we shove this bung with the long handle up into the bung hole and stop the molasses from running out of the cask until the tub underneath becomes nearly empty. I have been wet with molasses many days all day long handling this wet hose and stowing empty casks. We always have a strainer made of rope yarns to put over the tub to catch all the cane leaves that are sometimes in the molasses.

I remember once when I was mate in the brig *Agnes Barton* loading molasses for Boston. I attended the gangway in taking the full casks on board and running them in the tub. I broke out all full of little boils from being wet all day with molasses.

Getting now back to the *Agnes Barton* in Havana, we are now about getting our cargo nearly all on board consisting of about 650 hogsheads. Our brig was leaking very much and it would not do to go to sea short handed. Three of our A.B.'s were in the hospital with yellow fever so our captain shipped a Turk and we got an English boy who was a stowaway on this English ship from Liverpool. Our captain and the English captain became quite friends while in Havana. So he let us have this boy. One evening after supper our captain said me, "Mr. Tawes, you take the yawl boat and go on board that English ship and get a boy that the English captain said I could have." So off I went to the English ship, saw the captain, and got the boy. He was, as I thought, the most beautiful lad I ever laid eyes on. He appeared so happy to think he was shipping where he would now earn wages. His wardrobe was light for he was a poor boy 18 years old. When I had sculled about 30 yards from the ship—there was no gasoline in those days, everything was done by hand power—I will never forget an old English sailor got up on the rail and says to me, "Look here, matey, take good care of that boy and don't impose on him because he is English." "Oh," I says, "we will try to be good to him. We do not carry malice always." It used to be a custom in those days that when American and English sailors met in a foreign port, and after taking a couple of rounds of liquor, they would reap up the question of our old Revolution and fight it over again and end up with a lot of black eyes. I hope after this World War a better feeling now exists between the English and American seaman and the nations as well.

Well, we now have this Turk and English boy to replace 3 able seamen. No sailors were to be obtained in Havana; so many had died with yellow fever that most ships were short of crews. Our captain went to the hospital and took the 3 yellow fever patients out but they lacked a great deal of being well. In those days we had a maritime law that if an American ship left any one of its crew in a foreign port the ship would have to pay to the consul all of the wages due the man, all of his hospital bills, and three month's extra wages. This 3 month's extra wages has long since been abolished but his wages and hospital bill the ship has to pay even now. These three men served to increase our labor ever so much for we had them to wait upon besides the handling of ship such as reefing, making sail, and pumping. It was now November, one of the worst months to come up the Gulf Stream toward Cape Hatteras. I presume our captain would have taken these men if there were any prospects of them living before he would have put up the 3 month's pay for each man.

Well, we were all loaded and the day has come to sail. I will not forget as we were sailing out of the harbor. The wind was very scant and sailing close-hauled it looked we were not going to fetch out by the marine barracks. A lot of ships were laying there discharging cargo from all parts of the world their bows sticking out with long jib booms and anchors ahead that the pilot got scared and he began to holler, "Tener cuidado, tener cuidado, clew up gants, haul down jibs, let go ank." In good nautical English it is interpreted, "Look out, look out, clew up the topgallant sail, haul down the jibs, and let go anchor." Captain Knight took the wheel and yelled out, "Touch nothing." And in his good seamanship at the wheel she fetched around this bend and we touched nothing. Only a short time thence we passed out by the Morro Castle and we were at sea. My, I was glad. It saved us a lot of labor not to anchor to the windward of all these ships shorthanded as we were. There was no steam on any sail vessel in those days. All was done by hand which meant a lot of hard labor. And we were so shorthanded I hardly think I could have held out to get this brig underway twice in one afternoon.

Now we are at sea and it was Captain Knight's custom to give everyone of the ship's crew a dose of calomel and jalap on going into a yellow fever port and on the day of coming out. Captain Knight called us all aft to take our dose of 15 grains of calomel and 15 grains of jalap mixed with molasses. I took a dose of this going into Havana and it served me so bad that I refused to take any going out of the harbor to sea. I told the captain when I took another dose of calomel and jalap it would not be for a prevention; it would be for yellow fever itself.

Usually, when any of the crew escaped yellow fever while laying in the port, it would develop when they would get to sea which it did with our fine looking English lad on the second day out. This boy was taken sick and captain did all he could to save this boy. He was quite a good yellow fever doctor. His method first was a dose of calomel and jalap; then to produce a profuse sweat by wrapping the patient up in a blanket to head and ears, just leave his nose out to breathe, set him on a stool, fill a plate or pan full of alcohol and set fire to it. When the patient sweated profusely he would lay him in his berth well wrapped in this blanket and keep the sweat up for five days never allowing him on deck. In five days there would be a change for better or worse—if you live the 5 days, of course. Those that were well would have to wait on the sick after being well physiced. Then quinine would follow. Well, our boy was put in a house on deck. He was there alone but his case was attended as best we could for off Cape Canaveral awful northeast storms set in on us and take in the reefing, and the steering, and the pumping, for she was leaking badly, and attending to four cases of yellow fever patients, was a task no tongue or pen can describe.

I saw our boy was getting worse all the while. I think his parents must have been merchants for in his delirium he would ask you how much cheese you would like to have or how much coffee or tea, bacon, butter, and such other things as one kept in a grocery. I could see how it was. The captain never took this boy's home address. Before he got so ill on the 4th day I saw he was going to die and I took it on myself to get the name of his mother and his address so that I could write her. All I could get from him was that his mother was named Agnes Asoin. The 5th day, at 4 o'clock in the morning, this boy passed away. I held the light while the mate sewed him up in canvas. We sewed about a 20 lb. bag of sand to his feet and at 5 o'clock we put him overboard before he was cold. And all of his clothes were thrown over immediately. It is customary to lay a ship to and read a burial service when burying the dead but this ship was not hove to. She was running 9 or 10 knots when this lad was put over. Our captain was not even on deck when we pushed him over. I just heard a splash and that ended a fine English youthe whose mother looked many years with yearning eyes to see him return.

Now we are left with 3 yellow fever patients to attend to which was so hard on us to handle the ship and keep her pumped out, and in the month of November. Those who have traveled much from the Florida Straits can describe these storms prevailing at this season of the year. We had one man on board whose name was Adam. He was so bad I expected him to die before we got to New York. But he did not. One morning our old mate let a squall strike him which carried our mainsail away. There was no more sleep for any of us until this mainsail was repaired. We would work all day and pump ship every two hours. We would light lanterns and sew by them all night and pump ship every two hours. At last this is repaired and put on her. There is no telling what we suffered and endured on this passage.

We had an old lady passenger on board by name Mrs. Mockerby. She belonged in Washington. She was certainly a brave and enduring old lady. When the cabin floor would be wet, which it was often from the heavy rains and sea coming in, and by people passing in and out with wet oil clothing on, she would get off the lounge and on her hands and knees wipe up the cabin floor. I never thought the captain treated her with the respect he should have. Sometimes she would call the mate and I, gentlemen. The captain would say, "Hell, there are no gentlemen here." She would say, "Why not? They are gentlemen." She was the mother of the chief engineer of the Spanish gunboat that captured the American steamer *Virginius* carrying arms to the Cubans. They towed her into Santiago and there the Spaniards would take out some 10 or 12 of these Americans now and then and shoot them. I suppose they would have kept it up until they shot every one of them but an English man-of-war came over from Jamaica and stopped them. I think there was about 25 of them shot. The correctness of this could be obtained from Washington or other authorities. Our captain would say to this old lady sometimes, "Your son was much to blame for the murder of those men." She would say, "How so? He was hired for an engineer and he could not help it." "Oh well," he would say, "he could have slowed her down and not let them caught up with her." All this I thought was inappropriate talk to a helpless old lady.

This was one of my bad voyages; our provisions were short. We lay in Havana so long and our captain bought very few in Havana for the voyage. Captain Knight had some few barrels of flour he carried to smuggle to the Cubans when he got the chance. This flour had been on board so long that the steward could not make bread from it. But he could fry flap cakes out it. So we all lived a long time on flap cakes and molasses.

I have heard several comments made about going over the top during our World War. Well, I imagine it is comparable to a job I had to do one night on this brig. It was eleven o'clock and dark, rainy, and blowing a gale from the northeast. Our port main topmast backstay carried away at the topmast head. This backstay was hemp rigging 7 inches in circumference and very heavy. It broke in the splice under the service at the topmast. Fresh water from the rains had been getting into this splice for years and caused it to rot away. As soon as it broke the captain yelled out, "God d. such mates as I have got. They never know when anything is getting bad until it breaks. Splice an eye in that stay and get a ratline seizing. Get it aloft and seize it to the topmast head." We got a couple of lanterns on deck to give us light to make this splice by. Though this was in 1877, 48 years ago, I can now plainly see the water running off my south-wester hat showing brilliantly between me and the light while this splice was being put into this backstay. I was thinking of my luck and how I should make out going to this topmast head this dark, stormy night. Would I ever get back to the deck alive? It looked very doubtful, she was rolling so heavy. Had the captain been a kind-hearted man, we could have waited until morning before sending this backstay up when we would have daylight and see how to work. It was the backstay and we could have well dispensed with it until morning but oh, no, it must be done now.

The eye now spliced in we spliced 6 fathoms of 14-thread ratline for a seizing and, now ready, the mate says to me, "Mr. Tawes, you take this backstay aloft. The men will fall in behind and follow you up about 10 or 12 feet apart and lighten this stay up. When you get aloft haul up enough of this to allow you to get to the topmast head, then lash it to the crosstrees. Take a boatswain chair up with you. When you have enough of the stay up to reach the topmast head lash it to the crosstrees. Then go to the top of the mainmast head. Take the topsail halyards, hook the same to your boatswain chair, then fasten the stay to your chair about three feet below the eye so that you can handle it. When ready, sing out and we will hoist you to the topmast head and when there seize the stay to the topmast head and be sure to criss the seizing in the eye splice of the stay."

When I had everything ready I sang out, "Hoist away." Now going over the top this topmast was not less than 50 feet long. When I left the masthead I had to hold on to the topmast rigging to keep from being swung some 50 or more feet outboard and then in and have my brains battered out against the topmast or be thrown out of the boatswain's chair in the ocean. But the rigging narrowed up as I approached the topmast and when I got high enough to catch hold of both the port and starboard sides of the topmast rigging I felt safer. When the halyards were two-block at the topmast she could not swing me away. Then I took the eye of the topmast backstay, adjusted it to its place, and began to pass the ratline around the topmast head and through the eye on the backstay hauling the ratline tight with a marlingspike until I had the backstay well seized to the topmast head. When all was done I sung out, "Hello, below, lower away." I got back to the masthead, took the topsail halyards off my boastwain chair, hooked them in the cringle of the head of the topsail, took my marlingspike and chair down in the crosstrees, and I took hold of the backstay and went on the outrigger and put the backstay in the score out on the end of the outrigger and sung out, "Hello, below, set the backstay up." Now take in consideration the blowing, darkness, raining, and rolling, "going over the top" would be preferable to this job. But I did get through with it and to my surprise and pleasure came back to the deck alive.

Things went on as usual, sometimes a little better, until one night the molasses got loose in the between decks. Now when hogsheads of molasses start they can burst one another mighty.

The ship was rolling heavy and one of the tiers gave way and every time the ship rolled the loose hogshead would knock another loose. Then they began to burst open. Captain Knight called me out to get on deck as quickly as possible and with all the crew in the between decks to chock these hogsheads of molasses. I jumped on the top of them and threw old fenders, old rope, old sails, and everything possible to chock these hogsheads. They were as slippery as grease and how I managed not to fall in between these hogsheads and be crushed to death I do not know. The molasses would fly out of the bungholes up into my eyes and blind me sometimes. But I was quick and nimble in those days and I would jump from one hogshead to another. We managed to get them quiet after a while by throwing our old sails, rope fenders, and wood in between them. We lost about forty hogsheads from bursting and when she would roll the molasses would break on her sides like seas rolling upon the beach on the sea shore. It took this molasses about three days to find its way in the lower hold and in the limbers so we could pump it all out. So we pumped sweetened water three days and nights.

Now the gales were almost getting the better of us and being short of provisions the captain called me in the cabin and says to me, "What do you think about us going into Charleston, South Carolina?" I told him I thought we could hold out pumping and take care of the ship until we got up to Cape Henry and go to Baltimore. I was in the brig *Water Witch* once and we put into Bermuda and I had learned how people would make heavy charges on a vessel in distress. So we did not go into Charleston but pursued on our voyage. I did not know the trouble I was bringing on myself and the crew when I gave this advice. I believe the captain meant to make money out of it if he went into Charleston because when he got in the lattitude of Cape Henry he made no attempt to go in but proceeded on his voyage to New York. If he had put in Cape

Henry she would have been looked after by S. H. Travers and Son of Baltimore and there would have been no chance for graft if he had been so inclined. So we had to exist on flap cakes and molasses a few more days.

At last we were north of Barnegat. We got a pilot on board and at night it looked awful ugly and another storm was brewing. When I went below to get my supper consisting of flap cakes and molasses we were braced close on a wind. The land showed about two points on our weather bow. I knew we would soon have to tack her offshore which meant another 3 or 4 hours grubbing with bad weather if we were not driven up on the beach and wrecked altogether. I was feeling awful bad. I was so anxious to get in. I was so tired from pumping, reefing, and making sail that I was nearly given out. Our 3 yellow fever patients were very much better since we were now in cold weather but they were never well enough to turn to. We were saved the trouble of waiting on them so much and carrying their slops. When I had finished my supper and came on deck it was now coming on dark. But I could see no more land on the weather bow. The wind had hauled to the southeast and we were now heading our course for Sandy Hook. The Lord was good to us this night for about one o'clock in the morning we had anchored safely on the quarantine ground at Staten Island. That night turned out to be a terrible one. We had a gunboat by the name of *Huron* that went out of Cape Henry and was blown ashore between Cape Henry and Cape Hatteras that night and was lost. Some 40 men were drowned.

We are now in New York 22 days from Havana. One of the ruffest and toughest passages ever made by me. Our yellow fever patients were dressed to looked neatly and there was no yellow fever reported. And the death of the boy was never reported. We were all so glad to get in port and to get where there were provisions to be had no one said a word for fear of being quarantined. Our quarantine laws have so changed since that now such a thing can never occur again. The laws are such now that we have an American doctor who with the American consul makes out a bill of health which tells if there are any contageous diseases in the port, how many in crew on board, how many passengers on board, and so forth. The doctor comes on board and goes out nearly to sea with you to witness no one else gets on board. He then signs this bill of health, seals it, and gives it to the master of the vessel. On arrival in an American port the quarantine physician is the first man on board, and the only one. The custom house officer stays in the boat until the doctor has examined all the passengers and crew. I may add then that it costs nothing to obtain this bill of health in a foreign port, but if you sail without it Uncle Sam will surely fine you $5,000 and make you pay it.

We are now in the port of New York and docked ready for discharging and getting plenty of something good to eat. Captain Knight hired two Irishmen to pump her of nights at $4 each. We had two old wood pumps; there were no iron pumps in those days. The pumps had an iron crutch between them and a long oak handle and the bolt on this handle directly over the pump. When both pumps were geared up the handle would pump one pump and then the other. We were so used to pumping that Harry Travers and myself could beat these Irishmen badly. I remember one cold night while we were in the cabin we could hear these Irishmen pumping. It seemed that the two pumps going at one time was too much for them. They would soon give out. So they unhooked one of the pumps and pumped with one pump. They did this for quite a while and they got no suck. So they made a change, unhooked this pump, and hooked up the other. They pumped quite a while this way then one of them said, "Let us hook up the other again and try it that way for a while." Finally, one said to another, "Ah, Jimmy, you unharness the one and harness the other and the devil the bit of a suck do we get."

Finally, that money looked so good to me I suggested to Harry to say to Captain Knight that if he would give us the money he was paying those 2 Irishmen that we would do the night pumping. He agreed to give it to us. So Harry would lay down and sleep 2 hours through the night then I would call him and we would pump her out. We were so used to pumping that we could soon pump her out. Then he would go on the watch for 2 hours and call me and we would pump her again, and so all through the night, sleeping every other two hours and watch every other two hours. Then we would do our work and keep her pumped out through the day for our regular wages. We did this for something like 4 or 5 nights but I regret to say when pay day came we got only our monthly wages. This night pumping and watching was never paid for.

After our cargo was out we ballasted and sailed for Baltimore. It was now getting along in December, 1877, and the days and nights were very chilly. There were very many vessels sailing on the coast and it was most necessary to keep a bright lookout which should be at all times. It was my first watch this particular night from 8 PM to 12 midnight. At 12 the watch was called, wheel was relieved, and the starboard watch went below. I went down the cabin and, while I was there warming myself preparatory to turning in, the old mate, Mr. Wilson, came below. He began talking to me in a half dase. I suppose the warm fire made him sleepy. He says to me, "Mr. Tawes, how have you been heading along this watch?" I said, "South southwest, sir." He said, "About how fast has she been going?" I said, "Five knots, sir." "Has she made that all through the watch?", he said. "Oh," I said, "she has made 20 miles alright." He sat there and talked to me all of 20 minutes. He looked so sleepy and did not go on deck. I had kind of feeling that we would have a collision before morning.

Time was going fast and making an inroad in my watch below. So I went to my stateroom and turned in to try to get as much sleep as possible before 4 o'clock when my watch would be on deck again. I went to sleep.

We were now well down below Chincoteague. Well, 20 of 3 I heard her strike a ship—bang, snap, crack! I was called to get on deck as quick as possible. I jumped out as soon as I could and began to put on some clothing to keep from freezing to death as I expected the boat would be lowered to leave her to keep from being drowned. I got on my coat and boots which was about all I had to put on for in those days sailors never pulled off their pants while at sea. It was dark in my stateroom but I always kept my coat and boots where I could lay my hands on them as quick in the dark as I could in a light. Now being ready to jump for the deck I began to think of my $56 that I had stored away in my chest. The money I had worked for so hard, I loathed to leave it behind here now. I needed a light but had not time to get one. Well, I thought, I must find my money and all the time I did not know what was going on deck. I expected they would lower the boats and leave me but I stayed until I found my money. I think anyone would if they had pumped a leaky ship night and day, repaired sail and rigging, reefed and made sails, and waited on yellow fever patients as I did for more than a month. It was the hardest earned money of my life to the present time. Would you not take a big chance to save that hard earned money? I believe you would.

Well, now with my money in my pocket and my heavy clothes on I jumped for the deck and here was a great sight for me to see. The captain and mate were forward on the topgallant forecastle with lanterns in their hands doing something I know not what. I saw our jib boom poked through the mainsail of a three-masted schooner. Our sails were full and even yet pushing hard into him and we were about riding him down for he was deep-loaded with coal and we were in ballast high up out of the water. About the time I got on deck my watch was just getting on deck which showed I was not so long getting there after all. But it seemed a long time to me while I was trying to find my money. Being now on deck, and the wind blowing from about west northwest, in an instant I saw what to do to clear our vessel of this schooner. So I ran to the lee braces, threw them off the pins, and yelled out to my watch, "Starboard fore braces." I threw the forward sails into aback and backed her right off from the schooner.

A few minutes more and we would have had her sunk for everytime we rose up and down by the swell of the sea we were cutting into her. However, we broke two shrouds of her main rigging and pulled off her two chainplates. They caught into our stem lining. When we pulled them off we had about 3 fathoms of her 7½-inch hemp main rigging lanyards and chain plates hanging to us. When we got into Hampton Roads the next day I had an awful job getting them loose from our stem lining. I threw those heavy chainplates and rigging overboard in Hampton Roads where they are today if time and rust have not eaten them up.

When we were loose from the schooner our captain asked Captain Rose, the master of the schooner, if he wanted him to lay by him to take him and his crew off in case she went down. Captain Rose said he thought it unnecessary as he thought he could get her in port himself by nailing canvas over the holes in his schooner. So we filled away and proceeded on our course to the Chesapeake and went into Hampton Roads. It was a Sunday morning when I got this broken rigging, chainplates, and lanyards loosed from our bow.

All signs of wreckage now being cleared up that afternoon we took a Maryland pilot on board and proceeded toward Baltimore. I forget when we took out our ballast. But I well remember when we arrived at Wm. H. Skinner's Railway. Preparatory for hauling out on the ways a U.S. marshal came on board and put a libel on us and we could not get to haul out. We tried our best to get the marshal to allow us to haul out as she was leaking so badly. But he would not consent to it. Hence Harry Travers and myself had to set our old 2-hour watches and pump all night like we did in New York as the sailors had quit immediately on arriving. They were only shipped to make the run from New York to Baltimore, anyhow, and they quit the moment we arrived. The next day bond had been given and the U.S. marshal relieved us and we were permitted to haul out on the railway. We were now released from pumping after a two-month elapse of time without cease.

Here we caulked her from keel up, coppered her about a foot above the light water line, and chartered her for Rio de Janeiro to carry a cargo of flour. Now Mr. Wilson, the chief mate, quit and I was promoted to his place as chief officer of the brig *Agnes Barton*. We went over to Smith's Dock and there loaded 4,600 barrels flour and on the 2nd day of January, 1878, we sailed for Rio. We had, as most all the old Rio traders say, a mighty good run out. We were 49 days and 15 hours from Cape Henry.

I well remember we were 21 days on one tack in going through the doldrums at the equator. We had lots of rain but never stopped going for want of wind. I remember one night near the equator I felt awfully scared. It was a real rainy night. There was the most phosphorus I ever saw before or since in the water although I have crossed the Line several times before and since. The ocean for miles looked like fire as if the water was aflame about six feet above the water and though rainy, with stars and moon obscured, I could survey this flame of light miles and miles from the ship. I thought 3 or 4 times I would call Captain Knight, I felt so lonesome. But on account of him being so fractious when called out of his sleep I did not do so.

Having now crossed the Line and got through the doldrums we now took the southeast trade winds. This is the trade wind that blows south of the equator to the north of the equator. We have the northeast trade wind that usually blows from 26 degrees north lattitude to near the equator and the southeast trade blows from about 26 degrees south lattitude to near the equator. These two winds very near meet at the equator and cause the doldrums and there is where all the water falls that these two winds have taken up by evaporation and hot sun for 12 or 13 hundred miles on each side of the equator. Some rain falls here in the doldrums. Usually the winds are very light and changable causing the sailors to brace the yards from the starboard to the port side and vice versa. The water running down the braces and filling your jacket sleeves full of water when hauling on the braces is anything but pleasant.

In all this rain we fill every empty cask full of water, even to the yawl boat on deck. The sailors are busy as any laundry washing all their dirty clothes and getting everything in order against the next dry lattitude we get. On these long voyages we do not allow clothes washed out of the ship's water. This extravagance has brought misery on a many poor seaman. Sailors are so indifferent about their future needs that if they are not watched they will steal the water out of the casks at night to wash clothes. I have thirsted a great deal myself from this extravagance. It is worse than hunger.

It used to be our custom to give each seaman one bucket of water every Sunday morning to wash and shave himself with. After this he had to wash his face and hands with salt water throughout the week. It was always my custom to give them the weekly ration of one bucket each Sunday at sea until we had our water cask empty. Then I would give them this empty cask to fill and keep full whenever it rained. I would oftimes be compelled to make them fill it when it rained and even help them to do so.

On this brig, once our water was getting down, the sailors would appear to drink water when they did not need it. The captain told me to carry the bung dipper to the topgallant yard and hang it there and when a man wanted water he must go there to get it. And when he drank he must go to the top-gallant yard to hang it there. Water began to go further then because he would not go up after it unless he was real dry.

Having now got into the southeast trades the weather cleared up and the sun came out and dried all the wet clothes and the stuff. Wet ropes got dry and soft to handle and the sails dried out. It makes us all feel quite comfortable again for it takes a sailing vessel about a week to get through these doldrums, the winds are so light and baffling in them.

Though I got fooled mighty badly once in them. I was bound to Rio Grande do Sul with a cargo of flour in the schooner *City of Baltimore*. My brother John was mate with me. I told him, "John, you need not shorten sail for any of these bad looking squalls down here. It's nothing but rain; there is no wind in them." He says, "They are mighty bad looking, some of them." I says, "No fear, it is all rain." So one night about 2 o'clock in the morning I was at the wheel. I saw this ugly looking squall but I shortened nothing. I let it strike with the whole 12 sails set. Well, this turned out to be a bad squall. Indeed it was not all rain this time. John was below but when the *Baltimore* heeled over so low, and wind asquealing so loud, he knew that was no place for him. He jumped on deck and went to taking in sail. I thought it would take the sticks out of her. I kept her as close to the wind as I could to keep the masts in her. I was heading by the wind on a southwest course and when the squall passed I was heading by the wind on a northeast course. We saved everything but our two staysails. They were blown away. I do not know what we would have lost if John had not got on deck so quick and rendered the service he did. I remember seeing an Italian brig in Pernambuco once all dismasted. He must have got into such a squall. She was named the *Julio Caesar*.

I get off my course sometimes in writing this story but you must understand it takes a mighty good seaman to keep a ship steady on her course.

But to resume to our passage on this beautiful brig, which she certainly was, and Captain Knight was proud of her too. All of us would have been, if things had been more agreeable. Well, one morning in my watch below, Captain Knight called me out. A German bark short of provisions had just spoken us. He was about 70 days out loaded with bones from Buenos Aires bound to Falmouth for orders. We had, besides our regular stores, eleven barrels of beef and pork on deck. Captain Knight always carried a big stock of provisions to speculate on when he got the chance. He failed to sell his flour once and we had it on board so long that we sailors had to eat it made in flap cakes bound from Havana, Cuba, to New York. Well, we stored the old German with beef, pork, flour, and hard bread. Captain Knight told him he could have all he wanted. I bet our captain made a good spec on him. It is not every ship went as well prepared to fit out a ship at sea as we did.

Nothing occurred more than the usual happenings on a ship such as reefing, shaking out, and making all the time we could until we arrived in Rio de Janeiro. When we got there it was summertime and very hot. When it is summer there it is winter here and vice versa. The yellow fever was at its worse, being now about the last week in February, 1878. The harbor was full of ships of all nations. There were lots of Portuguese. I do not know why but they seem to die with yellow jack worse than all the other nations. On account the fever being so bad we were not allowed to go to the dock to discharge our cargo. We had to lay in the stream and discharge in lighters to save the lives of our crew.

There were quite a few other Baltimore coffee ships there at the same time. I remember well of going one evening on board the clipper barque *Aquidneck,* Captain Raffle in command. She was a mighty sailer. She and the clipper ship *Gray Eagle* were called the fastest ships out of Baltimore at that time. The captain and I talked considerably about our fast passage out. The old captain said our time was hard to beat, it was such a good one.

It was the law in those days to hoist the flag early every morning when any one was sick on board, under a penalty of $50 for not doing so. As soon as the flag went up a boat was sent from the hospital to get the sick man or men. It often happened to be more than one man sick on a ship at the time. One morning when I turned out I counted fifteen flags on fifteen different ships. Some two and three were taken from each ship. The hospital boat went ashore loaded that morning. Many of them to never return to their ships again because I used to notice when this boat was taking the convalescents back to the ship she would scarcely have half as many as she went ashore with. It was said if the doctors did not get the men immediately after being taken sick they would never get well. That is why the law was so rugged and enforced. It seemed all of our crew escaped.

We Baltimoreans had the custom of keeping our ships immaculately clean. We kept our deck holystoned. Crew's and officer's quarters were holystoned before going into port. Then all the crew were given a dose of calomel and jalap; the dose contained 15 grams each. You would know you had taken something unusual too when you got this dose in you. Lime water was used on the floors in all the crew's and officer's quarters every morning and in this way the quarters were kept sweet and nice and healthy. No spitting on the floors was allowed. American vessels suffered the least of any other nations with yellow fever in these unhealthy ports though I remember the captain of a very large Bath ship dying not far from where we were lying. I think our cleanliness and Mr. Perez, our consignee there, not allowing us to come to the docks saved the lives of some of our crew.

After discharging our cargo we took in about 40 tons of stone ballast for which we paid about 50¢ per ton. Many ports will not let a ship enter from a sickly port with dirt ballast. They say it carries the germs of yellow fever. There is no need of ballasting with dirt ballast in Rio de Janeiro for there are millions of tons of stone in those high mountains in Rio.

While laying at anchor in Rio we always took the boat up to the davits at night to keep thieves from coming along at night and stealing her. They will do this trick very often and then take her up some creek and sink her with stone. You may advertise all you wish but that boat is not seen anymore until you are gone. I remember one night about 8 o'clock we were taking our boat up. We were laying high out of the water then as our cargo was all out. I think Captain Knight had just come on board from the shore. I got down in her to hook her on for in those days I was as limber as a cat. I jumped on the davit fall, slipped down in her, hooked her on, and sang out, "Hoist her up." It was very dark and rainy. She must have laid up out of the water 10 or 12 feet. The sailors and the second mate hoisted her up. About the time she was up to the davits she turned more than half over real quickly and threw me overboard. I heard Captain Knight say, "Lower the boat quick; the mate will be drowned." The current was running very strong in the harbor of Rio. Anyhow, when I struck the water I went down a good ways but being a pretty good swimer when I come up I swam hard to stem the current. When the boat came down I was there to catch onto her and I was hoisted back on board safe and sound.

Our cargo out and ballasted with stone we cleared and sailed for Barbados. I forget how long we were on the passage, but more than a month. I well remember on this passage that Captain Knight got way out on his longitude. He was a man like other people I have seen. It would never do to tell him he had made a mistake. He was always right and the other fellow was always wrong. He could not error. It was the custom in those days for the mate to keep the dead reckoning. The captain worked the chronometer sights. The mate was not supposed to see them but once a week and that would be on a Sunday morning. The captain would hand him the chronometer sights to work up to check up his dead reckoning and practice.

It was this Sunday morning in particular he gave me the morning sights to work. About 9 o'clock he said to me, "What longitude did you put her in?" I told him. He said, "You are wrong; you are way out. You had better work that sight over." I did work it over. I could find nothing wrong with my work and I put my slate away. I would have taken a chance of a shipwreck before I would tell him he was wrong. The penalty would have been harsh words. I always did like to have peace and be agreeable so I just put my work away and said no more about it. That afternoon in the dog watch he said to me, "Mr. Tawes, did you work that sight over?" I said the same. "Well, by God," he said, "you are wrong. Bring me your slate here and I will show you your mistake in two minutes." He began the observations. Altitude corrected alright, lattitude correct, polar distance. "Ah," he said, "here is your mistake; it's in the polar distance. This is what put you so much out of the way." Said I, "Beg your pardon, Captain Knight. Of course you work Bowditch and I work Thomas but Thomas says when the lattitude and declination are of the same they are subtracted. "By God," he says, "I never made a mistake like that in my life before. I do not know how the hell I could have done it." He took my lattitude and longitude, placed them on the chart, and measured his course and distance for Barbados.

We were in the northeast trade wind then so we checked in our yards after keeping her off about 3 points and headed her for Barbados where we arrived about 3 days after. Here we consigned our ship to the house of John Decosta and Company, a very large business house in Barbados. He chartered to load a cargo of sugar in very large hogsheads. There was no sugar shipped in sacks in those days. This sugar was loaded in the between decks and our lower hold was loaded with molasses. So our cargo constituted molasses and sugar, all of which we took to Boston. While lying in Barbados loading a whaler put in there and on her was a shipwrecked crew. They were from a bark from Brunswick or Savannah bound to Buenos Aires that foundered at sea. She was a Boston ship under the command of Captain Charles Estus. Our captain was well acquainted with him and we took him and his mate, by name of Bryan, to Boston with us.

While lying in Barbados, this little instance I feel like telling just to show a little of human nature. We had pin holes all along the fife rail from forward aft to the break of the poop deck. Just abreast of the gangway there was a pin hole and often the sailors would put a belaying pin into this hole which would be a little in the way of going over the gang way. The captain always went ashore about 8 o'clock in the morning. There was a pin in this hole. The captain says to me, "Mr. Tawes, don't allow any more pins put in this hole." I said, "Alright, sir." I ought then to have drove a plug in the hole so the sailors could not have gotten another pin in the hole. But I was a very young man then and could not think of everything or to forelay for what might happen. But I went to all the sailors and told them not to put any more belaying pins in these holes abreast the gangway as it was the captain's orders not to do so.

About the second morning after this, in washing down the decks which we always did from 5:30 to 7 in the morning, one of the sailors had put a belaying pin in this hole abreast the gangway. At 8 o'clock, when the captain was going over the side to go down in the boat to go ashore, there was that belaying pin in the hole abreast of the gangway. Captain Knight swore at me in a rage of temper and threw it with all his force aft not caring where it went, whether it went overboard, who it hit, or whatever damage it might do. Mr. Sam Travers, from Dorchester County, Maryland, was making the round with us from Baltimore to Rio and back. He was setting in the cockpit aft reading and the belaying pin, a piece of locust about 18 inches long fitted into an inch and quarter hole, struck Mr. Travers on the elbow and give him great pain. Sam immediately went to the gangway and just as Captain Knight had got into the boat to be set ashore he says to Captain Knight, "What the hell do you mean by throwing this belaying pin at me and hitting me on the arm." Captain Knight jumped out of the boat and ran up the gangway. I expected there was going to be a fight but there was no fight. There were some ugly harsh words and Captain Knight discovered he had a match. So he said, "I will put you ashore." Sam says, "Alright, I can get home." So Sam went on board one of L. W. & P. Armstrong's ships that was loading there for New York and made arrangements to go home in her. But in about two days or so they made up again and Sam came back and went to Boston with us. Sam's father owned a quarter of this brig which I presume had something to do with the make up.

After we finished the loading of our molasses and sugar we cleared and sailed from Barbados for Boston. I forget how many days we were on the passage but I remember we went through the Vineyard Sound. Captain Charles Estus piloted us through. We arrived in Boston some time in May 1878. When the cargo was out I quit being on board of this brig one year lacking three days. It was, take it all in all, the hardest year of my life.

After being paid off I took the train for Baltimore, came down to Crisfield to see the people I always made my home with, Aunt Leah Sterling. She always told me to make her house mine which I did. She was a mighty good woman and I know she has been rewarded with a heavenly crown. She did so much good while on this earth.

Staying there a few days I went to Baltimore and shipped 2nd mate of the brig *D. C. Chapman* along with Captain James Tyson. This man was a different type man from Captain Knight. He was a kind, good man and a good disciplinarian. In his life he had traded a great deal around the Cape of Good Hope in the China trade. He was the only man I ever sailed with that could lay in his berth and tell when a ship was off her course by the least different roll she would make.

We left Baltimore sometime in May, 1878, with a cargo of flour. We were 56 days on the passage from Cape Henry. These Brazilians were very particular about damaged cargo. If they could see where drops of water fell on the barrel and stained it from the constant drip they would roll it out to one side and call it damaged. The heat in the hold of the vessel going through the tropics and this drip of water, even though it be slow, would turn the barrel staves very dark. We would often roll a few of the bad stained ones on one side while discharging and keep them there and at night, or when there were no lighters alongside, scrape the staves bright so they could not detect the stains on the barrels.

I remember one day we repaired our fore lower topsail. We got through with it just at nocking off time in the evening. The mate says, "We will put the topsail down the hold on the cargo forward and tomorrow morning at 8 o'clock when the watches are changed we will take both watches, that is the starboard and port watches together, and send the new topsail down that is on her now and get the one out of the hold we have just repaired and send it up and bend it." The next morning it was my watch. I had the eight hours out that night. Very early that morning my one man and myself got to work and washed her down for that was our custom at sea and in port, to wash her decks and swab the paint work around the deck. These coffee ships' paint was always kept as white as a lily and their white pine decks were holystoned about every two months forward and aft and kept whiter and cleaner than some housewives keep their biscuit boards.

After my sailor and myself got through cleaning ship I said, "George, we will send that fore lower topsail down." My other man was at the wheel which only left two of us to do the work. The captain had not turned out yet so we clewed the topsail up and aloft we went and unbent the topsail and sent it down. We took off the little fore hatch that led down in the hold forward and got the topsail out and sent it aloft. After getting the topsail out I forgot to put the hatch on and cover it with the tarpaulin, which I should have done. The neglect of it caused me to see many unhappy hours the remainder of the passage for while I was aloft she threw her bow under and a great heavy sea came rolling over the bow and many barrels of water went down the hold on the cargo of flour. I just slipped down from aloft as quick as I could and put the hatch on and covered with the tarpaulin. Then I went up and worked as fast as I could and bent the fore lower topsail and set it up before seven bells, when the mate came on deck. He, the mate, could hardly believe that two head of us could have done such a heavy job and in such short time. I was young and could work in those days.

I never breathed it to anyone about the sea coming over and the many barrels of water that went down the little fore hatch and wetting about 200 barrels of flour. The sailor George knew nothing of the consequences of it and never told it. But I was much worried about the black damaged barrels of flour coming out of the hold forward when ge got to Rio. I knew when all this flour came out damaged there would be an inquiry and when this inquiry came about then my man George would expose the whole thing. The blame I would have to bear would be so unpleasant to me. But to my agreeable surprise and pleasure when we discharged our cargo not a barrel came out black or in the least damaged. I supposed they soon dried in the hold when the warm air drew through the hold and with no more water falling on them they never colored or stained. No one on board ever found out they got wet either.

I do not remember of anything unusual happening on this voyage out more than to make sail, carry sail, reef sail, make it again and carry on the usual work that came along in the routine of a passage. There is always plenty to do on a ship at sea and in port. We arrived in Rio sometime in July which is a winter month in that lattitude and the weather is quite pleasant in that month. But it is never cold in Rio de Janeiro. It is too close to the equator to ever get cold as it lies in 22 degrees south lattitude. But it gets severely hot in December, January, and February and quite sickly. This time after getting to sea homeward bound I took the yellow fever and I suffered very much. The captain, James Tyson by name, did what he could for me but after coming on deck to stand my watch I was not much account for work the remainder of the voyage. I was so weak and run down and not getting the nourishing food that my system required. We had a fair passage to Cape Henry. We were 49 days from the Sugar Loaf Mountain to Cape Henry.

Arriving in Baltimore I was feeling so badly that I did not go back in this brig but returned to Virginia to visit my mother's relatives who were always kind to me. Here my Aunt Leah, a better woman than her never drew breath, persuaded me to give up the sea and try to make a living on shore. I came up to

Crisfield and here I met a photographer by the name of Peter M. Tilghman. Peter was a single man then as well as myself. We got together and concluded to open a novelty store such as picture frames and pictures, glass, cigars and tobacco, and many numerous things. Peter worked in the gallery taking pictures of people. I stayed in the store and sold goods and received the patrons of the picture gallery and entertained them until he could receive them in the gallery. I also sold goods in the meantime. We opened about the first of November, 1878. I stayed in this store all winter and on the 12th day of February, 1879, I married. In the spring things looked dull and I sold my interest and concluded I had better get back to sea. As I was not doing much in this store, and now being married, I plainly saw the necessity of making money.

III

1879–1880

ABOUT the first of April, 1879, I went to Baltimore to ship out or look up a job. As I was walking along Pratt Street I looked up at the office of Sam H. Travers and Son. His office was up stairs over a nautical instrument store kept by F. J. Sloan and Company. Captain Travers was in the act of hoisting his window when he saw me passing and he called me up stairs to see him. Now Captain Travers knew me well. I had been sailing in his employ 4 years. He owned two nice brigs and one 3-masted schooner namely the brig *D. C. Chapman;* the brig *Agnes Barton* (both of these brigs were of 600 tons capacity); and the 3-masted schooner *Wm. H. Knight,* all 3 seagoing vessels. Besides he owned several bay vessels. When his window was up he saw me passing along Pratt Street and he called me up. He says to me, "What are you doing?" I told him I had come up to go to sea again. He says, "I have chartered a small vessel to go to the West Indies and the captain not being a navigator himself requests one. Could you go as mate and navigator of her?" I told him I could and would be glad of the job. So I took this job at $40 per month. Afterwards, I was introduced to the captain whose name was Henry Palmer. He belonged around Church Creek, Dorchester County, Maryland.

I went on board and unbent the old sails and bent new ones, looked over her rigging and set it up quite taut, and otherwise got her ready for sea. On Sunday morning, the 7th day of April, we hauled out of Long Dock and sailed without the use of a tow boat. We proceeded down the bay and went out the capes on Monday. About the next day a fresh northeaster struck us and we had a nice run out. I was quite a young looking man for my age. In fact every one tells me that now though I am 72 years of age. However, on account of my youthful appearance, the captain doubted me very much that I could see for now and then he would say, "Mr. Tawes, you think you are runing the right course?" Said I, "Oh, yes, I do." We were skipping along very fast. The next day he got at me again about the course I was steering. Said he did not believe I was steering the right course. I asked him why he thought I was steering wrong. "Well," he said, "I have been out here 3 or 4 times and I never saw any of my navigators steer like you are steering." "Well," I said, "how did they steer?" He said, "They always steered south southeast while you are steering south by west." I saw in an instant that they were men who doubted their work in longitude and they were runing their lattitude down and kept her off west and run until they made the island they were bound to while I had no doubt about my longitude and steered as the crow flies to his nest straight for the Northwest Providence Channel. "Well," he said to me, "if we fall to the leeward and do not make the island we are bound to, which is Eleuthera, I will go down in Georgia and load hard pine and go home." Now to relieve him of his anxiety I hauled up a point and the Sunday following the day we left Baltimore I sighted Bridge Point on Eleuthera Island. There the cook and all then began to hug me so proud I had made the island so successfully. All confidence in me was restored from then on. The next day we arrived at Harbor Island, entered, and sailed for Rock Sound where we were bound.

I had been distracted with a toothache from about the second day from Baltimore until we arrived at Rock Sound. I turned out the first thing there at about one o'clock in the morning and sculled a large yawl boat about a mile to the shore to get a dentist to pull this agravating tooth. I banged at the door of his house and he would not turn out. So about sunrise the next morning I sculled this old, big yawl ashore again. There was some work about this sculling. I knocked at the door of the dentist and the servant girl told me I was too early, that the doctor did not turn out until 9 o'clock. I thought such lazy people ought to have to know the husk from the swine as the Prodigal Son did. I sculled back to the ship. At ten o'clock I sculled ashore again. This, the third, time I was successful in seeing the doctor. I spoke to him. "Ah," he says, "you are the young man who came to my door last night aren't you?" I said, "Doctor, I have suffered the greatest of agony with the tooth since I left Baltimore. I want it extracted." He threw out his arm and said, "I do not believe I have sufficient strength to pull that." Now he was the only dentist in Rock Sound and it was very discouraging to me to hear him say he could not pull this agravating tooth. I said, "Oh, doctor, try to gather up enough strength and resolution to take out this tooth." I could see the man was failing in health and I do not think he pulled many more after that for I met him shortly after that in New York on his way to Canada to seek health. "Well," he said, "come down to the office." Then he took out an old rusty pair of forceps. However, I was glad to have this aching tooth pulled with anything. So I got in his old chair and he let her go. After one or two big yanks that tooth and me separated and I was surely proud it was gone. I think my wife has it home here somewhere at this day.

After discharging our cargo at Rock Sound we took in part cargo of pineapples and proceeded to another island and finished loading and sailed for Baltimore. I forgot to mention that while on our way I saw a large schooner coming head on to us from the southward. I saw he had his ensign set which in those days he wished to exchange longitudes as a matter of courtesy. I worked up my longitude, wrote it in large figures, set our ensign and ran very close to him. My longitude as I remember was 76° 13′ west. His was 76° 15′ west. So we were practically together. This was the last time I ever exchanged longitudes with any ship though I went to sea more than 30 years after. I am sorry to say it is a courtesy which has become obsolete. We had a pretty good run to Baltimore though it was very squally coming out of the Gulf Stream off Cape Hatteras. After I got in the bay the captain, seeing the thick green water and the headlands on the bay he knew so well, said to me, "You go below and take your rest. We have got her now." Arriving in Baltimore we delivered a nice cargo of pineapples to H. P. Dyer and Company.

This voyage being completed I was wired for from Philadelphia to go out as navigator and mate with Captain J. C. Woodland bound to Nassau. I believe we went in ballast for a load of pineapples in Nassau. We loaded "pines" and came back to Philadelphia. We then chartered to go to Jacksonville and load lumber for New York at $8 per thousand feet. We loaded at the St. Johns Mill about 2½ or 3 miles below the city of Jacksonville.

When about loaded one of our sailors ran away. He was an Italian. He had a chest of clothing and quite some money in it, one or two hundred dollars. He left about a day before we were loaded. Sailors are a hard thing to get down south. The south furnished no seamen in those days and I presume it is the same today. Well, Captain Woodland found out where this Italian seaman had his things stored. It was in the house of some old colored woman. So that evening Captain Woodland went to this colored person's house and got the Italian's chest and other clothing and brought them on board. Then we dropped the vessel in the stream. About 12 o'clock that night this fellow came down from Jacksonville with a team to get his things. When he got to the colored man's house he learned they were on board the vessel. He had a particular friend in one of the crew so he hailed to this fellow to bring the boat on shore. As soon as he started to take that boat I was right at the davits to prevent him. I and this man on board came near to blows when I prevented him from taking the boat. I knew if the other fellow got on board the two of them would overpower me and the fellow would take his clothes and go, and perhaps the other fellow too. I knew the Italian on shore would not leave his money and clothes and I intended to die before I would let the Italian on board get the boat. The captain did not stay on board that night. He stayed in Jacksonville and came down on the tow boat the next morning to tow down the river and go to sea. When he got alongside I told him Manuel was on the dock and I believe ready to come on board. So the towboat took Captain Woodland ashore after him. He did not have a very pleasant time on shore that night as the man who brought him down wanted the dollar he had promised him. He had no money with him and he could not get where his money was. I could hear the teamster on shore cursing him and telling him he was going to lick him if he did not give him his dollar. I had a very unpleasant time that night for I stayed right at the davits to keep the sailor on board from getting the boat and the mosquitoes like to eat me up alive. Oh, I had a terrible headache all the next day with a lot work to do and awful hot it was, for it was in July.

We had a fair run to New York. I guess Manuel paid his way to Jacksonville to start a peanut stand, if he went at all. We chartered to load sulphur for Wilmington, North Carolina. Captain Woodland thought he would send me out in charge of her but it was lucky he did not for I should have certainly pursued my course for Wilmington whereas he turned back and anchored under Sandy Hook. I know I would have kept on for I could see nothing to turn back for but I afterwards found out for on the 19th day of August, 1879, a dreadful hurrycane struck in on the coast which did a great deal of damage to shipping. We were lying under Sandy Hook, both anchors overboard and payed out to the bitter end. When we did come out we came across a large 3-masted schooner bottom up. I heard the captain had two of his daughters with him. All were drowned.

On our way down the coast we put in Hampton Roads. Captain Woodland said he was feeling unwell so he put me in charge of her and went to Norfolk and hired a mate, Bill Diggs by name, who was well known all the way up and down the coast. He could swear the most gramaticle than any man I ever met. The captain went home. I proceeded to Wilmington as early as possible, discharged our sulphur at the Navassa Guano Works, loaded our lumber, and was in Baltimore 19 days from the time Captain Woodland left us at Hampton Roads. This was my first trip in charge of a vessel and I got through with it successfully and nicely. After this I went as mate again in the same vessel. Bill Diggs quit and went back to Norfolk. If I am right, and I believe I am, this was the first cargo of lumber from the south to start the building of the Johns Hopkins University.

Captain Woodland then took charge and I went as mate again. I think we then loaded corn and went back to Wilmington, North Carolina, and lumber back to Baltimore. We were longer on this trip than the last one. We then took in a part cargo of coal and finished cargo with kerosene oil in barrels. We left Baltimore on a Sunday morning on or about the 18th of October, 1879. We had a good strong breeze down the bay, wind from the north. The weather was not looking good and favorable. The next morning Captain Woodland said to me, "Don't you think we had better go in Hampton

Roads with weather looking like this?" I discouraged it by saying we can go much further with a fair wind than we can with a head one. Captain Woodland was a better judge of the weather than I was. At that time I was young, then only about 25 years of age. I have learned a great deal about weather since. Well, we went out of the capes on Monday morning— not to Hampton Roads. I had ample time to afterwards regret. We went swiftly down the coast, passed Cape Hatteras, got in a southeast storm which we wore out just a little before we all were worn out from reefing, and pulling, and hauling, trying to take care of the ship. Finally, we got down to the Frying Pan Lightship. The wind died out and we rolled around there for a few hours. The wind breezed up again from the northeast. We trimmed her sails and put her on her course.

About 4 o'clock the next morning we were in sight of Cape Romain Light. The wind commenced to freshen up and get strong. A sea runed across the poop deck which disturbed Captain Woodland and he came up on deck and said to me, "Don't you know when to take in sail?" I said, "I do." "Well," he said, "I think you do not. Clew up the mizzin topsail, also the fore and main topsails, and send three men aloft to make them fast." This being done the men came down from aloft and I was ordered to haul down the flying jib, and jib, and furl them. Then I was ordered to take in the spanker and put a single reef in it. I was then ordered to furl it and to lower the mainsail and put a single reef in it. I was then ordered to put a peak stop on it and take in the foresail and put a single reef in it. I was then ordered to put a peak stop on the foresail and double reef the spanker. Then I was ordered to double reef the mainsail and to double reef the foresail, the wind all the time increasing. Rapidly, I was then ordered to hoist up the double reefed mainsail and to furl the spanker and foresail. It was now along in daylight. I had already done enough pulling and hauling that morning to kill some people. I will here add that this was the first and last time I ever saw all three of the lower sails single reefed then double reefed before either one was set.

We were now running at a flying gate before the wind on a course somewhere about southwest. She was washing like a half tide ledge and the seas were boarding her heavily. Captain Woodland said to me, "Don't you think we had better get the hawser out and make it fast to the bits on each side and tow the bight so as to cut this sea down?" I then looked at the log and told him we were only 70 miles from Jacksonville Bar and that we had better heave her to and lay to until the gale blowed by or moderated. Then we could run down when the wind moderated. In those days St. Johns Bar only had ten feet of water on it at high water. To run down there then in a gale of wind and not get in, and not be able to drive her off the sea again, we might be driven on the beach and all of us drowned. The captain listened to me and we hove her to. And a good thing we did for it was Thursday, about the 23rd or 24th of October, and it blew a gale all day and night, Thursday, Friday, Saturday, Sunday, and Monday. Four days and nights we were hove to on the port tack, headed offshore and we drifted away below Jacksonville. I happened to get a noon observation and I found we were in the lattitude of Cape Canaveral. This was on Sunday. We then wore her around on the starboard tack and head reached back to the northward heading offshore all the time and trying our best from going ashore on the beach. I was watching our lead line all the time to see if we shallowed our water any for our safety depended intensely in keeping her from the beach. None of us had any idea of having such a long gale of wind when it first began to blow the Thursday before. On Monday night the wind shifted and blew a heavy gale from the northwest which caused a big cross sea. This gave us a terrible washing and the captain suggested wearing around on the other tack. I told him I did not think she would make any better weather. But he did wear around on the port tack and she made ever so much better weather.

The next day being Tuesday the weather cleared off and I got a noon observation. I found we were ten miles south of Jacksonville Bar. We turned all our reefs out and put her under full sail and that evening late we got over the bar and into Mayport. We towed up to Jacksonville Wednesday morning and docked at John Clark's Wharf. The cargo of oil and coal was for him. He came down while I was taking the tarpaulins off the hatches and I may add they were as clean and white as a boiled shirt for they were under water and washed for four days and nights. Mr. Clark spoke to Captain Woodland and said to him, "How is it this vessel would not insure? I tried my best to get insurance on this cargo and could not do it." Captain Woodland told him she ought to insure; she was built under inspection. When I heard him say this I thought to myself, Mr. Clark you owe me $200. Captain Woodland was so uneasy in this storm that he wanted to cut a hole in the cabbin floor and go down the hold and burst the heads in of all the coal oil barrels and let the oil run down through the coal and pump the oil out as it drained into the limbers. He wanted to do this to lighten the vessel up. We discharged our cargo and went down to the St. Johns Mill and loaded lumber for Washington, D. C.

I must relate a little incident that happened while I was in Jacksonville this time. About 4 months previous to this time we took a young man to New York with us as a passenger. He thought he was somewhat of a seaman. He had put in a little time on a pilot boat on the St. Johns Bar and when he came on board he said to me, "Whenever you want me to help you handle the sails, set the rigging taut, or to do any pulling and hauling day or night be sure you call me." His name was Ned Hudinal. This was in the month of July but poor Ned he was disappointed in himself for he was seasick all the way to New York and was practically useless to us as far as help. When we got back to Jacksonville in the latter part of October, 1879, and while lying at John Clark's Wharf discharging cargo, Ned came down to see us and would have us, Cris Woodland and myself, go over the river with him to see his father's orange grove and farm. It was on a Sunday afternoon that Cris, myself, and I believe Hiram Sterling, for Hiram was with us on this voyage. We had a big Newfoundland dog which we took along with us. When we crossed the river and landed we were going through the fields back of Mr. Hudinal's house. He saw us coming. He had 8 dogs including a bull dog. He was coming to meet us and hollering, "Keep your dog back. If mine gets on him they will kill him." "Yes, sir," said I, "I will because I do not want my dog to get hurt." He kept his dogs back behind him. I had about 5 fathoms of hambro-line with me and I tied it around Jack's neck and held on to him. The old man told me all about what a savage dog his bull dog was and related to me about how many dogs he had killed and when he got hold of a dog he never let go. He always killed them and that he never missed his hold.

Well, the old gentleman became very interesting telling me about how to raise oranges. His trees were as full as they could hold and it was the prettiest sight anyone ever looked at. The orchard was so clean. Not a spear of grass or weeds to be seen anywhere. I think he told me some trees would bear five thousand good marketable oranges. We had now become so engrossed in our conversation we had forgotton all about the dogs and the first thing I know the bull dog jumped on mine. But his long hair I think, and the quickness of my dog, prevented him from getting his never failing or deathly hold. In a second my dog had him down and was crushing the bones in him. I could hear them cracking and the other 7 dogs were snaping at him at the same time. I saw that Jack, for that was my dog's name, was handling himself so nicely, which pleased me so much, I just slacked the hambro-line and let him go in the battle unmolested. In a very short time old Mr. Hudinal hollered to me, "Take your dog off, he will kill mine." Jack was a very obedient dog and when I pulled the line and called him off he did so at once. The old man was much surprised at the alertness of my dog. I said to him, "Mr. Hudinal, I will take the line off my dog and let him go at liberty if you say, for he can take care of himself regardless of all of your 8 dogs including the bull." He said to me, "Don't do it for that dog of yours can give a bear a hard tussel." He gave us a sack of oranges and we bade him good-by, went down to the river, and crossed over to the vessel after having spent a very pleasant Sunday afternoon. I made about 50 voyages to Jacksonville after this but never met this old gentleman again.

After we finished discharging our cargo we took in a cargo of lumber and went to Washington consigned to Johnson and Wimsatt. I well remember on the 17th day of November, 1879, we were rounding Smith Point, mouth of Potomac River, with wind southwest. I thought, a nice fair wind but all three of our topsails were furled. We ought to have them set. I looked away up the river ahead of us. I saw a pungy boat with his topsail set. I said, "Captain Woodland, there is a pungy up the river there carrying his topsail." He said to me, "Yes, and dam him it won't be long before he will wish he had it down in his bunk for a pillow." So we sailed on up the river under lower sails which I was afterward thankful for in 2 or 3 hours one of the worst gales of wind struck us down from the northwest that very, very seldom ever blew harder. We lowered all of our sails down as quickly as possible to save them from blowing into ribbons. The spray flew all over us in solid sheets. The pungies were runing down the Potomac with about 3 hoops of their foresails up. Some with a few hanks of their jibs. Some could not make a harbor on the Potomac at all but just went before the gust of wind and made out to reach the Taskmakers below Smith Point and make an anchorage. The old man Gilly Carman, who lived in Crisfield, was in a very small clinker-built sloop called the *Masonic,* did reach this harbor by a very close call and was saved. As for us we put part of our mainsail and fore staysail on and runed her under Piney Point and anchored with our big anchor and layed there 3 days and nights. There was not a dry thread on me when we came to anchor.

After 3 days freezing weather it moderated and the breeze sprang up from the southwest. We got underway and proceeded on our journey toward Washington. After discharging our cargo of lumber we chartered to take a load of coal from Georgetown to New York at $2 per ton. We all thought it was a big freight for those days. We then chartered to go to Norfolk and load corn for Savannah, Georgia. Discharging this cargo we chartered to carry a cargo of lumber to Baltimore and got there sometime in February 1880. We chartered then to load corn for Charleston, South Carolina. Captain Woodland, wishing to move his family to Baltimore to live and school his children, put me in charge to make this voyage. Now, this was my second time to take charge as master and being the month of March it weighed heavily upon me. But here I was a young man, married, and one child to support. It compelled me to carry heavy burdens and being this was my occupation it was my duty to myself and family to go. I had some very heavy gales of wind to contend with on this voyage but I got through with it nicely and successfully. And I was building up a nice reputation around Gaff Topsail Corner and my future as regards the maritime was looking brighter and brighter all the time.

Merchants were getting acquainted with me. One I will mention in particular by name Ebon B. Hunting. This man befriended me a great deal in the years after. He is yet living.

I called on him at his office in the Calvert Building, Baltimore. He seemed glad to see me. We talked over old times and about our surviving all the merchant captains and vessels that were engaged in the southern trade out of Baltimore. In our conversation he gave me a very agreeable surprise. He said to me, "Tawes, you made more money for me than any of the other vessels." He was interested in more than a dozen. He continued, "Besides, I will say to you that due to my confidence in your seamanship and the vessel you sailed that I did not insure my cargoes under you." I said, "Mr. Hunting, this is flatering but you did not let me know it. And besides you took an awfull risk." "Well," he said, "I always charged her and you with insurance and after I had saved enough to pay the cost of a cargo insurance did not cross my mind any more." Well, I will say that I met Mr. Hunting in Charleston on this my second voyage. He was then a fine, young looking man full of business to the letter.

After making this voyage I resumed my old place as mate again. We then chartered to take a miscellaneous cargo to the West Indies. We discharged our cargo, loaded pineapples, and went to New York. We discharged our cargo and chartered to go to Cat Island for another load of pineapples, coming back to New York. Discharging our cargo of fruits we coasted to the different places along our coast. I have forgotten where and whither it has been so many years ago.

On the 11th day of October, 1880, I was in Richmond, Virginia. We had finished taking in our cargo and was going to tow down the river that night. It was on a Saturday night, I well remember, that Captain Samuel A. Travers wired Captain Woodland if he could spare me to take charge of one of his vessels loading there with cooperage for Matanzas, north side of Cuba. The captain brought me the telegram and I read it and I said, "Captain Woodland, if it is agreeable with you, and the captain of Captain Travers' vessel, I will accept the position." It was all dark then so I packed my things and cleaned up the stateroom that I occupied for it was my system in those days to leave everything clean and in good order behind me so that the next mate would have a clean place to go into. I put my things in charge of old Mr. Hopkins who had charge of the locks on the canal. I went up to the vessel and asked the captain if he was resigning. He said that he certainly was and to come on board and take charge. Captain Woodland got the mate that was on this vessel and proceeded down the James River that night.

The next day, it being Sunday, gave me an opportunity to take in the situation and Captain Flowers gave me the ins and outs about the vessel which was poor recommendation. He said that the vessel was awfully wet at sea and that she would not tack nor wear. In all she had a bad reputation but undauntedly I was not bluffed. I had then been more than 8 years at sea and I knew if others had got her in and out of port I could too. In about two days Captain Travers came down and brought me a mate and crew from Baltimore. Captain Flowers had packed and gone. Now my troubles were still heavy upon me. Captain Travers wanted to pile a great high deck load on the vessel and the shipper did not want any more to go on. Hough and Company were the shippers of this cargo. I was a young fellow and had to keep quiet but after a long argument Mr. Hough and Captain Travers came to an agreement and by splitting the difference up in the hotel that night and the next day they piled her up with these hoop poles. Everybody in Richmond felt sorry for me to have to go to sea in an overloaded vessel. In hauling down through the locks in the canal she struck a fender and fell over more than a streak. Oh, she was awful tender but I had made up my mind to throw the hoop poles overboard if I had got caught in a hurrycane on the way out, for it was then hurrycane season. The former captain and mate of this schooner, the *William H. Knight* was her name, were only coasters and could not take this vessel to Matanzas for at that time they were not navigators. But some years after did become navigators I did hear.

Well, I must tell you something about hoop poles. They are small white oak and hickory trees cut 15 feet long and split open from end to end. They were used in those days for making sugar and molasses hogsheads. These hogsheads were made large enough to hold one ton of sugar and 145 to 160 gallons of molasses. So you can just imagine the work we sailors had to do hoisting on board and stowing these heavy hogsheads. Sugar and molasses is no longer carried in hogsheads now. Even before I quit going to sea sugar was carried in sacks containing 300 lbs. to the sack. My little vessel *City of Baltimore* usually carried 3400 sacks and I brought up several cargoes of sugar from the north and south sides of Cuba and Santo Domingo, Antigua, and Demerara.

To persue my story we cleared from the custom house in Richmond, took a tow boat, and towed down the James River. On the way down Mr. Smith, my mate and a fine fellow he was too, and I went to work setting the rigging down tight. Also all of the head gear for everything was so slack that the rigging was almost hanging in a bight. By the time we reached Hampton Roads we had the old ship in a good, seaworthy condition for I think we were about 2 days towing down the river, there being 3 other vessels in the tow beside ourselves. We arrived at the Roads sometime after midnight. Now having everything in readiness to go I got underway immediately and went out for in those days I was very restless and was anxious to make time. And by leaving at such an early hour the Virginia pilots did not catch me and I saved about $40 pilot money for Mr. Travers, the owner.

I passed out of Cape Henry just before the day broke and with a fresh northwest wind I passed Cape Hatteras Shoals close aboard and shaped my course for the Hole in the Wall

Lighthouse. In the meantime the wind hauled around to the northwest with fine clear weather and we were scooting along nicely with this fair wind and rolly, top heavy ship. When about 140 miles from the Hole in the Wall we spied a dismasted brig. We runed down to her, lowered a boat, and Mr. Smith with part of my crew went on board. I did not want to be loosing time with a nice fair wind prevailing. He came on board and brought a lot of blocks and some rigging all of which was very useful to us. She had a cargo of white pine lumber in the hold. Her deck load was gone. Had I known as much about the Bahama Banks as I know now I would have gotton a line to her and towed her to the Banks and anchored her there, left a couple of my men to look out for her, and proceeded to Matanzas. And after discharging my cargo I would have cleared and come back to her and loaded that white pine lumber and proceeded to Baltimore or New York with it and made not less than $3,000. But I did not do it. About the next day, in the night, I made the Hole in the Wall Light and proceeded down the Northwest Channel toward Stirrup Key Light. Now here I was up against it again. I was never across the Bahama Banks in my life. I had no chart of it on board. In fact I was short of charts. Captain Travers compelled all his captains to find their own charts in those days.

Well, in looking around the cabbin to my agreeable surprise I found an old *Coast Pilot* compiled by Captain Edmund Blunt. I took this old book which was valuable to me and if I remember correctly, though it has been 47 years ago and I cannot be to definite about it, these were his sailing directions: get Stirrup Key Light to bear south 2 miles and steer west southwest 44 miles. Then steer south southwest until you run off the Bank south of Orange Keys. This Orange Key is a rock just above water right in the way of vessels crossing the Banks and not lighted. When I reckoned we were in about 10 miles of this danger I came to anchor. Then the wind changed to the west and I layed here two or three days to anchor waiting for a fair wind. It was squally and rainy all the time I laid here but the Bahama Banks anywhere is like laying in a harbor. The water is too shallow to get rough although no land is in view anywhere. But the water is so clear the bottom is visible all the way across, a distance of about 120 miles. On about the third day the wind came from the northeast which was a fair wind. I got under way and proceeded. I runed off the Banks and shaped my course for the Double Headed Shot Keys, passed by them in the daytime and the light keeper, a Mr. Thompson, came on board and beged for some potatoes, onions, and butter. I gave him what I could spare which every ship should do for a man who lives on a lonely rock where weeds would not grow and keep us a light, though he could catch all the fish and turtles he needed. He brought us quite a supply of both but having no ice it was little or no use to us. The weather here is always hot. We sailed on by this island and the next day the Pan of Matanzas began to rise in view bearing about southwest. And that afternoon we arrived in Matanzas safe and sound with all of our rolly cargo of hoop poles safely on board.

Now trouble come upon me again. I have heard shipmasters talk so much about their manifests and paying fines if a word was left out or spelled wrong. And all of this cussedness with the Spaniards. But I never had this thing to contend with until this time, my first voyage as master. I had the ship cleaned all over on deck and below. I had every can of lobsters, peaches, and apples all on my manifest and I was in hopes by all this precaution I would get off without having to pay a fine. I had my American flag flying from the mizzin and here come the custom house visitors on board for in Matanzas you have to lay at anchor about 1½ miles from shore. Here they came alongside and the interpreter says, "Captain, let me see your bill of health." I handed it over the side to him. He saw it was a clean bill of health and says, "How long were you coming out?" I told him eleven days. "Did you have any sickness on the way out?", he said. I told him none. "And all on board well?", he inquired. I answered in the affirmative. Then they all came on board, examined the crew, then came below in the cabbin and began to go through my papers. This old interpreter began, "There is a word left out in this manifest. That is $10 fine." In looking along he found another, the word *bundles* of hoop poles we left out. Well, I began to think, this will end me as master. When these fellows got through fining of me after awhile the old interpreter called me aside and says, "When you come ashore you bring me some of those cans of lobsters and peaches and bring your same pen and ink up to Mr. Antonio Fernandez's ship chandlery store and I will help you to correct up this manifest before we go to the custom to enter." I said, "Can't we do that here?" He said, "No, we cannot in the presence of these Spanish custom house officers." What a cute way that old rascal had to get my lobsters and peaches. But I would have been willing to let him have all the can goods I had on board and lived on salt beef and bread all the way back home for sake of not being fined.

After they left and gave me the privilege to come on shore and enter ship I hurriedly dressed myself and went on shore carrying with me a generous supply of lobsters, peaches, and my same bottle of ink and pen. I went up to Mr. Fernandez, the ship chandler, made his acquaintance and kept it for I went to Matanzas quite a few times afterwards. He assigned me to a private compartment where the old interpreter was in waiting for me. I took out the ship's manifest and wrote where he said write and got everything in shape to go to the custom house and enter. Which I did and got through without a hitch. I told him I had the can goods in the boat at the wharf but I was afraid to take them out. He said, "Leave that to me, I will get them."

After entering at the custom house I then went to our American consulate, deposited my register crew list etc. and came back to the ship chandler. There I met some American and English shipmasters. We then had a little something to drink to seal our acquaintance. I then asked Mr. Antonio Fernandez to send me out two laborers when the lighters came off after the cargo the next morning. I then went on board and got supper and turned in to take a whole night's rest which I had not had for nearly two weeks.

I forgot to say, in crossing the Banks on the courses mentioned, I threw the lead as fast as I could and I found 18 feet of water on every cast of the lead excepting two casts. I found 16 feet of water on these two casts. I have crossed the Banks several times since then but always had a chart of the Great Bahamas Bank and the courses are laid down on the chart to steer over by. But on none of these other courses did I find at anytime over 14 feet of water.

At Matanzas I discharged all my cargo in lighters. We loaded about 2 lighters. One day I was trying to get the captain of one of the lighters to move his lighter a little furthur ahead. I could not get him to understand me. But there was a real old negro man sitting on the side of the lighter fishing. He was so old he was useless for work any longer. He understood what I wanted the captain to do so he told him and the lighter was moved. I said to him, "You understand English don't you?" He answered me in very plain English. I said to him, "You speak nice English. Did you learn that here in Cuba?" He said, "No, I learned it in St. Thomas. There is where I was born." I said, "How did you get here?" He told me that just before slavery was abolished by Denmark—Denmark owned St. Thomas then—he was sold to slave holders in Jamaica. And just before the English abolished slavery he was sold to the Spaniards in Cuba. I think if any man had a hard fate it was this old fellow. I felt awful sorry for him. At about 3 o'clock PM the lighter was loaded and as the lighter was leaving the old fellow says, "Good by, captain. When you come out to Matanzas again bring me something." "Alright," said I, "what would you like me to bring you?" Said he, "Bring me an old jacket." I thought that was the smallest and simplest request one man could make of another. I ran down the cabin as quickly as I possibly could to get him one of my jackets to give him but when I got on deck the lighter had gotton too far from my vessel for me to even fling it to him. I made several voyages to Matanzas after this but never saw this pitiful old negro man again.

In about a week we had all our cargo out. I took in 35 tons of ballast, settled up with my consignee, sent Captain Travers a bill of exchange for about $1,200, and took about $250 in Spanish doubloons to defray my expenses in Jacksonville. I sold them to the Ambler Bank and by the rate of exchange I lost 8 or 10 dollars on them. I cleared for Jacksonville and sailed. Got caught in a heavy north northeast gale in the Florida Straits and I had to tack and wear every 4 hours. Could not see a thing it was so thick and stormy. I was expecting every minute to be thrown upon the Florida Keys when tacking to the westward and expected to be thrown upon some of the rocks or islands on the Bahama side when tacking to the eastward. I did not get any rest during this 48 hours but one morning, sometime after midnight, I saw to my great relief Jupiter Light so bright it almost lighted the clouds. I felt much relieved when I saw this light for I knew I was out clear of Abaco and I could put her on longer tacks, 12 hours or 14 hours, if I so wished. Jupiter Light has made me happy several times, this by sighting it dark nights, for it is very hard to keep an accurate dead reckoning of a ship in these stormy waters and currents runing 4 miles an hour to the northward and eastward.

After working 3 or 4 days with head winds and calms I arrived at Jacksonville Bar. Towed in over the bar with Jim

Philanny as pilot. Arrived in Jacksonville and reported to my consignee, a man by the name of Root. He directed me what wharf to go to and discharge my ballast. After entering at the custom house and paying my tonage dues I got a permit to discharge my ballast. Finishing this I hauled to the lumber wharf and began loading lumber. I took on board 170 thousand feet which was my cargo capacity. Cleared and towed down the river and crossed the bar December 4, 1880.

Had a good run to Cape Hatteras. Here a heavy northwester hit me and blowed my spanker away. It blew a heavy gale and began to freeze the ropes hard. And for the want of after sail I could not hold the beach and I drifted ever so far offshore into the Gulf Stream. This cold air on this warm water made the ghostiest sight I ever laid my eyes on before. For miles, before getting into the warm water of the Stream, it would seem I saw thousands of water spouts. Then it would look like forestry. This would pass off for a minute. Then next I would see some great city and to be honest I felt scared. After a while I drifted out of the cold water into the warm water and then I was enclosed into this vapor and I could see nothing but cities, towns, forestry, and ships of all kind of rigs. And this was all vapor rising off of this warm water. Sometimes the sailors would squeal out, "There is a ship on the port." I would jump forward to get the bearing of her and about that time she would disapear and roll away as nothing but mist. Now I was lying right in the track of ships from New York or Philadelphia bound south. All that night I never shut my eyes in sleep and none of the crew got much. I expected every moment to be runed over. All day the next day, the wind continuing to blow a gale from the northwest, we continued to see these phantom ships, cities, forestry, and water spouts. I was hove to all this time drifting to north and east. About 4 o'clock afternoon, just before dark set in, I happened to be looking to windward and just above the mist I sure see a topgallant and royal. Could see no ship but this was no phantom. It was really and truly a barentine runing before the wind. He just did run clear of our stern. He scared us all up quite considerable but a miss is as good as a mile.

We lay to all this night and kept the best watch we could. The next day the weather moderated and we made sail. The wind came up from the southwest and I did my best now to get to Cape Henry. We came in and proceeded up the bay and got to Baltimore on the 14th of December. It was thick snowing when I was going up the Patapsco River. Old Captain Samuel W. Travers owned ¼ of this vessel. He was in charge of the oyster police steamer at that time. He bore down close to me and hollered in a course and masculine voice, "What did you do with that spanker, boy?" I told him I left it in shreds off Cape Hatteras.

IV

1881–1883

I ARRIVED in Baltimore safely just ten days from Jacksonville, entered the vessel at the custom house, discharged our lumber, and loaded chemical and fertilizer for Wilmington, North Carolina. Got frozed up in Baltimore and it was sometime in January before we got away. I shipped this Mr. Swann, that was mate of her when I took charge in Richmond about 3 months before, and a good mate he was too. I also had my namesake, Captain L. E. Tawes, cook with me. A pair of nice fellows, too, they were. I got a strong northwester which turned into northeaster which gave me a good run to Southport 3 days.

In those days we had to take a pilot in over the bar and then take a river pilot to Wilmington. All this was compulsory backed up by the laws of the State of North Carolina. I took a river pilot by the name of Burrows. I made him sail her all the way up the river to Wilmington. This cold northeaster would sleet the rigging rainy and cold. This pilot had no mittins to steer with and only a pair of calfskin shoes. He certainly was snapper riged for this occasion. The wind was light and ahead all the way up to Wilmington, a distance of thirty miles. Now we could only work one tide a day which was the flood, of course, and we were 3 days getting up the river. This pilot expected me to take a towboat right up the river so he could set in the cabbin by the fire. And in about

6 hours we would be in Wilmington, he'd collect $35 out of me, and be back in Southport at home by night. But this time he struck a man that was never used to anything but hard work and no luxuries. Every day when we would get under way with the begining of the flood tide he would say, "Captain, if you will take the *Passport* to tow you up she tows cheaper than the other tow boats." I would tell him it would not pay me to tow up because with this rainy weather I would not be able to take off the hatches to work. I would just have to lay there idle until the weather cleared up. "Well," he would say, "I am afraid she will not tack. This river is so full of witch tides." "Oh," I would say, "I think she is working fine." Then he would begin to tell me about the logs and piling that the Rebels put down in the river during the Civil War. He would say, "She will not work through them. She will fail to tack and will go ashore on them." But I persisted. We would keep sailing although it would keep raining and sleeting. Well, we successfully sailed her through the Rebel logs and defences and after awhile we came around the bend of the river and there was Wilmington in sight. The harbor was full of vessels lying at anchor for in those days many Norwegian, Danish, Swedish, and other European barks and brigs came there to load naval stores and cotton. No steamers were runing from the south to Europe in those days. All business was done with sail.

As we approached up to the vessels he says, "Captain, we will come to anchor." I said, "For what? I am going up to the Carolina Central wharf to discharge my cargo and that is away up in the upper part of this city." "But," he says, "I cannot work her through this fleet of vessels." "Well," I says, "I will do it." I took the helm. I worked her up through this fleet of vessels and I never touched one of them. I put her up to the Carolina Central wharf nicely and moved her safely. No tow boat got his line on me that voyage. "Now," I says, "pilot, what do I owe you?" He looked at her draught. She drew

11 feet 7 inches. He says, "Captain, you owe me for 12 feet."
"Oh," I said, "11½." He says, "If a ship draws a fraction
over the 6-inch mark I am intitled to the whole foot by law."
He says, "I have had a hard time getting this ship up here and
I shall take all the law gives." I had a notion telling him he
ought to give me a new tooth brush as he took mine to clean
his teeth with and I threw it overboard. I will tell more about
this pilot later if I live to get so far with this work.

It rained about one more day then cleared off. Took off our
hatches and began discharging cargo. We lay here quite some
time waiting for a freight. I was offered $15 per thousand feet
on lumber to Aspinwall but Captain Travers objected on
account the heavy northers blowing there at this season of the
year. So we accepted a cargo of lumber to New York at $6 per
thousand feet. The tow boat captain and owners said to me,
"You got up to Wilmington without us but you will have to
take us down." When I got loaded one of my sailors tried to
leave but I had him arrested and put on board. The next
morning the wind came out from the northeast which was a
fair wind down the river. I just runed my kedge anchor out
in the stream over the stern and swung her to it, loosed the sails,
took the kedge line to the winch I had on the mainmast, and
hove the kedge anchor up to the stern. Hoisted the mainsail
on her and the way we went down the river without a tow boat.
Had a pretty good run down to Southport. The river pilot
left us. Then we took on a bar pilot and went on out to sea.

Had a heavy norther off Cape Hatteras. Wore this out and
by the time I was up off of Cape Henry a fresh northeaster set
in blowing and I came into Hampton Roads for a harbor. After
here a day or two we got a fair wind and we left Hampton
Roads and proceeded on our journey toward New York. Now
this was in the mischievous month of February, 1881. Got up
off the Delaware capes. Here we got a heavy northwester and
I had to work hard to hold the beach making very short tacks

so as not to get off in rough water. Had we failed we would have been blown off. The next day the wind was easterly and threatening so I went into the Delaware Breakwater for harbor. That night we had an awful gale of wind from about east northeast. There was an Italian bark out in it and when they saw they were going to be thrown up on the beach and be drowned nearly all of them cut their throats to keep from being drowned. Only about two of them did not cut their throats and were saved by the life savers along the Jersey coast. They told the story the ship was wrecked. This was the first and last time I ever heard of anyone cutting his throat to keep from being drowned.

My old friend Captain Coneal Woodland was in the Breakwater the same night. After about a couple of days the weather was not encouraging. But the wind breezed up from the southwest which was a fair wind, though cloudy. So after dinner I began to get underway. Captain Woodland hollered to me and said, "Tawes, what are you going to do?" I said, "I cannot lay here with a fair wind." He says, "The weather is not fit to go out." I said, "Well, I am going." So he got underway too and we proceeded. About the time we got out by Cape Henlopen good it set in thick snowing. Captain Woodland used better judgement than I did; he turned back and in the Breakwater again. I just proceeded on. About 9 or 10 o'clock that night I was up to Absecon. The weather cleared off beautiful; the stars came out nice and bright. I just kept going. The next night as I was going in by Sandy Hook about 2 o'clock in the morning, going along at a pretty nice speed for a vessel of my class, I saw something ahead that looked like foam to me. And I thought it was foam. I let her go into it head on. When she struck it I found it was heavy ice cakes. It broke a plank abreast of the forward chainplates on the starboard side and knocked the coffee pot off the stove in the cabbin. I then shuned all these white cakes of ice until I came to anchor on

get the best of treatment free if he has
served 60 days on an American
vessel. after entering at the custom house
at Tapahanock. which was the first
+ last vessel ever entered + cleared from
there, I got Boards + laid a tight dunnage
floor. about 9 inches above the ceiling
to prevent the corn from getting the
least wet. as I was to carry the corn
in Bulk or loose, I got a Pilot and
proceed to Beat up the River, I had
never been up the Rappahannock in my
life but I never Runed her a shore
from the mouth of the River to Tappahannock. now mind the wind had
been N or West ever since we left New
York. the Pilot got me up as far as Car-
ters wharf given the job up + left me
I laid her all day on Sunday. blowing to hard to forseed. Monday I got
under way and beat to Leedstown
Reported to a Mr John Baxter who was
to Superrted for buying the cargo. he
notified all the far mers and they began
to bring the corn down in sacks in
1½ or three bushel sacks I forgot which
I traded for a man named Phillips
who lived up to Fredericksburg. he had
a very fine man to Represent him I

Captain Leonard S. Tawes as a young man.

Jersey City flats. About two days after, Captain Woodland came in and anchored close to me. And I think my old skipper was a little cross with me. He said to me not in a very pleasant mood, "Well, I see you are not discharged yet." I had been bothered to find a dock to discharge my cargo on.

After being discharged, Captain Travers chartered the vessel to go to the Rappahannock River, Virginia, to load corn for Savannah, Georgia at 10¢ per bushel. Leaving New York I just flew down the beach with a strong northwest wind. It was blowing so strong when I got to Cape Charles I anchored under the lee of Smith Island. Laid there until the wind moderated. I then got underway and beat into the capes and worked her up the bay to the Rappahannock River. And I had to beat her all the way up to Tappahannock. There being a custom house here I had to stop and enter as my little vessel was under register. Also in those days I had to pay hospital fees at the rate of 40¢ per month for every man on board. But Uncle Sam permitted us to take the same from the crew when paying them off. A system that has long since been abolished. Sailors can now go to U. S. Marine Hospitals and get the best of treatment free if he has served 60 days on an American vessel. After entering at the custom house at Tappahannock, which was the first and last vessel ever entered and cleared from there, I got boards and laid a tight dunnage floor about 9 inches above the ceiling to prevent the corn from getting the least wet as I was to carry the corn in bulk, or loose.

I got a pilot and proceed to beat up the river. I had never been up the Rappahannock in my life but I never runed her ashore from the mouth of the river to Tappahannock. Now mind, the wind had been nor'west ever since we left New York. The pilot got me up as far as Carter's Wharf, give the job up, and left me. I laid here all day one Sunday, blowing too hard to proceed. Monday I got under way and beat to Leedstown. Reported to a Mr. John Baxter who was to supertend

procuring the cargo. He notified all the farmers and they
began to bring the corn down in sacks in 1½ or two bushel
sacks, I forget which.

I loaded for a man named Phillip who lived up to Fredericksburg. He had a very fine man to represent him; I have forgotten
his name. I well remember he had a bad scar. He told me he
got it while in the Rebel army. I asked him if he thought he
had ever killed a man. He said that he was sure of it. He was
engaged in conflict and while near the edge of a woods came
close in sight and he shot one of them. In a minute he would
have had another but just as he was taking aim for another
a bullet struck his gun and knocked the hamer off. It went
through his chin and came out under the jawbone which completely put him out of business for quite sometime.

The farmers would bring down 20 sacks of corn for a load.
I could pick out any one bag I choose, call it a weigh bag, and
average all the rest of them by this one bag. Then dump them
in the hold and give the farmer his empty sacks and a receipt
for his corn. Mr. Phillip would pay for the corn at Fredericksburg as the farmers presented them.

I had quite a little mishap lying at Mr. Baxter's wharf. I had
a brand new yawl just built in New York this time. She had
never been overboard but once and that was to take her to the
vessel from the East River near the Catherine Market. The
steamer *Mason L. Weems* was coming into the dock just below
me. She caught on the center. The captain or the engineer
could not get her to back up and she ran up into my stern and
cut my new yawl in half. Now I was without a boat. The
Mason L. Weems took the boat to Baltimore to have her
repaired. The captain of the *Weems* would not let me have
one of his boats. I wrote to Baltimore about it and when the
Weems came back from Baltimore the captain let me have
one of his boats.

After getting all the corn I was supposed to get at Leeds-town I went further up the river to a place called Port Micou. Here I finished loading, taking on board 12,414 bushels. I met an old captain up here who told me how to get across the shoals at Tappahannock. I was drawing 11½ feet of water. He told me when I went down to these shoals to anchor and lay until high water. Then get underway and keep a certain church steeple about 3 points open to the southward of the belfrey on the school house. This would take me through the deepest water and out over the shoal. I saw plainly the marks Captain Woody gave me and the wind was blowing hard from the northwest which was a fair wind. And the tides still ebbing I just let her run on the marks he gave me until she stopped. Then I lowered my sails down, anchored, and jumped in the yawl with my lead line and two men to pull her. I sounded in a zigzag way until I got down to Tappahannock. I found the best water on the marks he gave me. The tide then turned flood and we had a fair tide back to the ship. We got on board, eat dinner, then she floated and we got under way. And with a strong breeze we went scoot down over these shoals and on down the river. We anchored that night at dark though I could see both lights at the mouth of the Rappahannock which is Windmill Point on the north side and Stingray on the south side.

While we were loading I left Leedstown to go to Tappahan-nock to clear for Savannah. I went down in this new yawl I had built in New York. After I left the ship a while there sprang up a gale from the northwest. I had too much sail on the yawl. I thought she would turn over every minute. Runing before the wind I could not let go the helm to go forward and lower the sail. If I had she would have come to and turned over and drowned me. So I had to take the chance. It certainly looked like I had to be drowned that morning. Just before getting down to Tappahannock on the south side of the river there is a mud flat. I let her go down through this mud flat until I got to the point before getting to Tappahannock. When I rounded this point the wind began to moderate and I began to go comfortable. I made up my mind to never go into a sail boat alone again which I seldom, if ever, did. I went down to clear the vessel which would have saved me a day's time. When I came down in the vessel after clearing I got my dinner. And the wind moderating down to a pretty breeze I began beating up the river. It seemed like the wind blew from the northwest every day while I was up this river—and cold. The next morning, after laying at anchor all night and resting up, we got underway and proceeded down the river. Passed out by Windmill Point about 8 or 9 o'clock, having been up this river just 24 days. We went on down the bay and went out of the capes before night.

Had a good run to Cape Hatteras. Here our fair northwest wind quit. The weather looked terrible bad. My mate wanted me to run back to Hampton Roads. I knew whatever we were going to have would overtake us long before we could get to Hampton Roads about 130 miles distant. So with a strong southwest wind, and dark as a dungeon, I ran her back to Body Island. I got close to the beach that a life-saver warned me off by burning a Coston signal. After getting up to Body Island I doubled reefed her all around ready for the change that I knew was coming. I intended to put her on the best tack to keep her from the beach when the change came. If it had come from southeast I intended to head her offshore on the starboard tack. If from the east northeast I intended to put her on the port tack and head her offshore on this tack.

It was my watch below at 8 o'clock PM and I laid down telling the mate, Mr. Swann, to call me as soon as a change came. About 10 PM he called me and said, "Captain, come up on deck, here is the wind from the eastward." I got on my oil coat, boots, and sou'wester and got on deck as quickly as possible thinking how bad this wind is from east and setting me toward the beach. Now on any tack I put her I was feeling bad. But when I got on deck and looked at the compass, and oh my how it was raining and blowing, I saw the wind was from the northeast. Oh, my, what a relief. I just kept her off south by east and runed her so she would clear the outer Diamond Shoals. And the way we went with a fair wind. It blew hard for the first day, and cloudy and rainey. I did not see Cape Hatteras when I went by it. But I watched my log and when nearly 60 miles below Cape Hatteras, according to my reckoning, I began sounding for the Cape Lookout Shoals. And shortly I began to come up from 17 fathom, to 16, to 14, and finally 10 fathoms. I was then surely on the Cape Lookout Shoals then 64 miles below Cape Hatteras. Shortly, I droped down again to 14, 16, and 18 fathoms. I now well had her position. Now I had a long run of 120 miles before coming up on the Frying Pan Shoals. When the log registered 180 miles I began sounding for the Frying Pan Shoals. Shortly I began shoaling my water from 18, to 16, to 14, to 10 fathoms. I was now on the Frying Pan Shoals. This shoal is southwest ¾ west, 184 miles from Cape Hatteras. The weather kept thick all the time. When I reckoned we were down off the Tybee Light, still foggy, I had to lay to one day before I could see anything. Finally, a pilot boat spoke to me and asked me where I was bound. I told him Savannah. "Have a pilot?", he asked. I answered in the affirmative and told him I would have taken one a day ago if I could have found one. The wind continued to blow from the northeast and I had a fair wind up the river to Savannah thus avoiding the services of a tow boat.

On arrival in Savannah I found my consignee who was named Schley. And very nice people too. I beleive they were relatives of our famous Admiral Schley of the Santiago victory over the Spaniards. When I got my orders to go the wharf I got her underway and with the ebb tide and a fair wind I put side of the dock and avoided the services of a towboat again. A couple of State of Maine captains lying there in their vessels came on board and told me how nicely I did the trick. After discharging my cargo of corn and got settled up with I sent Captain Travers at Baltimore $900 and carried enough with me to Brunswick, Georgia, to pay all port charges there when I went to load lumber for Baltimore. I forgot to say that from the time I kept off at Body Island with this northeast storm that in 4 days I was in Savannah. I do not know what would have become of us if I had tried to run back to Hampton Roads.

After discharging cargo and settling up I took a tow boat and towed down the river and out to sea. The next day I went into Brunswick. There was a large bark about one mile behind me. When the Brunswick pilot spoke me and says, "Bound to Brunswick?", I replied, "Yes." "Well," he says, "are you very particular about having me to come on board?" He says, "That large bark needs a pilot badly. You know he draws so much more water than you do." I said, "Go to him. I do not care." I had a fair wind and I intended to run her in though I was never there before. This fellow was mighty happy to go after the bark as her pilotage would have been 3 times more than ours. This fellow violated the pilot regulations by not boarding the first vessel approaching the harbor. Finally, 2 pilots boarded me and began to swear like parrots because I did not take this first pilot that spoke me and leave the big-draught ship for them to bring in. I told them if they did not quit swearing about it I would refuse to let them bring me in as my vessel was light and I did not draw much water. I had not any hesitancy whatever in taking her in myself. Arriving in Brunswick all o.k. and moored I was notified to come up to the Masonic Hall at 7:30 in the evening. They were going to have this first pilot tried and take his branch from him for violating this pilot rule. I went up to the Masonic Hall and stayed around more than an hour and not a soul appeared. About two days after these two pilots, Club brothers by name, notified me again to come up to the Masonic Temple to try this fellow. I went and stayed about an hour and a half and no one appeared. The next day they came after me again. I went and as usual no one appeared. I think the matter droped as I was never notified again.

Here my mate, Mr. Swann, was taken sick with the southern fever and I had to leave him at the hospital. I had to come home without any mate. I never had the pleasure of having him again. He has now been dead many years at Baltimore. My friend, L. E. Tawes, went home. I never had the pleasure of having him again. He came home and did well runing as master of fish steamers for years. He saved himself of many hard nocks by not going to sea in merchant ships as I did. He married and has lived a most respectful life and is living at this writing at Baltimore.

I loaded corn and went to Wilmington, North Carolina. Loaded lumber and come to Baltimore. Took on a load of scrap iron and went to Richmond. I had a mate with me that I had known from childhood. His name was Allie Wilkins who was born and raised in Accomack County, Virginia, close to where I was born. We chartered to take a load of hoop poles to Matanzas from Richmond. It was now August, 1881, the very center of the hurrycane season. They were always a great scourge to me and I hated the most kind to go south at this season of the year. But having a family and young children to raise caused me to do many unpleasant things or jobs. After discharging the iron and loading these hoop poles, getting the vessel ready for sea, and getting sufficient stores and chandlery on board for the voyage, I cleared and towed down the James River. I escaped the pilots again and went to sea.

When about 35 miles down the coast off the Currituck Lighthouse, we were swiftly sailing along with a northeast wind and clear weather. But quite a heavy roll was coming from the eastward. Thinking everything was all serene away went my foremast head off. And here was trouble sure. The main topmast stays were bolted to the foremast head and it came about half way down the main rigging and there it hung. And it would swing and threaten to go through my foresail. So I took a piece of rope in my hand and started aloft under the protest of the crew because had these heavy spars hit me in their swing they would have nocked me 40 feet out of the rigging overboard. And had it swung through my foresail I would have gone ashore on the beach and lost ship and cargo. But I was resolved to do all in my power to prevent this. Well, on about the third roll I caught it and secured it to the main rigging. Then the crew cleared up the wreckage. As soon as possible I got the fore topmast and broken masthead on deck. It happened that the crosstrees did not come down. I went aloft on the foremast with great hazard and lashed the rigging so it would not slip off and secured a place by chain under the crosstrees for the peak halliards and got the foresail on her. During all this time I had drifted close to the beach. I wore her around and headed for Cape Henry. I rigged up the flying stay, set it, and put the flying jib on her. Making leeway with east northeast winds I just did fetch in by Cape Henry. The Baltimore pilots wanted to know if I needed assistance. I do not know what assistance they could give me for theirs was a sail boat. There was no steam pilot boats in those days for this was in 1881.

I went into Hampton Roads and wired Captain S. W. Travers that I was there with foremast head gone. What must I do, go to Norfolk or Baltimore for a new one? He wired me to come to Baltimore. I sent this wire from Fortress Monroe. I always thought that the Western Union people told the pilots about this for I had not been on board but a short time before a pilot came on board and says, "Captain, where are you bound?" I said, "Baltimore." He said, "I am your pilot. I have come on board to take you out of the Roads." I said, "I am not subject to pilotage. I am not going to sea. I am going to Baltimore." But he says, "You are." I said, "I will not take you." He said, "If you do not pay I will have a sheriff off here and take you ashore and hold you until you do pay." So I gave him an order on Captain S. W. Travers for about $40 for speaking me at anchor in Hampton Roads. Then I got underway and sailed her to Baltimore. Captain Travers would not honor the draught but they caught me in Norfolk about 3 or 4 months after that and put a libel on the vessel which cost more than the first cost of pilotage. I was never in favor of compulsory pilotage.

I got to Baltimore, put in a new foremast, got her rigged up all o.k., and in about 10 or 12 days I went to sea again. But I do not remember how long I was going out to Matanzas this time. After discharging my cargo of hoop poles I was chartered to go to Fort Pickens at Pensacola, Florida; Fort Jefferson at Dry Tortugas, Florida; and to Fort Taylor, Key West, Florida, to take powder from all three of these forts. I had awful strong east winds and I was not more than four days making the run over. Arriving at Pensacola I laid to on the state quarantine grounds and lay 8 days which gave me a nice opportunity to paint her up nicely and catch plenty of fish for fish were good. I lay at the mouth of the Santa Rosa River and here I borrowed a cast net from a captain who was on the quarantine with me. I have forgotten his name though I had been acquainted with him before. We used to go on shore and watch for the jumping mullets swimming along in schools then run out right and throw the cast nets over them. Sometimes we would catch them and sometimes we would miss them. This of course would be in sandy, shoal water. If we were real quick we would spread it over them before they got away. But they were usually plentiful and we always got about what we wanted.

Now the state quarantine ground had a very small place on the shore that we were allowed to use. We were never allowed out of sight of the quarantine boat. The shore line took in about the half of a mile the state quarantine was. It was a ridiculous thing in those days. Sometimes they would keep a vessel laying there to anchor for 30 days. I laid 8 days and got off well. If you had ballast in you had to throw it overboard without any help and they would charge you 50¢ a ton for the privilege. I knew I was not going to take in a full load of powder at Fort Pickens and I did not want to pay 50¢ a ton to throw it overboard so I told the doctor my vessel was cranky without plenty of ballast and that I wanted to keep my ballast on board. He consented. I was after saving $17.50 for my owners and I dumped it when I was released from the quarantine grounds.

There was other troubles arising which I had to overcome if possible. I knew that boarding house runners would be after my crew and in those days, and I believe today, all crews on American vessels can demand their discharge on arrival from a foreign port. So when I was released from the quarantine ground I just moved the vessel outside the line of buoys on the quarantine ground. When I started on shore, for I was 5 or 6 miles from the city, I met the sailor boarding house boat pulling for my vessel to get my crew. If he had got on board, in 5 minutes he would have all my crew dissatisfied and I would have had to pay them off. Then I would have been all alone. So I met him and said, "Where are you going?" He said, "I am going aboard that schooner." I said, "If you do you will take a trip to Tallahassee and serve time for she is yet on the quarantine ground." He said, "How is it that you are going on shore?" I said, "I have a special permit." The bluff worked fine so he turned back for Pensacola. The mate, a rascal, was quitting me then and I had him in the boat with me. He was a rummy and not much to depend upon. I had to pay him off right after he went from Baltimore to Fernandina, Florida, as a second mate. He was a badly run down man then.

After arriving in Pensacola and entered at the custom house, and getting the necessary needs for the ship such as stores and shipping one seaman to fill the place of a man, I must now have to act as second mate. I went back to the ship. I then made my second mate as mate. And a smart a little fellow I had before the mast, named Peter, I made him my boatswain. And I got them all counted but the cook.

I got underway and sailed down to Fort Pickens for the cargo of powder. Here I took in 500 barrels of powder. Then the sargent of the fort asked me where I was going next. I told him to Fort Jefferson and Fort Taylor, Key West, Florida. He informed me the Fort Jefferson was not at Key West but at Dry Tortugas. I told him my papers or charter party said so. But he said he had been stationed there for some years and that he knew what he was talking about. I then had to rig up the yawl with sail and sail 10 or 11 miles up to Pensacola to get a chart of Dry Tortugas. And this cook was determined not to go in the vessel with powder. The result was I had to take him along with me up to Pensacola, pay him off, and ship another.

There I saw the most gastly sight I ever saw in all my life. There was a large English ship laying at the wharf and the night before the crew went in swiming. While in, one them just gave a yell and down he went and did not appear to the top of the water again. The next day they dragged for him and got him just as, or a little before, I landed. They spreaded him out on the wharf and his right leg was bit off, the whole length of the leg. It was a bad looking sight to behold.

After paying off the cook and shipping another, procuring a chart of Dry Tortugas, and buying a barrel of salt beef of Bell and Bell, ship chandlers, I proceeded down the bay to Fort Pickens with a new cook. I will never forget how Mr. Bell braged on this barrel of beef. He said it was such nice beef. He said, "Captain, let me open it and show it to you." I said, "No, I will take your word for that." When I opened it the first lay on top was beautiful beef. But the next tier was the most commonest beef I ever saw. It was poor, leen, hard beef not fit to make use of. And my crew and myself had to eat this common meat for six or seven weeks or until we got to New York.

The next day we left Pensacola for Dry Tortugas. I had a nice wind and in 3 days I was up to Dry Tortugas. After the first day out I put the crew to moving the powder in each end of the vessel, that is in the stern and the bow, and began throwing the ballast overboard. About 2 in the afternoon, for that is when we all worked, we had it all out and restowed the powder and cleaned up the hold ready to take in cargo at Dry Tortugas. I set my flag for a pilot and an Indian came off. The wind was blowing fresh and it was so close to being night I would not let him run me in. So I laid off in the deep water all night. Unfortunately, the chief lost his boat that night. The next morning, when I had the day before me, I ran in and came to anchor just outside of the fort and I went on shore to report to the Ordnance Sargent. He told me I would have to go up to Key West and get men and a horse and cart to haul this powder from the different magazines to the ship. There was no men there. The fort was not garrisoned and he could do nothing. "Well," I said, "who is going to pay for all of this trouble going up to Key West and back here?" He said, "I do not know but that is the only way you will ever get the powder." I went back to the vessel nearly worried to death. I did not know what to do. I just felt like giving the vessel up and quitting like the mate and the cook did in Pensacola. But I had just built a home of which I owed for, I had a wife and one little baby boy all depending on me for a living, and if I left the vessel I would never be able to pay for my little house and would be in debt all my life. This was as bad as being blowed up by a cargo of powder. And for going to Key West and coming back to Dry Tortugas I could not think of it. And right here in the hurrycane season too.

I laid here in my berth for awhile and thought and thought and worried and worried about what was best for me to do. While waiting on board and worrying so much I would look at this great big fort built of brick, not less than three million in it, built away off here on such a small island that the fort covered the whole island. Away off in the sea, no land in sight anywhere, I just felt vexed that the government did a foolish thing to build such a fort. What good could it do I asked myself over and over. Yet when I made several inquiries about it I was told it was to protect the Gulf states from enemies sailing down the Gulf Stream between Cuba and the Florida Keys. This little island, called Gordon Key, afforded a splendid little harbor where our ships could put in and repair after a battle. As our ships in those days were all sail ships they could put in there and heave out, caulk the bottoms, and copper them without leaving their posts. The harbor is composed of coral reefs and plenty of fish. During the noon hour I would catch enough fish to last me until the next noon hour. I think it would take me a year to tell all about this fort. But worry never killed anyone or I would have been so long dead that I would have been forgotton by most immediate friends.

About eleven o'clock the wind drew around more to the eastward which gave me a leading breeze to the dock. I told the crew to man the windlass. I hove the anchor and got underway and sailed her to the dock and made her fast. The Ordnance Sargent, a good Irishman he was, came down and said, "Captain, why did you come to the dock?" I said, "In compliance with my charter party and I want you to endorse it now. I am ready for cargo." "But," he says, "Captain, I cannot give it to you. I would readily do so if I had men." "Well," I said, "you endorse on the back of this charter party—

Captain L. S. Tawes reported to me ready for cargo on this day October 1881." He did and signed it. Now charters had 20 runing days to load me. In all days in excess of this charters were to pay me $30 per day. Now runing days in a charter agreement mean every day including Sundays, rainy days, or what not. So by reporting ready for cargo at Saturday noon I made one and half days time equal $45 which I was paid for in New York by Laflin and Rand Powder Company.

On Monday I began to take all the precaution possible of which I could think. I got all the inch-boards I could find and nailed them over all the heavy iron bolts of which the ship was constructed on both sides, fore and aft. Having completed this job I began then to make a trade with the sargent. I hired him and my crew at $2.50 per day to haul the powder out of the magazines to the side of the ship. I gave the men, my crew, $1 per day of this money including their wages which meant to them $1.60 per day. To go to the furthest magazine they would have to go a mile. I let him have every man I had except the steward. He had to do the cooking and as stores were getting scarce he did not have so much of that to do. Well, I took some inch-boards and made me a shoot to lead from the top of the rail to the hatch. Then another shoot leading from the first one. I had the two shoots so constructed that the powder barrels would slip around at the hatchway and come down the hold to me. I took in and stowed 1,760 barrels of powder all by myself. Of course, I was not rushed because there were only two hand carts to bring the powder down in but I did do some work sure. I was in this place 17 days. Everybody thought I was lost as in Baltimore they thought Fort Jefferson was at Key West. And we had a dreadful hurrycane in the Gulf of Mexico while I was marooned at this Dry Tortugas.

I have one very little incident to relate in connection with this place besides all the good fishing, collecting of beautiful coral, shells, and sponge which abounds in plenty at this place.

Everybody knew that during our Civil War that our President Abraham Lincoln was shot by John Wilkes Booth and Booth, in making his escape, broke his leg. As I understand it he rode his horse away out in Southern Maryland, went to the house of Dr. Mudd who set Booth's leg for him. And for this bit of humanity Dr. Mudd was sent to Dry Tortugas, a penal prison at that time. They put Dr. Mudd in a cell here with one window where he could look out to the sea for there being no land in view there was nothing else for him to see. They had a little window about a foot square where they passed into him his food. I do not know how long he was put there for. Neither do I know how long he staid but I was told that the officers in charge at the fort got a little lonesome and took a boat and went across to Havana, Cuba, a distance of about 90 miles. I presume they indulged a little too freely in bananas and good liquor. From my experience sailing in the West Indies and South America for 35 years nothing will give fever any quicker than bananas and rum. Anyhow, as I was told, when they returned yellow fever broke out in the fort. Dr. Mudd was taken out of his cell and put to work on yellow fever patients. He burned powder and fumigated all the garrison and did such wonderful work saving lives that the government reprieved him and let him come home. About in the year of 1886 I saw in the papers where he passed away. Over this little foot square window he wrote with a small paint brush these words—*They who come here leave all hope behind*. And I was told not so long ago by an American naval officer, who had been there very recently, that those words were still there. Perhaps the setting of Booth's leg and the consignment of Dr. Mudd to this penal prison was the cause of many lives being saved at this fort. I could never have voted a Republican ticket if I had been a Mudd. But I understand they are staunch Republicans.

After laying here 17 days, and getting all the powder on board and getting my charter party signed the day I was through, I must now make preparations to sail for Key West, a place I had never been before. But I felt that I ought to give more description of Dry Tortugas and the fort. Tortugas in Spanish means turtle and should be called Dry Turtle Key. There are so many turtles there that the Spaniards named it Dry Tortugas. Besides, there are such dangerous shoals there and reefs it is easy to run out of 10 fathoms of water high and dry on a reef. And many a fine ship and valuable cargo has been lost here. On the inside of this fort, which is real roomy, there are many fine buildings and residences with beautiful finished walls. And not a soul into them. All vacant, built for Army officers to live in. Nice cisterns all full of rain water. I often thought were I close to this fort I could put in here and get all the fresh water I wanted.

After some maneuvering I got out of this place safely and sailed for Key West. After about two days I came up to Sand Key. The wind was blowing a gale from northeast. I did not know the way in and the pilot boat would not come off in deep water to board me. And I had to stay off in the stream all night it blowing a gale and the rain pouring down on me. I would work her up as far as American Shoal Light. Then run her back to Sand Key. In this way I put in a mizerable night. The next morning, when the pilot boat came out, I ran in on the banks where he was and got a pilot on board and went in the harbor.

Not feeling so good after standing out all night in a heavy northeast rain storm, on arrival here the first thing for me to do after entering at the custom house—for as I before said my ship was under register—I went to look for the Ordnance Sargent. I have forgotton his name. I told him my business with him. He was an Irishman and I have wondered if all our forts had Irish Ordnance Sargents for all three of these that I had been to were kept by Irish sargents. But this fellow was the most troublesome one I had fell in with. I could not reason

Schooner Maggie E. Gray *shown at Long Dock, Gay Street, Baltimore, Maryland. Both the schooner and dock are mentioned in Captain Tawes' journals. The* Gray *was built at Baltimore in 1867 and was wrecked in 1891.*

Currituck Lighthouse, North Carolina, built in 1875, assisted Captain Tawes in his coastwise navigation.

with him and besides he was full of John Barleycorn and kept so well he said, "There is the powder in the fort. You can go and get it out. There is no wharf at the fort and you can do what you please about it. The fort is not garrisoned. I have no men and no money." I took out my charter party and asked him to endorse on it the day and the hour I have reported to him. After I got his name on it I told him the government was paying me $30 per day for all the time I was loosing. Though pretty well soused he began to wake up a little.

We had been to two or three saloons together already and I may have taken one drink with him, but not more. He had a little horse and cart in which we drove around the town. I went to his house. He had 3 or 4 daughters which appeared to be very bright girls. He got the oldest to write 2 or 3 letters for him. I think they were to the War Department. Well, he did not know what to do. Finally, we drove down to the wharf where a man kept a store and, if my memory serves me right, his name was Mr. Philbrook. He had been a paymaster in the Northern Army. A man who knew his business; a man of brains. He showed Mr. Philbrook my charter party. Mr. Philbrook said, "The captain is alright. You have got to give him this powder alongside in the reach of the ship's tackles." "But," he says, "man, how can I do it, I have neither men or money?" Mr. Philbrook said, "If you will sign the papers I want you to sign I will advance the money you need. You go and get the Mayor's consent to haul the powder through the city. Then have the captain bring his vessel alongside of my wharf and you can have the powder hauled by teams to the ship's side as per contract by the government with the captain."

After getting the Mayor's consent to haul the powder through the city I went on board and the next morning I got underway and beat the vessel up the harbor to the wharf of Mr. Philbrook. And about the time I got her all moored and sails tied up it was 12 noon and I was very hot from the labor I had to do. I was just going down the cabbin for dinner when a police-man came down with a long envelope and handed it to me. The city council met that night and recinded the Mayor's consent and the powder was not allowed to be hauled through the city. But Mr. Philbrook told the sargent that I would have to go back in the stream or harbor and anchor as close to the fort as I could lay safely and get the small sponge boats and fishing boats to lighter the powder from the fort to the ship. I forget how long I was there getting the powder on board at Key West—about 4 or 5 days. After I finished loading, I cleared from the custom house, got my hatches all caulked ready for sea, and got my charter party endorsed by the Ordnance Sargent which showed I had nine and a quarter days of demurrage due me. I then went to the cable office and cabled Captain Sam W. Travers I was loaded and sailing on this day.

While getting underway I had a very old sailor named John who fell off the top of the mid-ship house on the deck and so injured himself that I had to pay him off and put him in the hospital. A bad start indeed. Now I had to look up another seaman. I found an old seaman on the beach broke who said he would go with me. I signed him on and when I got down to the boat he bucked and said he would not go. He was drunk as he could be and he had been quite a nuisance around Key West for sometime. Four fellows standing by looking on just took the old fellow and put him in the boat and dared him to get out. So off I went on board. He was so drunk he could not hold his head up and it draged through the water as the boat was on its way to the ship. When I got on board I got underway immediately and sailed from Key West on the 25th day of November, 1881, for New York. When this old chap sobered up and got the rum out of him he turned to be as good a seaman as I ever had in all my life.

After leaving Key West I made a vow to the Almighty God if he would see me safely in New York with this load of powder

I would never go with another cargo of powder as long as I lived. And I have turned down some good money several times after this. Quite a few times when I have chartered to go out to Santo Domingo I have had merchants to send for me. They wanted to see me and when I would get in their office they would say, "Captain Tawes, I have about a ton of maybe less or more. I have some real good money for you to take this amunition out to the President of Santo Domingo." I would tell them I did not want it. "Why," they would say, "you could put this amunition in your cabbin and you would not displace any room in your hold for cargo. And the President will reward you handsomely." That vow would come before me and I would refuse to carry it. There was only one line of steamers runing there then and steamers carry passengers and are not allowed to carry explosives like gun powder, gasoline etc.

We sailed from Key West the 26th day of November, 1881, for New York with no mate but just a lot of sailors of very little experience on schooners. And none at all in the way of navigation. The first night out I had another one of those heavy northeasters with heavy rain. I was on the deck the most of the time until I got clear of the Straits of Florida. Then we had usual fair weather until north of Cape Hatteras about 60 miles when we had an awful gale of wind from the northeast again. I had to heave her to and lay for 48 hours, 2 days and nights. The second night of this gale the sea had raised to a tremendous height and it was my watch below. It was 2 o'clock in the morning. I was lying in my berth for I was very tired at the time. A tremendous wave hit the vessel and it seemed to me she fell from the crest of the wave 50 feet before she took up and began to rise again. I drew myself up in a small knot expecting the powder to ignite from the friction in the hold. But to my agreeable surprise and joy she did not explode. In the 48 hours I was hove to I lost 20 miles backward from New York. Now the gale being well spent I got her underway and proceeded on my voyage toward New York. The night of December the 7th, about 8 PM, I passed Barnegat Light. The wind was blowing a gale from the northwest. The moon showed nice and bright. I think she must have been on a full it was so light. I kept her as close to the beach as possible. I lost my jib and flying jib by the heavy wind. I turned my storm trysail bottom up and bent it on for a jib. I had to do this to hold the beach. The next morning, December the 8th, I went in the Hook and worked her up to Jersey City Flats and came to anchor 12 days from Key West.

It was freezing and bitter cold. It was a quick passage for winter time. I went on shore and reported Messrs. Laflin and Rand Powder Company, 29 Murray Street. Here I was instructed that I would not be allowed alongside of any wharf in New York but to lay at anchor where I was and they would send barges out to me to discharge the powder in. So I hired the crew, my crew, at $5 each lump sum to get the powder out. Captain Travers came on to New York to see me and stoped at the United States Hotel on Fulton Street close to Fulton Market. In just about 4 days I discharged the 3,760 barrels of powder. My headquarters was at Hicks and Bill ship chandlers, 68 South Street. The United States Hotel and Hicks and Bill have passed away a long time ago. I think the United States Hotel was at the corner of Fulton and Pearl Streets. When I was making up my account to take to Laflin and Rand for settlement I made it up for $3,000 as per the charter party and $277.50 for 9¼ days demurrage. Mr. Bell said, "It is no use to make up any charge for demurrage. They are not going to pay you any." But they paid every cent of $3,277.50 squarely and without a murmur.

Captain Travers chartered the vessel to load salt for Norfolk. I had a pretty good run to Norfolk. Before leaving New York I asked Captain Travers to have me relieved at Norfolk so that I could have a few days at home. He sent Captain Henry Palmer of Church Creek, Dorchester County, Maryland, to come to Norfolk to releive me. I was in Norfolk a day before Captain Palmer got to Norfolk although he left Baltimore in a sailing vessel the same time I left New York. He was very much surprized to find me at Norfolk as he said he had no wind scarcily from the time he left Baltimore. He had no idea I was in when he arrived. I then took the Bay Line steamer to Baltimore and the Eastern Shore steamer home. There was no railroad going to Cape Charles then. No steamers from Norfolk to Cape Charles.

While I was home the Virginia pilots libeled her for the pilotage out of Hampton Roads while I was there dismasted the September before. I would not let him take me out and Captain Travers did not honor the order I gave the pilot. What forces compulsory pilotage? Why don't our government repeal all state pilot laws and furnish the pilots themselves like other nations do? It cost the vessel very heavy for the libel and the pilotage out of the Roads, a service they never rendered.

The vessel was chartered to load lumber for Baltimore which gave me a nice little stay at home and I was glad to have it. After the vessel got to Baltimore she was chartered to take a load of corn to Charleston, South Carolina. Captain Palmer, being only a bay captain, his mission was up on arrival in Baltimore and seeing the lumber discharged. I was then wired for to come to Baltimore and take charge. We put her on the railway at William Skinner and Son, caulked her and coppered her. Then loaded corn and I went to Charleston, South Carolina. Here my consignee comenced to work a sharp game on me. He would only take away the corn as he sold, evidently making a warehouse out of the vessel. He would not give me a receipt for what was piled on the dock so I hired my steward, a fine fellow if there was ever one, to watch this corn for me at night for $1 per night. The cargo was going out slow. There was a storage warehouse about one block or two from where I was lying. I steped over there and began complaining about how slow my cargo was going out and I wanted to know what could be done. This gentleman said, "I see you are being imposed upon. If you are anxious to get out quick bring your vessel over to my wharf and endorse your bill of lading to me. I will discharge your vessel at once and pay you your freight." This was a big lesson to me and served a good purpose in Galveston one time after this. The next morning I told my consignee if he held me up again I should put his cargo in a warehouse, collect my freight from the warehouse people, and he could take his own time getting clear of it. He never held me up any more and hired my steward to watch it of nights and paid. So my steward, David Friend by name, got $7 or $8 out of his job.

After the cargo of corn was out I went up to John C. Malonie's saw mill and loaded lumber for Mr. Ebon B. Hunting of Baltimore and went to Baltimore. Here I was chartered for the round trip out and Baltimore to Santo Domingo city by Fink Brothers and Company, wholesale grocery merchants. They ran a sugar house down on Long Dock. Their store and office was on the corner of Eutaw and Franklin Streets. I used to have to walk away up there to sign bills of lading for the outward cargo. I made 5 voyages altogether out to Santo Domingo city and back to Baltimore for them. I used to take out miscellaneous cargoes and bring back molasses. I used to make a voyage out and back every six weeks and I got along nicely with these people. They used to treat me so nicely. Mr. Rufus Wood was a partner and general manager. While I was in Santo Domingo I used to fill the hogsheads up to about 9 inches from the bung and the next morning I would run over them and refill to about 5 inches from the top of the bung hole. And if I delivered the cargo in Baltimore with a loss of less than 5% of the cargo Mr. Wood would make a present of

$50. That money looked big to me in those days. I used to pick up considerable little change in other ways.

Sometimes my good steward came near getting me in trouble with the custom house there. Once he bought a lot of cigars, bay rum, cigarettes, and other stuff that I knew nothing about. So when the vessel was searched they were found. Old Mr. Gray, then the deputy collector, made a lot of noise about it and said to me, "Why did not you report these goods and manifest them?" I told him they were not mine. They belonged to the steward. He said, "What were they doing under your berth?" I said, "He put them there. He told me he did." "Well," he said, "we are going to hold an inquiry or court here tomorrow. He won't swear he put them there." But he did. I met David up the street and he said to me, "Captain, if you will say they are yours I will sail with you until the fine is paid." I said, "David, you must say they are yours tomorrow at the trial and the fine will be much less on you than on me." I had on board two cases of Holland gin that the custom house detective did not find and they were safe there for they would not search us again. But I was frightened that I threw them overboard. That was about February, 1882, and I have often wondered if any of those flasks of good old Holland were found when they dug out those docks and made them wider after the big fire in Baltimore in February 1904.

The next day the trial at the custom house came off. David acknowledged the goods as his and they were confiscated and no fine was put on him. I have always thought how square and honest he was to acknowledge them. Had he not it would no doubt went hard with me.

About two days after, when the cargo was all out, David was getting out kegs of Talmond's liquors and other contraband goods and putting them in a yawl boat of a schooner he had shipped in. He was on his way home to Bucksport, Maine, where he belonged, to marry a young girl there. We had been discharged from the custom house as all cargo was on shore. While David was getting this contraband out of the hold I was standing talking to our custom house agent, Billy Lawson, who was employed as a custom house employee. I could not leave him and go over and tell David to quit, that a custom officer was or could be looking right at him. But I would not look at the vessel at all. I was trying to divert his eye in another direction. Captain Billy did not notice him, much to my gratification. I did not know that David had all these goods on board. He even had a piece of the first cross that was ever made on this side of the ocean. It was made by Christopher Columbus when he first landed on this side and was a large, coarse piece of wood in the rough, not plained, dressed and varnished like anyone would suppose in these enlightened days. But just rough wood set up in the cathedral in Santo Domingo city. He showed me this when he was leaving me in Baltimore at this time. It was a large piece. I am sorry I did not ask him for a piece of it. I suppose pieces of it today are distributed around Bucksport and Bangor. It so surprised me I said to him, "How did you manage to get a piece of this cross?" He said, "When that guide which showed us around the city showed us this cross I was determined then and there to have a piece of that cross. And as you know the cathedral is always open day and night. I took the hatchet and went up in there one night at midnight and cut this hunk off." They must have taken this cross from off exhibition for I went to Santo Domingo city seven times after that and I never saw it again. I never met David but once after that. He was then captain of a coal barge runing coals east. I had a German with me on these voyages to Santo Domingo city. He made another voyage with me to Jacksonville then he went home to New York where he lived. I have forgotton his name.

It was about August of the same year, 1882, while I was in Baltimore, that my brother John showed up. I had not seen him

Steamboat WILLIAM F. ROMER, *formerly the Rappahannock River passenger steamer* MASON L. WEEMS. *As the* WEEMS, *this vessel struck Captain Tawes' yawl boat while his schooner was loading corn at Leedstown, Virginia.*

Remains of the steamboat wharf at Leedstown, Virginia, February 27, 1967. It was at this port that the steamboat MASON L. WEEMS, *in 1881, cut in half the yawl boat of Captain Tawes as his schooner, the* WILLIAM H. KNIGHT, *was loading corn.*

Captain Leonard S. Tawes
as the young master of the schooner CITY OF BALTIMORE.

for ten years since we parted in Providence, Rhode Island. He had just got back from a voyage to China and the Philippine Islands. He brought to New York a cargo of sugar from Iloilo. I was very unwell at the time and the vessel was chartered to load cooperage in Baltimore for Sagua la Grande, north side of Cuba. He made this voyage as master in my place and I stayed home. He brought back a cargo of mahogany or Spanish cedar, I forget which. This being discharged we chartered to go out to Gibara and Borai on the north side of Cuba. We made the voyage in less than 30 days and back to Baltimore. We come home so quick that I walked in the door behind the letter carrier that was taking in my letter with the first bill of exchange of my remittance while I was taking in the second bill of exchange in my pocket. That is something that seldom happened in those days since mail service was not as swift in those days as now. And it could not happen now by a sailing vessel as there is so much better mail service from Cuba.

On two of my voyages to Santo Domingo I had a mate named James M. Nute. He was a good mate and a very industrious man though sometimes very comical. On one of my voyages to Santo Domingo the consignee out there gave us a barrel of molasses each. Our law requires the master of every vessel to make out his manifest and manifest all of his cargo and ship stores remaining on board before he reaches within 3 leagues of the land. I knew the custom house officials in Baltimore would not pass more than one barrel of molasses so I obeyed the first law of nature, self first. I manifested my barrel but did not manifest the mate's barrel. The custom house officer sat on the head of the mate's barrel all day keeping tally of the hogsheads as they were hoisted out of the hold. After awhile, or along late in the afternoon, the barrel was covered over with an old coat to screen it and to make it pleasant to sit upon. Just before night the custom house officer said, "What is this I am sitting on?" He pulled the coat off of it and discovered a barrel. Looking a little further he found it to be a barrel of molasses. Then in looking over the manifest he discovered that it was not manifested. They took this barrel of molasses as contraband and sent it up to the marine stores. The mate made a big howl telling them he was treated badly when he had 9 little children home with tongues hanging out to get into that molasses. "Oh," he said, "this is something awful." Mr. Wood came out of the sugar house and told the mate to keep quiet and he should have a barrel of molasses. He said, "Mate, give Mr. Sneeringer your address." "Now Mr. Sneeringer," he said, "you fill up a nice barrel of molasses and send it out to Mr. Nute's house." Mr. Nute did not have any children at all, nothing but a dog. I had to laugh at the way he got his barrel of molasses replaced.

When we were discharged we loaded general cargo under deck and empty hogsheads on deck. By Mr. Nute's suggestion we shipped a green hand who had never been to sea before. And he was very green. On our way out to Santo Domingo, right in the northeast trade winds, he seemed to have a cold. I said to him, "What are you snuffing about, Dodson?" He said, "I have caught a cold." I said to him, "How can you catch a cold out here in these trade winds and such fine weather?" He said, "I don't know unless it is staying out nights." "Why," said I, "I never heard of such a thing." So one night we were going along about 8 or 9 knots when 8 bells was struck. I came on deck to releive the mate and his watch but no one came aft to releive the wheel. So after a little while I got impatient. I went forward, pulled open the forecastle door, and not one of my watch had turned out. I yelled out in no pleasant voice, "What in hell do you mean by sleeping here like this? Why don't you get out and releive the wheel and the lookout?" They said, "Captain, we have never been called." "You have not?", I inquired. "No, sir, upon honor," one replied, "we have not." Dodson was supposed to be up on the topgallant fo'c'sle keeping a look out. I went up there to read the riot act to him for not calling the watch but Dodson was not up there. I looked all around the decks and in between the hogsheads but could not find him. So I thought he had fallen overboard and was lost. We all of us began looking in every place around the deck and found him sitting in an old shaking barrel abaft the mainmast to the lee of the main boom where the wind was pouring down on him from out of the mainsail. And he was dead asleep. He left a most important post and doubled himself up in an old flour barrel half full of old rope in the most exposed place on the ship. I said, "You rascal you, this is the way you keep a lookout, ha! I know now how you catch your colds. You leave your lookout post and sneak in a good hiding place and go to sleep." He said, "This is the first time." I said, "You mean the first time you got caught."

When I got out to Santo Domingo this time there had been an awful hurrycane and the harbor had filled up. I could not enter into the harbor but had to lay at anchor in an open roadstead and discharge and load my cargo which took me 30 days to do. I had on some goods for my own account. I had 3 large looking glasses for the coopers who worked for Mr. Zannetti. Of course, I intended to smuggle them ashore if I could have entered the harbor and got alongside of Mr. Zannetti's wharf. But now I was hampered and did not know what to do with these looking glasses. So I told Mr. Zanetti about them. He said to me, "How big are they?" I said, "One of them that I got for your head cooper is large enough to see your whole profile in." He said right away, "I want that one myself." He had 3 coopers, one white man and two colored men. I said, "The other two looking glasses may show more than half your profile. They are for your two colored coopers and they all three have marble brackets." He said, "What did you pay for them?" I told him, "$7.50 for the large one and $4.50 each for the two small ones." He said, "I will give you $25.00 for

the large one and you ask $18 each for the two small ones."
Oh, my, what a profit. Then I wished I had a cargo of them.
He also said, "I will see they come ashore without any trouble
to you." Which he did when his lighter came out in the roads
for cargo. I had in a lot of Rangoon rice and other general
cargo, besides 100 tons of hard coal. When the lighter was
loaded Mr. Zanetti said to me, "Put those 3 looking glasses on
top of the cargo in the lighter." Then he said to the custom
house officer, "Those 3 looking glasses are not manifested but
I want them to go on shore." And they went. Whether he paid
duty on them or not I never heard. He paid me for the glasses.
When I got loaded the coopers were mad because they did
not get the glasses they ordered. The boss cooper had to take
one of the small looking glasses and one of the colored coopers
got no glass at all.

I had a lot of rubber coats, very thin and light ones they
were. I paid $2.25 apiece in Baltimore for them. I told Mr.
Zanetti about them. For these he obtained $10 apiece. They
were the very thing for this climate for every 3 or 4 hours a
shower of rain comes and these coats, when bundled up, would
go in a pocket which the saddles have. And everybody rode on
horseback and they were very nice to have along. The whole
2 dozen were sold quickly.

But I must tell about another gauntlett I runed out there
the year before which came near getting me in trouble. And
nothing but luck caused me to escape. The Santo Dominicans
charged a heavy export duty on molasses and it seemed that
my consignee cleared his cargo short, and very short. He hired
the custom house officer to turn in 145 hogsheads when really
we had on board 320 hogsheads. We lay in the river 4 or 5
days after we were loaded and cleared waiting for good
weather to go to sea. The government talked strongly of
taking us back to the wharf and discharging the cargo to see
if the manifest was correct. All of this I heard when I came

back to Santo Domingo the next time. I did not know that Mr. Zanetti had cleared the vessel short but on this very voyage, on my arrival, I entered and deposited my papers with an American consul named Jones. Before I left a colored man by the name of Astwood had come out from New York and releived him. I cleared my vessel from this colored man and I must say he was a bright fellow. He could speak Spanish fluently. I think he was from Louisiana; I am not so certain. But to make himself popular with the Dominican Government he wrote to the custom house in Baltimore to find out how many hogsheads of molasses I landed there. Of course, that let the cat out of the bag. When he made his report to the Dominican Government, they put the custom house officer in jail for a long time and made Mr. Zanetti pay a fine of $800. I could never understand why Mr. Astwood should have done such a thing. It benifitted him nothing.

To begin the story of my trouble, I see the women wearing low cut blue shoes and high cut shoes and other kinds I just now cannot describe. So I took a notion if I were to bring out some of these shoes and smuggle them ashore I might make some money. That is what I was going to sea for anyhow. So when I was in Baltimore I went up to Tucker Smith and Company wholesale shoe house. Here I met Henry Ames who was clerking in there. I was glad to meet him. I did not know that Henry was a clerk there until I walked in. I knew Henry from boyhood. We used to go to school together in Pungoteague, Accomack County, Virginia. I said, "Henry, I am in luck to meet you here." Then I told him about what kind of shoes the women wore in Santo Domingo city, and that I was runing there for Fink Brothers and Company wholesale grocery. If he had the kind of shoes I was looking for I would spend $100 with him. He took great interest in showing me such stock as I tried to describe and I bought $100 worth of him. I took a sample out of the boxes and put the boxes down in the lazarette. And I put the samples in the cabbin into drawers that pushed under the poop deck so that I could show the samples to my customers. I always made it custom on arriving in a foreign port to have a box of cigars, a bottle of good brandy, and a bottle of good wine to treat the custom house officers when we have the custom house visit. That is when four, or probably six, will come on board together to examine the manifest and to see that everything is in compliance with their laws. I had these cigars, brandy, and wine laying in my stateroom on my bed which had a nice white spread on it.

When the custom house officers came on board there was a lot of them too. They give me the biggest surprise of my life. They brought a negro man with them to overhaul her in good shape as I suppose a real smugler they took us to be. This negro came in the cabbin and went through the 2nd mate's room, turned over his bed, opened his valise, and went through all he had. Well, can you imagine my feelings when I had my stateroom full of sample shoes. I began to think if they were only men's shoes I could tell them they were slop chest and all of them was for my crew as they required them. But the trouble was they were women's shoes. What in the world would I do about this thing? Must I pay a fine and serve time in a Dominican prison? My brother John would have to take the vessel home as he was mate with me. When he got through with the 2nd mate's room on the left, as you enter the cabbin, he went through the steward's room and gave it the same searching that he gave the 2nd mate's. When he got through with the steward's room he went into the mate's room, gave it the same overhauling that he gave the other two. Now my room was the next and the last one. I sure was feeling bad when he entered my room. But to my agreeable surprise he just looked at those cigars, bottle of Martell brandy, and bottle of wine laying on a nice white spread on my bed and said to me, "Everything is alright in here." He just turned around and walked out into the main cabbin where the Dominican elites were in waiting. I had them all to be seated around the table, got out my cork screw, and drew the corks. Took the wine glasses down off the rack and told these gentlemen to drink hearty and smoke to their heart's content. I have treated many times in my life but never any more cheerfully than these Dominican officers. About midnight that night the watchman, by the orders of Zanetti, opened the doors of the warehouse and I put all my contraband in. Then all was over and safe. Mr. Zanetti sold the goods and on leaving gave me a draught on Fink Brothers and Company of Baltimore for $279. I did well on this trip.

Another time I went there out of New York by the way of Jacksonville. I had a mate with me named Fletcher Gantt and a steward named Walter Barnes who had been with me 3 years. Two men that could not be excelled for character and duty. I had a whole lot of clothes left over from a voyage I just made to South America which our government made me carry as a slop chest. The sailors bought very few of them on this South American voyage and they were on my hands and I wanted to get rid of them. There was a man by the name of Lyon who used to keep the toll bridge that crossed the river there. I got acquainted with him. I told him I had a lot of clothes on board I wanted to sell and asked if he could not handle them for me. He said he could. We lay alongside of the custom house, so about 3 times a day I would put on a big lot of underclothes and walk through the custom house across the bridge on the other side of the river where Lyon lived and collected toll. His house had two rooms and I was so heavily clad the perspiration would be dropping off me. If anybody was at the house I would say, "Mr. Lyon, can't you give me a drink of water?" "Why certainly, Captain," he would say, "just walk in here." I would get in this private room and unstrip about 3 suits of underclothes and be releived from the excessive heat. At night I would get Mr. Gantt and Barnes each to dress up with a top suit of clothes and walk over the bridge and strip off. It was a hot job but they did it for me. I kept this up until I got everything in the way of clothing off the ship and Lyon paid me nicely every cent he owed me. This was years after I used to go there in the schooner *William H. Knight* but I must resume my story about her as I am not through with her as yet.

On this same voyage, that I lay so long in the river to get out, there was a schooner called the *Mabel* of Calais, Maine, laying in the roadstead. As I went in I was drawing much less water than he was. And I went on in over the bar in a nice smooth harbor. This got the captain of the *Mabel* very anxious to get inside though advised by the pilot not to go in. I could not much blame him for Santo Domingo Roads was, and is today, one of the roughest places in the world to lay at anchor. The sea comes in from the Caribbean Sea and strikes up against a high, rocky wall and then rebounds back, which causes a double roll. And the vessel rolls teribly in these roads. Then Captain Malony got the *Mabel* underway and tried to come in. She grounded on the bar, bilged, and she and cargo was lost. They cut holes in her deck to get the dry goods and cases of shoes out of her. She was loaded with general cargo and lighters and boats worked night and day to salvage the cargo. Very often I would see lighters going by my vessel and see the lighter men throwing bolts of dry goods under the wharfs. And some of their families would come along later and pick them out while it was night time. But these goods were all soaked with salt water and the river on the east side was adorned with the most beautiful colors where these dry goods were spread out to dry. One of the most peculiar things about this wreck was that negroes that never had shoes on their feet in their life were now wearing shoes. The American was looking after the salvaging this cargo but he could not stay there day and night to watch these lighter men.

Finally, after the cargo was salvaged, the ship was given up and sold for what she would bring. I wanted her but I would not put a bid on her. The captain would have thought hard of me had I put a bid on her. He was hitting the Santo Domingo beverage a little, anyhow, so I let a Dominican buy her. She brought $11. I was convinced that Malony was no longer connected with her so I went over to the consul and said to him, "I will give that fellow $35 for this bargain and give you $5 to make the terms." In about ½ hour to an hour he came to me and said, "Captain, the bargain is closed; the ship is yours." I gave him the $40 and it was up to me to get what I could off of her. She lay in a very rough place at the entrance of the harbor. I knew that my crew would not go aloft on this wreck and help me as they could. So I hired 2 English sailors that were on the beach there. They had got shipwrecked at Barahona, one of the worst exposed harbors on the south side of Santo Domingo, and had walked from there up to Santo Domingo city. They were about a week or ten days tramping up to the city. On arrival they applied to me for work. I had to have men to help me to discharge and to load and a good sailorman is always to be desired on a vessel provided he is willing to work. And necessity made these fellows very willing. John, my brother, was mate with me on this voyage. When I was loaded I hauled in the stream and anchored to get ready for sea. I was keeping these two fellows all the time. About 5 o'clock in the evening I came on board. I had been on shore all the afternoon fixing up my business with the consignee, clearing from the custom house, and so forth. When I came on board John said to me, "Len, I discharged them two Englishmen." I said, "What for?" He said, "They brought a lot of rum on board and they were getting our crew drunk. It made me mad. I set them ashore." He went down the cabbin and brought up 8 or 9 bottles of rum and said to me, "Look here what I took away from them." "They were well stocked," said I, "but when you set them on shore you should have given them their rum. You had no business keeping it from them." In a little while they came on board to receive their pay for the services they had rendered. After I paid them I said, "Jack, you are a hell of a fellow to bring all this rum on board here. The mate done right to discharge you." "Now," I said to one of my sailors, "set these 2 men ashore." And I said, "Here, you, take your rum with you."

It was now dark and I was on deck. When the boat returned I said to the man, "What is that in the bow of the boat?" He said, "It is the rum those 2 English sailors had. They told me to bring it back and give it to the boys and let them have a good time." I said, "Give it to me. I'll put it in the cabbin for future use." The next day I bought this wreck I went to look for these two Englishmen at once. I said, "Jack, I have bought that wreck out there and I want to strip her and get the rigging and all I can off of her. If you will work like you ought to I will give you $2.50 per day each. But you do all the the work that is done aloft." "Captain," one said, "we will do it or anything you say." I said, "Alright. Report tomorrow morning for duty." The steward prepared our dinner for us and the way we went down to the wreck. When we got there I saw we needed things we did not have with us. So I said, "Jack, we need a pin maul, another marlinspike, an ax, and hatchet." I said, "I will take my two men and go back to the schooner and get them." And I laid off some jobs for them to do while I was gone. Jack said to me, "Captain, if you will bring a little rum back with you, you take charge of it and just deal a little out to us, we will be able to do twice as much work." After getting back to my vessel and getting all the desired things, I put in the boat two bottles of his rum that he sent back to the boys two days before. I got back to the wreck, give them some rum, and we got to work stripping of her. The main deck was all under water but the top of the cabbin was out. When noon came we got up on top of this cabbin to eat. While eating I said to Jack, "Jack, that was pretty good rum I brought down with me, was it not?" "Captain," he said, "truthfully that is the worse rum I ever drank in Santo Domingo." I said, "You rascal, you, it's your rum; the rum you brought on my vessel and the rum you sent back for the crew to have a good time on. I intercepted it at the gangway. Now you are runing down your own goods." He was nonplussed. He could not say another word.

We worked hard all day pretty well naked as the main deck was full of water yet warm. About the first week in February it was and the climate was delightful at this season of the year. But when I went on board that night and turned in I kept feeling something like pins and needles sticking into me. I could not sleep. I did not know what ached me but the next morning I discovered I was all sunburned. The next day we went down to the wreck again and on this day we got the rigging all down on deck. Now the question that confronted me was what I was going to do with it. It was large 7-inch hemp rigging. But somehow in all my life I could conceive some kind of an idea how to master a bad situation whenever I was confronted with it. The wreck lay about 200 yards from the beach and the wind and sea set on this beach. So I took a coil of rope about 1½ inches in size and tied a piece of wood on it and let it drift on shore. Then I took the end of a coil of marlin and let it drift ashore the same way. I had two men on the beach to haul enough of the big line ashore to let the end come back to the wreck. We pulled this end back with the marlin and made the two ends fast to each other and now we had endless rope leading from the wreck to the shore. The sea was so rough and bad that it was impossible to take this rigging in the boat and go in the harbor with it.

So now we tied this 1½-inch rope to the rigging that we now had on deck and threw the rigging overboard. And the men on the shore pulled on this endless line and pulled all of this rigging ashore on the beach. And when it was all on the beach we went inside of the harbor where it was as smooth as a mill pond. Then we had to carry it on our backs at 200 yards across this sand point and put it in the boat and take it on board of the vessel just about ½ mile up the harbor.

The capstan and some other iron works and blocks, we had to put them in the boat alongside of the wreck and come across the bar into the harbor. The current at the bar of this harbor is always runing out which causes a sharp, dangerous sea to run. I had a big Newfoundland man steering the boat in across the bar. He always lorded it so over the other men on board and being a Newfoundlander I did not think fear ever entered his heart. I was sitting on one of thwarts of the boat, not thinking but what everything would go well, when quite a heavy breaker run up on the boat. And to my surprise this great big fellow fainted and fell sprawling in the boat. I had to jump over the top of him and grab the oar in time to keep her from coming side to and filling. If she had every one of us would have been drowned right there for the boat would have sunk with the heavy weight we had in her. And the tide runing out would have carried us out to sea and drowned every mother's son of us. But we successfully got everything on board safely and stowed in the hold. And all the while we were waiting for good weather to get to sea in. On my arrival in Baltimore the customs officials would not let me land this free of duty unless I cut the rigging up in pieces which I did and I sold it to a junker by the name of Woolford at the foot of Broadway. I cleaned up $148 for my two day's labor at Santo Domingo, giving the two English sailors $5 each.

We discharged our cargo, loaded, and went out again. When I got to Santo Domingo the harbor had shallowed up very much but I got in although the vessel had a close call getting in. But I did get in and discharged. Then I took in part cargo and had to go out in the roads to finish loading which was terrible hard work. She rolled so badly we lost two tierces of honey overboard and John, my brother, scolded the captain of the lighter for not hooking the hogshead hooks into the hogsheads good. He give John some back talk and made a jump to come on board to fight. But John jumped in the cabbin and got my Smith and Wesson. With fire in his eyes he just took aim at this half-breed and expected to see the fellow drop dead right where he stood. I prevailed on him not to shoot. But he did put a ball in the lighter side of his foot. Then the fellow said, "I do not want to the honey get lost. I am anxious to have it go on board safe." We never lost anymore honey or molasses. It made them more careful. When I went on shore the next day Mr. Zanetti said to me, "Captain, your brother made a big mistake to draw that pistol on that man. You tell him not to come on shore here anymore because if he does these natives will kill him sure." When I went back on board I told my brother what Mr. Zanetti told me to tell him. If John had shot that half-breed I would have hove up my anchor, got her underway, and been way out to sea on my way to Baltimore before they would have found it out on the shore.

When I had finished taking in cargo I told John to caulk the hatches and get all of the tackle down that we had been using to hoist in cargo. Also to get ready for sea and to send the boat on shore for me at 5 o'clock PM. I had to go on shore to sign bills of lading, settle up with the consignee, and clear the ship from the custom house and from the American consul. When I come down through the gate of the city at 5 PM now who would you think was in the boat waiting for me? Why it was John himself. I said, "John, how dare you do such a thing after the warning you have had from Mr. Zanetti?

You know they no more mind taking the life of a man here than a chicken." "I am not afraid of any of them," he said. He continued, "One of them lighter men passed by me just now and he tiped his hat to me." He also said, "I have that pistol with me and I could put 5 of them out of commission quick." I got in the boat, put all my papers in a safe place so they would not blow overboard, and said, "Let us get on board as quickly as possible." The next morning early with the land breeze we sailed for Baltimore. We got there safely some time in March. I remember it was very cold beating up the Patapsco River on a Sunday. John did not go with me again for a long time. It seems he quit to take charge of one of Captain Travers' brigs called the *D. C. Chapman.*

For the next voyage I shipped Mr. James M. Nute for my mate and he was a good mate too. But I feel it my duty to go back a little and tell you when John joined me. It was in August, 1882, that he came to Baltimore. I had not seen him for ten years. We were in a small Cape Cod schooner the winter of 1872-1873 runing oysters out the Chesapeake Bay or rivers to Providence. Sometime in February, 1873, we separated. We were only boys. I got to trading to Brazil and the West Indies before the mast, as 2nd mate and mate, and then master. He quit this schooner sometime the next fall. So 10 years after our separation he came to Baltimore at the time I was very unwell. He went out as master of my vessel to Sagua la Grande from Baltimore with a cargo of cooperage and back to New York with a load of mahogany. I went to New York and I took charge. He went mate with me out to Gibara, north side of Cuba, with a general cargo underdeck and car wheels and empty freight cars and a locomotive on deck. I got a mighty good freight on this business but I had to agree to go out on short manifest. I wanted to make money fast and I accepted the business.

I was chartered by Mosly Brothers, 56 Exchange Place, New York City. And here I runed the gauntlett. Before chartering, Mosly Brothers agreed in writing to pay my way out of any trouble I should fall into with the Spanish government on account of this shortage of cargo. I agreed with a stevedore to put all the cargo on board for $175. When I was ready to load, the stevedore said I was boycotted and he could not load me because the vessel had been discharged by non-union stevedores and the fine was 10¢ per ton. I told him I would not pay the fine. I said, "If you cannot load her say so and I will get someone else." "But," he said, "you have contracted to let me load her." I said, "Yes, but you say you cannot do it unless I pay a fine of 10¢ per ton." I telephoned up to the mahogany yard and asked them if they would load me for $175. They said they would with pleasure. This was a nice price and the stevedore did not want to give the job up. He wanted me to pay the fine and his price too. But, finally, we compromised by him paying to the union one half the fine and I the other. I always used the union stevedores ever after when I was in New York.

We loaded, cleared, and went to sea. We had a good run out. I have forgotton the days. I went down through the Crooked Island Passage. I had never been through this passage but once in my life. Then I was 2nd mate of the brig *Agnes Barton,* Captain Humphrey Knight, comander. We were bound to Santo Domingo and in the heaviest thunder squalls I think I ever witnessed. I was sure I would be killed by lightening that night. Anyhow, I learned nothing about the passage and the islands on this voyage so they were very much strange to me now going through here in charge of a vessel. And you may be sure I did not sleep much going through this passage. On getting through I coasted down the Old Bahama Channel looking for Cape Lucrecia. I made the light some time before the break of day. It was very dark and rainey at the time and I never left the deck but staid up and watched, it being my first time on this route. And with thick weather I had to use care and judgement to do this job safely. When the day broke there was the high, mountainous lands along the coast of Cuba. So I went to the foremast head and watched for the entrance to Gibara. It was too thick and rainey to see far but about 8 o'clock in the morning I made the sea buoy from aloft. I directed the ship's course for it and presently I made the outlines of the harbor and set the ship's course accordingly.

It was not long before I saw the custom house boat coming out with lots of men in her. Even Spanish soldiers were in her. I began to feel very cheap. The custom house collector was in her. I thought the whole thing had been exposed and began to see the Spanish prison doors open for me. There was one man who could speak broken English plain enough for me to understand. He says to me, "This Mr. Goviernier, your consignee. I am the American consul. Now Mr. Goviernier wants the mail." I said, "He cannot get it." I would not deliver the mail which contained the manifest bills of lading and consignee's letter. I just felt these were not the people I wanted to see. I said to them, "I will deliver this mail when I get at the American Consulate." So we brought the ship to anchor safely in the harbor. I started below to change my clothes. They were my old sea togs all wet and not fit to appear anywhere in. I always did like to have a respectable appearance in all my days wherever I happen to be. But these people were in such hurry they would not let me make a change and I had to get in the boat and go on shore with them. But whether it was to jail as smugler or to the American consul I did not know. I stuck to the ship's papers and my mail.

On my way ashore I had on a pair of shoes that Dan Morgan made for me. He was the bigest shoe maker ever lived in Crisfield and I beleive in the world. These shoes were as square across the toe as any scow and these young officers would point at my feet and make gestures length ways, then gestures cross ways, like if my shoes had been made by the yard and sawed off at the ends. Then they would look up at me and laugh. They wore nice light French calfskin shoes made up in a beautiful pattern and they were very beautiful in comparison to mine. When we landed they all dispersed leaving the consul and me together. I followed him sticking tightly to my papers though feeling embarrassed with my sea togs on and they all wet.

Finally, we came to the American Consulate. There was the eagle and the American coat of armor over the door. And oh, how my confidence was restored. How this great feeling of trouble left me. I thought this thing a thousand times when Germany was imposing on our rights and if I had been a public speaker I should have taken the platform and spoke in behalf of our Old Glory and how we should go down in our jeans and buy Liberty Bonds and keep our Old Glory wafting to the breeze. I cannot express my happy feelings when I got to the consulate's and all my troubles and suspicions were expelled. For I was now sure I was with friends. I said to the consul, "Here are the papers." He took out the ship's register crew list and the articles and gave me a receipt for them with the eagle stamped on them. "Now," he says, "let us go immediately down to the consignee and give him his mail." And the way we went.

Finally, we came to a large wholesale store. In there was Mr. Goviernier the man that met us out of the mouth of the harbor. When we were coming in the consul handed him his mail. He could not speak English but he was proud to get his mail for I think he was as much disturbed about this manifest shortness as I was. He told the consul to tell me to make my home with him while I was in the port. And I did enjoy some glorious Spanish cooking while I was in Gibara. We lay at the end of a long wharf which led up to his store. I, and my brother John, was up in the store one night and these Spaniards were weighing each other. John was always slick handed and on the counter were some small nail kegs. They came out from Europe in very small kegs. I do not think they weighed over 12 or 15 pounds. John backed to the counter and sliped one of these kegs up his back under his coat. When the Spaniards got through weighing me John steped on the scales. The Spaniard kept moving the pea on the scales and scales not tipping. The Spaniard began to hollor out, "Caramba," which is a great word with them. He weighed so much they could not understand it. They say over and over, "Caramba, muche carne," which means, "Gracious, much beef." When he was through he backed up to the counter, discharged those nails, and no one ever discovered it. They always thought that was his weight. That night, walking down the long wharf toward the vessel, I said to John, "By jingo, John, I did not think you were that heavy. And those Cubans and Spaniards were very much surprised." Then he said to me, "Did you see those small kegs of nails on the counter?" "Yes," said I, "what did that have to do with it?" He said, "I just backed up to the counter, sliped one of them up my back when they were not looking, and when they were through weighing me I backed up to the counter, sliped it back on the counter and they did not detect." I never could understand how he did such a trick.

We now got the locomotive and cars off the deck and were getting the cargo out of the hold. We were getting along nicely until one of the sailors, named Andrew, began to drink a little heavy and would be runing in the forecastle every 15 or 20 minutes. John was noticing this thing, and realy I was too, because when he was gone the winch that we were hoisting cargo with was hand powered. There was no gasoline or steam hoisting gear in those days. And when Andrew was gone the winch had to stop and wait until he returned. So John, getting impatient with him, said, "You have too much business in that forecastle. I want you to stay here in your place." He said, "I just go in there to get some tobacco. Cannot a man go and get tobacco?" John said, "It's not so. You are runing there to drink rum for I see it on you." I think after exchanging a few more words he called John a liar. By the time the word was out of his mouth John was into him and in a hugging and scuffling match which was a real fight. I happened to be abreast of the fore hatch when they ran up against me and nocked me down in the hold. We had in about 150 tons of coal, which was in the bottom of the vessel, and when I went down in the hold I fell summersalt and hit on my back between my shoulders on this coal right in between a lot of car wheels. My feet and legs went backward on each side of my neck and my skin hit the sharp edge of a car wheel and cut my pants and underpants just as smooth as a razor could have cut them, and made an awful gash through the flesh and into the shin bone. It was all of a 6 or 7 foot fall and, if in the fall the back of my head had fell on one of those car wheels, my brains would have been let out.

While John and this Andrew were fighting, another fellow, an Irishman, came down out of the rigging to help Andrew. John cleaned them both up. I had Andrew sent to prison and let him stay there two days to get sobered up. He beged so to get back on board I took him out and he was an alright man after this. John made the Irishman work as long as he could see before he let him have supper and we had no more trouble with that crew on this voyage. They afterwards behaved themselves and did their work like good men.

Mr. Goviernier sent a Spanish doctor on board and he treated my leg for it was badly cut. The doctor was on board to see me 4 or 5 times. He was a nice doctor too and when we settled up Mr. Goviernier paid the doctor bill and made me a present of $20 gold and I was much pleased with my consignee.

We cleared and sailed for Baltimore. I was at a loss to know which way to come home, whether I should work up to eastward and come through the Crooked Island Passage, or run down the Old Bahama Channel and come up the Gulf Stream. I had never been down the Old Bahama Channel in my life before and I was a little afraid of it. There was a Spanish captain there in a Spanish brig called the *Barrai*. I asked him his opinion on it and he suggested the Old Bahama Channel way and I took his advice and come home that way. I do not remember what kind of weather we had coming home but I think it was good weather. I well remember we were becalmed close to Cape Hatteras Light on Christmas Day.

We got in the Chesapeake Bay all in good shape and while coming up we had bad looking weather. Off New Point I made up my mind we were going to have a snow storm. I said, "John, we are going to have bad weather and I think we had better go under New Point and harbor." The wind was then northeast, light breeze, and cloudy. John said to me, "I thought we were bound to Baltimore not New Point." He said, "Let us keep going." It was his first watch below and about 9 PM it began to snow thick and blow. I went below and told him to get out and throw the lead, that I must try to find the Rappahannock. He came out and sounded and I steered a course that I thought would take us in there though it was impossible to see more than 250 or 300 yards. I was feeling mad with myself because I did not go under New Point and make a harbor while I had daylight and could see. But now I am caught out here in a snow storm dark and thick with snow. I must do the best I can. But luckily I made Stingray Point Light and I was pretty close to it too but I hauled her up a little to clear the shoals on Sturgeon Bar. I runed her for a while and I was so afraid I would run into some vessel

laying to anchor that I hauled down the jibs and brought her
to. The next day was Saturday and blowed a gale and snowed
all day. Sunday morning it cleared off. John and I went on
shore where there was a creek. They gave us some nice oysters.
We got back on board about noon, got dinner, cleaned all
the snow off of her, and about 2:30 PM the wind breezed up
southwest. We got her underway and went up the bay that
night. Got to Baltimore the next day, Monday. We had made
the round out of New York to Gibara and back to Baltimore
in less than 30 days.

We entered at the custom house, paid off the crew, discharged our ballast, cleaned up the hold, and got the vessel
ready to load a cargo for Fink Brothers and Company to go
out to Santo Domingo city. John went with me on this voyage
as mate which was the last time he went with me in this vessel.
This was the year of 1883. I believe I have described pretty
well all the particulars of this voyage already. When I returned
to Baltimore on this voyage and got the cargo out John quit
me to take charge of the brig *D. C. Chapman,* one of Captain
Travers' large vessels. He dismasted her on the way to Baltimore from Navassa loaded with Navassa guano. She drifted
or he ran her ashore on the north side of Jamaica and he lost
her. I then shipped a man name James M. Nute who made
the next two voyages out to Santo Domingo with me.

I was chartered to make four voyages that year but I only
made 3 of them. The harbor at Santo Domingo was filling
up so that I could not take a full cargo on the inside but could
only take part cargo and had to go outside in the roads to
complete my cargo out of lighters. These roads are the
roughest place in the world for a vessel to lay. This is the
second time I had to lay in this rough roadstead to finish
loading. I was getting tired of this rolling and the trade. I
believe I have described the particulars of this voyage already.
After making this round we went out to Santo Domingo again.

This time on arrival in Santo Domingo I could not get in the harbor at all but had to lay in these roads and discharge all my cargo and load molasses and honey which was awful hard work. It took us 30 days to unload and load this cargo and I was determined not to make the next and last voyage. So on my arrival in Baltimore I notified Captain Travers to get another captain to go in the vessel, that I was satisfied to quit. Between him and Mr. Wood they canceled this last voyage which was lucky for me for along some time in the latter part of August or September, or about the time I should or would have been laying in these roads, there came a great hurrycane and swept every vessel that was laying in these roads up against these high rocks. The vessels and their crews all perished. Had I been there I would have suffered the same fate.

After this last charter to Santo Domingo was cancelled I was chartered to take a general cargo, mostly bread stuff, provisions, kerosene oil, and many other things in general, to Demerara, British Guiana. On my way down the bay, or I will say at Cape Henry, the latter part of August the wind began to blow gently from the eastward. I never did care much about going out of the capes with an east wind and do not now in a sailing vessel. So I dropped anchor fairly close to Cape Henry. It was about 2 o'clock afternoon I said to the mate, "We'll lay here until midnight and see what this weather is going to do. If it does not cloud up and go to storming we will get to sea; if it does storm we will run back to New Point or Hampton Roads for harbor." I said, "Rig up the yawl, put the sail on her, and let us go on shore to the lighthouse." I was more restless in those days than I am now. So we rigged up the yawl, put sail on her, and away we went for the shore and lighthouse. When we got in on the sandy bottom in about a fathom of water I never saw so many female crabs in all my life. The water was real clear and bottom visible. The female crabs were so thick that they lay on top of one another apparently. And now they tell me there is never any there. That night at 12 o'clock midnight the winds changed to the northeast, gentler and clear. I hove up anchor and went to sea.

We had a long passage out. We had some of the darkest nights I ever saw at sea in this lattitude of the West Indies. One little, or I might say a big and important, incedent occured one day that I will never forget, it worried me so much. It was in the area of Martinique, though about 150 miles to the eastward of the islands; it was in the afternoon. I had my two pillows on deck to sun and get air. While they were up there a squall came up from the south and east which blew quite strong. I forgot about my pillows and in the squall they both blowed overboard. My mind was too much concerned about this squall to give the pillows any attention. But I saw them when they went over. When the squall was over, it did not last more than an hour, I got to thinking very much about my pillows. I knew I would not get any more sleep without them for in my case I could not sleep if my head was not still. My body may roll ever so much and it will not interfere with my sleep. But my head had to settle down on feathers and the crease my head would make in the pillow would scotch my head and keep it still when the ship did not roll too heavy. So when the squall had passed and the weather had moderated down I tacked ship and steered northeast, the opposite course I steered during the squall. After running back something more than an hour I saw them both. I lowered a boat, put two men in her, and sent them after the pillows. I steered the vessel northeast for awhile until I thought I was far enough from the boat and men. I tried to tack ship but the wind had moderated down and I could not get headway enough on the vessel to tack her. I made 3 or 4 attempts all the time getting farther from the men until I lost sight of them altogether. Then my worry became intense. I began to think I could get more rest and pleasure than Jacob ever got when he lay his head on a stone. A thousand diferent thoughts came through my mind. What would the world say about me putting 2 sea-men in a boat without water or provisions and leave them there to die? I then thought if they only knew their lattitude and longitude, with the trade winds blowing from the east and fair for Martinique, they could row there safely in two days rowing west. Finally, I got the ship to tack. I steered her back southwest again. Before the sun went down, to the joy of my heart, we made them out. I then steered for them. I think that was the most anxious three hours I ever spent in all my life. I never breathed my anxiety to any one on board; not even the men in the boat knew I was anxious about them. When I got down to them they said, "Captain, we only got one of your pillows. We rowed all around in diferent directions and could not find the other one." I said, "Alright, men, you did well. One pillow is enough for me. Bring your boat under the stern and hook her on." It is no cinch taking a boat up to the davits at sea for as the vessel rolls the boat swings out and back athwartship. The full length of the davit tackles make it awfully unpleasant for the men that are in the boat. Such a see-saw experience no one can imagine except those who have had the experience. The boat being brought to the davits safely and secured, we filled away and proceeded on our course.

When we got down in the lattitudes of Barbados we were threatened with a hurrycane it being in the center of the hurrycane season, the latter part of August. It had been a gale for 3 or 4 days, anyhow, and here is when we experienced that darkest night I ever saw. I told Mr. Nute, the mate, that the foresail, though already double-reefed, would have to come in. He and the sailors had to crawl on their hands and knees to get forward. Nothing in the world was visible. There was a tub of water on deck which had been there 3 or 4 days. He told me he did not know which part of the ship he was in until he got into this tub of water. He got the foresail in and tied it up.

We were then under very short sail and I was waiting for the blast of the hurrycane to strike. But, fortunately, it went by without hitting us with the heavy blast I was looking for. Had we been in an ink bottle it would not have been any darker. Finally, this spell of bad weather went by and the weather cleared away. Soon we began to get soundings on the Guiana coast. Finally, we made the lightship from which we took a pilot and sailed in.

The merchant who chartered us in Baltimore had been sailing in W. N. Perot's employ for years trading altogether to Demerara. I have always heard that Mr. Perot gave his captains the privilege of carrying any light merchandise they could stow in the cabin of his ships. He owned 4 of them, 1 barque and 3 brigs, and they were all named after rivers. The barque was named the *Delaware,* one brig was named the *Potomac,* one brig named the *Chesapeake,* and our brig named the *Mississippi.* This man that chartered us was named J. R. Marchant. He was a Mathews County (Va.) man. I think he sailed the brig *Mississippi.* He built up a splendid business in Demerara. So much so that he quit going to sea and stoped in Baltimore and chartered small vessels, loaded them, and sent them out to Demerara. He would have as many as five and six vessels on the sea at a time.

My consignee out there was named Birch and Company. My cargo was consigned to the order of the British Guiana Bank. Captain Marchant wrote a very indistinct hand and when he gave me the large envelope containing bills of lading, charter party, and consignee's letter to Birch and Company I never gave it a thought about my cargo being consigned to order as British Guiana Bank and Birch and Company looked so much alike to me. And I would never have detected it if I hadn't paid the duty on all the cargo and gotton a permit to land all of it at once. But I would have to go to the custom house everyday and sign papers and then go to this bank and go through a certain performance and then come on board and overhaul the cargo to get out certain goods. So one day coming out of the bank I looked up and saw the name British Guiana Bank. It dawned on me at once that my bills of lading was to order. I came on board and began overhauling the cargo to get out such goods as he had a permit to get out. I then looked at my bill of lading and sure enough discovered that my bill of lading was to order. I took my bills of lading up to Mr. Birch and told him I wanted to exchange bills of lading with him. "Why," he says, "I never heard of such a thing. None of the other captains coming here never required it." "Well," I said, "they did not know their business. I think I have been very lenient; I have been here nearly three days. I am sure you have had ample time to get it out of the bank and I want it." He pretended to look around for the bill of lading but could not find it. He said that it must be here somewhere but felt sure it was yet in the bank. I went on board and looked at that cargo going out and I without the bank's bill of lading. I went back into Birch's office and stuck there.

About 2 PM I went back on board. They were then getting out the cases of kerosene oil. I had all the salt beef and pork stowed down on the ceiling of the vessel so that if any of them leaked the pickle would not damage the flour and bread that was on board. Kerosene was a cheap article, anyhow, so I thought I would not hold them up on that. But I told Mr. Nute, the mate, that if I am not here when the oil is out, stop them, discharge nothing else. I knew the beef and pork was worth half as much as the ship was and I would have something in case Birch and Company should turn out not to be my consignee. I then went up in Birch's office and sat there. I was worried and I began to worry them. But at 4 PM they produced the bill of lading indorsed by the British Guiana Bank, deliver to Birch and Company. I gave them my bills of lading, took the bank's, and went on board very happy. I told Mr.

Nute to deliver all the cargo as they wished to come out. I made up my mind then and there that they would fail some day and burst Johnny Marchant. And so they did. He had hard luck after that. His horse ran away and broke Marchant's leg which had to be amputated. The last I heard of him he was keeping a coal yard in Baltimore for I used to buy my coal of him that I used on the vessel while I was going to sea.

After the cargo was out and I had my ballast in, three of the sailors wanted some money which I gave them. They went off but did not return promptly. The next day I went to look for them. One of them I got on board very nicely but two of them bucked and would not go on board. I could see they had been drinking. They told me they would not go on board. I told them I would see the American consul and get a warrant and have them put on board. They told me to help myself at that. Evidently, they knew more about the English maritime laws than I did. I went to the consul and told him I wanted a warrant for two of my men and have them put on board. Here I was informed by the consul that there was no treaty between the United States and Great Britain to assist seamen and put them back on board their ship. He told me to try to persuade them to go back on board since I could not have them arrested. This was a disappointment to me for in Spanish ports and Dominican ports I had no trouble about making them come on board.

I went back and talked to the two of them nicely and I succeeded in getting one of them on board. The other, a German, refused and I could not get him back. The mate and I took a stroll up town that night and on coming back on board we had to go down a long alley between houses to get on board. I was very much ahead of Mr. Nute and I met this fellow, Louis by name, in the alley coming ashore from the vessel. When I met him I grabed him and we were tusling hard. He was on top of me but I was hanging to him. Pretty soon I heard Mr. Nute coming a runing. He, Mr. Nute, was a powerful, raw-bone man. He hit this fellow 3 or 4 good, sound licks in the ribs. I could hear him hick every time Mr. Nute hit him. He then pulled him off me. I got up on my feet hanging to him and we led him down to the side of the ship. The side was low as there is a big rise and fall of the tide in Demerara, 6 or 7 feet. So we lowered him down on board. The steward came out and helped us. I sent the steward down the cabbin to get a pair of hand cuffs. We put them on him and put him down the fore hatch on top of the sand ballast and put the hatches on and barred them down.

The next morning we droped her off in the stream to anchor. I had to go on shore and straiten up with Messrs. Birch and Company and clear for Orchilla. I told Mr. Nute as soon as Louis sobered up and was ready to turn to to give him his breakfast and put him to work. He stuck it out until 10 o'clock in the morning. He came out of the hold, begged the mate's pardon for what he had done, and told the mate he was ready to go to work. The mate told him he must eat some breakfast first. I wish to add that we now do have a treaty with Great Britain to arrest crews and put them on board their ships. Great Britain seldom let one of their war ships come to the United States on account of the desertion of their crews. I think the treaty pertains to any British or American subjects fleeing from justice.

That afternoon, being ready for sea, we sailed from Demerara for Orchilla to load guano for Richmond, Virginia. I well remember when we were two or three days out of Demerara that I was expecting to see the island of Tobago. But I forgot to tell Mr. Nute about it. I had stood the middle watch and at 4 PM I went below. I had not been there long before Mr. Nute called me and said, "Captain, it looks like land here on the port bow." I knew immediately it was Tobago. I jumped out of my berth and went on deck as quick as possible for I did not know but what we were on top of it. And sure enough we were pretty close to it. I will never forget how those high, mountainous hills looked. It was dark, anyhow, and those dark, high peaks looked like they were touching the clouds. The strong equatorial current had set me very much to the westward. I luffed her up to clear any rocks or shoals that might be existing there. Tobago had no lighthouse on it. When daylight came and I could see good, and as soon as I saw I was out of danger, I kept her off and ran into the Caribbean Sea to the westward. This is the island that Robinson Crusoe was cast away on, so I have been told.

We had a nice breeze, fair, and fine weather. Along in the afternoon we made a beautiful island which belongs to England. We passed it to the northward of us. We sailed on to the westward, down the Caribbean Sea, and in about two or three days we made the little island of Orchilla. Night was coming on and I hove to well to the eastward of the island expecting to go in in the morning. When morning came the island was not in sight and I did not know which way it was. I took a morning sight to obtain my longitude. Then I ran to the westward until my longitude was up and no island was in sight. Now I did know my lattitude. I did not know whether I was north or south of it. I had to wait until noon to get my lattitude and when I did get my lattitude at noon I was 27 miles north of the island.

I now had my position in good shape and I ran for the island. In two hours I made it out dead ahead. Now I was determined to go in if I got there before dark. I did not want to let the current carry me away from the island again. As I approached the island I went to the foremast head to get the lay of the land and the entrance to the harbor. I was determined to go in and I let her run. I got the lay of the harbor alright and just as I was rounding the last point of the harbor,

Captain Barrett, the Governor of the island—for it seemed like all Governors of the island were old worn out sea captains—yelled to me to let go anchor at a certain buoy in the harbor, which I did. He then came on board and said to me, "Captain, you are an old trader here, ain't you?" I said, "I was never here in my life before." "Well," he said, "you came in here like a man well acquainted. I never saw a real stranger come in here like that before." I said, "I was determined the current should not carry me from the island again."

Of evenings I took fish suppers on shore with Captain Barrett. While I lay here loading, the captain kept two men fishing everyday to provide fish for all on the island including the laborers.

After taking in our cargo, which was about 325 tons of very heavy guano, which was not bulky but lay heavy in the vessel's hold, we sailed for Richmond, Virginia. It was strong trade winds blowing when we passed out by the east point. It was just like jumping out of a nice harbor into mid-ocean, right into a heavy sea. And, oh my, she did labor hard with this kind of cargo and began leaking which worried me very much for I did not like to hear the pumps going much when I was a long way offshore. We had a strong trade wind all the way across the Caribbean Sea and in 48 hours we had crossed the Caribbean Sea and entered the Mona Passage. After entering into the Atlantic we had moderate winds and hot weather until we entered the Gulf Stream. Here we encountered a hurrycane in which it looked like she was going to go down. I then made up my mind if she did take me to Richmond safely I would give her up as Mr. Ebon Hunting come down to see me just before I sailed for Demerara and asked me if I did not like to have a new and larger vessel. I said, "Yes, but how am I to get her?" He said, "If you can raise $6,000 dollars and take a quarter of one I can get her for you and you can have her on a half share." This was the best offer

I ever had in my life but I told Mr. Hunting that I could not raise $6,000 and that I did not think I would ever be able to raise that amount. I thanked him and declined the offer. But when I was in this hurrycane and in a vessel leaking badly, and all the water that touches this guano it immediately absorbed it, for this guano was fine as flour and the vessel was getting heavier and heavier all the time, I was resolved to go and see Mr. Hunting in Baltimore as soon as possible after I arrived in Richmond, which I did.

I went to Baltimore to meet my wife and our two little boy babies. After I met her at the boat and got her reconciled I went to the office of Mr. Hunting and told him I would like to have the vessel he spoke to me about when I was in Baltimore about 2½ months earlier. "Well," he said, "that vessel was completed and a man from New Jersey is sailing her." But he told me these same people were building another one. He said, "I will give you a letter to this man Emerson Rokes." He wrote a nice letter of recommendation to Emerson Rokes and I took it to him. He was in his office on Pratt Street, up a stairs. I went up and made inquiry if Mr. Emerson Rokes was in. He answered, "I am him." I said, "I have a letter from Mr. Hunting to you." I handed it to him. He read it over and said, "You are too late; I have engaged another man." I said, "Alright," and started to walk out. He said, "Wait a minute; you give me your address and if anything should happen, which occurs to my mind will, and you can take 1/16 interest which was $1500, I will let you have her. But you are to sail her on wages at $75 per month." I told him alright but he must let me know in three days as I would like to notify Captain Travers in time to procure a captain. I got my wife and two little boys and took the train for Richmond and in three days, according to his promise, I got a letter from Mr. Rokes that I could have the vessel then building in Bath, Maine.

I notified Captain Travers to procure a man to take my place as I was quitting to take charge of a vessel that Emerson Rokes was building in Bath, Maine. He wrote me back to stay by to attend to the unloading and to loading of her, buy the stores, and get her ready for sea, which I did. When this was all done he would have a captain there to take charge of her. All of this I did to my utmost best. I was on board of this vessel 3 years and 11 days. I left her at the same wharf I first took charge of her and loaded with the same kind of cargo which was hoop poles. And I must say I took quite a liking to the vessel as I suppose from our long association and the many storms she had safely carried me through. Even when I had gotten a couple hundred yards from her I had to turn around just at a street or wharf corner to take a last farewell view of her. I said, "Old girl, I may never see you again." And sure enough I never did for she was lost on the way out. She ran ashore on the island of Abaco bound to Matanzas. Her chronometer proved to be very much out. Luckily, all hands were saved and those hungry colored out there got a good feed. The captain afterwards told me that while they were trying to save their clothing these negroes had stole all the stores that were on board.

I must relate a little incident that transpired on my arrival in Richmond. My consignee was named Mr. Sneed. I got to his office a little early in the morning, quite sometime before he got down. When he came in I said, "Is this Mr. Sneed?" He said, "Yes." "Well," I remarked, "I have a load of guano here for you from Orchilla." He looked at me and said, "You do not mean that a young man like you is all the way from Orchilla with a load of guano in for me?" "Yes, sir," I said, "if your name is Sneed."

Mary and myself took the train down to West Point and the steamer *Danville* to Baltimore. Then Captain Travers and I had our last settlement. I came home and got there in time

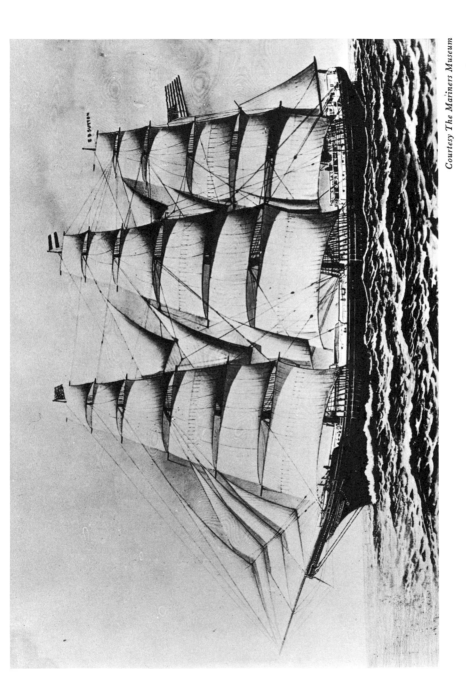

In August 1885 the City of Baltimore *sailed in company with this ship, the* E. B. Sutton. *Captain Tawes' brother John, then his mate, boarded the* Sutton *for a visit as the two vessels sailed along.*

The waterfront of Jacksonville, Florida, during the latter part of the last century when Captain Taves traded there in the CITY OF BALTIMORE. *The side wheel tug* R. L. MABEY, *which towed this schooner on the St. Johns River, is in the center.*

to vote. That was the first time in my life our ticket was badly defeated. We got Captain Don Lawson for judge of the Orphans Court. I was home for a short time. Apparently it was short to me for there is where I would like to have stayed the remainder of my life. But I had a living to make and I had to go.

V

1 8 8 4 – 1 8 8 5

A FTER being home a month or about I got orders to come up
to Baltimore, plank down my $1,500 for the 1/16 share and
proceed to Bath, Maine, to look after rigging of the schooner.
I think I got in Bath about the 4th of December, 1883. Her
hull was not finished. There was considerable joiner work to
be done. She was supposed to be finished and ready for sea
by the first of January, but the United Fruit Company was
building a steamer. I beleive it was their first steamer as all
fruit up to that time was brought to the United States in
sailing vessels. This steamer was laid down across our stern
and she had to be launched first. But when they got her engine
bedding in it cracked and they had to take that one out and
get a new one cast. My work being nearly finished I came home
and stayed a month until this steamer was launched. Then I
got orders to proceed to Bath as she was to be launched on
Saturday, the 2nd day of February, 1884.*

And she was. I will never forget that day. Our anchors
were brought down under the bow on sleds, or sleighs, drawn
by oxen that were shod. I never saw oxen shod before. They
just shackeled the chain to the anchors while they were on
the sleds and hove them up to the hawse pipes and put them

---

*City of Baltimore built by Goss, Sawyer & Packard.

on the bow. This being all done the stages were removed from her sides. I got on board before they were all taken down. Then they began blocking her up on the greasy ways. When she was up they sawed in two the blocks that were holding her and away she went flying down into the Kennebec River. She cracked and snaped terribly when she took the water. Monday, I got stores on board as she was all rigged and sails bent ready for sea before she was launched. Shipped a mate, Mr. Williams, a steward, and one man. On Wednesday took one of Morse's tow boats and towed to Belfast up the Penobscot and there took in 516 tons of ice for Jacksonville, Florida.

It is very interesting to see them load ice. They will take a horse and an ice plough that will cut a trench in the ice about two or three inches wide and perhaps two or three inches deep. They then lay it off in squares the size they wish the blocks of ice to be. Then they will let the water run out of the lake through a dam. They will begin to break this ice. The current running out at the dam will carry the blocks of ice to it. There they have a wheel full of cells to catch this flow of water which furnishes the hoisting power. This raises the blocks of ice some 20 or more feet. Then the ice runs across a scale and the weight is taken. Then it is pushed on a small railway which is about 200 or 300 yards long which feeds to the ship's hatches. The ice skips over this little track mighty, or surprisingly, fast. I beleive I was loaded in one day. But did not I suffer with cold while up in Maine in the winter time. Being now loaded I had to send down to Rockland to get a crew. Obtaining these I cleared and sailed on Friday, the 15th of February, 1884, for Jacksonville.

I was much worried to begin loading my first cargo on Friday. Then the first time I got her underway to sail her was on Friday. I thought I would surely have bad luck. I did have a long and perilous voyage to Jacksonville. I had a good run out to the South Shoal Lightship. I then shaped my course for Cape Hatteras. Heavy westerly gales came upon me and I could not hold my course. And when I passed the lattitude of Cape Hatteras I was 300 miles offshore. One night shortly after getting out of the South Channel, while it was blowing a gale from the westward and she was shipping heavy seas, rolling her rails under, and filling the deck with water, the halyards were all in a bunch and full of kinks from being new. I stood awhile on the poop deck looking at them going across the deck from side to side. I thought they would chafe out. The mate was below, it being my watch on deck. I thought a little hard of him for going below before the halyards were laid up on the pins securely.

I could not stand to see those halyards going from side to side chafing out so I jumped down on the main deck and began to straighten them up and lay them up on the pins myself. I was not there at work very long before she shipped a very heavy sea which cut my legs from under me and I could not gain my feet anymore. She rolled heavily and the big body of water would carry me across the deck aflying from side to side like it did the halyards. I was suffering intense agony for I expected to have my brains smashed in by the bulwarks or that I would be washed overboard when her lee sail would roll under. I went across the deck, I suppose between 30 or 40 times, always trying hard to get my feet so as to get up on the poop deck. The vessel was 33 feet in beam and I would cross the deck when it rolled just as quick as if I had been droped out of the air 33 feet high. It looked like I was gone but, fortunately, there was always an eddy of current coming back from the bulwarks which would catch me and never let me hit. Before I could get on my feet this big volume of water would go over to the other side at a flying rate. Finally, the seaman I had on the lookout saw my predicament and came and grabed me and held me until the big volume of water receded from me so that I could get to my feet. Then we both ran for the poop deck before the big volume of water came back again as the ship rolled. I had now what doctors so often recomend, a cold water bath. I was nearly frozen diped so long in water just coming down the coast from Labrador or Hudson Bay. This was about 2 o'clock in the morning, month of February.

When I got by the lattitude of Cape Hatteras the wind continued blowing from the westward which kept me offshore. I certainly was having a hard time getting to Jacksonville. But after considerable reefing, shaking out reefs, and pulling and hauling, I got to Jacksonville. I met a Captain Sweat in Belfast loading ice and hay for Jacksonville in a schooner called the *Penobscot*. He sailed from Belfast a few days ahead of me and we came in at the St. Johns River Bar at the same time. We hailed one another laying at the bar waiting for the tide to rise to go in. I saw I had beat him but I told him of the seige of westerly gales I had encountered since leaving South Shoal Lightship. I also told him when I passed the lattitude of Cape Hatteras that I was 300 miles offshore. He said that when he passed the lattitude of Cape Hatteras he was 700 miles offshore. I then began to think I did not do so bad. But I blamed sailing on Friday for it.

I arrived in Jacksonville on a Thursday, 28 days from Belfast. I began unloading ice on Friday. Terrible, this Friday business was in my mind. I finished unloading ice on the next Thursday, put her in her loading berth, and began loading lumber on Friday. Well, I thought I will never have any luck in this vessel and I will never make any money in her. Mr. Rokes and Mrs. Rokes were in Jacksonville when I got there. They came down in one of his other vessels called the *Brooxxe B. Rokes*. It was the first one he had built and named her after his wife. Captain Cleophas W. Bennett was in charge of her. My friend, Mr. E. B. Hunting, was in Jacksonville at the same time. I loaded lumber for him and went to Baltimore.

I did not sail on a Friday this time. It seemed I had got clear of Fridays. It was now the month of March. I had a reasonably fair run to Baltimore; made it in ten days.

Discharged our cargo of lumber and loaded a general cargo for Jacksonville and now I seemed to be getting along good. I remember I had to take out two long, heavy boilers for Dexter's saw mill. I experienced a strange phenomenon on this passage that I never experienced before or since. One fine morning, as I was sailing over the Frying Pan Shoals, the water was as clear and transparent as was ever seen anywhere on the Bahama Banks. I was in 16 fathoms of water a long way outside of the Frying Pan Light. I could see the fish all along on the bottom and there seemed to be lots of them. Something I never saw before or since.

I got down as far as Fernandina and right off this port, about 4 o'clock PM, I took a Jacksonville pilot, John Daniels. John was then a real young man and as he came on board he said, "I am the last pilot on board." After he was on board he said, "Captain, draw your fore staysail and fill away." The wind was from the south. We now had about 20 miles to beat down the coast to St. Johns Bar and it was a beautiful working breeze. The *Baltimore* was then new to me and I did not know much about her sailing qualities. I had not been thrown in company with any vessels. I think the pilot's boat was named the *Willie B.* It has been so many years ago that I have nearly forgotten. Anyhow, the first thing John said to me after we had filled away was, "Captain, you will see something that will leave you mighty quick working down this beach." I said, "John, she is a sailer, is she?" When he said that she cleans up every thing that comes around here, after making a tack offshore and standing inshore on the next tack, I saw that the *Willie B.* was loosing out. I said, "John, your boat is not keeping up with us." After standing offshore once more and tacking back toward the beach I saw we were beating him bad. Then I had to make a little fun of him. I said, "John, did you not say there was no other pilot on board? Are those two men on board capable of taking the *Willie B.* down to the St. Johns Bar? If not say so and I will shorten sail so that they can keep in sight of us. You know it is getting quite dark and I would be sorry if anything should happen to them by us leaving them so far behind." I never saw a man turn so red in the face before. He did not expect to see his boat beaten so badly.

We came to anchor about 9 o'clock off the bar, outside, but never got in until the next day in the afternoon. We had a young fellow working his way down from Baltimore full of aspiration. His name was William Bernet. He was going to make a fortune in Florida to hear him talk. The next day being Saturday there was a gentle breeze from the east. The tow boat *R. L. Mabey* came out and said there was not much water on the bar but it would be high water at 4 PM. If there was any show of crossing the bar they would come after me. I guess he came in about 40 feet of us so as to make us hear what he said. This boy could not understand why that tow boat did not take hold of us and tow us in. "Why," he said, "if I had known he was not going to tow us in I would have jumped on board of him." I said, "You would have jumped overboard too."

Finally, the schooner *Mary Lord,* being light with no cargo in, took a tow boat and towed in across the bar. I knew the captain mighty well. I met him in Santo Domingo the year before. Just before he got to the bar his yawl boat got loose from his vessel. The wind being to the east it was blowing this yawl for the beach where she must be broken up by the breakers. So I said to my mate, "I would be sorry to have Captain Lord loose his boat. I wish you would take the crew and my boat and go pick her up and we will take her up when we go in." He went and picked her up and lo and behold it was the pilot's yawl. She had a sail, oars, and everything in her.

Quite well equiped. After getting this yawl the boy began to nag me to let him have this yawl to go ashore. I said, "You astonish me. Don't you know there are large breakers on that bar and it's doubtful if that boat will live if you get in those breakers? You stand a big chance of being drowned." I could not discourage him at all. He wanted to get ashore and get orange growing. Nothing daunted him so I called the mate and crew to witness what I said to him about the danger of crossing the bar. I saw he was determined to go and I let him go. I made him take his trunk and all of his things with him. "Now," I said, "you must leave this boat ashore at Pilot Town." He promised me faithfully he would do so and under this promise I let him take the boat. Surprisingly to me, he crossed the bar safely but reached Pilot Town too late to catch the steamer to Jacksonville. This being Saturday, and no more steamer until Monday noon, was too long for him to wait. Two days were like a life time to him. So he bought some cans of beans and other provisions, set sail on this pilot's yawl, and started for Jacksonville 23 miles up the river.

At 4 PM the tow boat came after me and towed me in. We hamered heavily on the bar. We got an awful pounding and sliped the shoe off the keel. Fortunately, we got in. Had she been an old vessel she would have bursted open and sunk on this bar. While towing up the river I looked over to the south of me and said to the mate, "Mr. Mizzington, is not that boy there sailing up the river in that pilot's boat?" He said, "It looks like him." But it was getting late in the evening and cloudy and I could not see real clearly. The next morning, it being Sunday, before I got turned out I heard Captain John Floyd hollering at this boy. He yelled, "Where did you get that boat? What are you doing with that boat? That boat belongs to the pilots at the bar; you stole that boat." I then turned out, looked through the cabbin window and out on the main deck. This boy was there helping to wash decks to beat the band. I put my clothes on and came on deck. There was the boat lying alongside, his trunk and things in her all wringing wet for it had rained heavily that night. He had got lost at dark and got up Trout Creek and he was out all night in the rain. So much for being in such a hurry. I think Lindbergh would have been too slow for him. I said, "Boy, why did not you leave this boat at Pilot Town like you promised me you would?" He said, "Captain, I thought this boat belonged up here." "You promised me you would leave her at Pilot Town," I said. "Now you have deceived me." He began to beg me to let him stay on board until Monday. Said I, "What a cheek you have to leave me outside of the bar to get here the best way I could. You were through with me. Now I am up here safely you want me to keep you." I said, "No, sir. Get you a hotel or boarding house." He said, "Captain, will you let me put my things on board?" I said, "You treated me so badly I do not want you or your things on board. If anybody happens to steal any of them here you will want me to pay for them." He said, "No, Captain, I will not." I did not want to be too hard so I let him put his things on board and kept them for him for two or three days.

I discharged my cargo and loaded a cargo of lumber and went to Baltimore. Discharged my lumber and was up at Long Dock loading general cargo for Jacksonville when to my surprise a little market boat rounded up alongside and wanted to know if I did not want to buy some cabbages. And it was no other person than the same Bill Bernet. I suppose he found oranges in Florida did not grow in six months so he came to Baltimore and went down to North Point and bought or rented a truck farm. I do not know how long he did this farming but I am sure not long because in less than two years he was in Jacksonville running a grocery store. And in about 18 months he was out of this business. And then I lost the run of him. About 25 years after this I was in the oyster shucking business when a fellow came into my office selling empty bags and barrel covers. I gave him an order. He gave me his address or place of business in Baltimore and signed it Mr. Bernet. I then looked at him for a minute and said to him, "Are not you the fellow that went to Florida in the schooner *City of Baltimore* to start an orange grove and in about 4 or 5 weeks was farming down on North Point?" He said that he was so our acquaintance was renewed after an elapse of 25 years. What success he made in life I never knew. He must have succeeded for he would not stay in one place long if it was the least dull.

I runed the *City of Baltimore* steadily between Jacksonville and Baltimore for 18 months when the vessels began to bunch up as sailing vessels, owing to the irregularity of winds and weather, cannot run on schedule time. So in Jacksonville, the month of July, 1885, I received a letter from Mr. Rokes stating that the vessels were getting bunched up so that some of them would have to stop a while until they got separated. Or one of them would be compelled to go somewhere else to effect a separation. He also said in his letter that he could obtain a nice freight to an island in Brazil and wanted to know if I would go. I wrote and told him I would and to accept the business. To my surprise, when I arrived in Baltimore, I found he had chartered me to go to Richmond, Virginia, and load a cargo of flour for Rio Grande do Sul at $1 per barrel. My, I had no idea he was going to charter me to go so far. After the cargo of lumber was out I docked her, gave her two coats of copper paint, laid in stores for six months, and went to Richmond. He and his family, with some other friends, went to Richmond with me, staid a day or two, and went home to Baltimore leaving me sufficient funds to pay my disbursements at Richmond.

After being loaded I go to Baltimore to get a crew. Here I met my brother John and he agreed to go as mate with me.

I was mighty glad to get him too. On our leaving Baltimore, about I should say the 9th or the 10th of August, a little historical incident occured which I will always remember. General Robert E. Lee's son was on board the steamer with some other notable Virginians and the horse that Stonewall Jackson was riding when he was shot by one of his sentinels. They had been to General Grant's funeral and was returning home. Lee's son was a very large man and got off the train about half way between Richmond and West Point. This was August, 1885.

We arrived in Richmond with the crew and their baggage and got the ship ready for sea as quickly as possible. Cleared and sailed August the 12th, 1885, for Rio Grande do Sul, Brazil. Alex Curtis of the firm of Curtis and Parker, ship brokers at Richmond, was manager of the tow boat company at Richmond. He had 3 vessels there ready to tow down and said to me, "Let your vessel be towed down with this tow. You can stay up here and clear your vessel and we will pay your fare to Old Point and go down on the Chesapeake and Ohio Railroad." I objected and he wanted to know very particularly why I objected. I told him if I went to Old Point by rail the pilots there would catch me and I would have to pay pilotage. And I wanted to evade them if it was possible. I had been caught once by landing at Old Point and sending a telegram and I do not like to pay for something I do not need and do not want. So I kept my vessel in Richmond until she was cleared from the custom house. Then I notified Mr. Curtis and I went down in the next tow. I always believed Mr. Curtis notified the pilots at Old Point when we left Richmond for they were on the lookout for me when I got to the Roads. Though, I may be wrong in thinking Mr. Curtis did this.

Anyhow, we arrived down to the Roads about 9 o'clock PM. There were 4 vessels in the tow. It was real dark and the wind was blowing strong from the southwest. I saw the pilot boat's red light on my port side bearing down on me. I heard him holler at the tow boat but I could not understand what he said. But in about 5 minutes I saw a row boat coming and he was hollering, "Hello, on board the *Baltimore*. Take my line." I told John I was not going to take him but John said, "Must I take his line?" I said, "Yes." After he got alongside he said, "Captain, I have come to take you out of the capes." I said, "If that is what you came for you may go back to your boat. I do not need you." "But," he said, "I was sent here to do this." "Well," I said, "I do not need your services. I will take her out myself." He says, "You will have it to pay." I said, "I know that." He said, "Are you ready to settle?" I said, "The vessel is not out the capes and there is nothing due you." The tow boat was towing us all this time. The wind was blowing hard and the spray was flying over him profusely all this time that we were arguing about the pilot's money. And I am sure he was wet, every thread on him to the skin well soaked. Then he was lost in the darkness from the pilot boat, we had towed him so far. How he ever made out finding his pilot or his pilot finding him I never learned. As soon as the tow boat stoped towing us we got underway immediately and went out of the Roads. At 12 midnight I passed out by Cape Henry and proceeded on my long journey.

The next morning at 6 o'clock I heard the pumps going. I came on deck and said to John, "Why are you pumping her out? That bilge water will turn all this paint work around the decks black." He said, "I think it is about time she was pumped; she has 12 inches of water in her." This was a surprise to me as she had always been so tight. But she was truly leaking. We began to look everywhere that we could to find the leak. In going down the fore scuttle hatch we found it was the bow ports leaking. I got a caulker in Baltimore to caulk the ports when we got the lumber out. Whether he did not give me a good job or whether the ports shrunk while we were laying head to the southward, while we lay in Richmond in the hot sun loading, I will never know. But I do not think the caulker gave me a good job. The vessel was going fast with this strong southwest wind and, when she threw her head into the sea that was prevailing, the water coming in through the seams of the ports with such a rush would nearly nock you out of the bow. The wind, now as I have said, was blowing so strong from the southwest that it was a hard and tedious job to get back to Cape Henry. And after talking it over with John I decided to put her in Bermuda and caulk the ports there. I decided with this southwesterly wind I could get to Bermuda with a fair wind as quick as I could beat her back to Cape Henry. And I would then be six hundred miles on my journey. It looked like we were going to damage the flour which worried me very much especially as the charterer had given me an order on the consignee at Rio Grande do Sul for $60 provided I did not have over 60 barrels of damaged flour on board. I never expected to get this $60 as I supposed all of the ground tier to be wet.

After sailing for Bermuda for 2 or 3 days it died out calm. John said to me, "Len, I can go overboard in a boatswain's chair and caulk those ports and save the expense and time of going into Bermuda." So we riged up, he on one port and Mr. Clark, the 2nd mate, to the other. And when she would raise her head up out of the sea they would drive ocum into the seams. There was no chance to pitch the seams to keep the ocum in on account of the water. So while they were caulking I sawed out some boards 3-inches wide, the length of the seams, and padded them on the inside with some salt sacks cut the width of the boards and tacked on the inside so as to cover the seams and keep the ocum from washing out. I champered the edges of the boards nearly down to nothing to keep the sea from taking hold of them and washing them off. Then I nailed them on with 10-penny nails. We began

[157]

this job immediately after dinner and by sunset we were all through. Now we felt pretty safe to resume our journey and not go to Bermuda. We now had the ports tight and no more leaking. It takes brave men to go overboard in the ocean and caulk ports but John, my brother, was equal to dificult and hard jobs.

We now had no more worthy to mention but just proceeded on our voyage until Sunday, the 29th of August, when we fell in company with the full-rigged ship *E. B. Sutton,* Captain Carter, in lattitude 31° 32′ north, longitude 45° 12′ west, from New York for San Francisco. He was 10 days out while I was 17 days out. So far he had beat me one week. With his speaking trumpet he hailed us and asked me to come on board stating he would give us some late papers. It was very moderate and smooth just at the northern limits of the northeast trade winds, sometimes called the doldrums, that is between the trade winds and the variable winds. We lowered our dinghy over the side and my brother John went on board as I never cared to leave my vessel when at sea. John stayed on board of him about an hour and came back. Captain Carter sent me a little box of green apples which was quite a treat after being nearly three weeks at sea. He asked John if we had been struck by the hurrycanes that went up the Gulf Stream since we had been out. But it appeared we had got too far to the eastward of its track to give us any trouble. After John got back we took the boat in on deck and secured her. The ship was close to us all day. It was so calm it seemed we could not separate. But at night the winds began to breeze up gently from the northeast and we both began to get steerageway.

The next morning the trades began to blow their gentle zephers in earnest and we were leaving the variable winds and the doldrums behind. I trimed the *Baltimore's* sails close to the wind and I began to out-wind the ship. We were in sight of each other all day Monday, Tuesday, and until Wednesday noon when I could just see him from my foremast head bearing four points on my lee bow. I had out-winded him that much. We now had fresh trades and were progressing along at a nice speed toward the equator but trying to hold our course to the wind in order to clear Cape St. Roque. After runing 1,700 miles, and about two weeks after, I saw the *E. B. Sutton* again.

It was a rainey morning with shifting winds and gentle breezes, what we call doldrums on the equator. In these doldrums on the equator it rains and rains. Here is where we catch all the water we need. We refill all the empty casks and the sailors wash and clean all their dirty clothes. These last about 4 days or it generally takes a sailing ship about that long to get through them which gives ample time to get every-thing on board clean. And we all get tired of being wet so long for in hauling on the ropes leading from aloft the water runs down your jacket sleaves profusely which makes anyone very uncomfortable even though the weather be warm. After about the 4th day of this we begin to look to the southeast and see a break in the clouds. The winds begin to breeze up from the southeast and the sun comes out. We have crossed the Line and are now in the Southern Hemisphere. We are now runing lattitude up, trudging down the Brazilian coast toward Rio de Janeiro or Rio Grande do Sul, toward River Plate or the Horn, if bound there. I never fell in with the ship *E. B. Sutton* any though the captain wrote a letter to his family, sent it on board of me, and I mailed it from Rio Grande do Sul. I suppose he was well around the Horn before the letter reached his family.

We fell in with nothing else to break the monotony until one Sunday morning we saw the island of Fernando de Noronha, the peak of which looked like a church steeple. But as we sailed closer to it we saw the shape of the island on its lower land. On this island is where the Brazilians send their worst convicts, a penal colony. We had nothing more to break the monotony but to reef our sails as the winds increased, to shake them out when the wind decreased, look at the sun through the day away to the north of us, and look at the southern stars as we would raise them above the horrison, such as the Southern Cross, the Magellan clouds, and many other southern stars that are never seen in this lattitude until we were nearing Rio Grande do Sul. We had sailed through the southeast trades and were in the variables where the winds blow from every direction.

I will not forget as I was steering in for the coast that one of those pamperos struck us and blew like the dickens. The cringle gave away in my mainsail but before much damage was done to the sail I had it down and stuck another cringle in it. I then put the sail on her, and stood in for the land on the port tack thinking the wind would come out from the northwest and clear off like it does with us. But instead it came around from the southwest and south and cleared off. Just the opposite from us which put me on a lee shore. And this wind from the south was quite cold. I had to carry sail very hard on the starboard tack to get her offshore again in safety. Then it got foggy for 2 or 3 days. I will never forget while down in this lattitude that day it was quite moderate. John said, "Look, Len, there is an albatross." I thought it was the most beautiful bird I ever saw, a great, big, beautiful bird. It was the first one I ever saw, this being my first time so far south. He had been in this lattitude several times before trading to River Plate and also around the Cape of Good Hope to Australia, to China, and the Philippine Islands. After laying 3 or 4 days in this fog it cleared off. We got observations and the ship's position. We sailed in for Rio Grande do Sul. We made the light in the night time. I must say the land here is very low and you are very close to it before you see it.

We lay around in sight of the light until morning when a tow boat came out. He asked me where I was from. I told him the United States. He spoke very good English and asked me what United States. I was not thinking there was more than one United States but after he asked me I told him United States of America. He then threw me a heaving line by which I pulled in a large hawser, made it fast to one of the bits forward, and waved to him to go ahead. And he pulled us in over the bar and into the mouth of the river. Here we had to anchor and take a small tow boat up to the city.

I had to pay, as I thought, a big price for this tow. Some how this boat so reminded me of one I had seen in Richmond and on the James River. Her name was *Mary*. I said, "Captain, I have seen a tow boat just like her towing on the James River." He told me it was the same boat. I said, "How did you get her here?" This old Norwegian used to trade in a brig of his between Richmond and Rio Grande do Sul. His family went with him about all of the time and he raised his children on board of this brig. He wanted to stop ashore so he bought this tow boat in Richmond to make his living towing around Rio Grande do Sul. After he bought her in Richmond he dismantled her and put the smokestack, propeller, pilot house, and everything he could get off her that made her unseaworthey, and decked her over, put a mast and sail on her, and undertook to tow her to Rio Grande do Sul. He put the mate, who was going to marry the old captain's daughter, in charge of her and one of his sailors with him. She was stocked with provisions and water. After a few days out of Cape Henry there came a great storm and the tow boat broke loose and was lost from the brig. When the storm was over he sailed around and around in the location where she broke away and at last he had to give her up for lost and pursued his journey under great grief and stress. After sailing 7 or 8 weeks he arrived at Rio Grande do Sul and to joy of the old man's heart he found the *Mary* there. She had beat him out by 3 or 4 days. The girl and the mate were married. He got him a home to live and put the mate in charge of his brig. They were then on a voyage somewhere. He got his tow boat all put in order and was doing well in the towing business.

When he got me up to Rio Grande and docked at Thompsen and Company's wharf I was just 63 days from Richmond, 9 weeks at sea. I got my cargo out and I was very happy to find none of the flour damaged on the ground tier. I presented my letter to a Mr. Fettison, in charge of Messrs. Thompsen and Company's business there, and he gave me a draught on New York for $60. I then chartered through a Mr. Berg, a German broker there, to go up to Pelotas, fortunately a fresh water river, to load a cargo of dry hydes for Boston. I was fortunate to get up into this fresh water for her bottom was all covered with sea geese and they all droped off the bottom the first night we were there. The next morning the *Baltimore's* bottom was just clean as if she had just come off the railway.

I must say a little something about the people I met here in Pelotas. I thought they were the most manerly and friendly people I ever met. I reported to an old gentleman, a very polished man, who was to furnish the hydes. His name was Cordero. I was shown the wharf where to haul in. There was a Holland brig there, just finished her cargo of dry hydes, bound to Boston. Her name was the *Diana,* Captain Weringa. Captain Weringa was somewhat under the influence of wine, or something stronger, for all I know. Anyhow, he said to me in not a very becoming maner, "Why, that is a mighty low freight you are getting on dry hydes. $6.30 per ton is too cheap. You must be a cheap John. You can't do much to carry hydes all the way to Boston for $6.30 per ton. Besides it will take you so long to get there." "Well," I said, "I have got to go home, anyhow, whether I have a low freight or a high freight, whether my vessel be a slow or a fast sailer." "I suppose," said I, "from the drift of your conversation you have a smart vessel under you." He replied, "She is not lazy." "Then," I said, "you have all the advantage over me; you have a smart vessel and a big freight."

I hauled in to the very wharf he hauled out of. I laid there 22 days loading the cargo of dry hydes. I took in 26,500 hydes, droped down to Rio Grande do Sul, cleared, and sailed December 5th, 1885, for Boston. I met another old Hollander there in a brig called *Hebe*. I went on board of him. I knew he was an old trader there. I have forgotton the captain's name but he appeared to be a pretty nice old captain and I wanted to get the advantage of his experience there. So I asked him how far offshore should I stand on the port tack before I tacked to go up toward the equator. He said to me in his broken language, "Now, Captain, when you get out let her go aist, aist, aist, never mind the nort." From the drift of his advice anyone would think I ought to go to the Indian Ocean or away around the Cape of Good Hope. But when I got out I spread all my sails. I soon left every vessel that came out with me. I kept her on the port tack 3 days and nights. I had just made 500 miles. I thought of the old captain's advice but I had made up my mind not to heed it any longer for I wanted to get her on the homeward tack. So after supper I talked it over with my brother and I concluded to take her and stand to the north. I was then in lattitude 35° 49′ south, longitude-west.

I will add this is where we had an awful accident. After we had tacked ship, in getting the topsails shifted over, I had a man to fall from the mizzin masthead. In falling, he hit the ship's side on the port quarter and broke his right leg just above the knee and his right arm just above the elbow. I was at the wheel holding her by the wind at the time. I saw him when he left the masthead, and heard the oars rattle in the beckets hanging on the monkey rail. I knew he had hit the ship's side. We were running about five miles per hour at the time. I rolled the wheel down and let her come around on the port tack. I then left the wheel, ran forward, and threw the fore sheet off—also the main sheet. Time was so important that I could do all this myself quicker than I could give the orders to have it done for, when a man is overboard and you want to save him, there is no time to waste.

Fortunately for him the small boat was not lashed. It had been raining all the afternoon and was raining then and the mate had been scrubbing this boat and cleaning up the ship in general for painting coming up through the tropics, while the weather was fine, which was always my usual custom. While cleaning up the decks at 5:30 PM John said to me, "Len, is it worthwhile to lash this boat across the main hatch for the night?" I said, "No, I do not think we will have a storm tonight and if it does come out we can soon secure her. Just lay her across the hatch." It happened to be a very fortunate thing for him that she was not lashed for the ship with jibs to windward, fore and main sheets off, and spanker trimed by the wind, she was hove to by the time she had tacked. I jumped for this dingy boat now ready to be launched. Having no fastenings on her whatever, I would not take the time to turn her around as the crew were in the attempt of doing. I said, "No, men, we will launch her bow first." I was really expecting to see her fill half full when we launched her. We now had her on the ship's rail ready to go over. But I said, "Men, wait until the *Baltimore* rolls down close to the water." When she did I hollered out, "Launch her." And to my agreeable surprise she never took in a drop of water. I now started to jump in the boat to go after him for in those days I was as quick as a cat. But the 2nd mate, Mr. Dan Clark, a fine fellow who unfortunately was washed overboard off the schooner *Ida Lawrence* off of Cape Hatteras seven years after and was lost, said to me, "You stay on board, Captain, I will go get him." I said, "Work quick, Mr. Clark, time is precious." Another man jumped in the boat with him and started. I took my spy-glass and ran to the head of the same mast he had just fallen from and to my surprise not one of them knew I had tacked. They were rowing straight astern from the masthead. I had to wave to them to pull to the windward, the ship had been tacked. I could just see from masthead a dark object in the water which I knew was him. They began to pull toward him but the vessel was drifting from them and dark was now coming on. I could no longer see him, it being a rainy, dark evening. But in this lattitude the sun set 25 minutes after 7 on December 8 which gave us a long evening. It was fully 8 PM when we got him on board.

I tacked ship as soon as the boat could be taken on board and steered her by the wind. I put Antone in the cabin. His name was Antone Nordstrum, a Norwegian. He must have been an expert swimmer for he had gotton off his left rubber boot and his left arm out of his oil coat. I don't see how he did it but the right boot was on and the right sleeve of his oil coat was on. I sawed some flour barrel staves about 1½ inches wide, tore up some of my shirts in ribbons about 2½ inches wide, champered the edges of these staves with a plain so they would not hurt him, and I rapped these domestic ribbons around these staves until I thought they would not be uncomfortable to him. And when I thought I had sufficient quantity of them I straitened up his leg and set it to the best of my ability, put these splints on, and wraped them tight to keep his leg in place. I did the arm the same way and laid him in his berth and put one man to wait on him who was a nice fellow and did the work splendidly. This poor fellow lay in his berth 59 days before I got to Boston, from the 8th day of December, 1885, to February 5th, 1886, before I could get him to a hospital. The doctor at the Marine Hospital in Boston told me that I made a splendid job with his arm but not so well with his leg as I did not put a pully on it and keep it stretched out even and that one leg was shorter than the other. It is hard to imagine what this poor fellow suffered laying in that berth coming through the tropics suffering intense heat. And then coming around Cape Cod in the dead of winter. Two years after, I went to Boston with a load of coal. I went to the hospital to inquire for him. I learned he came out some time in early May. He was in there 3 months.

After tacking ship in the lattitude of 35° 49′ south, longitude 42° 12′ west, I stood on this tack 17 days which put me in about 20 miles of Pernambuco on Christmas Day. I tacked ship and stood on the port tack to the south and east 40 miles. Tacked again and cleared Cape St. Roque. With all of the Hollander's advice I persued my own ideas about making a passage to the equator and hit it nicely. Shortly after passing Pernambuco, just before taking the northeast trade winds, we had a calm spell in what is known as the doldrums. The band on my fore topmast had sliped down causing the fore topmast stay to become slack and useless to carry the jib topsail on, a very important sail. This band had to be raised up in its place and John, my brother, had to go up there if it was to be done. He had to set in a boatswain chair at the fore topmast head the most of the afternoon to complete the job. Anyone would think this was just a simple job to do but to be at the topmast head when she was rolling heavy was surely a bad job. He said to me when he got back on deck, "Len, that was the meanest dam job I ever done in my life." I carried this topmast off about ten years. After the next one I put in her I had hounds cut in the topmast so the band could never slip.

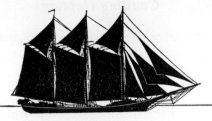

VI

1886–1887

I OBTAINED strong trade winds and made 1,468 miles one week. I just thought I was going to make a quick passage to Boston but there was too much bad weather in store for me to endure. When I got up in the cold northern lattitude I came very near not getting to Boston at all. I crossed the equator one day at exactly noon. On this day I had no lattitude at all. After a few more days I passed through the northeast trades and got into the variable winds. Now with a great deal of pulling and halling, reefing and making sail again, steering and navigating, we made the No Man's Land and lighthouse on Gay Head. I passed into Martha's Vineyard, went by Holmes' Hole. All the vessels I was in company with went in for harbor. The sun was just setting. The weather looked too good to anchor but when darkness set in I was awful sorry I passed Holmes' Hole that night for the chart I had was given to me by a Nova Scotian, at Rio Grande do Sul, which belonged to his father. When darkness came on, and I saw about 2 or 3 times more lights lit up than this old chart showed, I was about lost. About then the wind began to blow a gale from the northwest. I began to haul up for the north shore and when the Bishop and Clerks Light bore north of me I came to anchor. The next morning early here came a big fleet of vessels from out of Holmes' Hole, strong wind from the northwest, runing to get

over the shoals. I said to the mate, "We will get her underway."
We hove her short. The sea was quite high and before we had
got her underway she fell back on her anchor with a jerk and
broke the shank off the anchor. Lost both flukes. I sailed in
company with the fleet and crossed over the shoals. Then the
fleet began to disperse, some going one way and some another.
But there seemed to be none of them going to Boston. I
seemed to be alone going by Cape Cod Light. The next day
we were in Boston Bay. It was mighty cold and freezing. That
evening it began to snow heavily and to blow a gale from
the northeast, or about north by east. Fortunately, I made the
light on the Minot's Ledge. It was then snowing so thickly
that nothing was visible at any reasonable distance. I had
only been on the port tack but a few minutes when I saw a
big light right ahead of me. He was burning a tar barrell or
something similar. I saw in an instant he was lost. I did
think I would hang a lantern over my stern and becken him
to follow me. But someone on board said to me, "If he follows
you and he should get into trouble you will be blamed for it."
I did not do it but have always felt convicted since for not
doing it. It proved to be the *Mary A. Killen,* a fine vessel with
a cargo of sugar in from Surinam, Dutch Guiana. He went
ashore on Scituate that night and was lost. It was a trying
night to me.

After sighting Minot's Ledge Light, which gave me a grand
departure, I laid off the chart just how far to go on the port
tack. Then to put her on the starboard tack to fetch the Boston
Light. And the sweetest music of my life was the whistle of
this light when I heard it. But now we all began to watch, peep
through blinding snow, to try to see the light. Finally, I saw
the gleam. Was it the white snow or was it the cap of a sea?
Anxiety was weighing heavily upon me. John, though cheerful,
said to me, "Len, if we miss that light it will be all up with us.
We shall have to climb the golden stairs." But the glimmer

began to get brighter and sure enough on my starboard bow there undoubtedly was becoming visible through the blinding snow one of the most beautiful scenes of my life. When John saw the Holy City, the New Jerusalem, coming down from God out of Heaven, none of his scenes surpassed the beauty of this. I ran up fairly close to the light. I can now in my mind see the snow flakes passing between my eyes and the light on this rock. After runing sufficiently close to this light to discourage all doubts, I kept off about west by north, or west by south, I forget which it has been so many years ago. The light was quickly out of view on account of the blinding snow. In a very short space of time after the light was obscured I came to anchor in the Nantasket Roads, gave her my big anchor—the small anchor being lost—and about 40 fathom of chain. My mind then began to relax from the strain. It was then about one o'clock in the morning. John, the mate, asked me if he should tie the lower sails up. I said, "Just put peak stops on them and let the men get below." I did not want the crew to get frost bitten.

The next morning the sails and deck were all full of snow and it was so cold the vapor was rising off the water so that nothing was visible close to the water. Two tows came to me and asked me if I wished to tow up. I told them it was so cold that I prefered to lay there until the weather moderated. The next day we were all frozed out. It took 2 boats to tow me up to East Boston where we discharged the cargo of dry hydes. There certainly was a big change in the weather after I got up to the wharf and under those big warehouses. I was consigned to a merchant by name of Thomas E. Proctor, a very fine gentleman. After we entered at the custom house, which was now the 5th day of February, 1886, I paid off the crew and began discharging the cargo. We got the crippled seaman to the hospital.

Five days after my arrival in come the fast Holland brig *Diana,* Captain Weringa. I met him on Commercial Street and I could not help make some fun of him for I had beat him 27 days on his passage, enough time for him to have gone down to the West Indies and get a load of sugar and come back. So I said to him, "I suppose you are with a cargo of sugar from the West Indies are you not?" He evaded my question by saying, "Oh, do not squeeze my hand. I got it all frost bitten while out in this blizard and I am all badly stove up."

After discharging the hydes I made a short run down to Promised Land, New York, took in a load of fish scrap, and went to Wood's Hole, Massachusetts, discharged, and took a load of fertilizer to Richmond, Virginia. Then I had to pay the pilot for speaking me at Hampton Roads about 7 months previous. We were some time getting up the James River. It was April and the river was high with freshits coming down so strong we could neither sail up or tow up for a week or more. We were a long time getting discharged, there were so many vessels arrived there all in a bunch at the same time. They had gathered together in the river below during the freshits.

After the cargo of fertilizer was out we chartered to load a cargo of pyrites, a very heavy cargo. It is something like copper ore. This cargo being in we towed down the James River; we were bound to Port Royal, South Carolina. I do not remember when we passed out of Cape Henry but I well remember the storm I was caught in just south of Cape Hatteras. This pyrites was so heavy that it filled her hold not quite half full which kept the lower part of the hull so stiff and unreactionary that all of the reaction had to come from the upper part of the hold where no cargo lay. With the wind from the southwest blowing heavy I stayed on the port tack until I was well in toward the land. Here the wind moderated and the current, which usually runs strong in this vicinity toward the northeast, carried me well into the bight just south of the Diamond Shoals. At 10 minutes past 12 midnight I saw Hatteras Light which was bearing north northeast approximating my position, which was uncomfortable close. The light then shut in and I never saw it again that night for at that time the heavens closed in with utter darkness and the wind blew a gale from the southwest with heavy rain, severe blinding lightening, and heavy peals of thunder. Now my vessel was nearly a new one and to loose her would lame me for life. And I thought so much of her. Really, I loved her. She was smart, sailed well, would handle well, and I could tack her or wear her at anytime. But now here were the Diamond Shoals laying offshore of me bearing, as near I could judge, southeast by south which had to be cleared if I put her on the starboard tack. And if I put her on the port tack she would have to go ashore on the beach. I thought it over for a few minutes which was the best thing to do, whether to put her on the port tack and let her go on the beach where all the crew could be saved, besides her sails and tackles, or put her on the starboard tack offshore and carry hard sail and force her out fast. The faster we went offshore the less the current would take us up in this bight.

Bearing in mind that if we struck on these dreadful Diamond Shoals, that not only the ship would be lost but every man on board would be drowned, I chose the latter. I put her on the starboard tack, took the wheel myself, and told Mr. McKinsie, my mate, to get extra sheets on the foresail and mainsail so that they would not carry away for they were full sail, not reefed. The spanker was reefed. I told him to come aft and sound. When we had sholen to 10 fathoms of water I told him to lay the lead in on deck and quit sounding. If it got any shallower I did not want to know it for I was sure I was close to the Diamond Shoals. I was carrying such hard sail that I could feel the deck working under my feet she was under such a strain. We had a hatch close to the wheel on the poop deck for going down the lazerette. It was made of white pine, about 4½ feet square. I was resolved in mind to take this hatch and jump overboard and float on it in the hope some passing ship would pick me up. I was certain with this heavy cargo in, and the gale that was then blowing, that the good ship *City of Baltimore* would not last over 15 minutes. But I used all my best seamanship to keep her a clean full and by.

After the elapse of 3 hours I told Mr. McKinsie to sound and we got 22 fathoms of water. I then told him to reef her down to put her under easy sail. After we got her reefed down I observed she was loggy. She was not riding as she ought to so I ordered the pumps sounded. And bless my time she showed over 2½ feet of water in the hold. As soon as the sounding rod came up I said to Mr. McKinsie, "She has got 3 feet of water in her." He said, "I do not think so." I went down the lazerette aft and through another hatch into the lower hold. He went down the hatch forward leading into the chain locker and lower hold and I saw him from aft way up forward over the top of his boots in the water. This convinced him that she had sprang a very bad leak. The morning came. With it this heavy south southwest wind had moderated and hauled to the west. She was leaking so badly I thought sure she was going to sink. I was now anxious to put her ashore on the beach and save her sails, cables, and tackles but this westerly wind kept me off to sea. I must say the crew, even to the steward, all worked faithfully at the pumps and as the sea went down we began to gain. The ship must now be reacting back in her old place and was not leaking so badly so I headed her for Norfolk where we arrived in a couple of days in safety.

I could never tell why these two shoals at Cape Hatteras are called the inner and outer Diamonds unless they are the reapers of so many rich harvests. I have known a lot of nice vessels to be lost there with valuable cargoes while I was going to sea.

After I got to Norfolk I wired Mr. Emerson Rokes, the managing owner. He arrived the next day. Before he got down I busyed myself looking up a wharf and warehouse to put this pyrites in and the best I could do was to get a wharf and warehouse for $3,000. I thought it an outrageous price so I told Mr. Rokes when he came down that we would caulk the centerboard well and try the butts above water and I would proceed to Port Royal, South Carolina, without hauling out. When the crew found out we were not going to dock her and caulk her bottom the mate, cook, and crew demanded their pay and quit to the last man and I was left all alone. I got some laborers and shoveled the pyrites from around her centerboard well.

We were laying about three or four miles below the city, down the river, so I had to get a tow boat to carry laborers, caulkers, and supplies down to the ship. The captain of this tow boat proved to be Captain Ed Hudgins who long before this shot his mate and killed him dead on board of the schooner *Maggie E. Gray* from Baltimore bound to Rio de Janeiro. This was in the year of 1878, just 8 years before as this was in 1886 I was having this work done. Well Captain Ed went home as a prissoner or passenger on the ship *Gray Eagle*. He was tried and cleared early in the year of 1879.

We put 28 bails of oacum in the centerboard well and butts. Then I sent to Baltimore for a full crew, mate, and steward. I had Captain Hudgins to meet the Baltimore steamer in his tow boat and take the crew down to the vessel before anyone could tell them I put into Norfolk leaking. As soon as breakfast was over I got her underway and proceeded out of the Hampton Roads and persued my voyage to Port Royal. None of this new crew ever knew I put her into Norfolk leaking. We were ten days getting to Port Royal. We watched the pumps carefully and did not have much trouble in keeping her free.

After discharging this pyrites we chartered to load timber at Beaufort, South Carolina, for Philadelphia.

We arrived in Philadelphia all in good shape some time in June. When the cargo was out we went over to Cooper's Point, docked her, and put her in splendid order. Then chartered to go to Jacksonville and load lumber for Baltimore. There being no cargo obtainable in Philadelphia for Jacksonville we had to go out light. We towed down the river as far as Chester, anchored, and filled our water. I remember this was on the 4th of July, 1886. It was awfully hot weather. I pulled off my shoes and stockings that night and left them on top of the cabbin. That night there came a heavy squall of wind and rain. It was sometime before day the wind came out from the northwest, which was a fair wind down the Delaware. It was very dark as yet and I had to feel around the top of the cabbin to find my shoes and stockings. I was very much in a hurry and I put these cold stockings on and oh, my, how cold they were to my feet. And shoes also all ringing wet. After getting underway I ran down keeping the range lights on. And I remember going down through the bulkhead channel with the New Castle ranges on before the day broke. Had a good run down the Delaware and passed out of the Delaware capes.

Before night on the 5th of July, 1886, after being to sea three or four days, I had the worse soar throat I ever had in my life. The wind kept fair all the time. I did intend to put into Southport to get medical aid but the wind kept fair and I kept her going. Then I made up my mind I would put her into Charleston to get medical aid for I was about dieing. When abreast of Charleston the breeze was fresh and fair so I pursued my course and suffered. Then I made up my mind I could not suffer like this and pass Savannah, Georgia. When off Savannah the wind was still northeast and fresh. I passed on taking the chances of loosing my life to save a fair wind. I then shaped my course for Jacksonville. Had an unusual good run out for summer time. As soon as I arrived in Jacksonville I put myself in the care of Dr. Mitchell. He was then the marine doctor there. He soon got me well and it was the greatest relief which he gave me. I can never forget him. Here we loaded our cargo and proceeded to Baltimore.

On this voyage we had a very disagreeable sailor on board. The mate, Mr. McLeod was his name and a mighty nice man he was too, one day lost his temper with this fellow and he punched him between the eyes. On arrival in Baltimore this fellow went before Commissioner Rogers and got a citation for him. I got hold of it through the shipping masters there and I slipped on and told Mr. McLeod to go immediately up town. I told him to go into a boarding house to stay and that I would pay his board and wages. After staying up town 3 or 4 days he got lonesome and concluded he would go to sea in another vessel. I paid him his wages and board bill. I heard the vessel he went out in was lost with all hands. By this unruly seaman a valuable and precious life was sacrificed. I now have his picture in my album at home.

I discharged and loaded on the Emerson Rokes Line for Jacksonville. I had been away from Baltimore for a year and it seemed nice to get back on the Line. There were four vessels of us runing on this Line but when we began to bunch up it was my luck, either good or bad, to be sent somewhere else. I must mention the names of these 4 vessels which runed on the Rokes Line. Their names were the *Brooxxe B. Rokes,* Captain C. E. Bennett; the schooner *City of Jacksonville,* Captain Louis Stilwell; the schooner *City of Baltimore,* Captain L. S. Tawes; the schooner *Frank M. Howes,* Captain Josh Rich. There was such shallow water over Jacksonville Bar that no steamers runed there. Railroads were insufficient to accomodate the growing commerce of Florida and sailing vessels were required to carry on the growing trade. But Uncle Sam built jetties there and the strong current coming out of the river has deepened the water so much that steamers run on schedule time now.

To resume to the sailings of these vessels again we would sometimes leave in company with one another. The *City of Jacksonville* and the *City of Baltimore* were built on the same moulds and they were rigged and manned just the same. And there was no reason why they should not sail the same. But Stilwell always said he could beat me sailing. I do not know he thought he could beat me handling a vessel but out of four opportunities three of them were to the contrary. We came out over the bar together once bound to Baltimore and the first day out he took up his carpet from the cabbin floor and set it for a sail. This was the first time we got hooked up together. This shows how zealous we were to beat one another and to prove which was the fastest ship. Well, this time he beat me to Baltimore by an hour and 20 minutes. The next day the Baltimore papers came out in big letters that Captain Stilwell beat the *City of Baltimore* on the passage home. Most all the Jews along Pratt Street knew me and when passing their door they would run out and pull me in and more especially the old man Row, a famous clothier on Pratt Street. He ran out, pulled me in and said, "Hello, Daws, I hear Captain Stilman has beat you home."

The next time that Stilwell and I got hung up together was off of Cape Hatteras. He was from New London bound to Jacksonville. The wind was blowing fresh from the southwest and we both tried our hardest to beat around the Hatteras Shoals. We both would tack close in to the Diamonds to get in out of the Gulf Stream current but neither one of us could make it. We worked hard all the day. I now intended to stay in company with him and catch the same winds he did. I did not intend he should beat me again if possible. He was trying all the strattegies possible to beat me. We were both right at the Diamonds close in when night came on. He put his

Captain Sam Messenger of the British brig BERTHA GRAY,
photographed at Rio Grande do Sul, Brazil, December 1893.

Photo by Robert H. Burgess

The unique Queen Emma pontoon bridge at Willemstad, Curacao, in 1962. Captain Tawes describes this bridge as a result of a visit to that Caribbean island in the schooner CITY OF BALTIMORE *in 1896.*

Photo by Robert H. Burgess

The Dutch freighter THERON *enters the harbor at Willemstad, Curacao, in 1962 just as the schooner* CITY OF BALTIMORE *did 66 years earlier. The pontoon bridge, pivoted at its end at the dock, at left, lies parallel with that dock. In its closed position the bridge connects with the extension from shore, at right center.*

vessel on the starboard tack. So did I. We were now side and side going like two scared horses heading south by east into the Gulf Stream. We ran together like this until midnight. I concluded this was no way to go to Jacksonville. So at midnight I tacked, stood in on the wind heading west by north. He kept going. The next morning sometime I made land close to Body Island, 35 miles north of Hatteras. There were lots of vessels scattered along the beach from Body Island to Cape Hatteras.

We now began working down the coast towards the Diamond Shoals and trying to find Stilwell. I wanted to get in company with him again so much. I had a steward with me, McKinnon by name and a good fellow, and the most interested fellow in this sailing match you ever saw. He went to the masthead several times that day looking for Stilwell. Sometimes he would think he saw him and sometimes not. That evening late a squall came out from the northwest and I let her go with a mad rush to get by the Diamond Shoals. And go by we did in good shape. Then wind came from the northeast and down toward Jacksonville we proceeded in fine shape with a fair wind. Every day, 3 or 4 times, McKinnon would run aloft looking for Stilwell. Sometimes he would yell, "Captain, up here to the masthead, I think I see him. Is not that him there just abaft the port?" I would look at this vessel. I am satisfied of its being him. Then we would come below and give it up. But the last day out before we got to Jacksonville McKinnon went aloft again and yelled out, "Captain, there he is right abeam 5 or 6 miles offshore runing down toward Jacksonville." I went aloft and took a look and I decided that surely was him. About 4 or 5 o'clock that afternoon we got to the bar. Two pilots came to us. Bob Gordon was one of them. I took one of the pilots in. I told Bob Gordon that the *City of Jacksonville* would be at the bar in an hour for I saw him offshore of me about 6 miles. Gordon, the pilot, tied his small boat to the sea buoy and staid there all night waiting for the *City of Jack-sonville* to come. But he did not come that night. Gordon was in a small boat and she liked to rolled him to death that night for there was a big sea runing.

We got up to Jacksonville, discharged our cargo, and was at the lumber yard loading when Stilwell arrived. We were just through dinner when he came on board. In a jolly way he said, "Now I know you have got it laid in for me. Now say all you have to say." I said, "Go down the cabbin and get your dinner. You will be better able to stand what we have to say on a full stomach." The weather was warm and we were all on top of the cabbin under the awning when he came on board. But McKinnon could not wait for him to eat before he was pouring it on him in such language as this, "Now, Captain Stilwell, your vessel cannot sail with the *Baltimore* in speed. She is no comparison to us. I would bet anything in reason that if you sailed with us, saying you discharge your cargo, load, and sail with us at the same time, we will beat you to Baltimore." "But," says Stilwell, "this was not a fair beat." "What," says McKinnon, "to beat you over a week from Cape Hatteras to Jacksonville and then you say it was not fair?" "I do not see that," said Mack. I could hear all they said up through the skylight which was open while Captain Stilwell was eating his dinner and Mack was waiting on him. Captain Stilwell said, "You know, I went across the Gulf Stream which was a much longer way while Captain Tawes stayed in on the coast and got a northeaster and strait down the coast with a fair wind. And this northeaster I did not get though I thought to go across the Gulf Stream and catch a southeaster and beat you fellows shamefully bad. But my calculations on the weather did not materialize." When he got through his dinner and came up on top of the house under the awning I never said a word about the beating he got. I thought Mack had given him enough.

We loaded, sailed, and left him there. It was quite sometime before we got together again. It think it was sometime the next January, 1887, after making two or three voyages between Jacksonville and Baltimore that summer and fall. We got together in Baltimore by being detained by ice. I am not just able to say now, it has been such a long time ago. However, we were loaded and ready to sail together. Now there was a lot of talk around the broker's offices and shipping circles about who was going to beat. Mr. Emerson Rokes, managing owner of both vessels, said the one that gets there first he would present him with the hat of his choice made to order by R. A. Taylor which was the leading hat maker in Baltimore at that time. I said to Mr. Rokes, "Why he has got the advantage of me." "Why how so?", said Mr. Rokes. I said, "I have two hundred barrels of kerosene oil on deck which is bad for my crew to get over of dark nights to handle sails. And he has clear decks. His crew can get around twice as fast as mine in handling sails and reefing etc." "Well," he says, "I will take him into the wharf and put 200 barrels of kerosene oil on him too." Nowhere was two vessels of the same size, model, and rig loaded just the same and bound to the same port. Could it be the captains or the vessels that was to be beaten?

Mr. Rokes wanted to have us towed out of the harbor together but on account of the association of the tow boats in those days we had to take the same company's tow boat out that towed us up. This made Mr. Rokes mad and he would not let any association tow boat tow us out. We found a tow boat runed by Captain Sam Meekins which did not belong to the association. And he had to take us out one at the time. He was not big enough to take us both together. My vessel was the first one towed out of the harbor just outside of the Lazaretto Lighthouse. Then he went back to get Captain Stilwell. The wind was northwest and fair to sail down the river. I just put enough sail on my vessel to move her along slowly as I did not want to take any advantage of Captain Stilwell because the least thing he would form some excuse and say it was not fair. When he came out of the harbor he would not make sail. He just let her jog along real slow. Here I was waiting for him to make sail and come up with me. Here I was killing time waiting for him. This thing went along like this for five hours or more. When I got to Sandy Point I hove to and waited for him to come up. It was now between sunset and dark. He came across my stern. He hailed me and said, "What are you laying there for?" I said, "To give you a fair chance." Before I could get her payed off and filled away he had gotton 3 or 4 hundred yards ahead of me. I dressed her up as quickly as I could and steered her as straight down the bay as I could runing as close to Poplar and Sharps islands as I dare to make a straight course to Cove Point. I lost him some time during the night and never saw him again on the passage until he arrived at St. Johns Bar just 20 minutes behind me. He then said it was not fair as he went into Hampton Roads. I never stopped anywhere. I went to the capes and put out to sea though the weather was threatening. When I went out I went through considerable before I got to Jacksonville.

On the way down I witnessed a phenomenon I never did see before or since. One night I saw Cape Hatteras Light, Cape Lookout Light, and Hatteras Inlet lights all at one time and Cape Lookout Light is 64 miles from Cape Hatteras Light.

Here we lay becalmed. In a short while the wind came out from the northeast and blew a heavy gale. I went flying down the coast on a southwest 3/4 west course. Jacksonville being a barred harbor I had to run her down under short sail on the last night out so as to arrive there in the day time. All of this time Stilwell could run her under full sail and catch up with me provided he was a long way astern. This of course I never knew. It was foggy the morning we arrived and I could not see very far.

This race was all the talk around Gaff Topsail Corner and in the ship broker's offices. Captain Bill Fooks, who used to be an old Rio trader but was now on shore selling the Baltimore Copper paint and other marine paints, was into one of the ship broker's offices. He heard the Jersey and Delaware captains talking it over within themselves and saying to one another how Stilwell was going to beat me out to Jacksonville, intimating that Eastern Shoremen could sail a pungy boat alright but they were no equal to a Jersey man making a passage and handling a vessel at sea. Now Captain Bill was an Eastern Shoreman himself and had been to sea a great deal of his life so he took it up, so he told me afterwards. "Now," he said, "gentlemen, you are misjudging your man. If Stilwell beats that Eastern Shoreman to Jacksonville he had better keep his rubber boots and oil skins on all the way out for that Eastern Shoreman he is going up against does not know what comfort and easy living is. He has roughed it all of his days and he has got strictly to his ship all the way out." Well, I beat him 20 minutes and R. O. Taylor made me the first hat and the last that was ever made to order for me. Captain Stilwell said the race was not fair because he went into Hampton Roads and I did not. He got rid of a lot of bad weather that I had to contend with.

We are now in Jacksonville together discharging and loading. We got loaded at the same time and towed down to Mayport waiting together at the bar for sufficient water to get across. There was 9 vessels of us there waiting. It was about the first of March, 1887, when the prevailing winds are from the west which make the tides run low. I believe we waited there a week for a chance to get to sea. I had my wife and my two youngest children with me which were a little disadvantage to me as my wife always was a nervous and scary kind of a woman. But I did not let her hinder me much.

Now it was all the talk in Jacksonville about who was to beat to Baltimore. Dr. L. Engle, who owned two tow boats at that time, had instructed Captain Crawford to tow us out together. Captain Stilwell had two passengers to go with him. One was named Jack Williams. Both of these gentlemen loved the water and was much carried away with this race to Baltimore. Jack Williams and his brother-in-law would have come up with me but having my family with me they took passage with Captain Stilwell. While lying at the bar at Mayport Jack Williams said to me, "Whoever beats to Baltimore I am going to present him with an 8-day bell to hang up in his skylight." Captain Crawford was a Jersey man and I suspected he intended to favor Stilwell.

On a Sunday evening Captain Crawford and the bar pilots had a gathering on board of Captain Stilwell. I watched this thing for about an hour from my deck and I concluded I would go on board of Captain Stilwell and see what it all meant. My wife said to me, "You can easily find some excuse to leave." However, I pulled my dinghy alongside, got in, and started for the *City of Jacksonville*. About the time I got half of the way over the pilots and Captain Crawford began to leave. I hailed the pilots and asked them would there be water enough on the bar the next morning to get out. They said there would not be water enough in the morning to get out. So I turned around and went back on board and contented myself.

The next morning I did not rise as early as usual but at about 6:30 the steward came down in the cabin and said, "Captain Tawes, Captain Stilwell has gone out." I jumped out, put on some clothes, come on deck, and went aloft to the mizzin masthead and looked over the town of Mayport. And to my surprise and disgust there was Stilwell crossing the bar and putting out to sea. I had an idea some kind of a scheme was being concocted when they were gathered together on Stilwell's deck the evening before. I told the pilots it was a mean trick they had served me but that night on the evening tide I got out. And so did the other seven vessels. Now Stilwell had 12 hours start on me.

I had a pretty nice run to Cape Hatteras, 2 days and 18 hours. Had considerable thunder, lightening, and rain. It was amusing to see my two little children playing in the cabbin. Their mother was seasick and laid either on the sofa or in the berth and let them go at random around the cabbin and amuse themselves as the best they could. When the ship would make a heavy roll they would squat until she made it. Then they would jump to their feet and go on with their playing until the vessel would give warning she was going to make another heavy roll, which they always do. But how two little children could catch on to this was somewhat of a puzzle to me. And they never got seasick.

I rounded Cape Hatteras sometime on Thursday and just about at night I was about 12 or 15 miles north of Hatteras Light. There was no lightship off the Diamonds in those days. The wind began to breeze up from the northwest. There was a little clear streak in the sky in the west. I had no idea it was going to blow a gale of wind so I put her on the port tack and stood offshore thinking that at midnight the wind would go around to the northeast. Then I would tack her and head right up for Cape Henry. But my calculations on the weather this time badly miscarried for at midnight it was blowing a real gale from the northwest. I not only had to reef her to low sails but it blew so hard I had to heave her to and lay 3 days and nights. It got up an awful big sea. Finally, it moderated enough on the 3rd day to let me make a little headway under close reef sails. The first I hove her to. When I got every thing set and trimed I came below. My wife was nearly scared to death. I said to her, "Why is the trouble?" "Oh," she said, "if I was only in Crisfield. I know we will never see home again." I said, "Mary, there is only one thing that worries me."

She says, "What is it, what is it, oh, what is it?" "Why," I said, "I am worried about these poor North Carolinamen living in rickety houses along this coast in such a gale as this." The *City of Baltimore* was a strong-built vessel, easy to handle with a good crew, and I felt as safe as if I had been in a fine brick building in a city.

Well, the next Thursday, after being blown off more than six days, I fetched in right at the same place along the coast I left from the Thursday before. Now ten days from St. Johns Bar the wind was still blowing a gale or so from the northwest. There was seven or eight of these vessels got back under the beach at the same time I did. Most of them that came out from the St. Johns River when I did. After getting close under the beach I turned the reefs out of the fore, main, and mizzin sails and began working up the beach making short tacks to keep in smooth water as much as possible. There was an awful strong current setting down this beach. Driving as hard as I could drive we were only making one mile an hour as it took 3 days to work from Body Island to Cape Henry, a distance of 72 miles.

I soon worked away from this fleet of vessels that were in company with me, just about 10 or 12 miles below Body Island Light, excepting one little 3-master smaller than mine. This fellow was certainly a tough match for me. He was a good sailer and I was anxious to know who he was. Any vessel that was a match to the *City of Baltimore* for working to the windward, I wanted to know who he was. I carried full lower sails and tied reefs in all around, that is fore, main, and mizzin. At night he would beat me a little as he would keep close under the beach. I was too afraid of getting on the beach at night and being in the rough water I lost by it. But during the day when I could see I kept as close to the beach as possible for safety. And I would catch up on him, being a larger vessel and carrying more sail. I always stayed on deck standing toward the beach and let the mate have her in charge when standing off. We were making 2-hour tacks. This would give me a short while below to warm myself and maybe catch a nap. This thing went on like this until we got nearly up to Currituck Light. Then I was so tired I told Mr. Hughes to let her go off until 12 midnight. I wanted some sleep. At 12 midnight I came on deck and stood her in toward the land and let the mate go below. The next morning when daylight came I surely was surprised and hurt to see how this other little 3-master had beat us. I quarled with the mate and told him he did not attend to her in his watch or that vessel would never beat us like that. But I suppose he was no more in fault than I, as I stood her off four hours and got off in rough water while he stood close to the beach all night and kept in much smoother water.

When daylight came I got close under the beach where the current was not so strong against us and we began to go up the beach pretty fast. When this little vessel got up far enough to head in the cape he let her go in. I kept my vessel on the port tack and stood across the mouth of the Chesapeake as close up to Cape Charles as I dare to go with safety. Then I tacked and stood in the bay. My little friend was way down in Lynnhaven. He was headed off somewhat and I was favored with a slant. It was blowing very fresh for it seems it can do that in the month of March. We were heading in the bay now very fast when this little 3-master tacked toward the northeast coming out of Lynnhaven. I saw that I had him. I caught a big favorable slant by tacking over toward Cape Charles. He was now on the port tack coming out of Lynnhaven. I said to Mr. Hughes, "I am going to get close enough to this vessel to see who he is." For the last three days I had been anxious to find this out as I was with all smart vessels. We kept getting closer and closer to one another. I said to the mate, "We are going to cut him off." I was on the starboard tack which gave me the right of way. And sure enough we cut him off. He came so close to us under my stern he hollered at me and asked me where Stilwell was. I told him in Baltimore I supposed. But to my surprise this little vessel was the *Frank M. Howes,* Captain Josh Rich. He had left Jacksonville long after we did.

I was now 13 days from Jacksonville Bar and being blown off for a week I could not think otherwise than Stilwell was in Baltimore. Now the *Frank M. Howes* was a Jacksonville trader and whoever got to Baltimore first would be entitled to load the outward cargo first as we sailed for the Emerson Rokes Line. "Now," I said, "Mr. Hughes, we have got to use our utmost skill to beat the *Howes* to Baltimore. If not we may have to go to Jacksonville light or load to go somewhere else off the Line." I did my very best working to the windward all day and found I was the best man working to the windward. That night the wind went down very light, or hardly any. I was caught in the bight just below the Wolf Trap. I would have anchored and took a night's rest, which I was very much in need of, had I not been in company with this other vessel. We made nothing the whole night. The *Howes* was becalmed over on the Cherrystone side of the bay a long way to the eastward of me.

The next day was Monday and the wind breezed up from the eastward. The *Howes* now had a big advantage. I had expected the wind would breeze up from the northwest again but I got left on this expectation. This was the first east wind I had seen since I had been north of Hatteras. I was now 14 days from Jacksonville Bar. The *Howes* gave her the sheets and up the bay he went all drawing while I had to beat out from back of the Wolf Trap. He now had a big start on me and my case almost looked hopeless for with a fair wind he could lead me. When night came I think he was ten miles ahead. And as night drew the wind freshened and blew heavy, backed to about east northeast, and rain began to pour down. The spars cracked and snaped, they were under such strain, for I was carrying all the sails we had. And steering north by east this was the highest course I ever steered going up the Chesapeake with an easterly wind. It was very dark and I was anxious to see Sharps Island Light when I went by. I kept my lead in hand most all the time sounding to keep from runing ashore. When I went by Sharps Island I never saw it. About midnight it began snowing thick and fast. I came near runing into a steamer and I concluded it would not be safe to run her any longer. I was surprised to find I had only five fathoms of water and sticky bottom.

Really, I did not know how far up the bay I had gotton. The next morning I found I was close on the western side of the bay and Sharps Island was bearing east southeast. The course I steered I did not know how I got there. Now all my crew were out of tobacco and were crazy for tobacco. There was a 3-master laying to anchor as much as two miles from us. The wind was now northwest again, it seems, in its old usual place. The mate and crew wanted to lower my big boat and pull up to this schooner and get some tobacco. I said, "No, the wind is too heavy for you to row that boat and you will all be blowed away and I will be here with no boat or crew." They said, "Captain Tawes, we can row that boat." I said, "No, you can't." Then one said, "Will you let us drop a long line out to the stern? We will hold on to the line and if we cannot row her up we will pull her back by the line and hoist the boat up to the davits and say no more about it." I consented to let them do this for I know if they wanted to go to all of this trouble and labor they must surely wanted tobacco. It's something I never used in my life. They lowered the boat and droped her away astern and began to row up to the vessel. I found they could do as they said they could and I let them go ahead and row up to this vessel anchored so far up the bay from us. When they got there they did not get even a chew of tobacco. They were all out. This vessel proved to be the *Howes*. The captain asked my mate what ship he was from. He told him the *City of Baltimore*. He asked him when he came to anchor. He told him it was after midnight. My mate asked him many tacks he made coming up. He told him three tacks. Then Captain Rich asked the mate how many tacks we made. Mr. Hughes told him none but just headed strait up the bay.

We got the boat to the davits and got breakfast. And just about that time there came a tow boat down the bay and Josh Rich took him. There was no other tow boat in sight but in kindness and justice to the captain of the tow boat, before he started towing the *Howes* up, he ran down to us and threw a big plug tobacco weighing a pound over on our deck. He went back and picked up the *Howes* and started towing him up the bay.

I said to the mate, "Mr. Hughes, cannot we get the snow from off these masts and get her underway?" He was a game Irishman and never said no to any of my wishes. There was considerable ice and snow frozed on the forward part of her mast occasioned by the ship laying head to the wind at anchor. I was afraid some of the slabs of ice might fall when hoisting sails and cut their heads and faces or otherwise injure the crew. They took oars and sticks of wood and went aloft and beat all the ice and snow from off the mast. Then they came below and cleaned the snow and ice from off the decks. Then we hove the anchor short, loosed the sails, and hoisted them. When the spanker, mainsail, and foresail was on her we proceeded to break out the anchor and put the jibs on her and filled her away on the port tack. The sun was getting up high and all along the western shore it was blue and smoky like I know there was going to be plenty of wind that day. And it was too. We could just head up the bay with a good, clean full. The *Frank M. Howes* was now quite a good long way ahead. But when the wind began to increase we began to come up on him good and fast. Before they got to Thomas Point we went by them rapidly. After we passed Sandy Point a tow boat came out of the Magothy River and asked me if I wanted to tow up. I replied, "Yes, if you can catch me." He came after me as hard as he could drive but we could beat him. When I got to Seven Foot Knoll I had to bring her to anchor. The wind was blowing such a gale it would have been difficult for us to beat up. I came to anchor and paid out 45 fathoms of chain and she now lay safely. Then the tow boat came alongside and said to me, "Captain Tawes, this wind will go down tonight and at 12 midnight I will come after you."

As good as his word he came alongside and told us to heave up and we would start. The wind had fallen as he said and he began to tow me along pretty good. At the sun rising we were at Fort Carroll. Then that blue, hard looking streak began to show all along the shore line and the gale arose from the northwest again. Soon our tow boat could not take care of us. He signalled for the help of another boat. Now with two boats we began to make headway in spite of the gale. Sometime about noon we were made fast at Jackson's Wharf. Captain Somers, a retired old sea captain now a stevedore and was my stevedore, came aboard and told me that Captain Stilwell had not arrived in Baltimore yet. He said the *Frank M. Howes* was laying in Annapolis and that he was going to get my cargo out before the *Frank M. Howes* got to Baltimore. And sure enough he did. He got my cargo of 250,000 feet of lumber out in 3 days and I was on the berth loading for Jacksonville when the *Howes* arrived. I well remember taking out the material to build the lighthouse at Mosquito Inlet. I had about cleaned up all the cargo going to Jacksonville at that time and I had in a 1,200 dollar freight, which in those days was a good one.

When I arrived, the *Sun* paper and also the *Baltimore American* came out in big letters that Captain Tawes of the schooner

CAPT. TAWES WINS AGAIN.

Another Race from Jacksonville to Baltimore—A Rough Trip.

The proudest man in Baltimore yesterday was Captain L. S. Tawes, of the schooner City of Baltimore. For the third consecutive time he has beaten the schooner City of Jacksonville, Captain Stillwell, in good weather and in bad, and when he came into port yesterday morning his rival was still down the bay somewhere battling with the adverse winds. Both vessels had to contend with a series of northwest winds, and Capt. Tawes was sixteen days making the trip, which is usually made in seven or eight days. Once he made it in five days. Much interest has been taken in the races between these vessels. They are both staunch and swift; both belong to the same line, and are commanded by first-class seamen. It will be remembered that the outward race was won by the City of Baltimore in just thirty minutes. This was the closest contest they have ever had, and made the interest in the last race all the greater. On the return, they both left the wharf at Jacksonville, Fla., on Saturday, February 28, the City of Jacksonville getting off twelve hours ahead. There was some detention at the bar on account of low water, and they did not cross until March 7. The City of Baltimore then had a fine run to Hatteras, getting north of that place at noon March 10. That night a strong gale set in from the northeast, and she stood off shore, not being able to get back to land until the following Wednesday, six days after. The first gale lasted for three days, and there was no more favorable weather until Sunday. There was then no chance of getting in the capes until she could be got back to the land, and this Captain Tawes resolved to do, if he had to go south of Hatteras. Monday, the 14th, the wind blew a gale and heavy seas were shipped, which stove clear through the shutters, and stove in the back and water cask. On Wednesday she got into the land at Body Island, and worked up the beach, getting into Herring Bay on Monday, where she anchored, and on Tuesday came up to the mouth of the channel, where she lay all day on account of heavy winds, and was towed in yesterday by the tugboat Edna. The City of Jacksonville has two passengers on board, who said on leaving Jacksonville that they would give a bell clock to the winning vessel. About eighteen months ago Captain Tawes beat his rival between the two ports by one week. The only race won by Captain Stillwell was the first one, about two years ago, which he won by two hours and forty minutes. The City of Baltimore is consigned to Emerson Bokes, with 245,000 feet of yellow pine lumber consigned to Wilson, Hunting & Co.

Courtesy of Enoch Pratt Free Library

Column from the "*Baltimore American*" of March 24, 1887, describing the race between the schooners CITY OF BALTIMORE and CITY OF JACKSONVILLE. *Captain Tawes refers to this news release in his journals.*

City of Baltimore had arrived but Captain Stilwell was in the lower part of the bay and would soon be up. Mrs. Stilwell, then living in Cape May or New Jersey, saw these papers and came right to meet her husband and be with him while in Baltimore. She was stopping at Mrs. Emerson Rokes' while she was hourly expecting her husband to arrive. About the day before I sailed from Baltimore, after being in port a week nearly or it was six days, I met Mrs. Stilwell on Pratt Street and she was weeping and sorely distressed. She was apprehending that her husband must be lost, vessel and all. I did my very best to dispel her of this idea. I told her of the heavy westerly gales I had to contend with coming up from Jacksonville and that in these heavy winds he had been blown off. And as soon as these westerly gales ceased, and the wind changed to the south or east, she would certainly see him coming in, which was the case.

I lost my clock which Jack Williams had promised me and I also never got the suit of clothes which Doctor L. Engle said he was going to give me if I beat Stilwell to Batimore. I may say here that Doctor L. Engle was the owner of the tow boat that towed us out over the bar. He had instructed Captain Crawford to tow us out together on one hawser so that we could sail evenly together. But when he heard that Captain Stilwell had stole a march on me, that Captain Crawford had disregarded his instructions, he said he would give me a nice suit of clothes if I did beat Stilwell to Baltimore. And he told me that himself when I got back to Jacksonville. But somehow I suppose the doctor, having so many things to attend to, it slipped his memory. The doctor was an honest, square-dealing man and I do not think he intended to forget it. He has passed into the beyond and I will never get them. But I felt quite rewarded in beating Stilwell for all the hard labor and sleepless nights I indured.

I made about one more round to Jacksonville when the vessels began to bunch up. To get us separated I was chartered to load coal for Galveston, Texas, at $3.40 per ton for the Houston Gas Light Company. One of his other vessels, named *Brooxxe B. Rokes,* had sailed for Galveston about two weeks ahead of me. For Galveston, he got $3.60 per ton.

I sailed from Baltimore about the 22nd day of May, 1887. I was sure of having lots of southerly winds and probably a long passage out. Working down the Carolina beach I fell in with quite a lot of vessels working down. I was up on top of the cabbin making a staysail. The *Baltimore* worked ahead of all this fleet except one little 3-masted schooner which seemed to be cleaning everything up. Pretty soon he got close enough to me for me to see who he was and behold it was the *Minnie and Gussie,* Captain French. He bore the name of being fast and usually cleaned up everything on the coast. He was a Jacksonville trader. I knew her well and the captain knew me. We were then off Body Island Lighthouse. As soon as I saw it was Captain French I quit sailmaking and got all the sails giged up, trimed the sheets to suit my eye, and took the wheel myself. For about 35 miles we had it and I cut him off several times. He worked hard to beat me but he missed it. The wind was from the southwest and he stayed right by me. I runed down close to the Diamond Shoal and on the starboard tack I let her go south by east on the wind. He stayed by me. He thought I was bound to Jacksonville and he did not want me to get away with any laurels. And he followed. He thought I would tack pretty soon and come back under the coast. But I made up my mind if he followed me I would take him to Galveston. At 10 o'clock that night he was so far into the Gulf Stream that he tacked. I carried off the laurels and I never fell in company with him again but met him a few times in New York and Jacksonville afterwards.

Nothing occured of note excepting head winds and squalls as usually occurs at this season of the year in these lattitudes. We made the Hole in the Wall all in good shape and runed for

Stirrup Key Lighthouse. Just as we were abreast of the light an anchored fisherman came out to us with fresh fish which he wanted to dispose of. The pile seemed not as large as most fishermen would have when they came out to us on previous voyages. I said to him, "Is that all the fish you have?" He said that it was. "How much do you want for them?", I said. "I will give 50¢." He said, "Oh, no money Captain, just poke, poke." I told the steward to get up a nice piece of pork out of the barrel and give to him. All the time we were runing along with a fair wind from the northeast at about 5 miles an hour. I see him looking back astern of us toward the Hole in the Wall which had been out sight for quite awhile. Then he said, "Captain, did you see any other vessels come around the Hole in the Wall when you did?" When he asked me this my instinct suggested that he had not told me the truth about the fish he had and that he was holding back fish for the next vessel that might be coming along. So I jumped down in his canoe, lifted the cover in the stern locker, and oh what a nice pile of fish he did have. "Now," I said, "I know why you were so interested in other vessels coming around the Hole in the Wall when I did. You were holding these fish for them and putting me off with a scanty mess." "Now," I said, "give me all those fish or you will get no pork." The Bahama Islanders know how to trade and beg. I got all of his fish and he had to go back to Stirrup Key and catch more before he could trade with another vessel.

On the Bimini Islands they will come on board and bring the most beautiful shells and shell work and corral to sell and trade. They will begin by asking a high price for these pretty things. After they exhaust the ship's crew of their cash they will then begin to trade for clothes. When they can no longer trade they will begin to beg for a mess of potatoes and onions. Then beg for pork and beef. They will probably want to buy some butter and lard. I have had them to ask me for everything on the ship even to medicine out of the medicine chest for a sick woman on the island. They will hang on the vessel and we will tow them for miles while this promiscuous trading and begging is going on. Yet they will pilot us along these islands close into the shore so that we will avoid being caught in the current of the Gulf Stream which runs very strong. Sometimes vessels are caught in these strong currents and carried back to the north-ward of the Great Abaco which case would delay the voyage several days. Such has occured to vessels. Often this is the route vessels drawing over 12 feet have to take. If less than 12 feet we go across the Bahama Banks an interesting trip I have herebefore discribed.

After crossing the Bank we steered a course for the Double Headed Shot Keys, a great boulder of rock portruding up out of the sea with a large, tall lighthouse on it. A man by the name of Thompson kept the light in those days. He too, like the colored fellows at Stirrup Key, will bring off fresh turtle or fish for trading for potatoes, onions, or any vegetable you have on board to spare. I always accomodated the best I could a man living on a bald rock, keeping a light, excluded from all civilization who deserved to be treated well. He came out to see us. He seemed to know me very well. He told me that Captain Robertson in the schooner *Brooxxe B. Rokes* had passed there one week ago. I thought myself he is getting along awful slow. If he does not do better I will catch him before he gets to Galveston. After accomodating Mr. Thompson to such of my stores as I could spare, and runing down until I sighted the Pan of Matanzas, I then shaped my course to make Dry Tortugas. And then about west northwest for Galveston. From Dry Tortugas to Galveston I was one week.

Here I found Captain Robertson with his cargo about half out. I had to lay in the stream and discharge in lighters. There was not water enough to let me go up to Houston. When I got my letters I had one from my sister bearing to me the sorrowful news that my owner, Emerson Rokes, had passed away. I sure regretted to hear this. I lost a friend and so did the *City of Baltimore* for he was an energetic and prosperous man and there is no telling the good he would have done. He was only 54 years of age at the time.

Captain Robertson got his cargo out and sailed 3 days ahead of me for Pensacola to load lumber for Philadelphia. I sailed for Apalachicola to load lumber for Philadelphia. I got to Apalachicola, a hundred miles further to go, and loaded and sailed before he got to Pensacola. He neglected to haul the *Brooxxe* out before he left Baltimore. He was so long getting up to Pensacola, and then so long getting from Pensacola to Philadelphia, that the worms got into the bottom so badly that they had to cut the old bottom off and put a new bottom on her. I had gotten my cargo out and left Philadelphia for Jacksonville a long time before he got to Philadelphia. The putting on a new bottom cost $2,600. I made one or two rounds to Jacksonville and back while these repairs were going on. After being repaired he went to Jacksonville, discharged his cargo, and loaded for Baltimore. He sailed from Jacksonville for Baltimore one day before I left Baltimore for Jacksonville. Then came a strong northeast gale which carried me to Jacksonville in good time. I discharged my cargo and loaded for Baltimore and to my surprise he had not got to Baltimore yet. And I was 20 days in Jacksonville this time discharging and loading. I just made up my mind that the *Brooxxe B. Rokes* was lost.

I was lying at Jackson's Wharf in Baltimore and Captain Greene of Delaware came on board and said to me, "What color was the water casks on the *Brooxxe B. Rokes* painted?" I said that I did not know but I believed white. "Well," he said, "I saw her water casks off Cape Hatteras when I passed by there the other day." And he said he saw her yawl and other equipment and we together had figured out that she was gone. It was then sometime in December, 1887, and it was a wet, chilly day. While Captain Greene was in the cabbin discusing the loss of this nice vessel Woody Milbourne, a mere youth he was then who has married since and raised a family in Crisfield (he made this voyage to Jacksonville and back), put his head in the cabbin and said the *Brooxxe B. Rokes'* boat is alongside. I went on deck and looked down into the yawl where two men were setting. I said, "Whose yawl is this?" They said it was the *Brooxxe Rokes'*. I said, "Where is the *Brooxxe Rokes?*" In a flash it occured to me that they had been picked up at sea and brought in by some other ship. But they told me she was at anchor out in the harbor. I said, "Is she alright? Any of her spars or rigging gone?" They said, "No." I said, "I am glad to hear that." I said, "Where is Captain Robertson?" They said, "He has gone up to telephone." After awhile he came back and came down the cabbin. I will never forget what I said to him and how sorry I was after I said it. In those days I guess I was rough, having rough men to deal with. But my greeting to him was this, "Man, where in the hell have you been?"

It was now December and I had not seen him since the last June in Galveston. He had only made 2 voyages in 7 months. I had made 3 in much less time. They sold the vessel to Captain Wilbur Tall of Dorchester County, Maryland. When he got in charge of her the *Brooxxe* made as much time as I did. She could make trips as fast as I could. This was January, 1888, he brought her and he was very prosperous with her until the 7th day of April, 1889. In an awful gale of wind she was lost and all hands perished. There passed away a mighty nice man that I aways admired. Also his brother Guy Tall who was mate with him. This proves that the right man is the success of the ship both in her sailing qualities and her earning ability.

I must now pick up my friend Stilwell again as I do not believe I mentioned our being together in Jacksonville and Christmas Day, 1887. I sent up that morning and got a quart of whisky and made eggnog and called all my crew in the cabbin and treated them. Everything was moving along cheerfully when about 10 o'cock Stilwell came on his deck and sung out to me a cheerful, jolly way, "I just want to get another chance at you." I said, "You do, eh?" "Well," I said, "I hope I will not meet up with any of your immediate friends for I am the poorest man you ever saw to console people that are in deep trouble." Stilwell went down his cabbin and never mentioned sailing to me again during his life. He was a man you could not help admiring but he would certainly stretch the sailing qualities of his vessel. He sold his interest in the *City of Jacksonville* to his brother-in-law, Captain Charley Ross, and built him a larger one and named her the *Douglass Gregory*. He lost her in a dreadful hurrycane in September, 1898.

VII

1888–1891

WHEN MR. ROKES passed away in 1887 I was put in rather
an awkward position. He owned the controlling interest in the
vessel and I had only around 1/16th of her. She was a nice
vessel. Captains from Maine, New Jersey, and Delaware were
trying to buy his interest. I tried my best to get some people in
my own home town to take some stock in this vessel that I
might hold on to her but not one would listen to my appeals.

I fell in with a man by the name John G. Johnson who came
to my relief. He said to me, "Tawes, you just keep on sailing the
vessel and I will watch and let you know when this estate will
be settled. I am well acquainted with the executer of this estate.
We used to be school boys together. And from him I will keep
posted and let you know in due time when this vessel has got
to be sold." Mr. Rokes left a widow and one daughter.

In November, 1888, Mr. Rokes' brother, Leander Rokes,
chartered the vessel to go up the Little Choptank River to load
oak piling for Boston. I always believed he took advantage in
chartering this vessel. He owned the piling. Well this was certainly a dirty, hard job. Great, long oak piling had to be hoisted
out of the water and put in the bow ports. Sometimes some
of them were so heavy they sank. We would have to put in the
big end of our piling then turn the next piling around in the

water under the bow. Then hoist up our end, get it in the ports, then slip the tackle to the middle of the heavy oak log and raize it up by the capstan; and then have a tackle in the hold leading to the winch and put it in the hold. The big end of one log would lay alongside of another's small end and in this way they laid closely and made good stowage. I had to use the farm labor up there for help and they did not understand this kind of work. And though willing and hard workers they would sometimes work right dead against you. We were about 30 days getting this cargo in. I had to get my mail from a store kept by Mace & Woolford. When we were loaded I had to go up to Mace and Woolford's to get my check cashed and pay my store bill. We left the store about 8 PM to go on board. I had a sailor named Scot. He bought him a new pair of rubber boots and got over the tops of them before we left the landing.

Shortly after we left the store the moon rose, and a strong northwest wind rose at the same time. It was cold and freezing. We reefed our sail and kept working down the river. The wind blowed in hard flaws at times. I had my sheet rope so rigged that you could slip it as quick as you could fire a gun. I gave it to Scot to attend. I told him to let it fly off as soon as these strong puffs knocked her down so low that she would take water in over the gunwales. He had it in his hand but a short while when he let her knock down so low that she filled a quarter full. I said, "Scot, why did you not let that sheet fly off?" I had to jog her along and run ashore on the side of the river and bail the water out of her. We then pushed her off when the water was out and started beating down again. With Scot tending the sheet rope, with my right hand I was steering. Having mittens on my hands I was afraid I could not let the sheet fly off quick enough and I gave it to Scot to tend to.

I had not gone long when a heavy puff hit her. I could not let her to the wind quick enough and Scot did not let the sheet

fly and she came very near turning over. She got lots of water
in her this time. I said, "Scot, why did not you let that sheet
fly?" I said, "Scot, you will drown the whole of us if you do not
do better than that." We had then gotton below any houses and
where no one lived. I joged her ashore again, bailed her out,
and by the moonlight I saw a lot of drift wood on the shore.
I said, "Who has got matches? We will pick up a lot of this
wood, make a fire, and stay here tonight. The gale is too fierce
to attempt to go any furthur."

They searched themselves and not any of them had a match
to start a fire. I stood there by the side of the yawl countem-
plating whether to stay there with no fire and freeze to death.
Or to attempt to go to the ship we must all be drowned. Finally,
old Scot said, "I am going to freeze to death." I knew his boots
were wet inside so I said, "Hoist the sail up. We will try it
again."

Now the further we got down this river the broader it was
and the rougher was the water. I could not trust Scot with the
sheet line anymore. So I took the sheet line in my left hand
when tacking to the port side and in my right hand when on the
starboard tack. The water was coming over the bows so fast
it kept 2 men constantly bailing it out. The boat was more
able on the starboard than she was on the port. It had got
so bad I could not fill the sail on the port tack. So when I
had gotton down in the vicinity of the vessel I had to let her go
a long way on the starboard tack until the vessel was all of 3
points abaft the beam. Then I tacked and let her kind lay to or
jog for the vessel. It appeared to me I had more than a mile to
do this drifting in but I fetched the ship alright. And oh, my,
how the wind was squealing through her rigging. It was terrible
to listen to. Chris, my mate, said to me, "Captain, why did
you come on board such a night? When you got close to the
vessel I expected to see that yawl go down and drown every one
of you."

We got the stores out of the boat and I went into the cabbin to put on dry clothes telling Chris to drop the boat astern, which he did. And before I got my clothes near changed he put his head in the cabbin and told me the boat had sunk laying astern. I never knew until then the risk I had taken in getting on board that night. I had about half a ton of stone ballast in her. This was on Saturday night. I lost my rudder and oars. The next morning we got the boat up along side. Chris got the throat halyards of the main and mizzin on the boat and was about to make an attempt to hoist her up. I saw in an instant that the boat would break in half if he did this so I told him not to hoist her up. To loose this boat would mean delay of another week in procuring another one, say nothing about the cost. These stones had to be thrown out of the boat overboard and the boat bailed out before hoisting her up.

Now who must I ask to get in there in icy water about 3 feet deep and almost dive down and get these stones and throw them overboard? Really, I could ask no one. It was now blowing fresh from the northwest and freezing. I would have been called inhuman to ask or order any one of my crew to do this. So to save my boat, and the temper of my crew, I jumped down in those icy waters and scratched around in the water and threw all those stones overboard. Then I took a bucket and bailed her out. As soon as I had done this I told him to take halyards off of her and drop her astern. Then I went in the cabbin to the fire and put on dry clothes. I do not remember of taking a cold from it. That afternoon the wind moderated and we went to the lee shore in the boat and walked all around the shore looking for our rudder and the oars. We succeeded in finding two of the oars. The other two, and the rudder and tiller, we never found. How we ever got on board with five men in and some stores has always been a puzzle to me. But we did it.

Monday there was no chance to sail out of the river. I went up to Mr. John H. B. Woolford's. I bought a nice turkey for our Christmas dinner. I got full of cake and wine for they were making big preparations for Christmas. I told of the chance I took in getting on board on the Saturday night. The old gentleman remonstrated me for not coming up to his house with all my crew and spending the night instead of going on board in such a storm.

On Christmas Day, 1888, the sun rose beautiful and clear. We got under way and broke out our anchor as the sun was rising and proceeded on our way down the Little Choptank River. Got in the bay sometime before noon and proceeded down the bay that night. It got stark calm. We had to anchor near the middle grounds back of Smith Island. I did not like my anchorage as the bottom was hard sand. I was very afraid the wind would come to west or northwest and blow me ashore. I was afraid my anchors would not hold here and away to the leeward go. So I let the crew go below and staid up and watched myself.

At midnight there came a light breeze from the southwest. I got underway and proceeded to work down the bay as I was dissatisfied with my anchorage. When day came the wind had got to the south with thick fog off Smith Point. I came near being run over by one of the Merchants and Miners steamers. I was on the starboard tack and blowing two blasts of the fog horn. He ran across my bow too close for comfort. That night about 9 o'clock, when abreast of Windmill Point, the wind shifted and blew like fury from the northwest. We got all light sails in and stowed away and reefed the spanker and set it. We were now going down the bay like a scared dog under reef spanker, full foresail, staysail, and jib. Chris and I talked it over and concluded we would come to anchor under the Buckroe shore until morning and see if the fury would not subside a little. He went forward to get the anchor ready. While he was forward I made up my mind not to anchor but go to sea. I told the man at the wheel to keep her off southeast by south, and when I was slacking off the spanker sheet and in rendering around the bit it made her tremble from stern to bow. Chris, feeling this trembling, came aft and said, "Captain, what are you going to do?" I said, "I am going out." "What," he said, "in a time like this?" I said, "Yes." He said, "We will not be able to hold the beach." I said, "I think she will." And out of the capes I went. I carried this northwester to Barnegat. The wind then backened to the southwest and gave me a nice run over to Gay Head and a mighty nice run through the Vineyard Sound and to Boston. The nights were long of course, but I was at the Sow and Pigs Lightship when she lighted up. And I saw Boston Light before it was put out.

I had only been to anchor on Boston flats two hours when here it came out from the northwest blowing a gale. I was just 3 days and 5 hours from the time I kept her off in the Chesapeake Bay to Boston flats. A mighty good winter passage. Seldom beaten by a sailing vessel. If I had anchored under Buckroe shore I would have lost a nice run. I told the mate and the cook, who was Bob James a well known Eastern Shore cook, that if I got to Boston before New Year's Day I would go to French Brother's Market and buy the bigest turkey he had for our New Year's dinner. Bob baked it in nice shape but I missed getting my dinner on board that day.

If I had known Mr. Leander Rokes' intentions he would not have seen me that day. When he left me at Church Creek, Maryland, he gave me his address in Thomaston, Maine, and asked me to wire him as soon as I arrived in Boston, which I did. I then bought my turkey and all that was needed for a New Year's festivity. Late in the evening I got a wire from Mr. Rokes to meet him at the Boston and Maine depot at 11:30 or 12 that night. I was then so tired I could hardly stand on my feet having been on them all night coming through the Vineyard Sound and around Cape Cod and up Boston Bay.

When I first got his telegram I did say I would not meet

him that night, but after reconsidering I thought it might be some very important business and that I would go. And I did. I came to find out he only wanted to come on board and stay and save his hotel bill. If I had known that was his business he would have gone to a hotel or walked the street that night for I was awfully tired the next day. I had to go ashore with him to be a witness to any conversation that he might have with the man he had sold the piling to as he was not a reliable man as he said. And I had to stay by him all that New Year's Day 1889. I told him two or three times that I wanted to go on board. I was anxious to get into that turkey but I did not tell him so.

When noon came he took me into Young's Hotel or Restaurant for dinner where hundreds of people were dining. He took the bill of fare and looked it over and called for the cheapest bill of fares on the list. I have regretted many times since that I did not call for the highest bill of fare on the list, which I believe was about $2.50, for it was a mighty tony hotel. Well, that day he and the buyer of the piling came to terms. He was to put them on a wharf. The purchaser was not to move them until Mr. Leander Rokes was satisfied. He ate and he slept in the vessel until she was discharged and ready to sail. I wish to add that Mr. Rokes went home and I have never seen him since. I heard he bought a lime kiln in Nova Scotia which did not turn out well.

We took in a few hundred barrels of apples at a low rate of freight and sailed for Baltimore. We were ten days to Baltimore. J. S. Hoskins had her chartered for Jacksonville and Palatka. While in Baltimore this time my friend John G. Johnson, who had been looking out for me all this time, said to me, "Tawes, we have got to act. Jim Bond wants to settle the estate and the vessel has got to be sold. Now how much money have you got and how many friends.?" I said, "I have very little money and few friends." "Well," he said, "let's go see him." Here was 10/16ths to be handled. Johnson and I went to see him and talked a while. No one in the world knew what was going on. If they did I would never have succeeded in getting the vessel. Mr. Johnson got Mr. Bond down as low as he could and then Mr. Johnson said, "Jim, I will take her. Here is so much on account. I will give you the balance in a short while." Now the way was open for me to keep the vessel. I got Mr. Wm. H. Skinner, a shipyard man, to take a 1/16th and others took some. I took 5/16ths. Johnson loaned me $1,050 for which I gave him my note. Gray, Irelan & Co. took 1/16th. John G. Christopher, in Jacksonville, Florida, took 1/32nd and Mr. Ebon B. Hunting, in Baltimore, took 1/32nd. This left Mr. Johnson holding 4/16ths. Now I was boss of my business. I must say that Hoskins did what he could to block this deal when he found it out but he was too late.

1888 and 1889 were 2 good years for freighting and I made some money. When August, 1889, came around I walked into Mr. Johnson's office and I said to him, "You have my note which I want to pay off." "Why Tawes," he said, "you havent the money have you?" I said, "I have." He said, "You have been doing well haven't you?" I said, "I have. Let me have the note." He took it and I began to figure the interest on it. He said "No interest, just the face of the note." I drew him a check for a $1,050. He certainly befriended me. He was a Catholic and I wish there were more of them.

I traded between Jacksonville, Fernandina, and Baltimore steady for about a year. When I did not think I was doing as well as I ought to be doing I chartered to load coal and cooperage for Matanzas. As usual I had favorable winds. I got underway at quarantine ground in Baltimore on Saturday morning with wind from the north. The next day I went out the capes with the wind from the northeast. This northeaster runed me to the Hole in the Wall. When it hauled to the southeast I just fetched by the Hole in the Wall Light close on the wind.

Then I had a fair wind to Stirrup Key, cross the Bahama Banks, and went into Matanzas the next Sunday just 8 days from Baltimore. My spanker boom never came across the deck from the time I left Baltimore. I was consigned to Zanetti, Dubois & Co. I got my cargo out and chartered to load molasses for New York.

There were some Rockland captains there loading and I had lots of dunnage on board where I had been running lumber. I gave two of these captains quite a lot of it. These captains were named Hart and Hooper, schooner *Mabel Hooper*. They had their families with them. One day they all went on a picnic and they asked me to join them. I was at work when they came on board and I jumped in the boat and went off unconcernedly. There were 4 or 5 boats. It seemed that this picnic had been in preparation some few days ahead. We rowed down the harbor and went up a river on the south side of the harbor until we came to a road crossing the river. On the bank was a Spanish guard house or barrack. They kept watch on all teams crossing the river here. We landed and the Spanish officer in charge welcomed us. Then the women began getting out cakes, doughnuts, and all maner of good cooking. We had some red snappers and groupers and the captains began cleaning these fish, some peeling the potatoes and onions, all of which they brought with them. The Spaniards very kindly loaned us their cooking utensils and these Maine people made the nicest fish chowder I ever eat. These down-east people do sure know how to make nice doughnuts and fish chowders. I felt very much embarased for I did not bring a thing along. I did not know anything about the trip or the nature of it until I had landed at the Spanish barracks. Anyhow, these people gave me a harty welcome and a nice time.

After dinner was served the Spaniards furnished the music, for which they were well equiped with a nice band, and the ladies and men went to dancing. Captain Hooper's daughter would not dance with the Spanish officer and he was a splendid dancer too. Her father tried to persuade her to dance with him but she declined. The other Maine ladies danced with the Spaniards in general. Well, we all had a nice day but I would have felt better had I taken some of my stores with me. And I felt a little at odds being an entire stranger and a southern man at that. We had to pull back to the vessels that evening against a strong head wind, and I tried to make up deficiency by pulling hard on an oar all the way back to the ships after spending a pleasant day.

I finished loading our cargo of molasses. In order to trim the vessel I took ten hogsheads on deck at my risk, eight of them just fitted head to head across the main deck at the break of the poop deck. But on the main deck, and on each side at the gangway, these holes in the pin rails were large enough to get lashings through to secure these two hogsheads. I bunged all ten of these hogsheads and left the two vent holes on each side of the bungs open. These vent holes were about 5/8ths inch in size and, to keep the sea water from getting into the hogsheads, I tacked a strip of leather over them so that they would close down over the vent hole, when a sea shipped over them, and cut the sea water off.

After sailing from Matanzas everything went well with us until we got within 60 or 70 miles of Cape Hatteras. Here we got caught in a fearful storm. The mate I had with me was a careless, indifferent fellow and he let this gale hit us with our topsails on her, it being my watch below at the time, and he never called me. It is a wonder we did not get the vessel stripped of her sails and rigging but I jumped on deck and got all hands out, got the topsails clewed up, jib topsail and flying jib in, tied them up, and her reefed down. The seas came over us so heavily that these ten hogsheads were many times out of sight. I expected to see them break away and go overboard or smash on the deck. Had I lost them I should have had them to pay for as I could not get them insured on the deck. I signed bills of lading all under deck, all in good order and condition, and in which condition I promised to deliver in New York. In this storm she labored so hard that she threw the glasses out of their racks and all the pots out of their holes on the stove. We weathered the storm all o.k. and got to New York safely and the ten hogsheads of molasses too. By having these ten hogsheads on deck aft enabled me to carry ten more in the hold forward which made my freight count up good.

After the molasses was out I hastened to go to Baltimore light and load coal for Palatka at $2 per ton and back to New York with a cargo of lumber at $8 per thousand feet. This made me up a very nice round. When I got back to New York to John G. Christopher I agreed to take a cargo of salt to Jacksonville for $400 he to pay all expenses whatever, tow boats, wharfage, and stevedoring. Then I chartered to load a cargo of lumber for Conyextine & Company Mill at Jacksonville for New York. We got along nicely on this voyage and had a good run out to Jacksonville for summertime for it now was August, 1890. Got there safely, discharged the cargo of salt, and put her at the lumber wharf and began loading the lumber which was all on the dock waiting for us. We put on plenty of help and loaded her in 3 days and left for New York. We made the round trip out and back in 28 days. I paid the crew off for one month. I knew I had made a nice voyage and could afford to be liberal. The mate I was giving $40 per month. He worked hard to forward my interest so I gave him a $100 and made no figure as to what was coming to him. It made him so happy that tears of gladness came in his eyes. I just wish I could always do something to make people happy. But when a man is pinched tight on low freight and continued bad weather, which often prolongs the voyage, he cannot afford to be generous.

After my cargo was out I chartered to take a general cargo to Brunswick, Georgia. After discharging this general cargo I

British steamer VEDAMORE *which Captain* Taws *boarded on December 12, 1898, to replenish his stores after his schooner* CITY OF BALTIMORE *had endured continuous gales while bound from Black River, Jamaica, to Chester, Pennsylvania, with a cargo of fustic.*

*The harbor of Captain Tawes' home town, Crisfield, Maryland. The
schooner at right is the* A. VICTOR NEAL.

*The Windmill Point screw-pile lighthouse, situated in Chesapeake Bay
off the mouth of the Rappahannock River, Virginia, was mentioned by
Captain Tawes in his journals. The lighthouse was dismantled in 1965.*

was to proceed to Darien, Georgia, to load a cargo of lumber for New York. In order to save the pilotage out of Brunswick and into St. Andrews Sound I got a tow boat to tow me through a cut or canal in the land and tow me up to Darien. One of these pilotages each way would have amounted to nearly as much as the tow bill and it was done in half the time and with less than one fourth the labor. Had I sailed from Brunswick to Darien I may have had to gotton her underway 3 or 4 times. But by taking the tow boat pulling in the hawser was the most of our pulling. I well remember towing through a very narrow passage through a low, marshy place.

Just before I took this freight from Darien I had been getting good freights. But about this time a bill was passed in Washington known as the McKinley Bill. As soon as this bill went in force freighting business went all to pieces. I do not know that the McKinley Bill had anything to do with freighting business but I know something seriously happened to the freighting business when it went in force. When I had been getting $8 per thousand on lumber to New York I was now getting $6.37½ which was a big cut.

After I was loaded and got a tow boat to tow me down, and was about ready to leave him, a pilot came on board to take a sail down the river and over the bar at my expense of $44. It gave me great pleasure to tell him I did not come in over the bar at St. Andrews but that I had towed through from Brunswick and I was not subject to take a pilot out. He said, "Yes, I know but I thought by me being on board it would protect your insurance." My second pleasure was to tell him that I did not insure my vessel that way; that I was insured whether a pilot was on board or not. Tow boats usually stand in with the pilots in these southern waters and will not tow your vessel unless a pilot is on board. But this tow boat captain never said a word but took my hawser and towed me down the river and out to sea without a question about the pilot. This certainly made me happy for I never like to pay for a service that I did not require. I got to New York safely, discharged my cargo, loaded a general cargo for Jacksonville, discharged, and loaded a cargo of lumber for Baltimore. Arrived in Baltimore on the 17th day of January, 1891, six days from Jacksonville. Not so bad for a winter passage. Docked her on January 28 for painting and general overhauling. Launched from the ways on February 3, finished caulking top sides on February 6. On the 11th of February finished loading a cargo of coal for San Juan, Porto Rico.

On the 14th sailed from Baltimore for San Juan, Porto Rico and we arrived on the 5th day of March, 1891, after having many storms and adversities. Had one sailor on board which gave me lots of trouble from time to time. One night in a gale of wind, in hauling down the flying jib, he cursed the mate. I called him to account about cursing the mate and he gave me the same kind impudence. We then clinched and began to scuffle. He being a big fellow was getting very much the best of me when the steward, Bert Adams, ran out of the galley and hit him with something which he did not seem to mind. Then the mate hit him with a belaying pin which stunned him. He then asked for mercy which I granted on condition that he would behave himself for the balance of the voyage and do his work which he promised to do. And he did the balance of the voyage. I never had to speak ugly to him any more and all the remainder of the crew did much better than they did before. I thought what a treat to have such a good crew. Porto Rico belonged to Spain then. Had I reported him to the American consul, whose name was Stewart, from Mathews County, Virginia, I am sure he would have discharged him as a bad character. But I could not see the use of discharging a well behaved, orderly man. But I afterward learned my mistake, which I will relate later.

I tried my best to get a load of sugar or molasses for New York, Philadelphia, or Boston. And after laying there a few days trying I thought I would go light to Jacksonville, Florida, and load a cargo of lumber for south of Hatteras. I got along nicely, arrived at Mayport, and left the ship there. Took the train and went up to Jacksonville to enter the ship. There was a colored collector there by the name of Lee. I had with me all the necessary papers for entering but Mr. Lee was the most precise collector I had ever met. He says to me, "Captain, where is your foreign clearance?" I said to him, "I do not know." He says, "I cannot enter your vessel until you produce it and if you fail to produce it I shall have to fine you $500." I said, "Mr. Lee, I have entered from foreign ports in about all the custom houses on the coast from Boston to New Orleans and you are the first collector that ever asked me for a foreign clearance." He said, "That is the law." He read it to me and said he would have to enforce it.

Now I had to have my vessel entered in 48 hours or I would still be fined $500 in accordance with our marine laws. It looked like this colored collector was going to catch me for a fine anyhow. I had remembered seeing this Spanish clearance knocking around in the cabin just before I arrived at Mayport. I found the train was leaving that evening for Mayport and I just barely had time to catch the train and get back to Mayport. When I got there I found the mate had let the vessel drag on shore that day with the big anchor on the bow. I could not help asking him what he thought I carried that anchor for. I looked around the cabbin that night and to my joy I found this Spanish clearance. And I worked the most of the night getting the vessel off on the high water. We got her off and anchored her in the stream. I may have rested 2 hours that night. I am sure not more. Got my breakfast next morning and caught the train in time to go up to Jacksonville and enter in the 48 hours that the government allows. I made a point to always keep the foreign clearance ever after and I may say here to surprise of my relatives and that this was just the beginning of my trouble in this voyage.

I chartered to go up to Jacksonville and load lumber for Baltimore. When I got up to Jacksonville this half-Indian from Gay Head, Massachusetts, had me arrested. The United States Court was then in session. They put me under a $500 fine which John G. Christopher, a merchant there, stood for me. I employed a lawyer, Messr. A. W. Cockrell & Son. He said to me, "Captain, I will do my best for you but you are now in the hands of the Philistines." He said, "Look here at this photographed letter." This letter was written by the U. S. Marshal to the different postmasters throughout the northern district of Florida for them to name the Republicans that they might know as they wanted to draw them to serve as jurors in the United States Court. He says, "Captain, this is contrary to law. So you see what we are up against." Under the Republican administration the district attorney was a white man. I cannot say more of him. I never liked him afterwards. He put a colored jury on to try me and Mr. Cockrell would challenge 3 of them. He would put 3 more colored men on and the case went against me and cost me heavily. I never had my feelings hurt so bad in all my life. I could stand before Mr. Lee and take the oath on entering and clearing my vessel without much regard for his color because I knew I was doing it before or in regard to our Stars and Stripes. But this jury got me. I have some good Republican friends that I like ever so much and would be willing to do anything for them in reason. But I wish they would never ask me to vote for them. I paid my fine and court cost. And when I was through Mr. Cockrell said to me, "Now, Captain, get your cook away. They are going to arrest him." It was then late in the evening, I would say sundown, when I got out of the court house. I told Bert not to come to the vessel since they were going to arrest him but to go some where and board until I was loaded. I would pay for it.

My vessel laid about 2½ miles down the river below Jacksonville at the time. I went down on board and I might say all broken hearted. I had not been on board but a short time before Bert came on board. I must say I almost felt mad at him for coming on board for I had just runed the gauntlet of the U. S. Court and I had enough of it to last me my life. Bert had only been on board about 20 minutes when here came two marshals on board. I was in the cabin and heard them ask for him. I said, "Bert, they are after you." I said, "Hide here under my berth." I then went to the cabin door. They said to me, "Captain, where is the cook? I have a citation for him." I said, "I left him up in Jacksonville." They said, "He is here for the people up here in the saw mill saw him pass through." They said, "Give us a lantern so we can find him." I said, "I will not." Then they replied, "I will arrest you again if you do not give us a lantern." I said, "Arrest all you please but no lantern." Some stayed on board while the others went up in the saw mill to borrow a lantern. No one there would let them have one. Well, I thought, the world is not altogether against me even if Ben Harrison is President of the United States as they could get no help around the saw mill.

This saw mill was runed by George A. Decotts, a very noted and honest gentleman who would not uphold such indignities. At this writing he has long ago gone to his reward. One of them drove back to Jacksonville to get a lantern. The other stayed on board to keep watch. After a little I sliped below. I was so well used to the cabin I could get around in it about as well in the dark as lighted. I got back in the after cabin. I said in a low voice to Bert, "I am sorry you did not take my advice. This is going to give me a lot of trouble." He said to me, "Captain, one of those forward steps to the entrance in the forward cabin is loose. The nails have rusted by so much exposure to salt water. If you can manage to get that step up I can crawl in there and hide." He was a small fellow and could get in so I managed to get the marshal away up forward to feel the sail cover and the foresail to see if he was there. He felt the sail cover and I left him for a minute up forward and I went down the forward cabin as a pretext of some kind, probably to get a drink of water. And coming out I took the loose step off and went forward to join the marshal.

In 2 or 3 minutes I heard Bert get in the steps. Now this step had to go on again. It was not long before I formed an excuse to go back in the cabin. In coming up I placed the step in its place. So now I felt at ease. I had him hid in good shape. Then in a short while I said to the marshal, "It is getting late. It is nearly 11 o'clock. You want to go home and I want to go to bed. I will no longer be contrary. You may have a lantern and look where you like." So I lighted a lantern and he looked all over the ship to his satisfaction. And when the other marshal came back from Jacksonville he said to him, "We may as well go home. I have searched the ship all over and he is not here."

After these two U. S. Marshals had gone it became apparent that I must do something with Bert. It would not do to let him stay on the vessel as the stevedores and others of the crew would report him. And I would have another court case on my hands to defend. I called Bert out from under the steps and discussed the matter with him. He was now beginning to view this matter seriously. Something had to be done. I had had all of this U. S. Court I wanted. I was filled up, even gorged.

Now there was living on the other side of the St. Johns River a man by the name of Thomas Cook. I used to carry to Baltimore very often 50 or 100 bags of roots to make medicine of. I have forgotten the name of this root. He told me he married a Miss Waters from around Princess Anne, Maryland. They were nice people, reliable and obliging. I had only been to his house about twice in my life. So I said, "Bert, there is a man living across the river that I know and I will take you over there if I can find his house."

It was now midnight and we put off in my small boat and rowed across the river to just about where I thought he lived. Every home on this side of the river had little wharfs built out 40 or 50 feet from the shore to where their boats would have sufficient water to float on low water. Mango trees would be growing thickly on each side of these landings and it was pretty hard for me to tell exactly which was Mr. Cook's wharf. But I was pretty certain I could tell his house when I saw it. After getting across the river I stoped at one of these wharfs. I said to Bert, "I will stop here. You stay in the boat and I will walk up and look at the house and see if it is his. If so, I will come back and let you know."

It seemed in those days I never feared danger. But I took the risk to be shot at or being eat up by dogs. I walked all around this man's house, looked at it in good shape, and concluded it was not Mr. Cook's. I came back to the boat and told Bert it was not Mr. Cook's house. So we droped down the river further passing very close to the mango trees so as not to miss the next wharf as it was very dark. Finally, we came upon another boat landing extending away out in the water. I said, "Bert, we will tie up here until I go up and take a look." I walked around this house taking a big chance to be shot or eat up by bad dogs, but it happened I never heard a bark at neither house. After looking at this last house I went up to I fully decided this was Mr. Cook's so I began to holler for Mr. Cook. The old gentleman answered and came out in his nightgown, all white looking like a ghost, and says, "Who is this calling me out such a time of night?" I said, "Mr. Cook, this is Captain L. S. Tawes of the schooner *City of Baltimore*. I have just runed the gauntlet of the U. S. Court of here to Jacksonville and I got beat all to a frazil. Now they are after my steward. I have come over here to see if you would not keep him for a few days until I finish loading. I am sure he will be safe here with you and Mrs. Cook." This old gentleman had been to sea himself. He used to go as supercargo of ships trading around Cape Horn away back in '49 when the California gold fever was on. He knew how to sympathise with me and he readily took Bert in and kept him for me until I was loaded.

I never got back to the vessel until 4 o'clock in the morning. I was all raw sitting so long and rowing this boat so much that night. I was nearly wore out and very much unfit for a hard day's work which was now before me, such as looking after the stevedores loading the ship and trying to get a full crew of seamen to go with me when I was ready to tow down the river.

Now the next question was how am I to get Bert on board without some of the crew finding it out for in those days Jacksonville was a barred harbor, and I have laid at Mayport as much as 20 days at one time waiting for a full tide to get to sea. And besides it took one high water to get down the river and another full tide to get across the bar and out to sea. So I told Capt. Montcalm Broward, the captain of the tug that was to tow me down, where my steward was stopping. So after I was loaded and cleared from the custom house, and was ready to go down the river, he told me to go over to Mr. Cook's in my small boat. He would slow down when abreast of Mr. Cook's and for me to bring him on board his tow boat and he would take care of him until we could get to sea. I may as well add here that a strange man wanted to go down the river as passenger on Captain Broward's boat. The *Kate Spencer* was the name of the tow boat that did most of the towing on the St. Johns River at this time. Captain Broward felt a little suspicious of this fellow being deputised as a marshal. So he said to this fellow, as he afterwards told me, "Now I do not mind carrying you down to Mayport but there is one thing I want to know. Are you in anyway connected with this U. S. Court now in session at Jacksonville?" The fellow said he was not. Well he said, "You may go down with me on those conditions, but I will warn you right here if you are connected with court now in session, and you give me any trouble, you will remember Montcalm Broward all the days of your life." Captain Broward was a big, strong man physically able to punish most any man. He was a gentleman, every inch of him, and fearless. He ran the Cuban blockade during the Cuban-Spanish war in a boat called the *Three Friends* built, I believe, for the purpose. He got in close quarters with a Spanish man-of-war one night on the coast of Cuba and when the Spanish man-of-war got to firing at him to stop or heave to he opened fire at the man-of-war and made his escape.

He had a brother, by name Napoleon Broward. He was also a steamboat man but after he became Governor of Florida he had the *Kate Spencer* built and ran her as a passenger boat between Jacksonville and Mayport. She was a boat of a good lot of power. I got him to tow me once from Jacksonville down to Wilson & Hunting's saw mill, a distance of about 4 miles. When we got clear of the wharfs in Jacksonville he let her go down the river at full speed. I was fastened alongside of him. I knew he was not used to towing vessels and I did not want my vessel tore up. So when we were in about a mile of the saw mill where I was going I just said to him a matter of precaution, "Captain, how far do you think my vessel would carry you now if you were to stop and reverse your engines full speed?" He said, "You would almost stop instantly. This boat has the power." I said, "She will carry you half a mile." He said, "No." There was another old steamboat captain on board who was of the same opinion as Captain Napoleon.

I had in 180 thousand feet of green lumber and with that weight, and the weight of the vessel, I was sure he could not hold or check my headway as he thought he could. So I said, "Just slow her down to half speed, please. I am afraid you cannot hold her." He cut her down half speed, as I asked him to do, and when he went back on her the *Baltimore* just went on and on. There was a schooner laying at the wharf by the name of *St. John,* from Belfast, Maine. I saw we would have to go up in her stern and tear her up so we had to run into the wharf. It came near breaking two planks in the *Baltimore.* I hated this so bad to have these scars in a new vessel. He felt a little bad over it himself. The last time I saw him he made a speech in the big Plant Hotel at Tampa on the 4th day of July, 1904, just 20 years after. He was then a candidate for Governor, was elected, and served as Governor. He died October 1, 1915. He did everything from boyhood up. He cooked on tow boats and worked up to master. He worked in a log camp as a youth, fished on the banks of Newfoundland, and coasted in sailing vessels on our coast. When he was through making his campaign speech in the Plant Hotel at Tampa I went up and shook hands with him. I said, "You do not remember me do you?" But he did. He told some of his friends that were with him that he put me side of a saw mill wharf in Jacksonville and that I was terribly worried because a little paint got rubbed off the ship's side. Florida lost a good citizen when this man passed but he was nominated for U. S. Senate at the time of his death and would have been elected had he lived.

I must now go back to towing down the river. It would be about 8 PM when the tow boat would be passing abreast of Mr. Cook's home and it was dark. The mate was in charge of my vessel and Captain Broward was towing her down on a 50-fathom hawser. This would place the tow boat 300 feet ahead of the *City of Baltimore.* I was watching for him and when I saw his lights up the river coming down I and Bert got in my same dinghy that I took him over the river in. And when Captain Broward slowed down I put Bert on board of him. It was dark and none of my crew saw this. Then I dropped astern, threw my painter on the vessel, jumped on board, dropped my boat astern, and we proceeded down the river under full speed. Got to Mayport safely some time that night. We had to lay at Mayport two days waiting for a good high tide to get over the bar. When the tide was right to go to sea Captain Broward came alongside, put Bert on board, got our hawser, and as soon as we hove up our anchor towed us out to sea. The crew were all greatly surprised to see Bert come on board from off the tow boat. Now we are out to sea and thankful to be clear of the United States Court for the northern district of Florida.

I said I would never go to Jacksonville again. And I did keep my word except on two occasions. On arrival in Baltimore, after discharging my cargo of lumber, I chartered to Lord & Height to load cooperage for Mayaguez and Ponce, Porto Rico. I had just had the vessel recaulked and she appeared as tight as a jug. But the caulkers neglected to caulk at the forward end of the centerboard well where the white pine wedge comes up in the king post. Harry Skinner raked about all the loose oakum out of this place with his pen knife and said, "There is a place needs caulking." He told the boss caulker about it. But anyhow this place was not caulked.

It seems everything went bad while loading this cargo of hoops, heads, and staves. While loading, Mr. Edward Height, the charterer, dropped dead and his successor cleared me for Ponce first instead of Mayaguez. And in the meantime I had a negro cook arrested for stealing my pistol some two or three years before and I had to be up to the police court under a fine of $500. I was never so sorry in my life for having him arrested. It took up so much of my valuable time. The vessel was now at Locust Point loading. No one knew what trim she should be in but myself and I had to wait in this court so long I was just really on nettles to get away and be on board. And then it seems I had to appear in court again as this case was now before the grand jury. I was on pins and needles. I could not keep still and I would ask the policeman every little while how long before my case is called. He would say to be patient and it will be called in a short while. I walked to and fro. I could not keep still. So in order not to have to come back to court again I was determined to evade the evidence I had against this negro, Ed West by name.

I had all the evidence necessary to convict him. It was like this. I was laying up the Frederick Street dock, Baltimore, loading for Jacksonville with general cargo, when Captain Jim Cris Nelson came up from Crisfield with a load of canned goods. He was with Jack Ward in the schooner *Jacob Barnes*. Jack had a lot of young people with him as passengers and crew. I knew, or thought, Captain Jim would like to be separated from them so I told him I was going down home that night on the steamer and to come on board of my vessel and eat and sleep. I had splendid accomodations on board of my vessel and I wanted to make Captain Jim Cris comfortable. Chris Woodland was then my mate. I had this pistol under the pillow in my stateroom. I went home and when I got back I said to Mr. Woodland, "Where is the cook?" He said, "He has been arrested for drawing a pistol on a woman. He is now in jail." "Well," I said, "I will go up and get him out." Chris said, "You don't need that fellow. When you left he piled his supper dishes in the dish basket and left them in the middle of the cabbin floor." "Oh, well," I said, "if that is the case he may stay there. I do not need a man like that." I shipped another cook, loaded, and cleared for Jacksonville. Somewhere between Body Island and Cape Hatteras, on my way down to Jacksonville, I looked under my pillow and my pistol was gone. I knew immediately that Ed West stole her. If I had given all the circumstance to the foreman of this Grand Jury a bill would have been found and I would have had to appear in court again. But I was determined to get rid of the case. When the foreman of the Grand Jury read the warrant he said to me, "Now, Captain Tawes, please relate the evidence you have in this case." I said, "Sir, I left my vessel to go home to stay 2 or 3 days and when I returned my pistol was gone and I sincerely believe he stole her." He replied, "You believe he stole her. Would you have a man arrested because you believe he stole?" I said, "Yes sir." "Well," he said, "that will do. You may go." Which I was happy to do.

I got over to Locust Point just in time to do some little arranging of the cargo and she got loaded all in good sailing trim. Now the first cargo I took in was to be landed at Mayaguez. The last half was to be landed at Ponce. In clearing the vessel Mr. Height's successor cleared me for Ponce which turned out to be wrong as the case will show for itself later.

VIII

1892–1893

I THINK I left Baltimore the 2nd day of January, 1892. When we got to sea I took a heavy gale of wind from the southeast and when it shifted to the northwest I carried rather too much sail on, and in driving her head on in this old southeast head sea she began to leak. I always had her pump tried every night at 8 o'clock, leak or not leak. We were now getting in fine weather, fresh northeast winds and going like a scared runaway horse. And at this particular night at 8 o'clock we tried the pumps. The crew pumped and pumped. No suck. I was in the cabbin and I began to feel shaky for if there is anything disagreeable to my ears is to hear a pump going and not getting a suck. So after about an hour I went forward, drew the box on the forward pump, and sounded. It wet the line up so far I could not tell how much water she had in her. So I got me a long pole and ran it down in her and when I measured it I found she had 47 inches of water in her hold. I went to the mate and said to him in almost a whisper, or I believe I took him forward where the crew could not hear me, and I said to him, "Did you pump her out good last night?" He said, "I certainly did." He asked, "Why?" "Well," I said, "if you did a plank has droped off of her. She now has 47 inches of water in her with all the pumping that has been done." I was very much worried. I did not know what to do. I went below and looked

[222]

at the chart. I found Bermuda laid northeast of me about 200 miles and with a fresh northeast wind it would take 4 days to get there. Nassau laid about 400 miles to the westward of me so I said to him, "We had better go to Nassau to save the ship and cargo, and possibly ourselves." He said, "Captain, I believe we can keep her pumped out. Anyhow, let us pump all night tonight and see how it looks in the morning." He was a very game mate and a worthy, hard working man. So we pumped all night and I let her go on her course. I steered her all night and the mate and men pumped all night and by the dawn of day the next morning we had her sucked out. I got the steward out, Walter Barnes by name, a Kent County young man, and put him to cooking a midnight dinner. All the crew worked willingly and faithfully. I then ordered all ship duty suspended with so that the crew should have nothing more to do than to keep the ship pumped out by pumping every two hours and steer and keep the sails in trim. With all this trouble and anxiety I had a splendid run out to Ponce in 12 days.

But it seems our trouble was yet existing. Now all the Ponce cargo was at the bottom and the Mayaguez cargo on top. It was taken in last. I got extra help and piled the Mayaguez cargo in high piles on the deck to get the Ponce cargo. There being no wharfs in neither of these two ports, all the cargo had to be loaded in lighters. This was in 1892 and I found the same conditions existed when I took a trip in a steamer around the island there years ago in one of the A. H. Bull steamers, 1925. When we had got the cargo out of the fore hatch down to the keelson a sailor I had, by name Tim, hollered on deck to me and said, "Captain, I have found the leak." I looked and there it was pouring in at the forward end of the centerboard well where Harry Skinner had picked it out with his pen knife. This sailor Tim, being a handy man with a caulking iron and caulking mallet, jumped on deck, got these tools, and in five minutes the good ship *City of Baltimore* was tight as a jug. Thus ended the pumping.

After turning the Mayaguez cargo over and over and piling it in different piles we finished discharging the Ponce cargo and got the Mayaguez cargo restowed in the ship's hold. We cleared and sailed for Mayaguez. On arrival I entered at the custom house, got a permit, and began unloading in lighters. I must here state that we had some molasses shooks and heads which were stowed under deck as these are such a fine quality of staves and heads they had to be stowed under deck where they could keep dry. Now these molasses shooks and heads were to go to a colored cooper there although my consignee there was a very nice white gentleman by name of Bravo. When I got down to the molasses shooks a great many of them had rotted from the excessive heat in the hold where they had got wet. Some of them were in excellent order where they were piled high up toward the deck. I did not know this Mr. Molina at all. So one evening when I went on shore with a lighter load of cargo I met him. He came up to me and said, "Your ship is no good. She leaks. Look at my shooks here all rotten." He kicked a bundle of them and they all fell to pieces. I said to him, "She does not leak at all. I will stay on shore tonight and you may go out to her. Stay on board tonight or you may send two of any of your most reliable men and stay tonight and if you find the vessel leaks two buckets of water tonight I will give you $25." I said to him, "Do you expect a cargo shipped on a ship's deck and come across the Gulf Stream in the dead of winter to come out here perfectly dry?" All the time the cargo that was on deck, although all full of Gulf weed or Saragossa weed where the seas had been runing over so in the heavy winter gales I experienced on the way out, were as bright and nice as the day they came on board in Baltimore because they were in the air and not closed up tight. I did not want this leak to be reported on me as it would be detrimental to me in getting a cargo of sugar back to the United States. The insurance company might raize the insurance rate or refuse to insure at all.

After I got my cargo out and went to Mr. Bravo to collect my freight he said to me, "Captain, you will have to extend your protest." Now I had to use some diplomacy to keep from doing this as every insurance company in the United States and Europe would know it and my vessel would get a bad reputation from carrying dry and perishable cargo and the cargoes which the most money is in for high freights. Now I said, "Mr. Bravo, what is the use to put me to the expense of extending my protest? (The cost of extending a protest was $10 in those days.) I am sure you do not have a general average insurance. This cargo was all a wood cargo and you only have a total loss insurance." He says, "Captain, I believe you are right." I did not have to extend my protest. I settled up with him and sailed the next day for Mayaguez on the south side of Cuba and loaded sugar and cleared for Sandy Hook for orders.

It was now early in March and we had usual March weather. I remember I had a strong southwest wind and driving for Sandy Hook. It was a clear day and Sunday. The sun shone brightly. I had my position nicely both lattitude and longitude. I remember at noon I was about in the lattitude of Cape Henry, though well offshore, when about 4 o'clock in the afternoon a heavy gale struck me from the northeast. It was a terrible storm. Having my position so nicely I knew exactly how Cape Henry bore and I bore away for the Chesapeake. About ten o'clock that night I made both lights at Cape Charles and Cape Henry. It was blowing so hard that no pilots were out. They had gone to harbor. In those days I was a good pilot on the Chesapeake Bay and its approaches so I had no trouble. I ran her into Hampton Roads and came to anchor under Sewell's Point in a good harbor which far exceeded being at sea laying to in a hard northeast gale.

Next morning I looked as far as I could up along the Buckroe shore to see if I could see a bay freighter coming down. I soon saw one coming down running under foresail. I was pretty sure he was bound to Norfolk. This was very shortly after breakfast. I dressed myself up in my go-ashore clothes, put on my oil coat, southwester' hat, and rubber boots. I took my good hat and shoes under my oil coat, lowered the boat, got 4 men in her, and when this bay schooner was nearing us we put off for him. When he got in speaking distance I asked him where he was bound. He said, "To Norfolk." I asked him if he would take me up with him. He said, "Yes." He rounded his schooner up to the wind. My crew put me on board. I then pulled off my oil coat, southwester', and boots and threw them in the yawl boat. Then I told my crew to meet me at Old Point that night about 8 o'clock. It was blowing hard and it did not take long to get up to Norfolk. I then went to a telegraph office and I particularly asked them if I could send a message to New York privately as I did not want anyone to know it. I did not tell them the reason which was I did not want the Virginia pilots to know I was in the Roads. I thought to get my orders and sail the next morning before they found out I was from a foreign port. I wanted to save the pilotage out which would have been $40. I wired to New York to the sugar broker I was to report to and told him I was in Hampton Roads. I asked him if he would give me my orders. I went back to the telegraph office and to my surprise and joy there was a telegram with orders to proceed to Philadelphia and report to the Franklin Sugar Refinery. This saved me from going to Sandy Hook which would have taken a week to go there and back to the Delaware.

I thought to go to sea the next morning, but the weather got worse instead of better and I had to lay in the Roads for a week. Chris Woodland was out in all this long storm and had to abandon his vessel, the *Lewis Ehrman*. She was loaded with Orchilla guano, a very mean and unsafe cargo. It is very heavy

and fine like flour and soaks or absorbs every drop of water
that touches it which ladens the vessel more and more every
day she is at sea.

I knew the *New York Herald* would soon report me in the
Roads bound to Philadelphia. After being in there 2 days
there came the pilot boat. The wind was light and the current
so strong, it being a sail boat, he could not work up against the
tide. When he made his first tack alongside of us he hailed
like a roaring lion, "Hello, board the *City of Baltimore.*" I was
down the cabin sewing, making hatch cloths. I said to all,
"Keep below. Don't answer him." He tacked off and tacked
back and hailed again. When he tacked back he was too far off.
The strong tide had carried him far away. This was on Tuesday.
Thursday it was snowing and blowing a strong breeze. He
could stem the tide this time. He tacked up alongside and
hailed. I was eating dinner. I said, "Keep below, boys, don't
anyone answer him." It was only a few minutes and he was
along side and hailed again. He said, "What's matter on that
City of Baltimore? Are you all deaf on board of her?" This
time I had to come out. He said to me, "Captain, where are
you bound?" I said, "To Philadelphia." He said, "Will you have
a pilot?" I said, "Man, it is not fit to go to sea now." North-
easterly weather and snowing, the barometer was falling. He
knew the wind would be to the westward tomorrow and clear
up and so did I. But I was not taking him on board. Sometime
that night the wind came out from the northwest and freezing
like every thing. I began getting underway before light. I
broke my anchor out before it was good and light and out the
Roads the *City of Baltimore* moved. I never saw any more of
the pilot and if he came out he found, as an old sailor saying,
that we had "paid him off with the jib halliards." Of course,
by the laws of Virginia, I owed this pilot bill. But I never
thought compulsory pilotage was a just law and escaped it
whenever I could.

I went out of the capes and had strong northwest winds up the beach to the Delaware capes. I guess the Delaware pilots thought I was a coaster as they never spoke me and I did not seek them either. So I got in the Delaware capes without a pilot. I saved two pilotages on this cargo, one at the Chesapeake and one at the Delaware. I thought I would freeze to death beating up the Delaware. It seemed to me I never saw it so cold. The wind was yet blowing from the northwest and the tacks were so short I did not have time to go below and warm myself. When I got up as far as Bombay Hook, and saw the land covered with snow, I could easily realize how those northwest winds should be so cold, they coming down the Delaware from off those snow covered lands. After I got up above the Pea Patch I took a tow boat and towed up to the Franklin Sugar Refinery, docked and discharged. It seemed that the marine insurance company heard about this leak from one of their representatives, an old worn-out shipmaster usually. They found the cargo of sugar going out dry and in good condition and were well pleased.

When the cargo of sugar was out I chartered to load coal for Cienfugos and a cargo of sugar back to Delaware Breakwater for orders. After we got loaded with a cargo of coal we towed down to Chester, anchored, and filled our water out of the river. We carried about 1,600 gallons. We got everything ready for sea. There was a Portland schooner going to Cienfugos and he sailed 6 hours ahead of me. I forget what kind of weather we had on the passage out but I do know we went into Cienfugos side by side after a passage of 17 days.

While lying at the wharf there discharging, our crew went ashore on Sunday with the crew of a Delaware vessel laying close to us on the opposite. It was a very long wharf and a railroad track was laid on it. Vessels discharged their cargo in the cars on this wharf. When Sunday came work was suspended and these two crews of Yankee blood thought they would go on shore and take the city, expecially when they got well stimulated with the red essence of sugar cane. I think it was about two o'clock in the afternoon I heard shooting. The police were chasing our crews down this long wharf. The Delaware captain said to me, "There falls one of your men." The fellow soon righted himself and came running toward our vessels. It seemed the fellow got his foot in a broken plank in the wharf. He was not hit with a bullet. My crew jumped on board and hid themselves down in the vessel's hold. Also did the crew of the Delaware vessel. By the time my crew had been down in the hold the chief policeman and four or five others started to jump over the rail of the vessel. I ran to the rail and shook my head and said, "No, no," and then I pointed my hand to the American flag flying at the mizzin topmast head. When he saw that flag he backed down and never came on board. I wanted my crew to help discharge cargo the next day and I had them too. I will here relate it is the custom to fly the national insign every Sunday when laying in a foreign port. Old Glory was a power in those days. I think since World War I she is twice the power and is recognized by all the nations of the earth. We got our cargo out, loaded sugar, went to Delaware Breakwater for orders, was ordered to Philadelphia, and discharged.

This was 1892. It was real hard times. Harrison was President and there was a panic on. I laid over to Coopers Point a month and nothing to do. I remember Captain Jim Conwell and Captain Jim Fisher, both Delaware sea captains, coming on board to spend an evening with me. I was getting worried having nothing to do. I happened to say to them, "These are hard times. I don't know what will become of me." Jim Fisher, an always cheerful man, said to me, "Why, Tawes, cheer up. Never let nobody know you are poor. Let them find that out themselves." I got tired and took a run home. I saw L.E.P. Dennis and he chartered me to come to Crisfield and take a full cargo of fish scrap to Jacksonville, Florida, at $2 per ton. When I was getting under way to leave Philadelphia for Crisfield some two or three captains standing on their vessel's decks hailed and asked me where I was going. I told them I was going to Crisfield to load fish scrap for Jacksonville. They said, "How in the world did you find that? We have been laying here 2 months and wired and wrote from one end of this country to the other and found nothing."

I came to Crisfield and all the dry scrap I could get in her was 257 tons and this by lowering two big water casks down in the hold and rolling them over each tier of sacks as they were stowed. These casks held 165 gallons of water each. When the cargo was on board she was very much down by the head and out of trim for sailing. I ask Benson Dennis to let me have a few empty sacks to fill up with sand to put on her stern to trim her. I did not think it would take more than one and a half dozen. But we had to fill 70 sacks with sand and carry them on board before we had her in trim. Old Island, the place we lay, was then and is today noted for its beautiful white sand. When we were loaded Mr. Dennis' fish boat, under the command of Capt. Wash Milligan, towed us out in Tangier Sound. We lay there at anchor getting the vessel ready and waiting for a fair wind.

In a day or two we got a strong northwest wind and left about 9 or 10 in the morning part of the day. When we broke out the anchor and filled away she went down Tangier Sound as fast as any sailing vessel ever went. We runed down as far as Cape Henry and finding the weather unfit to go to sea I turned and headed her for New Point. I came to anchor quite a while before night with New Point Lighthouse bearing east. I saw a schooner that looked very much like the *J. S. Hoskins*, Captain Bennett in command, but he lay so far out I was not sure. Shortly there came a canoe out the creek, Pepper Creek by name. He had in oysters, eggs, and vegetables to sell. I bought some of the oysters of him. Then he wanted to get to this other vessel to sell some of his oysters and vegetables. But he was rather afraid to risk it. I said, "Captain, I will go with you." I wanted to see what vessel it was anyhow and in those days I seldom saw danger. So I jumped down in his boat and went out to the schooner with him and when I got near to her to my surprise and joy it was the *J. S. Hoskins*. Captain Bennett was glad to see me and prevailed on me to stop and take supper with him saying he would put me on board of my vessel at bed time. I asked the New Pointer if he needed my company to go back with him. He said he could get along alright alone and was not afraid. I told him he would have no northwester or offshore wind before he could reach his home and he went away satisfied. Bennett was quite surprised to find I could run in so far under the land. I stayed with Bennett, got supper, and we talked over many different things. And at bed time he put me on board.

The next morning when I turned out lo and behold here was Captain Woodland in the schooner *H. S. Lanfair* at anchor. He came in sometime that night. Now here was Bennett bound to Savannah, Captain Woodland and myself bound to Jacksonville. "Ugh," I said to myself, "there is going to be something doing now to see who gets there first." I think this was a Friday morning. On Sunday morning we all three got under way and started for Cape Henry. In about two hours after we got underway I had the lead. About 1 PM there came a bad squall and rain, bad looking weather. We all turned back for New Point. Captain Woodland came to anchor about a quarter of a mile up ahead of me and Captain Bennett came to anchor about a quarter of a mile below me. After supper Captain Woodland came alongside of me in his yawl to spend the evening. Now I said, "I would be mighty glad to have you on board but how about us droping down on board of Bennett and all three spend the evening together." Captain

Woodland says, "That is a fine suggestion." So I jumped in his boat and we went on board of Bennett. Now Captain Woodland prided himself as having the fastest vessel that sailed the coast. Captain Thom Bartlett of Belfast, Maine, told a yarn one time in Jacksonville that the *Lanfair* went by him so fast one time that his mate said to him, "Captain Bartlett, there is a pretty shot, ain't it? Look at that bird flying astern of the *Lanfair*." Bartlett said he looked and it was the log. The *Lanfair* was going so fast that the log was not touching the water but flying in the air. Captain Bartlett was always a joky kind of a skipper.

After spending the evening on board of Bennett, and we were about leaving to go on board, Captain Woodland began clearing his throat. "Ugh, ugh, ugh," he said, "my vessel is foul. I have not had her out since April." It was now September. I began to nudge Bennett with my leg. It was dark and he could not see. I did this to call Bennett's attention that Captain Woodland was worrying. He was afraid I was going to beat him. We bid Bennett "Good night." He put me on board of my vessel, bid me "Good night," and went on board of his.

The next morning Captain Woodland got underway and broke anchor first. Bennett was next, and I the next. Now we were strung along in a row steering for Cape Henry. Before we had got as far as York Spit I came upon Bennett. I hailed him and said to him, "Bennett, your vessel looks beautiful this morning. Why she looks so nice she reminds me of a young girl dressed going to church." "Well," he said, "she has got to set in a back pew." I went by Captain Bennett and in a couple of hours I picked up Captain Woodland and went by him. Now I was in the lead for Cape Henry.

We had the wind from the southwest, pretty and clear weather. I presume I was 4 or 5 miles in the lead and nearly down to Cape Henry. I was setting in the cabbin door reading. I happened to look astern and lo and behold the wind had struck from the northwest blowing a storm. They had their topsails clewed up and their lower sails across the deck on the starboard side while I still had the wind from the southwest, which was not to last long. I jumped to my feet and ordered the fore topsail, the main topsail, clewed up quick. I did not succeed in getting them clewed up before I had the shift of wind. Now my fore and main topsails were to the windward of the spring stays which made them very difficult to handle. However, after a while we got them clewed up sufficient to tie up and all the other light sails furled. Now we were sailing along very fast. Bennett and Captain Woodland behind me were coming with great white waves under their bows.

It was now Monday noon and we all passed out of Cape Henry almost together. I may have passed out the capes 3 or 4 miles ahead of them. The *Baltimore* now seemed to be doing her best yet I wanted her to move so I said to the mate, "Mr. Cosden, I think she will bear the fore topsail. Don't you think you can hoist it over the spring stay furled and set it?" He said, "I think so." This man seldom if ever said no to anything I wished done. He got at it, hoisted it over the spring stay in a bunch, loosened it, and set it. She seemed to bear this so nicely I said to get the main topsail over the stays in the same way and set it. She seemed to bear this sail nicely. I said get the mizzin topsail over and set it. She seemed to behave nicely under the three topsails. Now I said, "Give her the outer jib." Now she was all dressed up and flying apparently.

I looked astern to see what my friends were doing. They had as yet made no more sail but they saw how nicely I was gliding full-dressed. They could not stand it any longer so they dressed their vessels up with all light sails. It was a pretty sight to look at. Three beautiful three-mast schooners just flying down the Carolina beach.

There was no lightship off the Diamond Shoals in those days. Just the lighthouse on the shore from which you had to get your bearings and judge your distance. I was always afraid to get too close to the beach at night. Captain Woodland ran close to the Diamond Shoals while I kept further out. In this way he made up all he lost to me that day and the next morning he was one mile ahead of me. But at noon I made up this mile and was one mile ahead of him. Bennett was all out of sight and could no longer be seen astern.

That afternoon it blew strong from the northeast. I was running boomed out under foresail and mainsail and fore and main topsails set. Captain Woodland took his topsails in about the middle of the afternoon. I kept mine on her when daylight went down. I was so far ahead of him that his fore and main booms were below the horison.

The weather was then looking awful ugly. The sky had a tinge of red and blue. It was now hurrycane season and I really thought one might be brewing. I wanted to pretend to Captain Woodland that I was going to carry those topsails all-night; but to tell the truth I had no idea of such a thing. I was real anxious to see dark come. I wanted to shorten sail badly but I did not want him to see me. But when dark came I took those topsails in and my foresail too. I was now under cautious sail but yet going very fast.

About 2 AM I was off Fernandina Lighthouse which is about 20 miles north of St. Johns River Light. So I hove to and laid by the wind off and on until daylight when it got so I could see good. I went aloft and I looked toward the northeast to see if I could see Captain Woodland coming but he was no where to be seen on the horison. I then kept off and runed down to St. Johns Bar and laid to for a pilot. After I laid there about 3 hours here came the *Lanfair*. I sailed in over the bar and anchored at Mayport. Captain Woodland took the tow boat and towed in to Mayport. They put his hawser to my

stern as a matter of precaution. I was drawing less water than
he.

There were then many shoals in the river at this time. So
they towed me up ahead of him and in case my vessel took the
bottom he could not come up and damage me. He would take
the bottom first. After his line was gotton to my stern we hove
short and gave the tow boats our line. We then broke our
anchor out and proceeded to tow up the river. We had these
70 sacks of sand on the stern that we took on at Crisfield.
John Woodland, Capt. Carneal's son who was mate with his
father, said, "Look, look younder, Pa, Captain Tawes has
taken a lot of his cargo out of the hold and piled it on the stern
to trim her." Now we left Cape Henry Monday noon. We
were in Jacksonville quite sometime before Thursday noon. I
moored in the dock stern up where the Clyde Line steamers lay.
Captain Woodland came to anchor in the stream.

We went up to Ellis & Hussey store where all the captains
meet and buy their stores also. Here we met a lot of Delaware
and Jersey captains. We all knew one another in those days.
Some down-easters used to trade there too. What I mean by
down-easters, vessels belonging in the New England states; all
old traders to Jacksonville. Pretty soon some of these captains
said, "You must have had a good run down did you not?"
One said to Captain Woodland, "Carneal, when did you come
out of the capes?" He said, "Monday noon." They said, "You
certainly had a beautiful and speedy run down." Another said,
"Tawes, when did you come out of the Capes." I said, "Monday noon." They said, "Good God, you fellows had a race.
Who beat? Who got to the bar first?" I said, "I hove to off
Fernandina Light at 2 o'clock this morning." Captain Woodland said, "I saw you when you hove to." I said, "You did?
You can see well for a man of your age. As soon as it
got light I went aloft to look for you. And I could not see you
anywhere on the horison." These skippers began teasing him

about telling me I beat him. Then he told them that I took a lot of my cargo out of the hold and piled it on the stern to trim her for sailing and with all this earnest zeal I was entitled to some honors. I thought the joke was such a nice one I never corrected it. I let it go that way.

We stayed in the store until about noon. It was getting time for dinner. I said, "Your vessel is in the stream. I am laying in the dock. You come on board with me and get dinner." Now as I was laying in the dock stern up we had to climb on board over this sand. He stepped on it and said, "This is not cargo. What is this? Is it sand?" I said, "Yes, that was such a good joke when you told those skippers in the store that I had taken my cargo out of the hold and put it on deck I would not correct it." He said, "Did you have this on board when we were under New Point?" I said, "I did. I put it on board at Crisfield to trim her."

After we got our cargo out I chartered to John G. Christopher to load a cargo of lumber to got out to Mayaguez, Porto Rico, at $7 per thousand. So I lost no time. I loaded and cleared and I was consigned to the same house that I was consigned to about a year before when I was loaded with cooperage from Baltimore. It was Bravo & Company, good people all right.

While I was there they had an election in our country. There were two other American captains there, one from Maine. The other was Andy Hubbard; both Republicans. I was a Democrat and of course I was in favor of Cleveland. Mr. Bravo told me he had a son in New York and had advised him to cable him one word if Cleveland was elected. His son cabled him this one word and Mr. Bravo told me. I went on board and dressed my vessel up in all her colors and came ashore. These fellows said to me, "Mr. Tawes, what are you doing with all your flags set?" I said, "In honor of Grover Cleveland; he is elected." They said, "How do you know?" "Well," I said, "I am sure he is elected. Instinct tells me that."

I would not tell them what Mr. Bravo told me as he requested I should not. "Well," they said, "you being so sure you got your choice of presidents you ought to treat." I said, "I will."

This same old colored cooper, who said my vessel leaked and caused his molasses shooks to rot about a year before, was along with us. He was a rich old fellow and associated mostly with the white people. He led us in a very choice and up to date restaurant and after the four of us got seated I said, "Gentlemen, what will you have?" Mr. Molina said, "I will take champagne." I said, "Not on me. I will set up anything in the house you may choose to drink except champagne." Mr. Molina said to me, "After getting your choice of presidents you refuse to treat to champagne?" "I do," I said.

We stayed in this restaurant rather long and there came up a squall. The mate did not take these flags in and they got blowed to pieces badly. I was put to it to know how to get my flags repaired. I had a Mexican working on board and he told me an old lady lived close to him who had two girls that were very handy with the needle and he was sure they would repair my flags for me. So one evening I took the flags ashore and to their house, being guided by Peter. The young ladies put my flags in nice order for me and their charges were very reasonable. When I went ashore after the flags Andy Hubbard was along. Andy suggested sending out and getting some cake and wine and treating them. After drinking wine and eating the cake they began to entertain us with their Spanish songs. We spent a splendid evening there but on leaving the old lady said she would like to come on board and see the ship. I told them through Peter, the interpreter, I would be glad to have them and said that when it suited I would come on shore for them.

I had a splendid steward by the name of Walter Barnes. I told him we were going to have company for supper and to get up a nice one, which he did, I went ashore after them in my big yawl. Andy was with me and got some wine and brought it on board with us. I think Andy got some whisky and mixed it in the wine to make them happy. They sang their Spanish songs and entertained us nicely until time to go on shore and home.

Two or three days after this Andy gave a supper and we all met again on board of him and we spent another pleasant evening. These were real pretty girls and Andy was making love to one of them. I left Andy there as Mr. Molina was going to load him with a cargo of coconuts for New York. Molina told Andy after he got up to his loading port, which was open to northers, that he had better get under way and go to sea for 2 or 3 days as a norther was coming. Andy knew his dodge. He did not have the coconuts hulled and ready and he knew if Andy was away his lay days were not counting. He wanted to save $30 a day of demurrage for 3 or 4 days which would give him time to get the coconuts hulled and ready to go on board. Andy told him when that anchor was broke out all the cargo would be on board and he would collect all the demurrage due.

Andy told me all about this when I met him in Baltimore some months afterward. He also told me that as he was about leaving the mother of these girls asked him when he was going to marry her daughter. He told her just as soon as he got his share of his father's estate, that his father was a very rich man. When he died he left in his will that his estate should not be divided until the younger was grown which was then only five years of age.

I was in Mayaguez in 1925, 33 years afterward. I went to see Peter and he was glad to see me. He had lost his old squaw by death and had married again. I asked him what had become of the two girls. They had married and were doing well.

From Mayaguez I went to Orchilla to load guano for Baltimore. The island was then governed by Captain Rivers who used to sail out of Baltimore in the South American and West Indian trade. He had about 50 men on the island working under him gathering the guano out of the crevices of the rocks with large spoons. It took quite a lot of food to feed these men and he kept two men fishing every day to keep them in fish. And he usually sent out in the harbor after me to come on shore and have a fish supper with him. Fresh fish is a nice change when one has been living quite some time on salt beef and pork. Capt. Rivers knew this from his past experience in life having been so many years at sea himself. He had his son Will on the island with him.

I may add, at this time of the year, November, they usually had the "roughs." The "roughs" at this season of the year was a long, heavy sea rolling in the harbor from the sea. All other seasons it was smooth in the harbor. It was now the "roughs" were on. So much so that they could not lighter the cargo out to me. About 4 o'clock in the evening Will came after me to go on shore to get a fish supper. He came after me in a rudely constructed flat bottom boat that he built himself. She was square at the stern and sharp at the bow. While Will was rowing the boat toward the shore he faced me. I was sitting in the stern of the boat. He was not particularly noticing which way he was rowing. I could see he was rowing toward the eastern or outer point. I thought he was rowing that way to get to the windward and then row up the shore line to the wharfs.

We were very busy talking about Demerara. He had been there quite a few voyages with his father in the brig *Stephen Bishop*. Pretty soon I noticed the sea about breaking outside of us. I said, "Will, you better keep her out in deeper water. If you do not we will get in the breakers." He said, "I thought I was rowing up to our landing. I never noticed I was rowing over toward this east point. I will get her away from here because sharks are real thick here. Why they even come up to our landing and eat the fish heads and bones where they clean the fish."

About this time I looked to the starboard and sure enough there comes a great white breaker. Will threw her stern to it. It hit us in the stern of this rudely constructed boat and knocked me at a flying speed right by Will over the bow. It turned the skiff bottom up with me underneath of her. I sounded but could not touch bottom. I looked for Will but could not see him and concluded he was under the boat. I held onto the boat with one hand and runed the other under the boat and pulled Will out. The next big wave came and shot us inshore in a double quick speed. I sounded with my feet though I expected to loose both of them having just heard such a fearful shark story. But to my joy I touched bottom and they were both on me. The next, or third, breaker hove us up to the beach. I let go the boat and hurried for the dry land. I lost my hat and slippers and they were never found. Captain Rivers saw our misfortune from his house. He sent a squad of men down there to get the boat up on the beach and render any help we might need. When I got up to the house Will let me have a suit of his clothes to put on. I wrung mine out and hung them on a line and had supper. Then Captain Rivers and I swopped sea stories and our experiences until nine o'clock when my boat came after me. I went to get my clothes off the line and to my surprise the trade wind they have there had dried them even though it was night. So I took Will's clothes off and put mine on and went on board.

One more noticeable thing as regards Captain Rivers which I must mention and may be beneficial to some people if they try it. I saw something white on his head one day and said, "Captain Rivers, what is that you got on your head?" He said, "Salt." I said, "Why do you put salt on your head?" He said, "My hair got to coming out and I thought salt would stop it." He said, "I never saw a bald headed man in my life who

Captain A. Anderson who relieved Captain Tawes on the CITY OF BALTIMORE *for a voyage in September 1899.*

A scene re-enacted many times by Captain Taves. This view depicts the services of the pilot boat RELIEF, *built in 1891 as the first steam pilot boat of the Virginia Pilot Association and active during Captain Taves' period, being refused by Captain George H. Hopkins, at left, as his four-masted schooner* DORIS HAMLIN *entered the Virginia capes on January 6, 1937.*

always went to sea. Now I do not mean those who go to sea just a while and stop and go again for a month or two. I mean regular seafaring men." I do not know whether there is much in it or not. I went to sea for 35 years. I am now 76 years old and have a good head of hair and not much tinged with gray even.

After loading nearly 500 tons of guano, which was on the 6th day of December, 1892, Wednesday, the 7th of December, we sailed for Baltimore. There being no customs house here, or any government officials, there was no clearing to be done. Signing of bills of lading was all that was required. We had a rough and stormy voyage home. I ran down on the south side of Cuba, came around Cape Antone, up the Yucatan Channel, and up through the Florida Straits. From there to the capes of the Chesapeake we had no more good weather.

Just north of Jupiter we encountered high seas. About 5 minutes of 12 midnight we lost our fore topmast. I must say it was carelessness on my part as about at this time she began to plunge hard in a head sea. I thought it would be such a short time before 12 midnight when the watches would be changed. All hands would then be on deck and with the taking in of the jib topsail by all hands the job would be done so easy. But 5 minutes before 12 away with the fore topmast which surely did give everybody on board a job. Now the jib topsail was overboard full of water. The topmast and all of the stays hung from the jib boom to way abaft of the fore rigging. It was a bad mess. I had to heave to and lay to the wind until we got the rigging and jib topsail on board. The topmast being so heavy we could not get it on board. So we lifted the rigging off it and let it go to Father Neptune.

We followed the Gulf Stream up and when nearly in the latitude of Cape Hatteras we experienced a heavy northwest wind which kept us in the Gulf Stream. It was so cold that the vapor would rise off of this warm Stream water and form many remarkable scenes. Sometime you would see a great forest rise up with all the shape of large trees. Then in a few minutes this forestry would disappear and a great city would appear. Then this scene would disappear and in its place a thousand water spouts would appear. About this time your heart got to pulsating to its highest. These water spouts would disappear and in their place large, staunch full-rigged ships would appear to be runing directly head on for us. These imaginary scenes would appear and disappear as long as we would be in the Gulf Stream and these strong northwest gales would blow. All it was vapor or steam rising from this warm water. When the big seas would break they would emit great volumes of steam.

Sometimes the man on the lookout would holler out, "There is a big ship on the starboard bow, sir." I would start to run forward to see. And about this time this big phantom ship would break into fragments. But one evening about 4 o'clock I looked to the windward of me and above the top of the vapor I saw a royal and topgallant yard heading right for us close to. Shortly I saw it was a real barkentine. There was no phantom in this ship. She was a real ship. He scared me terribly for I thought he would sure run over us. But he just cleared our stern nicely and quickly disappeared from sight through the mist.

During this cold northwest wind we could not obtain an observation although the sun would be out clear and bright. But the horizon would be obscured. I was keeping dead reckoning as best I could but I knew the Gulf Stream was carrying us to the northeast as the Stream runs in that direction in the lattitude of Cape Hatteras. And that took us more and more from the land. I thought if I could only obtain an observation to find my position. The vessel had been laying to for 3 or 4 days and nights under storm trysail, reefed mainsail, and fore staysail. All this time we were shipping big quantities of water, decks continually full, and some of it was getting in the hold.

And Orchilla guano is fine like flour and all the water that got on it the guano would take it in like a sponge and never went to the pumps. This of course caused her to become deeper and deeper laden and I was sure if I did not soon get her in she would become unmanageable or sink. One or the other.

All this time the sea was high and water warm which caused all this vapor to rise. I had began to think if we did not soon get an easterly to drive us toward the land the Stream would take us up to the Georges Banks. I went down the hold one day to take a look with a lantern in hand. I walked around on the guano and I could see drops of water in different places in her decks falling on the guano. This gave me a lonesome feeling for all the water droped on this guano made her less seaworthy.

At last, on a Christmas Day it was, this old northwester wore out. The sea was high and we were rolling heavy. Clouds began to rise in the northeast. I saw a change was coming which I was real glad to see. Just after dinner we wore her head to the westward and put the foresail on her. This foresail was heavily soaked in water and hard to hoist. We had no power on board, all pulling was done with hand. The long looked for northeaster was on us with much rain falling. I steered on a west course as by my dead reckoning and judgement Cape Henry bore that course. Though I knew it was a long way west of us I runed her all the afternoon under full foresail, reefed mainsail, reefed spanker, fore staysail, and jib. I was in an awful hurry to get her out of the Stream and far enough to the westward to be in cold water when the wind came to the northwest again which would surely follow the northeaster.

As night came on it got to blowing real heavy. I had to take my spanker in and foresail too. Also the jib. Now the sea began to get real heavy. I was on deck all night. The next morning, when the steward brought me a cup of coffee, I would not dare to leave the deck to drink it. I just stood on the poop deck and drank it amid the rain, the wind, and spray. The sea was now getting so bad and boarding her so heavily that I had to keep her off 2 points, west northwest. The sea would come over the weather rail, run across the deck, hit the lee bulwark, and go fifteen ratlines high in the lee rigging. I was worrying. I thought I would have to heave her to again and that would mean when the wind came out to the northwest again to clear up I would still be in the Gulf Stream and in the rising vapor and no observation to obtain my position. Presently, the Stream seemed so choppy that I must be approaching the western edge of it. It is always rougher on the western edge than in the center of it. I was still undecided whether to heave her to or keep runing.

I felt so bad, my old flannel shirt all ringing wet, that I said to the mate, "Mr. Cosden, you just look out for her until I run below and put on a dry shirt." I hated to leave the decks for a moment, but down I went. I pulled off my oil coat, under coat, and vest. Then I took off the old water-soaked shirt and put a dry one on. Then I thought of a case of brandy that Mr. Bravo gave me in Mayaguez. I pulled this case of brandy out from under the berth, got a hatchet, and broke it open. It had been on board of me for six weeks and I had not even sampled it. I never was much of a drinker in my life which was the one particular reason this case of brandy went so long undisturbed. I took out a bottle and in my haste I got back on deck again. About half way thinking that this case of brandy would never be used anyhow I just grabed a case knife out of the pantry and broke the head of the bottle off. I took a good drink of it. It was good liquor too. I put the broken bottle back in the case and went on deck. In about 5 or 10 minutes I concluded that the *Baltimore* was making much better weather and I just there and then gave up the idea of heaving her to. And I did not heave her to either.

I had a sailor on board by name Bill Hopkins. Bill had a pair of rubber boots with the heel off. I did not know this until I was getting well up in the northern lattitudes. One very cool day he put these boots on and I saw the heel off. I felt real angry with him when I saw it. "Now," I said, "that is a pretty nice pair of boots to come in on the coast with in the winter time. Why didn't you let me know you had no boots? I would have bought you a pair. Now I am going to warn you if you lay up a day on our way home I will dock you wages for everyday you lay up." Bill was a good sailor and never laid up a day. I used him for my thermometer. The decks were full of water and that night I was runing to the westward. In a while I would say, "Bill, is the water getting cold any yet?" He would tell me , "No, sir, the water is yet warm." I would then know I was yet in the Stream and a long way from the coast.

Just after taking the drink of brandy the ocean was feather-white with breakers. I did not know what to think. I might be approaching Hatteras Shoals it looked so bad. I guess it was when about 8 o'clock in the morning I said, "Get up the deep sea lead and we'll get a sounding." We took the lead forward to the bows and I rounded the ship to the wind. About the time I thought her headway was sufficiently slowed down I yelled to them forward to heave. I had a man in midships to hold the slack of the line and as soon as it tightened with no bottom he sang out to the mate aft, "Watch and watch," and he let go the line. The mate let the line run through his hand until sixty fathoms run out. I said to the mate, "Mr. Cosden, did you get bottom?" He said that he did. I said, "If you did we will all be drowned in two hours."

The Gulf Stream runs so close to Hatteras and we were yet in the Stream which I knew by the current and the way the sea was runing. I had my doubts about his getting bottom and I could not be satisfied until I took a sounding myself. I told the crew to take the lead forward again. I then kept her off and got headway and rounded her up to the wind again. As soon as I thought her headway was sufficiently dulled I passed the word forward to heave. So over went this 28-pound lead again. By the time it tightened in the man's hand amidship he hollered out, "Watch and watch," and he let go. It then came to my hand away aft to where I was standing. As soon as it tightened in my hand I payed out the line just as fast as the lead would sink. Finally, 60 fathoms run out and no bottom. I knew then I was still in the Gulf Stream. We filled her away and steered a west northwest course. We were shipping big seas over our decks and even threatening to wash our water tanks and casks overboard from their lashings. But with all this danger and hazard she must get to the westward out of the Stream before the wind shifted to northwest, which it invariably does in the winter to clear off. About 10 AM I hove to and sounded. Let 60 fathoms of line run out and no bottom. At noon the sea was not so bad as at 10 o'clock which indicated we were getting to the westward of the strong current of the Gulf Stream. I hove her to and sounded. Let 60 fathoms of line out and no bottom. The rain all this time was falling in torrents and had been doing so since the evening before. I was so thankful she was making better weather, for to have laid her to so far out in the Stream would have meant the loss of the ship and all hands. The dry shirt and drink of brandy I took this morning gave me the courage to run her in such desperate weather. Thousands of tons of water boarded us during this forenoon. At 4 PM I hove her up and sounded again and yet got no soundings. But we were now out of the Stream for Bill Hopkins said the water was now very cold. At 8 o'clock that night I sounded again. We got soundings in 50 fathoms of water. I kept her off and ran her until 10 o'clock that night. I sounded and got 25 fathoms of water. I set her storm trysail in the mizzin and hove her to on the starboard tack for the night.

I had been on deck all night and all this day until now, 10 o'clock tonight. I felt tired though the excitement of the night and day seemed to keep me strong. But now I was all in. I told the watches to keep a good lookout and now, having a fine position, I went below and turned in. I was sure I had plenty of room to drift safely all night, believing to be 25 miles from the land. I went to bed just contented as anyone could imagine. The *Baltimore* was as sweet a vessel for laying to as any that sailed to make her living. The rain water pouring down out of that trysail just over my head soothed me in a deep, refreshing sleep.

The next morning the wind shifted to the northwest. As soon as the wiry edge of this northwester had blown off I took in the storm trysail and tacked in for the land. At noon I got the sun which I was so glad to get. Her altitude put me in lattitude 36° 22', just 34 miles south of Cape Henry. I kept her on the inshore tack and a little while before dark there was my native land in sight of me. I then tacked to the north and at 2 o'clock the next morning I was up to Cape Henry. The moon was shining brightly, the wind moderate, and sea smooth. The pilot hailed me and said, "Hello, on board the *City of Baltimore.*" I said, "Hello." He said, "Heave to. I will put a pilot on board of you." I hove my vessel to and went below and got three $5 gold pieces, put them in my pocket, and met the pilot at the gangway. When he came alongside I said, "Pilot, here are $15. Take this and let me off. I am sure you had rather stay down here and get a deep draft ship that will pay you a handsome figure." He said, "Captain, I cannot accept this." I said to him, "What terms will you accept and let me off?" He said, "The full pilotage." I said, "You may come on board." He was still in his small boarding boat. I remarked, "I cannot pay a man full price and do his work." He said, "Why, of course not." He was very polite about it. He came on board and took charge. Had it not been Christmas week I beleive I could have bought him off for $20 but he just wanted to get home for the occasion. I conversed with him about the long northwest gales we had been having and a few other things in general. And then I went below and turned in and slept until 7 o'clock and sought a much needed rest.

I washed and had breakfast and then I looked out for her and told him to go below and rest. The wind was moderate and we were proceeding slowly up the bay. After dinner I laid down and the pilot took charge. About 3 PM Sunday I came on deck. The wind had breezed up from the southeast and it was a little foggy. The breeze was freshening and the *Baltimore* had begun to move up the bay a little swiftly. Finally, I see the pilot looking anxiously around to the west northwest. I said, "Pilot, what are you looking for?" He said, "Smith Point." If my memory serves me correctly the Government had a lightship anchored there, the ice having sometime previously to this carried the lighthouse away. However, in a short while between us, we made the lightship. When abreast of her I saw the weather was going to set in thick. I set my log at Smith Point and put her out. After 3 or 4 hours he said, "Everyone be attentive and listen to see if we cannot hear the bell on Cove Point." I listened. So did he. And not the sound of a bell could we hear. Finally, I walked to the stern to look at the log. I saw it registered 35 miles which put us 3 miles past Cove Point. I said, "Pilot, we will not hear Cove Point bell." He said, "How do you know? You seem to be so positive about it." "Well," I said, "I put my log out at Smith Point and it registers 35 miles which is 3 miles above Cove Point." We let her go right on through the thickness of the fog until dark and then between the fog and darkness we could not see from forward to aft. I feared we would have a collision with some other ship. I said, "Pilot, we must bring

this ship to anchor." So I ordered the helm to the starboard
to bring the ship up under the western shore to shoal our water
and get out of the track of the steamers. I had the lead in
hand and was sounding. I wanted to get in 5 or 6 fathoms
of water and anchor. But he was so scared of us runing
ashore that I had to bring her to and anchor in 9 fathoms of
water. I said, "Pilot, we are in the middle of the bay." He
said, "No, we are real close to the land."

The next morning the wind was blowing strong from the
northwest and clear. There we were in the middle of the bay,
sea rough, and the anchor hard to heave up. But after a lot of
hard labor we got her hove short, got her underway, and
proceeded up the bay. In those days I never took a tow boat
below Sandy Point. If one ever came alongside and you gave
him any inducement at all he would never leave but follow
you all the way up the bay. So when we go up abreast of
Sharps Island one of Pat Dougherty's tow boats came alongside and says, "Captain Tawes, would you like to tow up?" I
said, "No." "Well," he said, "there is lots of ice up the bay
further and you might get stuck in it." "Oh, well," I said,
"there may be enough to make a julep." Then the pilot broke
in and said, "You are mighty decided about not taking a tow."
I said, "Yes, I don't want to have him following us all the way
up the bay. No other tow boat will ever come to us as long as
he is alongside." The pilot was much dissatisfied because I did
not take the first boat that spoke to us. He wanted to get to
Baltimore before the Christmas holidays were over. No blame
to him for that but the expense of this pleasure was coming
out of me. He was real anxious for me to take a tow.

When we got up to Annapolis the strong puffs coming out of
the Severn River blew my flying jib away. We saved what we
could of what was left of it and kept going. When we got a
little above the Magothy River, and the waters of the Patapsco
River began to show up, the pilot said, "Look there Captain,

see the Patapsco how full of ice it is." "Yes," I said, "pilot, that sure looks bad. But we can run up to it and not in it to get fast. If we find it too heavy we can turn around and go back to Annapolis Roads and anchor." If I had hit him between the two eyes he would not have gotten mader. So on we sailed and presently the sun went in the clouds and then showed the beautiful, clear water of the Patapsco with not a speck of ice in it. I said, "Pilot, look at the river now. It looks like a different river altogether." He said, "Yes."

With this strong northwest wind we could not head up the river any further than the Seven Foot Knoll. One of Pat Dougherty's tow boats came up to me and said, "Captain, would you like to tow up?" I said, "Yes, what are you going to charge me?" He said, "Thirty dollars." I said, "No." He said, "What do you expect to pay?" I said, "The clear water rate, $15.00." So off he went. It was very cold and with night coming on the pilot was real anxious to get home. The tow boat turned and headed for Baltimore. The pilot let his wrath out on me. He said, "You are incapable of sailing a vessel. Don't you know if the winds come around to the northeast tonight you will be carried ashore on the Bodkin Bar?" I said, "And don't you know as soon as I am reported there will be a tow boat here tomorrow morning to tow me up for $10?" He said, "Haul down the jibs and we will come to anchor." By the time I got the jibs down the tow boat turned around and came back to me and said, "Give me your line." I said, "How is that, pilot? It does not pay to give all they ask." I paid him the regular rate and we came to anchor that night in Canton Hollow at 9 o'clock. The anchor was so frozen on the bow that we had lots of trouble getting it broken so we could get it overboard. The pilot was not long in asking me to set him ashore. If I had a home in Baltimore I expect I would have been in just as big a hurry. He probably had been away from his home not exceeding a week. I had not seen my family for more than 3 months.

The next morning Captain Bennett came alongside and said to me, "Tawes, did you leave any guano in Orchilla? You look so deeply laden. You must have all from the island on board." I got up in Frederick dock to discharge the cargo. Then came a big freeze, a terrible freeze. Some vessels down the bay inbound had no provisions on board and they suffered before they could get to Baltimore.

While lying in this dock waiting for a thaw there came on board a West India man by the name Percival Dorsett. He wanted to charter me to go out to Rum Key, a small Bahama island. I was to take out some general cargo and some machinery for ginning out sisal, a kind of long fibre for making second class rope. I was to take Mr. Dorsett out, and an engineer, free. I may as well say that Mr. Dorsett being a stranger to me, though he talked like a money man, I required him to put the amount of my charter, $1,250, in the Continental National Bank to be paid to me when I returned and discharged the cargo of salt. And a good thing I did or I beleive I should have got nothing for making the voyage. I never got out of Baltimore until about the 9th or the 13th of February, 1893. Was in Baltimore about a month and half. Mr. Dorsett got tired waiting and went to New York and took the steamer for his home.

We had quite a long passage out, meeting with adverse winds. The island was small, principally inhabited by colored people. The only whites were Mr. Percival Dorsett, his sister, and father who was a Justice of the Peace. I wish I could describe the inhabitants of the island properly. It would make anyone laugh. I laid to anchor in the harbor called Port Nelson and ferried our cargo ashore in small boats. I was worried to know how I would get this engine and boiler on shore. They had no lighters and their boats were small. But I conceived the idea at last. I had some heavy planks on board that I used to secure my deck loads of lumber when I was carrying lumber. They were 3 inches by 10 inches by 33 feet long. I took 3 of these planks and laid them across 2 of these largest boats and lashed them good to both of these boats, which made a kind of catamaran. Then with my hoisting winch I lifted the boiler from the deck and gently laid it on these 3 planks. It loaded these two boat's gunwales to the water. I was glad when these boats got to the beach safely. Then I had to get the bed plates ashore the same way. They had to get them up on the island by hand. I do not remember seeing a horse or oxen on the island. They cleared away a place on a small square by cutting down the bushes and small trees and after getting all the parts of the machinery set up, and steam up, the chief blew his whistle, something the natives had never heard before. Of about 200 standing around they began to run and got tangled up in the bushes they had cut down and fell over the top of one another. The machinery was working well before I left and was getting out lots of sisal. I brought some of the samples to Baltimore with me.

I do not remember anything unusual happening on our way home. More than the usual reefing, steering, keeping her pumped, and keeping a good lookout which we always did, good weather and bad, until we got north of Hatteras. Here we got a severe norther which lasted two days and was very cold. Then it breezed up from the southeast and began to blow a smart breeze. At 8 o'clock in the morning we were, as I judged, in the lattitude of Body Island which lays in 35° 49', about 70 miles from Cape Henry. The second mate came on deck to take his watch and said to me, "Captain, we are going to have snow." I said, "No, we are not." He said, "I can feel it in the air." I could not beleive it and the *Baltimore* was sliping along so nicely I just let her go. At about noon the wind began to cant to the east and freshen up and the snow was sure falling. Finally, it canted to east northeast and blew hard. At 2 PM I was getting well up to Cape Henry as I was pretty sure though

I had seen no land since I left the West Indies. But I had a good observation of the sun the day before and I knew pretty well where I was. I knew I could not be far from Cape Henry. I laid her to for a while to see if I could hear the whistle on Cape Henry, and I could hear nothing. I now began to feel sorry I did not listen to Mr. Clark and get her offshore that morning while the wind was southeast. But now it was too late. The wind was blowing harder or increasing all the time and the sea was getting larger and larger all the time. I went down the cabin and looked at the chart and saw there would be no diference in either tack I put her on. There was no chance to get away from the land.

The mate I had seemed to have very little judgement in a time like this so I called the second mate aft and talked with him a little. Then I said, "Dan, we are not far from Cape Henry and we have got to get in the bay or we will be up in some man's corn field tomorrow morning as the wind is blowing straight in on the land and increasing. My reckoning puts me now right in the lattitude of Cape Henry but there is most always a current setting south along this shore and I beleive I am 5 or 6 miles south of it yet. Now the course up this shore is north northwest and with the wind east northeast we can head up this beach and have one point on the compass to spare for leeway. I am going to let her up to the wind and want you to get all the sheets in by the wind and in good trim for I am going to keep her off and run her for the beach. I want you to go out on the end of the jib boom and watch out for the beach and as soon as you see it I will bring her up on a wind and let her head up the beach. In this way we will be able to see Cape Henry Lighthouse when we get up to it. And we must do this quickly as we only have about 3 more hours of daylight. After it gets dark we will never be able to see it." Poor Dan began to shake in his knees he was so scared. However, we got all the sheets in by the wind. Dan went out on the end

of the high jib boom and I kept her hard off and ran her before
the wind for the beach. A nervy thing to do but this was our
only chance. In a very short while Dan hollered out from the
jib boom, "Breakers on land in sight." I immediately brought
her up on the wind heading north by west. Sure enough there
was the beach close under my lee all white like a clean sheet
spread upon a bridal bed. Now I kept her on the wind just
skining outside of the breakers. Now the most impossible thing
was happening. We were shipping heavy seas over us and
in these rough seas coming over us were lots of shells and pebble
stones, like the masons here in Crisfield mix in cement, washed
up from the bottom by the strong current and breakers. In a
little while I saw we were getting too close to the breakers. I had
to make a short tack off. When I had gotton far enough off I
found an English steamer laying to waiting for it to clear off
so he could get in. When I came around on the starboard tack
and headed up for the cape he followed me and just kept a
little offshore of me. I suppose he thought I was surely going in
the cape though the snow was falling thick and fast. Just before
dark I sure enough made Cape Henry Lighthouse and I do not
know of anything in this world that gave me more releif for
I was now sure of getting in the bay. It was snowing so that
I did not see the lighthouse more than 3 or 4 minutes before it
was out of sight. The steamer followed and got in safely. I
saw him the next day going up the bay.

Now I felt happy to think with this leading breeze I would
get far enough up the bay to make a safe and comfortable
anchorage. But my trials were not over for in a short while,
after passing the cape, the wind canted to the northwest, which
was dead ahead. And I had to beat to the windward. I would
keep her on the starboard tack for just a short while and as I
would think I was getting over close to the Thimble Shoal I
would put her on the port tack. In a short while I would think
I was getting over too close to the Middle Ground as half an

hour would appear like two hours. I did this 3 or 4 times and when I would tack a hogshead of snow would fall out of the leach of the spanker on top of me. I was now getting tired of this job, even sick of it, and was resolved to bring her to anchor as soon as I could find some sticky bottom. I took my 28 lb. lead and in my anxiety I could throw it as easily as I now could throw an 8 lb. lead. Finally, I found some sticky bottom. I ordered the jibs hauled down. Before the jibs were down good I brought her head to. I did not want her to get off from this good holding ground. I went forward and cleared her big anchor and when she got sternway, and everything was clear, I let it go over. And it went clear too. That was my business there; I could not trust anybody to let go that anchor. There was so much depending on it I paid out 50 fathoms of chain and when she came head to that old big anchor clinched her right there. We got all the sails furled but it was blowing so hard we could not get a light to burn in the rigging. I did not worry much about the light not burning for I felt sure nothing would come down the bay to go to sea that night and nothing would come in from the sea. We did not drag our anchor but rolled our rail under all night and kept our deck flooded with water. When I got below and could sit around the stove and get warm, and watch the snow banking up against the two forward windows, I thought how fortunate I was to get in the bay. It appeared like heaven to me in contrast to what it would have been out along the coast had I not got in.

I imagined I had gotten up the bay as far as Back River and sure enough the next day when the weather cleared away Back River bore west. It blew a heavy gale from the northeast two days. Then the wind moderated and I got underway and proceeded up the bay. When I got in Baltimore I found I had done the right thing to have my freight money deposited in the Continental National Bank for there was no one there to represent the cargo. It seems that Mr. Eugene Blake was to store the cargo of salt. He went to the custom house, entered the cargo, paid $1,000 duty, and got a permit to discharge the cargo. I gave him the job of discharging the cargo and paid him for doing so with his own labor. The cargo went direct from the ship's hold into the warehouse. Had the cargo not fallen in the hands of Mr. Blake I do not know how long I would have been detained. Being a man of means he just put the business through without any detention.

When the cargo was out I chartered to take a general cargo to Jacksonville, discharged the cargo, and went up the St. Johns River to Satsuma Heights to load dry cypress for Hodges & Godfrey. I guaranteed to take on board 150 thousand feet on 9 feet of water. They guaranteed the 9 feet of water. When the 150 thousand feet of cypress were in I only drew 8 feet 9 inches. I wired to Jacksonville for the tow boat to come after me. I thought while the tow boat was on her way up the river I would get some sticks and stake the channel off so that Captain Broward would have no trouble or detention when he got up to the vessel. There was plenty of water at the mill which was on a small branch extending in from the main river about half a mile up. But there was a small bar at the mouth of this little river. I went out in my yawl to sound out the best water. Behold, I could only find seven feet of water on this bar. I went back to the mill and said to Hodges, "Look here, where is that 9 feet of water you guaranteed me?" He said, "Captain, it is out there at the mouth of the river." I said, "You had better come out and show me where it is for Captain Broward will be here soon, and I want to have the channel stuck up for him so that I can get away." He came out and we sounded all over this bar. Seven feet was all that could be found. "Well," he said, "Captain, the *Kate Spencer* is a powerful boat and she can jump you over this bar." I said, "Mr. Hodges, that is a big jump—1 foot 9 inches—and I do not beleive that she can do it." "Oh, yes, she can," he said, "for this is a narrow bar only about sixty feet wide. I am sure she can do it."

In a few hours here came Decott's smallest boat, Captain Willie Roberts. This made me feel bad. I told Captain Roberts about this bar and that he had better tow me half a mile up this small river so that he could get a good headway on coming down so as to jump her over this bar. When we got down to it this small boat just got headway enough in the *Baltimore* to get her plumb on the bar. Then we sent for the *Kate Spencer* to come up. Captain Broward tried to jump her over this bar by backing up close to and go ahead at full speed. But the *Baltimore* was fast; she would not move. He broke his 8-inch hawser twice. Then he came around to her stern and tried to pull her back into the small river with no better results. He broke my chocks and cut my stanchions down. Also my davits fell down and the yawl boat fell in the water from off the stern. About this time I was getting sick of this job and I said, "Who is going to pay for these repairs?" Then we gave the job up and went down to Palatka, about 10 miles, to get some lighters to lighten the ship. Mr. Hodges talked very nicely about it. He said, "I will pay you $30 a day for all the time you loose." This agreement was in the charter party anyhow. We got two lighters at Palatka and towed them up to the ship and he took his mill hand and began taking out the cargo. Finally, when enough cargo was out so that Captain Broward could pull her over this bar, he did so. Outside of this bar we began taking the cargo on board again. At about two o'clock in the morning we had it all on board. Mr. Hodges came in the cabbin and called me out. He said, "Captain, there is some of this cargo in the hold not stowed. When you get to Jacksonville hire some stevedores to stow it up and I will pay the bill." We then figured up the demurrage he owed me, which was two days. This was agreeable, but I said, "Mr. Hodges, how about the damage to this vessel's stern? I expect you to pay this." He dimmed on this. I said, "Alright, I will lay in Jacksonville on demurrage until these damages are repaired. Or I can rig her up temporary and go to Baltimore and have these damages repaired while I am discharging and in that case there will be no time lost. No demurrage and the carpenters in Baltimore are practical and will do it in much less time than in Jacksonville." He jumped at the idea and said, "Captain, if you can get to Baltimore the way she now is have her repaired there and send me the bill."

I had her repaired in Baltimore and sent Mr. Hodges the bill several times and never heard from him. I registered him letters. I would only get the return receipt. Some 2 or 3 years after this I happened to be in Jacksonville and I met him in Ellis & Hussey's. When he was on the outside of the store, I did not want to approach him in the presence of the different captains in there, I said to him, "Mr. Hodges, I want to know what you intend to do about that bill for repairs." He said, "Has not that bill been settled yet?" I said, "No, sir." He said, "I am now going down to the Indian River on a business trip and as soon as I return I will look this matter up." I said, "Mr. Hodges, I have written you several times, I have registered letters to you and all I ever got from you has been the receipted register card. Now this thing has got to be cleared up before I leave Jacksonville. If I do not hear from you in 3 days I shall proceed to collect through the court after the third day." Not hearing anything from Hodges & Godfrey I went to the office of A. W. Cockrell & Son and made a complaint. He said, "You can do nothing with that bill. You will have to appear at the court house in this county. And they will have the trial put off from court to court until they wear you out." So I left Mr. Cockrell's office knowing now their reason for not giving me any attention all these 2 or 3 years. After walking about 300 yards down the street it appeared to me that this was a maritime case and could be brought before the U. S. Court. So

I turned around and went back to Mr. Cockrell's office and said to him, "This is no county case. This is a maritime case and should be brought before the U. S. Court." Mr. Cockrell said, "Captain, you are right. This is a U. S. Court case. I will write out a Bill of Complaint for you to sign. I will send the marshal after the both of them and bring them to Jacksonville for a hearing." If I remember, the bill amounted to $130. When the marshal arrived at Satsuma Heights and served the citation, and told them he wanted both of them to accompany him to Jacksonville, they were much surprised. They said, "How much is the bill?" He told them. They said," I will give give you a check." It was much cheaper than closing down the mill to come down to Jacksonville.

I finished loading in Jacksonville and got to Baltimore, discharged, and chartered Tate Muller to take out bread stuff and other miscellaneous cargo to Demerara, British Guiana. While loading cargo in Baltimore I could see my mate was failing in health and I should have advised him to quit and go home to Chestertown, Maryland, where his mother lived. But somehow I hated to do this. He seemed so attached to the vessel. This was a mistake I made which I have always regretted. We loaded and left Baltimore on the 11th day of June, 1893, went out of the capes on the 13th and arrived in Demerara on the 4th day of July, 1893. The mate laid up off duty just 4 days before we arrived in Demerara. We were 17 days from Cape Henry to Demerara which was good passage for summer time.

Just to show how small this world is I will create a little incident that happened. On or about June 16 it was blowing a gale of wind and we were laying to at the time. When just as night was coming on I noticed a full riged ship hove to. He was directly under my lee about 2 miles and I began to feel uncomfortable. This ship was deep and he would not drift to leeward fast as I would as I drew so much less water. So I slacked off my storm trysail sheet, which I always used in heavy gales, kept off, and ran down close in this ship's stern. I waved my hand to the captain. I saw her name was the *Fawn* of New York. I ran down about 2 miles to the leeward of him and rounded up, took my storm trysail sheet in by the wind as I did my mainsail sheet, and I hove to for the night. The next day the ship was out of sight and I never saw her again. About 8 or 10 months after this I was in New York. Just about dark I went across south ferry for Brooklyn. My vessel was lying at Red Hook. I wanted to get on board of her. After getting across the ferry I wanted to get on the street car going to Erie Basin. I got on the car that I suposed was the right one but I was not certain. I happened to get a seat by the side of a great big man. I said to him, "Does this car go to Erie Basin?" He said, "Yes, I am going to Erie Basin." So I then felt quite comfortable. Finally, he said to me, "Have you a vessel at Erie Basin?" I said, "Yes, but I am not in to the dock. My vessel lays at anchor at Red Hook." He said, "What have you got in?" I said, "A cargo of sugar. I am from Guantanamo, Cuba." After a few minutes I said to him, "Have you a ship at Erie Basin?" He said, "Yes, I am master of the ship *Fawn* of New York." I said, "Captain, do you remember ever laying to about one third the way across the Atlantic when a three-mast schooner was laying to windward of you? And he ran down across your stern and to the leeward of you and rounded up and hove to for the night?" He said, "I certainly do."

Now we were strangers no longer and when we got off the street car we stood on the sidewalk and talked for two hours. He wanted to know where I lived. I told him Crisfield, Maryland. He wanted to know if there were many seafaring men here. I told him I was the only one that did not know enough to make a living home in my town. This made the old fellow laugh cheerfully. Then he asked me if I lived in the town. I told him I did not make money enough to live in the town, that I lived just outside of the town in the suburbs where I could count my income whenever I heard a hen cackle. He said, "I expect you have fruit trees." I said, "Yes." "How many kinds have you?", he inquired. I said, "I have apple trees, peach trees, pear trees, and grape arbors." I told him no story for I had from two to three of each kind. But I did not tell him that I bought apples and peaches out of every peddling wagon that come by the house. I guess he thought I had hundreds of them. He said, "Why, you are certainly well off; what do you go to sea for?" I said, "Just to wear out my old clothes." I never learned this old captain's name but he told me he lived in Springfield, Massachusetts. After having a pleasant two hour's chat we separated and I never met him again as many fellows and brothers have done before.

I must now go back to my old ship in Demerara. As soon as I arrived I sent my mate to the hospital. Now, without a mate, I had lots on me to do. Sometimes I would have to be on shore to attend to business and then be back on board. Besides, it was now the rainy season and I had to be there to see that the hatches were put on when these heavy showers came in order to keep the cargo dry. The burden there was heavy but I was young and used to nothing but hard work all my life. When the cargo was out and I collected my freight, got my business fixed up, and was about ready to sail, I went to the hospital to get the mate. The doctor, a very fine English gentleman, told me my mate could not go with me as he was too ill. You may imagine my feelings. I went to his bedside and told him what the doctor said. His feelings could not be imagined by any one to be left in a foreign country among strangers, to get well or to die as the case may be. I can not forget the change in his countenance, the expression on his face and in his eyes when I told him. I told him I would leave all his wages with the American consul which our marine laws compel us to do with seamen left in a foreighn port. I told him that when he wished any to send to the consul and get it. He was now in the consul's charge and he would look after him and pay his bills. I can never forget the looks of his eyes as I got to the head of the stairs ready to go down. He raised up on his bed and took his last look at me.

I was now minus a mate and there was none in Demerara to be had. I shiped a seaman and took a man aft to stand the port watch. It was that or nothing. I sailed from Demerara July 14 for Barbados after being in Demerara 10 days. I was 4 days getting to Barbados. I consigned my vessel to the house of John Decosta. After laying there three days I chartered to go to St. Johns, Antigua. On Saturday, July 22, I sailed from Barbados for St. Johns to load a cargo of sugar for the Delaware Breakwater, U. S. A.

On this run from Barbados there happened one of the most rare coincidences imaginable by mankind. I ran very close to Guadeloupe, or just to the windward of the small island of Petite Terre. I saw from the strong northeast trade wind and high sea there prevailing I could not fetch to the windward of the island of Desirade so I kept off and runed down between Point Chateaux, a point of land extending in an easterly direction from the island of Grande Terre, between this and Desirade. It was now coming on dark and awfully stormy, blowing heavy with much lightening, heavy thunder, and rain. It looked so much like a hurrycane was on hand that I was much alarmed. After being sure I was all clear of the island of Guadeloupe I hove her to for the night under reefed sails. I stood the first watch myself at 12 midnight. I called Peter, the man I had acting as mate, and left him to run the middle watch from midnight until 4 in the morning. I told him to be cautious in watching the weather as it might turn into a hurrycane, this being the mid of the hurrycane season. After giving him all the precautions possible as to runing the watch I went below to stay until 4 AM, if not sooner called. Fortunately, I was not called during my watch below.

At 8 bells I was called. I came on deck and Peter said to me, "Captain, the mate has been on board." I said, "You are a fine fellow to leave in charge of watch, to go to sleep and dream such dreams and tell me about it on such a dark, stormy night as this." He was standing at the wheel steering. My watch had not got on deck as yet to releive him. He said, "Captain, it is an honest fact. He came around on the poop deck here, looked in the binnacle to see how we were steering, went around on the lee side of the poop, and went forward. The other man on the watch forward saw him too." I said, "What time did you see him?" He said, "Shortly after I took this wheel at 2 o'clock and I went forward and asked the other man. He said he saw him. He walked all around the main deck here and then disappeared." I said, "You have been asleep on the watch and dreamed all of this nonsense." He said, "Captain, I have not been asleep. Honestly, I have been awake and have not slept a wink on this watch." I made up my mind they were both mistaken or even worse than that, liars.

It was an awful bad night. The next morning at daylight, at 7 AM, I sighted the island of Antigua bearing northwest by north and kept off it. At 8 AM I set the spanker and flying jib. At 10 AM I got a pilot. At 1:30 PM came to anchor in the harbor off St. Johns, Antigua, furled all sails, and got up tackle ready to take cargo. I had a very quick run from Barbados to Antigua, being only two days. It may seem strange that I should remember these incidents and dates since 1893—it now being 1930-37 years ago. But I am not depending on my memory for I now have the log book spread out before me, the very log I kept myself, being without a mate at the time. And the log I kept I am not ashamed of. I am willing to compare it with any that has been kept by the most practical. I brought all my log books home with me when I sold the *City of Baltimore* in 1904 after being master of her for 20 years, 5 months, and 9 days. I wish I looked them up when I first began this narative for I should have had a more definite system in this writing.

Tuesday, the 25th day of July, we began taking in cargo. I see by the log book we took in 29 hogsheads and 60 barrels of sugar. We loaded and sailed on Saturday, the 5th day of August, 1893, for the Delaware Breakwater. After a passage of 18 days we came to anchor in the Delaware Breakwater. August 22 it was and we escaped a heavy hurrycane. Bursted our foresail on the way in. Had to give her 55 fathoms of chain on the big anchor and 30 fathoms on the small anchor. We laid our lay days out, 6 lay days, and was ordered to Philadelphia. When I got my orders a Delaware Bay pilot came to me and said, "You are going to Philadelphia?" I said, "Yes." He said, "I am your pilot." I said, "You are not. I am not subject to a pilot. I came in the Breakwater without one." He said, "That makes no difference, you are subject to a pilot." I said, "You will have to show me before I take you." It was not long before he brought me the statutes of Delaware. Then, of course, I saw he was right and I was wrong. I said, "Alright, you can come on board tomorrow morning at 7 o'clock. That is when my lay days expire." He said, "I will go off with you when you go." I said, "No, I have my wife and children on board and they are all the company I care for."

There were then 7 or 8 vessels laying in the harbor waiting orders. The captains were all sitting out in front of Frank Maul's ship chandlery store entertaining one another. It was then between 3 and 4 o'clock in the afternoon when one of these ship masters said to me, "You have got orders to go to Philadelphia?" I said, "Yes." One said, "Are you going to tow up?" I said, "No, I have a pilot, and a pilot and tow boat both are too much of a luxury for me. No, sir, I shall sail her up to the Greenwich coal piers before a tow boat gets a line on me if it takes me a week." The pilot was standing by. In a few moments he called me aside and said, "Look here, do you need a pilot?" I said, "When I am coastwise and not subject to pilotage I always sail her up and down the Delaware myself and I cannot see the reason I cannot carry her up the Delaware Bay with a cargo of sugar as well. I can with a cargo of lumber up and a cargo of coal down." He said, "Look here, if I am not on board by 7 o'clock in the morning you get her underway and go on." Sometimes before 6 o'clock in the morning I hove her short and got the sails on her all ready to go. At 7 o'clock I broke out the anchor and proceeded out of the Breakwater. There was no pilot to be seen anywhere. He just thought he would get on board and I would take a tow boat and tow to Philadelphia. He would sit down in a chair, smoke cigars, drink my liquor, make $42 in one day, and not lay his hand to a thing. But the idea of sailing her up the Delaware meant 3 or 4 days and a lot of work, which was not so pleasant. I, for one, cannot see the unreasonableness of using the public's money to build an expensive breakwater there for a haven for shipping and then let Delaware appoint a few of her choice citizens to levy a tax on the ships that use it in foreighn trade. I sailed the *Baltimore* up as far as the 14-foot Bank and took a tow boat and towed to Philadelphia for $30.

When I got to Philadelphia and docked alongside of the sugar house an officer came up to me and said, "I have a warrant for you." I said, "No, you haven't; it's somebody else you are looking for." He said, "Are not you the captain of this vessel?" I said, "Yes." "Well," he said, "you are the man I am after. You come with me to the Board of Health office." I went with him and asked these doctors what I was arrested for. They said, "Did not you take your wife and children on board at the Breakwater?" I said, "Yes." "Well," they remarked, "you have violated a quarantine law. You will now go with us up to the City Hall." I well remember the old quarantine doctor who said to me, "You plead guilty. It will be better for you." They fined me $17. A fellow went my bond and charged me $3. It cost me $20 which the City of Philadelphia, or the State of Pennsylvania, beat me out of and ought to refund me that money with interest for I had passed the United States Government quarantine at the Breakwater which would permit me to go anywhere in the United States without any restrictions as far as quarantine laws are concerned. I then had the doctor OK the certificate of health. But I was so surprised I never thought to put up a fight. Besides, it did not pay me as I wanted to proceed with my work.

A year or so after this I came to the Delaware Breakwater for orders with another cargo of sugar when I was boarded by a U.S. quarantine doctor and he passed me and gave me his certificate of inspection. I said, "Doctor, I have a wife and children living about 60 miles from here and I would like to see them. Can't I send for them and bring them on board?" He said, "Yes." "But," I said, "I might be ordered to Philadelphia and I will be fined if I take them on board." He said, "No, you will not. This bill of health I am giving you is paramount to any state law in the union. You send for them if you wish. I will see that you are protected." It happened that I was ordered to New York. The quarantine physician never looked at any of my crew when I gave him the doctor's certificate from the Breakwater. He just passed me on.

In referring back to my Demerara-Antigua voyage, when I got my cargo of sugar out I went over to Cooper's Point, docked, cleaned her bottom, painted it, and chartered to go to Kings Ferry, Florida, to load lumber for Demerara. While there we had a severe hurrycane. I was consigned to Messrs. Mozelle and Brother. Mighty nice people they were, too. We had an unusual quick run to Fernandina. By the log book I see we were only 4 days. We took a tow boat and towed up the St. Mary's River to Kings Ferry. We loaded in a reasonable time and went down to Fernandina, took on necessary stores, and cleared. Towed out over the bar. Captain Steve Chadwick was master of the tow boat. We had an unusual long and disagreeable passage. We were 34 days as the prevailing winds were east often blowing heavy with a high head sea. Arrived in Demerara on the 17th day of November. As soon as we got the ship safely moored I entered at the custom house and got permit to discharge cargo. I went immediately up to the hospital to inquire for my mate, Mr. Cosden, that I had left there more than three months past. To my sorrow and regret I learned he had passed out on the very day and the very hour that my two men saw him walking around the deck. I am totally unable to account for such a coincidence. I have to leave this to the High Power that can account for all mysteries.

Here, after discharging my cargo of lumber, I chartered through Messrs. Booker Brothers to load sugar for the Delaware Breakwater for orders. We took in a cargo of 4,233 sacks of sugar and sailed Saturday, December 9, 1893, for the Delaware Breakwater. On Friday, the 29th day of December, after a passage of 20 days, we came to anchor in the Breakwater. Another pleasing incident I feel it my duty to relate is that we brought warm weather and a fair wind to the Breakwater. Just as I got to my anchorage every bit of the wind was gone and we never made a fire in the cabin until we came to anchor. The next day the wind was from north northeast and snowing. After quarantine the doctor boarded us and gave me a bill of health. I went on shore and wired to my agent in New York for orders. I also bought a nice turkey from Frank Maul for our New Year's dinner which my steward, Walter Barnes, roasted in prime condition.

IX

1894–1895

JANUARY 1, 1894, I got orders to proceed to Philadelphia. Got there by towing up. Pilots did not bother me this time. I beleive I discharged at the Spreckels Sugar Refinery. January 6, finished discharging sugar. We now chartered to load coal for Guantanamo, Cuba, with sugar back to New York direct. On Wednesday, January 17, cleared from the custom house, got crew and provisions on board, and towed down as far as Chester. Here we filled water casks, caulked hatches, and got the ship cleaned up and ready for sea.

We got underway and sailed down the river. In my company was a schooner towing down. I have forgotton her name but she belonged to Port Jefferson, New York. I saw she had on a deck load of cars and I said to the mate, "That schooner is bound to the West Indies for that cargo of cars was offered me when I was in Philadelphia." I sailed along down the Delaware River about as fast as the tow boat pulled him. Just about at sunset we were down as far as Bombay Hook and he came to anchor. I proceeded down Delaware Bay that night. At about 12 midnight I went out by Cape Henlopen and to sea. This was January 20, 1894. Thursday, February 1, we arrived at Guantanamo, 13 days passage. After I had been there 9 days

I was introduced to Captain George Dayton of the schooner
I remembered seeing when sailing down the Delaware. I said,
"Was that you towing down the Delaware when I was sailing
down?" He said, "Yes." I said, "What kind of a passage did
you have out?" He said, "We had miserable, bad weather with
heavy gales and high seas. It was hard getting along." He said,
"What kind of a passage did you have?" I said, "We had a fine
run down the Delaware that night, passed out to sea a little
after midnight, and we just came right along all the time. We
just took in the light sails and reefed the spanker once." I
said, "Why did not you run down the Delaware the night we
were together?" He said, "My vessel did not steer good and
I was afraid to run down in the night time." That is one thing
my vessel would do. She steered good and with a proper man
at the wheel I never doubted the course I steered. We just
made 9 days by running down the Delaware that night. I
was loaded and on my way toward New York before he got his
cargo out. But we had a long lay here waiting for a berth or
lighters.

I had a very fine consignee at Guantanamo this time, Bueno
by name, which in Spanish means "good." And he certainly
was a good man. I had nine days demurrage due which he
paid promptly without a question. I went up to Guantanamo to
clear, which was 18 miles from where we lay, to unload and
which is Caimanera. This is where we unload and load cargo.
The town is small and is where the stevedores and laboring
people live, principally. Usually, the train goes up in the morning and never goes back in the afternoon. If we clear and want
to go to sea the next morning with the land breeze we have to
get a hand car and pay two men to propel it down to Caimanera. This always cost $5 but on this day when I went into the
office of Mr. Bueno he said, "Captain, there is a train going
down to Caimanera leaving here at two o'clock. I have been to
the American consul's and notified him to get your papers ready

and clear you so you can catch this train. I am working as hard as possible to get bills of lading and manifest ready and, by the way, you have not had your breakfast yet." Spaniards eat their breakfast at 11 o'clock and their dinner at 5 o'clock. I told him I had had no dinner. He said, "I will take you to a restaurant and interpret your orders for you because we have got to hurry to get you cleared and ready to take the 2 o'clock train." So we put off to the restaurant. Getting there he said, "What do you wish to eat?" Now I had been down to Caimanera for more than two weeks living on ship food for there was not much to obtain down there. So I ordered a very extravagant dinner and I asked him if he would not have dinner with me. He said he had not the time to eat. I ordered beef steak, dry rice with curry, eggs, a bottle of Bordeau table wine, cheese, and guava jelly. He said, "When you get through eating come to the office." When I was through I asked in Spanish how much I owed him. He shook his head and said, "Otro hombre paga" which is, "the other man had paid." If I had known he was paying the bill I would not have ordered so much. When I got back to the office he paid me the nine day's demurrage at $35 per day, by indorsing on the bill of lading, which was deducted from the sugar in New York.

On Saturday, the 10th day of March, 1894, at 5 o'clock in the morning, we sailed out with the land breeze and proceeded with all possible haste to New York. On Tuesday, the 27th day of March, after a passage of 17 days, we came to anchor at Red Hook in the harbor of New York. The American Sugar Refinery had very little room for storing sugar so they gave me $20 per day to lay and hold the sugar. This looked good to me with nobody on pay but the mate. I accepted it. I laid at anchor at Red Hook for about two weeks when my good luck came to an end. I chartered to Suzarty and Whitney to take a general cargo out to Maracaibo, Venezuela. They told me there would be no cargo to be put on deck. A broker by the name of Watson was the ship broker in this deal. I had to notify the sugar house people that I was chartered and I would have to have the sugar taken out. The agreement was that they would take it out when I needed the vessel. I had to put the cargo out to a sugar house over in Brooklyn not far from Newtown Creek. I got a tow boat and went to Red Hook after the vessel. When I got on board I told my wife, who was there on board, that I was going to make good money on this voyage. She always looked on the blue side of everything. She said, "You don't know, you have not got it yet." "Why all the hazards of the sea are now overcome. It is just as good as the cash in hand," I remarked.

After we hove up anchor and in towing up through the Buttermilk Channel it came up a gale of wind and began to snow thickly. The tow boat was put to it to take care of us and in docking at the sugar pier we went head on into a Nova Scotian schooner amidships. We broke out our bowsprit, jib boom, and fore topmast. Our bob-chain just slid right up on him and he being light just laid over to us. As luck would have it we did him very little damage. The end of my jib boom fell end on in his waterways on the other side opposite from us and made a round hole like a cannon ball had been fired in it. Then we fell alongside of him sort of wrecked up. I thought I would freeze to death before I got all the wreckage on board such as the broken jib boom, the jibs, and the heavy chains hanging to it. When I got the wreckage on board and the vessel well secured I went on board of the Nova Scotianman and told him I would pay his damages. I sent a carpenter on board of him. He put a graving piece in his waterways and smoothed up his rail where my bob chain roughed it up when I ran into him. His repairs cost me $3.51, mine cost me $319.62. My wife's prophecy came out as she had said.

As soon as the sugar was out I towed over to Pier 14, East River, close to the foot of Wall Street, and began taking in cargo for Maracaibo. At the same time I was having the bowsprit, jib boom, and fore topmast made. I got them in, rigging all set up, and ready by the time I was loaded. So I lost no time repairing. To my surprise and disappointment I see the stevedore measuring my deck. I said, "What does this mean?" He said, "There is a deck load of cars to go out." I was nettled; I saw that I was swindled. But I had it to do because my charter party called for under and on deck. Suzarty and Whitney did pay for putting them on board but I had to get them off at Maracaibo. I never cared for broker Watson anymore or Suzarty and Whitney either for that matter.

We finished taking in our cargo, caulked hatches, and lashed the deck load of cars for which Suzarty and Whitney gave me a coil of rope. We got under way close to the Statue of Liberty on Monday, the 23rd day of April, 1894, and sailed for Maracaibo, Venezuela. On Thursday, May the 8th, we came to anchor in Maracaibo after a passage of 16 days, which was good. I think this was the hottest port I ever got into. I was told that the devil went there to have a game of cards with the boys. He panted and blowed then he told the boys he could not stand it any longer and must go home and cool off. We worked hard and sweated getting these cars off. Then we got the cargo out and got orders to proceed up the Lake Maracaibo about 66 miles. The water was fresh and clear; so blue it looked like ocean water. We were now very close to the equator with great high mountains on both sides of the lake. But if I remember rightly the hills on the western side were scarcely visible from the eastern side. The pilot told me there were white Indians up in these mountains and they were bad people. One day I look to the westward. I thought I saw the smoke from a steamer. I said, "Practica, vapor, vapor," which in English is "Pilot, steamer, steamer." He said, "No, Captain, mokeets mokeets." I said, "We will be eat up by mosquitoes." He gave me to understand they were blind mosquitoes and

Photo by Robert H. Burgess

The lighthouses at Cape Henry, Virginia. The original, at left, was built in 1791 and its replacement in 1881. Both of these served as beacons for Captain Tawes and his schooners while trading out of Chesapeake Bay.

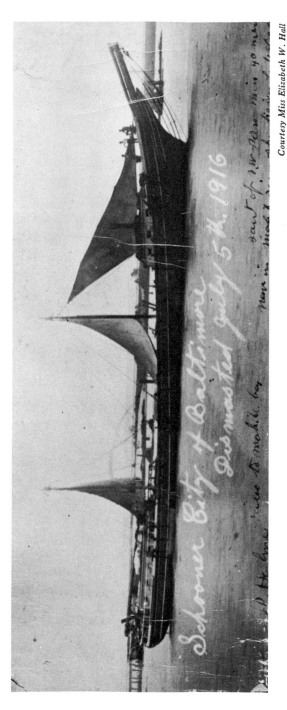

The CITY OF BALTIMORE *under jury rig approaching Mobile after being*
dismasted in the Gulf of Mexico, July 5, 1916.

would not bite. The mate had just put on some fresh paint. They got into that and messed it up. They go in large schools and we were only bothered once more with them.

We arrived at our anchorage and took in boxwood which we were to load with partly. This is the kind of wood that rules are made of. It was round and the heaviest wood I ever attempted to handle and bad to stow in the hold. We were up this lake 13 days before we got back to Maracaibo. Here we lay six days loading divi-divi. This is a dye stuff principally used in dying leather. In size I would say it looks something like the hulls of a hickory nut. We got the wood as level in the hold as possible and laid mats all over the wood in the hold. Then we stowed one tier of bags over the mats. When this was done we emptied the bags that afterward came on board. We did this to keep the divi-divi from going down in between the wood.

In emptying the bags we very often saw a centipede going in the hold with the divi-divi. I remember one in my berth. Sleeping, I rolled over and my underpants string passed over my other naked leg. I thought sure a centipede had crawled over me. I jumped out my berth terribly scared. I striped my bed, took off the sheets and shook them. The same with the pillows. I found nothing. I then took off the mattress. I then took up the springs and swept out the berth. Yet I found nothing. It dawned upon me that it was my drawer string that passed over my other naked leg. In those days underpants had strings and we tied them over the socks. Finally, we finished loading the divi-divi. The hold was full. We then took on board about 40 cases of balsam cababia, 10 gallons in each can, and about the same quantity of cocoanut oil.

I cleared from the custom house for New York, paid the tow boat bill, and sailed for the mouth of the lake. During this short time a rebellion broke out somewhere in Venezuela and the government took the tow boat away to transport troops. It was impossible to sail out over the bar on account of adverse winds setting in over the bar daily. They would soften down at about 9 or 10 o'clock at night and come up in the morning. At 9 or 10 in the morning these winds would be blowing hard and at about 3 o'clock in the afternoon when the sun would bear southwest of a certain mountain it would then blow a gale from east. It blew so hard that my shirt sleeves would whip on my arms while on deck. I had to keep 45 fathoms of chain out by the hawse pipes to keep from draging on shore. And here I laid to anchor 28 days. It was hard to lay here with crew's wages counting up daily. And I feared worms would eat her bottom off while the crew were eating the top off. I worried a great deal about the difficulty I was in. Here is when I first observed that my mustache was turning gray. Our food was getting scarce and worse still our beef and pork were spoiling. When the steward was boiling the beef it smelt so bad that it was awful to walk on the lee side of the galley. I must say that I had a good and agreeable crew. They never made any complaint about the provisions. They did their work faithfully without a murmur.

There was a Danish barque laying close to me in the same predicament as I was in. I think he was bound to Hamburg, Germany. He had a good sailing yawl and often came aboard of me. We tried to make one and the other as pleasant as possible. But one day he came on board of me and said, "I have a man sick with yellow fever and I am going to lose him." I said, "I am sorry, but do you really think he is going to die?" He said he did. "Well," I said, "I have been in yellow fever quite a lot in my life trading to Rio de Janeiro. Let me take him in hand. I might save him." He said, " I will be glad to." The captain spoke good English. I told him, knowing that I was coming to a sickly port before I left New York, I had all the old medicine destroyed and had my medicine chest recuperated with new and fresh medicines. I went with him on board his vessel and took a look at the man. He had him on a bed on top of one of his hatches and canvas over him in a kind of wigwam fashion, or like a house top. I saw he was surely sick with high fever. His face was red almost like fire. I went back on board and got two of my capsules containing 10 grains of calomel and 10 grains of phenobarb. I had them put up this way to make them a light dose. Doctors of today would say they were 9 grains too heavy, but all the captains I sailed with had them made up 15 grains calomel and 15 grains of jalap. I remember going into Havana once when the captain made us all take a dose of this calomel and jalap. It pretty near killed me but I did not get the yellow fever. Four of our crew did and a fine, beautiful English boy died with it and we buried him at sea. When I got back to the Danish barque I told the captain to give him one of the capsules. The captain and the mate had a time getting him to take it but they succeeded after a bit. It was now 2 o'clock afternoon. I told the captain to give him the other one at 6 o'clock which he did. I then gave him another favorite prescription of mine which was as much sulpinate of quinine as a 25 cent piece would hold piled on top of it four times in a four ounce bottle of water, and 4 to 6 drops of elixir of vitral. I shook this up nicely and told the captain to give the ill man 2 teaspoons full every 3 hours after the capsules had acted nicely. The next day I went on board of the Dane and found the man much improved. And the next day he was yet better. On the third day he was out of his wigwam on deck and he got well. This was the second life I had saved.

One afternoon a small vessel came down from Maracaibo to Fort San Carlos, which is the name of the fort there. The wind was then at its fury. It was about 3 o'clock and the sun was bearing southwest of this mountain. I said to the mate that I believe that schooner has 200 plantains on board for me. I wrote Mr. Pender, my consignee, to send me down 200 by the first vessel that left Maracaibo as my provisions were getting scarce. I said that we will have to go on shore in morning and see while the wind is down. The mate said, "Captain, we can go now." I said, "Yes, it is easy to do this right before the wind but you can't get back." "Yes, we can," he said, "for I and the 2nd mate can pull that small boat against anything." I said, "When you get on shore you will not be able to pull her back." He said, "I would like to prove it to you. Just let us try it." I said, "You may try, go ahead." They got in my 14-foot dinky and they went sliding fast before the gale. They were ashore in a short time. They went on board of the schooner just down from Maracaibo but there were no plantains on board. Now for the task of returning which they found they could not do. As fast as they would straighten the boat head to the wind, and before they could get on course, the wind would blow her back. Finally, Mr. Smith said, "We will give it up and go on board at 10 o'clock tonight when the wind falls." But the commandant of the fort would not allow any one to leave the fort after 6 PM. About 4 Venezuelan soldiers came down to the water's edge and took the boat and carried her up into the fort and secured her. I think they gave them some supper and a blanket each and put them in a house of no sides; just a roof to keep the rain off. I saw many of these kind of houses while I was in Venezuela. There were some donkeys in the same house which were given a nice bundle of green grass for their supper. The mate and 2nd mate took these bundles of grass from the donkeys and used them for pillows. At 6 o'clock the next morning they came on board. They had no plantains. I said to them, "Why did you not come back on board last night?" They said, "Captain, the wind would blow the boat back as fast as we could put her out." They related all the circumstances as I have written above.

On another day the Danish captain came on board of me in his nice sailing yawl and we took a long sail up the lake toward Maracaibo city. After we got up about 4 miles we saw a settlement along the lake and we went in there and landed. The people seemed nice to us. It seemed these people followed fishing. I cannot properly describe them as regards their race. I think they must have been two thirds Indian and one third Spanish. I thought the young ladies were the prettiest I ever saw. There was one young lady that seemed to take an interest in us. As far as I know we may have been the first real white men they ever saw. As best I could understand one old man asked me how I would like to have that girl. I did not know what to say or how to answer him. They had a big lot of fish that they had just caught, big jumping mullets large and fat. I told them that if they would let us have some of those fish that I would bring them some sugar tomorrow. Sugar was very high in Venezuela at that time as the government would not let any be imported, trying to force the people to raise their own sugar. I will add here that everything to eat in Venezuela was high. Duty on a barrel of flour imported in Venezuela was $10 a barrel and everything else in proportion. To have stored up out there the cost would have been immense. On the promise of sugar they let us have a nice lot of fish. We were all getting quite hungry on board of my vessel and I am sure it was quite same with the Dane. We went on board and my steward, Walter Barnes, cooked them for supper and we all had a glorious meal. The next morning the government sent a small launch that would help us in tacking and we got out over the bar and went to sea. The Venezuelan government owes me today $980 for detention at the bar. And I am sorry to say I never paid those people for their fish, the only obligation I never met in all my life. And though it has been 36 years since I made it I wish I could pay it. But I do not know how to do it. I meant well at the time as I had plenty of raw sugar on board at the time from when I had been running sugar from Cuba all the winter.

When I got out of the Gulf of Maracaibo and away from the mountains we had regular gentle breezes and went to New York in 22 days. This was a bad voyage. I made no money. We got out over the bar at Maracaibo July 10 and arrived at New York August 1 after a passage of 21 days. After discharging our cargo in New York business was dull coastwise and not brisk offshore. I chartered to go to Baltimore and load flour for Rio Grande do Sul. My second mate, that was with me on my voyage to Maracaibo, I now made him my mate. He was a nice fellow. He was by name John Sylvander. Unfortunately, while I was lying at Jackson's Wharf in Baltimore where I was loading, he fell overboard one night and was drowned. Now I had to do the best I could in getting a mate. I had not much time to look. I was getting pretty well loaded so I shipped a German and I think I got the meanest man out of Baltimore and the least capable to serve as mate. He knew nothing and would not let anyone else know anything. I had to put up with this fellow until I got to Rio Grande do Sul. We were 59 days on the passage from Cape Henry.

We went out of the capes October 15th and on the 18th of October we were caught in a dreadful hurrycane. For 2 or 3 days I saw this was brewing and I had all light sails tied up and tried to have everything in shape for it. I had on the deck 15 thousand feet of white pine lumber, 15 kerosene barrels of strained tar, and 75 barrels resin. I had this in on my own account. It cost me $465 and I could not get it insured. I told the mate to lash it down. He did it about like a ten-year old boy would have done it. When he got through I took two of my crew and lashed it myself in a way that I thought she would have to turn over to loose it. And in order to put her in nice sailing trim, I unshackled my starboard chain from the anchor and draged it aft and turned it across the deck from one side to the other just at the forward end of the lumber I had on deck. This chain was 75 fathoms long, stud lengths about 1½ inch. I am sure this put her in nice trim for sailing and you want a vessel in nice trim too when you are bound to a port six thousand miles ahead of you.

When we were 8 days at sea, on Thursday, October 18 at 3 o'clock in the morning, the hurrycane began from the south southeast and kept going around in the left hand way until it got to the north northeast. We could not get the sails in fast enough. The mate did not know anything about reefing a schooner's sails. I did get the mainsail double-reefed and set. I then lowered down the spanker and got the reef tackle hauled out. Then we had to leave it and go lower the foresail and take in the flying jib and jib. By the time we could get back to the spanker, where we left it a little more than half down, all the hoops on the mast were broken. We lowered this down and tied it up. By this time the mainsail, though reefed, had blown in ribbons. Then the fore staysail halyard parted and down it came. By this time our yawl boat was washed from the davits with all the oars and spars we had in her. The clouds were so low that they seem to touch our topmast heads. We were now without a rag of sail on her. It was now a case of keep off and run her. It was now a question whether she would keep off with no sail on her. I went aft and rolled the wheel up and to my agreeable surprise she did more than hundreds of vessels would do. She kept off without a rag of sail on her and when she did get before it she just flew like a mad horse running to escape danger. She was an easy steering vessel under most all circumstances. I had one of the men bring me a rope and I tied myself to the wheel. Finally, she was steering so hard I had to call for another man to come to the wheel to help me. Between the both of us we were keeping before the wind; she was going fearfully fast. Finally, I looked ahead and there was one of the largest seas I ever saw coming from the south, the course we were running. When I saw this large sea coming for our bow, I thought sure all the masts would go out of her over the bow. I never pass Johnstown, Pennsylvania, but I think of this sea. That high land there reminds me of it, though this sea was not quite as high as this land is. We went into it head on. I saw both anchors lift up on the top-gallant forecastle and the bow went into it deep and the great volume of water began running aft when the bow began to rise. I knew the stern had to settle in proportion to the bow. So I said to the seaman at the wheel with me, "Stop turning the wheel and take a solid grip and hold on for your life." He was not lashed at the wheel as I was. I looked aft when the stern settled and a great volume of water came and covered us up head and ears and pressed down heavily over the wheel. By good luck none of our bones were broken. When this sea that came over aft met the big sea that came over the bow her decks were even full from the bow to the stern. It seemed to me she had slowed down when she plunged into the heavy sea. To my surprise, and delightfully so, our masts stayed in her.

The poor fellow at the wheel with me began to cry and said to me, "Captain, are we running for the beach?" I told him we had plenty of room and our dependence was to keep her before the wind. And we did the best we could at this. The mizzin topsail blew out of the gaskets and we lost it. Not another heavy sea boarded us but the tops of the seas blew over us and kept our decks full of water. Fortunately, I never lost any of my deck load of lumber, tar, and resin. But if the severity of the gale had lasted 2 more hours I would have lost it all. The most unbeleivable thing to relate is that this 75 fathom of big chain was just floating around the deck and going from side to side as the big volume of water would go from side to side when she rolled. It got full of all kinds of knots, dips, and bowlines. The end of it was hard to find after the storm was over. It took us about 3 days to get it cleared up. At about eleven o'clock I ran in the cabin to look at the barometer. I saw she was rising. Then I knew we were running out of the hurrycane. It was bound north and we were steering south.

At 5 o'clock that afternoon we put the full foresail on her. It was one week before the sea went down to normal. It tore us up so that it was 8 days before we got her underway again. To give an idea of the force of the wind my main gaff, with not a rag of sail on it, went out against the main rigging and stayed there like it had been lashed. With all of her rolling it never swung from the main rigging. I had some stove bolts on board, 2 inches long, and with these I would screw the mast hoops together chamfering the ends to fit one another. In this way I could get one whole hoop out of two broken ones. And I had a few spare hoops down the lazarette. But now my most desirable sail was blown away and I had all of ten thousand miles to sail before I got back home. I had an old mainsail down in the lazarette. I got that up and repaired it in the best shape I could and reused it. The remainder of the voyage I took care of it like a mother would look out for a sick child. When the weather looked bad or the wind would blow a little fresh I would take it in and tie it up knowing it would do me lots of good in fine weather. Now we were fully underway again.

We sailed on without much trouble except we fell to leeward of the Rocas, the island I have heard captains talk so much about. There was one house on it. I suppose it was a fisherman's house. We progressed along down the coast of Brazil rather close. It was my watch below. One night, from 8 to 12, the mate was in charge of the watch on deck. At 12, when he called me and I came on deck, it appeared to me I never smelt coral stronger in my life. I expected her to strike bottom at any moment. I had the fore and main topsails clewed down on the cap as quickly as possible and tacked her offshore. Then I said to the mate, "When you smelt that coral why did not you call me?" He had the impertinence to tell me I should have been on deck myself. I guess with such an incompetent man on deck as he was, he was about right. But I runed my watch and I could not stay on deck all the time. Everything went along now fairly well until I got out of the tropics and in the variables south of the southeast trade winds. There the weather became changeable and stormy and we got one of those pamperos which bothered us for a couple of days. Then the weather became good and we proceeded on our voyage.

On Saturday, the 9th day of December, we arrived in port 63 days from Baltimore. On the 13th day of December I discharged the mate. He said he would not leave but I brought charges against him before the American consul and after a fair trial I paid him off. He was the only man I ever discharged in a foreighn port but this man I could not sail with any longer. He had runed out all my crew and here I was over six thousand miles from home. No mate. No crew. No one on board but my faithful steward Walter Barnes. Finally, there came into port a Swedish bark from the East Indies with a cargo of rice. The crew on this bark had been on her 3 years and the time they had signed for was up and they shiped with me. They wanted to get to New York so they could get back to Sweden. They were all good sailors but, excepting one man, could not speak English. I took him aft as my best man in the place of a mate just to stand the port watch and to call me in case squalls were rising. He knew no navigation whatever. No one can realize what I have gone through and had to contend with in trying to make an honest living. Just see the position I was now placed in over six thousand miles from home and with a crew that could not speak English. I could make signs to them in the day time and being trained seamen they knew what I wanted done. But these signs would not work at night and it was bad. I lost my jib topsail one dark night because they could not understand me. Yet with all of this I was much happier with these men than I was with that mate on board. He came on board two or three times before I left Rio Grande do Sul to see if I would not take him back. He said he was sorry to see me sail without a mate. But I was determined he should never get on my ship's papers again.

While I was in Rio Grande do Sul this time there was Captain Sam Messenger, master of the British brig *Bertha Gray*. I had met him once before in Fernandina, Florida. While here he was a big help to me. He loaned me his boat to use while here to get back and forth from on board to the shore. There also was in the port the schooner *Ellen Crusoe* of Portland, Maine. The captain of her was nice and helped me what he could. I was taking a survey boat from New York to Detroit, Michigan, 10 years ago, in 1920. I stopped at Portland to coal and water. I inquired for this Captain Bergman. I was told he got married some time before this and went on a voyage to sea. He, his wife, and none of the crew were ever heard from again. I also stopped at Yarmouth, Nova Scotia, to coal and water and in-quired for Sam Messenger. He was then dying and no one could visit him. I was very sorry I could not go to his house and shake his hand.

While lying at Rio Grande do Sul I took a trip up to Pelotas, about 30 miles by train, to visit a friend there I knew by name Peter Alvarez. It was on Christmas Day and I had dinner with them. Nine years before this I loaded a cargo of dry hydes there for Boston. There was one station we had to stop at on our way up. I got out of the train and looked up at the sun. It was real hot and I was sure we would have a squall which we did. It tore my flags up very badly there being no one on board but my steward and he did not see the squall coming. I spent a pleasant day in Pelotas. I could see that Mrs. Alvarez had aged a lot in those 9 years I was absent.

We sailed from Rio Grande do Sul January 2nd, 1895. We had irregular winds very nearly up to the equator and we did not make the time we should have made. We saw Cape St. Roque on February the 4th from which I took a new departure in lattitude 05° 27' south, longitude 35° 24' west. I crossed the equator on February the 7th, 36 days out. While working and struggling to get up to Cape St. Roque I was not giving Barbados much thought, thinking it was just a short run. To my surprise, when I worked up the course and distance by Mercator's sailing, I found it bore northwest by north 1,820 miles. I was much surprised to find it was so far but to my agreeable surprise I made the 1,820 miles in ten days, an average of 180 miles a day. But I met strong northeast trade winds and was 43 days to Barbados. My old quadrant which had served me faithfully many years was now failing on me but I wedged her up with match sticks. By this method I kept her in adjustment and made Needham Point Lighthouse at Barbados right over the bow just as well as if I had the best sextant in the word and the best mate to take the observations of the sun for me.

When daylight came I took a pilot and run into Carlisle Bay and anchored. The negro boatmen there were very amusing. About 8 or 10 of them were hanging close to the vessel. They were not allowed on board until the quarantine doctor came on board and gave us a clean bill of health. And while laying close to the ship first one and the other would yell out to me, "Captain, I am a boatman; I will do all your boating night or day." Then another would holler, "Captain, he is no boatman; I am the real boatman." Then another would yell out, "Captain, my name is Yankee Sam; I do all the boating for all the American captains that come here." Then he would holler out, "Thank you sir, thank you sir," trying to convey the idea that I had engaged him so that the others would leave and he would be alone. When the doctor came on board I knew better than to promise.

After I got permission to go on shore I consigned my vessel to the house of John Decosta & Company. While in this house I saw a lot of sea captains sitting around a table getting ready to take a drink. These captains were English, German, and Scandinavian. They asked me if I would join them. I always like to be sociable and I joined them. There were 14 of them altogether. They asked me about my passage up from Rio Grande do Sul, how long I was coming up, and other conversation usual among seafaring men. I looked around and I counted. I thought, well it will cost me $1.50 to treat then I will go to the custom house and enter. So I asked them all what they would have. They all named their choice of drink and when it was over I said, "Gentlemen, you will excuse me; I have to go to the custom house to enter." So I said to the waiter, "How much are these drinks?" He said, "Nothing." I looked at him and said, "Come on, how much are these drinks?" Again he said, "Nothing." I said, "Look here, I never allow liquor or cigars charged to my ship and I want to pay for them." Then these captains all spoke up and said, "Captain, there is no charge for these drinks. This man is paid to stay here and wait on us and give us any kind of drink at any time a day we wish and it is all free." "Well," I said, "this is new to me." People would think that captains and mates would be in there drunk all the time, but I am sure there was the least drinking in this place than in any other in Barbados. They would go there early in the morning and take a drink and they seldom took another. Free liquor was not much in demand.

After laying here a few days I chartered to go to Guantanamo, Cuba, to load sugar for the Delaware Breakwater for orders. I had not been here but a couple days when in come my old friend Sam Messenger in the brig *Bertha Gray*. Here I got his boat again to use at my pleasure. He chartered to go to Guantanamo to load sugar for Delaware Breakwater for orders. He said to me, "Tawes, which way are you going to Guantanamo?" I said, "I am going to run down between St. Lucia and St. Vincent and down on the south side of Haiti and on down to Guantanamo." He said, "No. The best way is to go through

the Mona Passage and down on the north side of Haiti."
That way did not appeal to me but we sailed the same day and
I went by his suggestion which afterward I regretted. It was
very hot coming through the Mona Passage and that night I
got a strong gale from the northwest. I reefed her all 'round
and put her on a course that would bring her close to Silver
Bank. I never gave the shores of Haiti a thought. She made
so much leeway that night that if daylight had been one hour
later I should have run ashore on Cape Frances. As soon as I
saw land ahead I tacked ship and shook the reefs out of the
lower sails and stood offshore. This was Friday, 22nd day of
February. Saturday we went through the Windward Passage.
There were two passages, the Mona and the Windward passages. By listening to Captain Messenger we were in sight of one
another most of the time. Sunday we were off Guantanamo
entrance. I was ahead of Captain Messenger but the wind died
out on the west side of the harbor and I drifted out. He was on
the east side, got a little slant, and got in before sundown. I was
left on the outside. That night a strong norther came up and I
was not certain that I could stay close to the land. I had been
there 3 or 4 times before and I know the way in and I worked
her up to an anchorage. But without a pilot and I had to pay a
fine of 30 or 40 dollars for coming in the harbor at night. Such
was the Spanish law.

The war broke out between Cuba and Spain while I was
there this time. The Captain of the Port came on board in the
evening and gave orders that no one should be on shore
that night at the peril of their lives. The next day I heard
that the Cubans were approaching the town and that they had a
fight in which several Spaniards were killed and wounded and
that Spaniards did not bring their wounded in until the next
night. They did not want the Cubans in the town to know that
they had lost any troops either killed or wounded, fearing the
Cubans in the town may rise. This war did not cease until

1898 when the Americans joined the Cubans and got all the Spaniards out of the island. The Spanish flag flew on this island about 400 years.

After I finished loading sugar I had to go up to Guantanamo city, 18 miles, to clear. My friend Captain Messenger went up the same day. I had been using his boat again at Caimanera to boat on board water, wood, and other things necessary for the trip to Delaware Breakwater. I said, on our way down from Guantanamo, "Captain Messenger, you have been kind to me to let me use your boat. I will send her over to you tonight." He said, "Look here, boy, I hate to see you going in on the American coast in the month of March with no boat. You keep her and return her to me in New York." "But we may not meet in New York," said I. He said, "You can leave her at Gokey's Shipyard." "But I might lose her," I said. "Have you thought how much insurance must I put on her?" He said, "Fifty dollars." I said, "Will that satisfy you?" He said, "Yes." I runed my hand in my pocket, hauled out $50, and handed it to him. I remarked, "Ain't this as good as an insurance policy?" He said, "Yes." We sailed the same day for Delaware Breakwater. I beat him a day or two. We both got orders to go to New York. There I met him along South Street one day. We exchanged greetings and after a little chat we said "Goodbye" and we never met again. In my memory I will always cherish him. I have his picture in my album at my home where it will always be kept for he assisted me in time of need.

I will try to describe the river we filled our water from at Caimanera. I never went to the mouth of it myself but my crew always went in the row boat up to it to fill water at its mouth. I should say it was forty feet wide; the water was fair and not to say real good. But sailors in those days could not be too choicy. I had been to Caimanera quite a few times before this and always took on water. I was very much surprised to see this small river runing through the city of Guantanamo and the women

[287]

washing clothes on the rocks by the side of this stream. They wash clothes different from our people. They lay them on a rock and beat them with a flat paddle or thin board. Many times they break the buttons on them. I think this is the custom in all of the Latin Republics. In this little stream at Guantanamo they throw about all their garbage and refuse. Then after this water runs 20 or 25 miles below we seamen fill our casks and drink it on our homeward bound voyage.

After getting our sugar out I docked and painted at Tregarthen's on the East River. Then I chartered to take in some general cargo for Santo Domingo city. But I had to go by the way of Jacksonville, Florida, and finish loading with lumber. When ready to sail it was on Saturday. I towed out close to the Statue of Liberty and anchored. The next morning was Sunday. It was raining and blowing from the northeast. It was not fit to get underway but I knew it would not be long before the crew would want to go on shore if I lay there. And it would give me a lot of trouble getting them back if I got them back at all. Every man on board was new to me excepting my faithful steward Walter Barnes. So I said to my mate, Fletcher Gantt, who I afterward found to be a fine mate, "After we get breakfast we will heave short, put the fore staysail on her and wear her around on her heel, go down to Sandy Hook and lay until we get good weather and go to sea from there." I knew I would have my crew if I went there. After getting the anchor up and got her headed for the Narrows I put the foresail on her and she began sliping along at a pretty good gate and I had got nearly down to Norton's Point. I could see all the old Jacksonville traders lying under the Hook that had left New York 2 or 3 days before. I will just name 2 or 3 of them. One was Captain Charley Smith, schooner *Mary J. Russell;* Captain Charley Sawyer, *James A. Simpson;* Captain George Steelman, who was afterward lost on or near Abaco in the schooner *Mary Lee Patton.* There was always a mystery about this vessel. She ran ashore on Abaco with sails set and breakfast and coffee pot set on the table ready for eating. And not a soul of the crew were ever heard from.

These vessels were laying at anchor under the Hook as I have already said and there seemed to be a half dozen of them. I then looked to the eastward and there was a clear streak just a little about the horison. I said to the mate, "Put the mainsail on her and the jib and flying jib. I will take a little run to sea and look at it and if it does not suit me I will run back and anchor under the Hook with these other southern traders." I then put the spanker on her and she began going off so nicely I said, "Put the topsails on her, I am not going back." I remember there was a big heavy swell rolling in from the eastward which was sufficient to warn me of approaching danger but I did not regard it but let her go south southwest. I looked ahead and saw two ships emitting big volumes of smoke. When I got close to them I saw they were the cruisers *New York* and *Columbia* ploughing their way to Sandy Hook. I was going along fine but when the night came on, oh, how I wished I was back under Sandy Hook with those other Jacksonville traders. But it was too late, there was no getting back. It was now blowing strong from east northeast and increasing. I said to Mr. Gantt, "Clew up the topsails and furl them good and take in the jib topsail. There is a heavy storm now on us and we have got to reef her down all round." I was at the wheel. Shortly he came to me and said, "Captain, we cannot clew up the fore topsail. There is something wrong up there." I said, "Yes, I know what it is. The shell on the fore topsail sheet block is cut down by the topsail sheet chain and I forgot to have it repaired in New York." It was such a bad storm and now I could ask no one to go out to the end of the fore gaff and render the chain through the block so as to clew it up. I told him to go aloft and cut all the hoops from the topsail, take the topsail halyards off the topsail, and lower the foresail down, topsail and all together. The *Baltimore* was tearing through the water like a mad race horse. It was dark and rain falling in torrents. In a very short while he came aft again and I said, "Did you get the foresail in? I have felt no difference in her steering." He said, "I did not take it in. We have the topsail in and furled." I said, "How did you manage to get that fore topsail sheet clear?" He said, "That Frenchman went out on the end of the gaff and cleared it up, got the topsail in, and tied it up." I began to feel as big as old Goliah to think I had such a noble crew. In this storm tonight I shall be able to handle this vessel without any difficulty. The way she was rolling and going, and dark as a cellar, I would not gone out on that gaff for a million dollars.

We took in our spanker, tied it up, reefed the mainsail and the foresail, set them and took in flying jib and jib. We were now under safe and snug sail and steering south southeast with wind 2 points abaft the beam. We were making 10 knots an hour. But, oh, how dark and rain falling thick and fast we could not see very far. It was my watch on deck from 8 to 12 midnight. It was usual for the captain to take the first watch when outward bound, the mate to take the first watch homeward. It is easy to memorize by saying, "The captain takes her out like a man, the mate takes her home the best way he can." I would have felt happy if I was sure there were no ships anywhere near our course for a collision would have meant death to all of us. About 10 o'clock that night a vessel passed close to our port quarter showing his red light. My heart came up in my throat for a minute. He was on the starboard tack standing in toward the coast. The weather was so thick that he was out of sight in 3 or 4 minutes. Red to red, perfect safety, go ahead. My red light was shining toward him. A miss is as good as a mile and I had no occasion to change my course. At 8 bells midnight watches were changed. I called Mr. Gantt and I left him in charge of the port watch cautioning him to keep a bright lookout and to call me in case of approaching danger. I told him I would lay down on the lounge and have the flash or torch light ready. About 2 o'clock in the morning I heard the man on the lookout forward holler, "Keep her off, keep her off!" I ran out on deck bareheaded in the cold rain and I hollered, "Keep her off, keep her off!" Mr. Gantt sang out to me, "No, Captain, we do not want to keep off. There is his green light in opposition to ours." In a minute or two, or as soon as my eyes had got use to the darkness, I saw his green light on our starboard bow. Mr. Gantt was right and we ran clear of this vessel. He was showing his torch light which was a bright one. We ran so close to him I saw the stitches in his sails when his torch light was shining on them. He was laying to under very short sail. The remainder of the night we never saw another vessel. I was glad to see the day break to have daylight and see around the horison.

We went to Cape Hatteras in 37 hours, a distance of 337 miles. Here the wind died out and we did some terrible rolling for there was a big swell on. We rolled around here for a few hours and it breezed up from the east again and this wind took us to St. Johns Bar. Got a pilot and tow boat and towed up to Buckey's saw mill one week from New York. I was much pleased when I looked in and thought of those vessels still in Sandy Hook and in a thick fog. When they got to Jacksonville I was loaded and gone and did not have the pleasure of meeting them.

Arriving at the sawmill where I was to load I hauled in astern of a vessel from Maine. The captain was a nice man. It was late in the evening and I wanted to learn how he found things going at this mill. He told me they were so close at this mill that you had to buy what wood you needed and everything else you needed in the way of stanchions, lashing planks, etc. I said I had been on a long voyage out to South America and all my lashing planks and stanchions had been used up as fire

[291]

wood. The old gentlemen said, "You will pay for all you get here." That night while in bed I got to thinking about a ten-gallon keg of rum I had on board. The government in those days would pass a ten-gallon keg of liquor manifested as ship stores. I had had this on board some time and it was getting quite aged and mellow. So I thought tomorrow morning when I meet my mill man and get through talking business I will offer him a drink. And sure enough when I met him and introduced myself and he showed me the pile of lumber I was to take in I asked him if he ever indulged. He told me he did. I said, "I think I have something on board that will suit your taste. Will you try it?" He said he would. On board we went. I got out the bottle and glasses and told him to help himself. To be social I took some too though, in all my life, I never cared much for liquor. When he had drank his I asked him how he liked it. "Why that is nice liquor." I said, "If you like it I will fill up a bottle and put it up on this rack overhead and you can come on board and drink at your will." This mill was about 3 miles below Jacksonville city. I had to go up there to enter at the custom house and I stayed most of the day. When I got back and looked at the bottle I found it ¾ gone. I thought to myself this is going to work out alright. I filled it up the next morning and I went to town again. When I came back my bottle was just more than ½ gone. The next day, or the third day, my hold was getting full. To start the deck load I had to have strips to lay across the deck, also stanchions. So I went to Mr. B. and told him I had to have stanchions. I said "Have not you a random lumber pile here I can get them out of?" "Oh, yes," he said, "come with me." I went with him to the random lumber pile. He said, "You see anything in here that will suit you?" I said, "Yes." "Well," he said, "take your crew and come up here and get what you need." I got the strips laid on deck and stanchions up and began the deck load. In about two days I had my deck load on. Now I had to have heavy lashing planks 3 by 10 inches, by 33 feet long. I said, "Mr. B. I have got to have lashing planks to secure the deck load. I would like again to see your random lumber pile." He said, "Come with me." He showed me the pile. "Bring your crew up here and get what you need," he said. I took my crew and got 5 or 6 lashing planks 3″ by 10″ by 33 feet long.

For the benefit of the reader I will tell what a random lumber pile is. It is left from ships loading a certain size and schedule of lumber that could not carry quite all of the order that was cut. The captain is not supposed to carry any more than a load and what is left of the cargo is piled out in the mill yard. With the remains of other ship's orders left behind this is all put together and called random because of so many different sizes piled together.

After I got my lashing planks on board and deck load lashed I needed about 1200 feet of inch-boards for dunnage. I had chartered to load sugar back to New York from Santo Domingo. Boards make nice dunnage to lay bag sugar on. I thought to myself he has been good to me. I will not ask him for anything else. I will buy the boards I need. So I went to him and I said, "Mr. B., I going to load sugar in Santo Domingo for New York and I want to buy 1200 feet of inch-boards for dunnage. Will you sell them to me?" He said, "Come with me." He said, "You take what you need off these two piles. I am not going to charge you anything." I took the crew up to these two piles and I got about 1600 feet of boards and they never cost me a cent. Sunday, the 19th day of May, 1895, we went to sea. And after experiencing calms, storms, head winds and fair ones, without incident on the ocean for nineteen days, we came safely to anchor in the roads at Santo Domingo city.

My outward cargo was to the President of Santo Domingo. To hurry up the unloading he sent some of his colored troops out of the fort down to the ship to help unload. He turned the ship over to an Italian merchant there to load her for New

York. My outward freight was to be paid in American gold in Santo Domingo. Mr. Vicini sent one of his clerks down to tell me that I would need dunnage for sugar and that he would furnish lignum vitae for dunnage if I would take it to New York free of freight charges. I told the clerk to tell Mr. Vicini I would need no dunnage. The next day he sent the clerk down to see me again with this free offer of dunnage. Lignum vitae is the heaviest wood in the world and this Italian wanted me to take it to New York for nothing. I said to the clerk, "You go back and tell Mr. Vicini that my charter party calls for a full and complete cargo of sugar, that I had plenty of dunnage, and that I would not carry his lignum vitae even if he paid me for it." When the cargo was out I was ordered to go to Palenque, 20 miles down the coast, where Mr. Vicini owned a sugar plantation. When I got down there and moored ready for cargo the overseer of the plantation said to me, "Captain, there is a locomotive on the track there that Mr. Vicini wants you to take to New York." I said, "Did Mr. Vicini mention the rate of freight he will pay to take that locomotive to New York?" He said, "The same as sugar." I said, "It will drop to pieces with rust before I take it to New York on any such terms." Just before I finished loading the overseer came. He said, "Mr. Vicini does not want you to leave that locomotive but to take it on board. When you come up to Santo Domingo city to sign bills of lading and clear, if you and he fail to come to an agreement as to the rate of freight on the locomotive, then my consignee and his consignee could make the terms." This looked good to me. It took me half a day to get up my heavy tackles to hoist this locomotive on board. I was scared all the time I was hoisting this locomotive on board fearing that something might happen to the crew such as break an arm, mash a hand, or something. But in about three hours we got it on board safely. As the hold was about full of sugar I had to carry it on deck. It was taken apart as much as possible. It was in 8 or 10 pieces. I put the smallest pieces down the hold on top of the sugar but the big, or boiler part, I carried on deck. I lost a day's time and suffered anxiety with this locomotive as a swell sets in the harbor of Palenque causing the vessel to roll which increased risk and labor. We lashed securely all we had on deck and then sailed for Santo Domingo city arriving late in the evening of July 4.

On Thursday, July 5, I went on shore to sign bills of lading and clear for New York. Also to settle up with the old President for the balance due me on outward freight. I had $1,500 due me. I told him I wanted $100 cash. He ran his fingers in his right vest pocket and took out two $100 bills. He passed me one. I would have asked for $200 if I had known he had them. Now there were $1,400 due. In about half an hour or so he handed me Mr. Vicini's draught on New York, 60 days sight, for $1,400. I said, "Mr. President, I want sight drafts." He said, "That is not the custom here to give sight drafts. They are always 60 day." I said, "I cannot get these bills sighted until I get to New York and then I have got to wait 60 days before they are paid. What am I going to do for money to pay off my crew and other expenses?" "Why," he said, "you can have them discounted." I replied, "Then I will have to pay 6% to have this done. My charter is payable in American gold on proper delivery of cargo. I have performed my part of this obligation. You pay me in American gold." He said, "Captain, if your crew knew you had $1,400 in American gold on board they might assassinate you." I said, "It will be no loss of yours; just give me the gold." I knew he could not raise $1,400 in American gold and my aim was to make him pay the discount which he suggested me to do. I said, "Now, you pay the discount." He gave me $14 to pay for the discount and I signed his receipts. He said to me, "Captain, you missed your calling." I said, "How so?" He said, "You should have been a lawyer instead of a sea captain." In a year or so he was assassinated which put an end to the President of Santo Domingo.

From the President's office I went to the office of Mr. Vicini to sign bills of lading and get my clearance papers. When I got there he handed me a chair and spread the bills of lading before me to read which showed I had in 4,115 sacks of sugar and the different parts of the locomotive. But there was no mention of freight on the locomotive. I said to Mr. Vicini, "What freight are you paying on this locomotive?" He said, "Same as sugar." I jumped out of the chair so quick my head almost knocked some of the cobwebs, which were in abundance, off his wall overhead. I said, "Your overseer at Palenque told me that you said not to leave the locomotive and that in case we could not agree that your consignee and mine could make the terms in New York." "Yes, yes," he said, "that is right." I said, "Before I sign these bills of lading you give me a letter to my consignee, A. H. Bull and Co. in New York." He gave me the letter but it was in Spanish. I left the bills of lading on his desk and took the letter to the American consul and had him to interpret it for me. It was just like he said it was. I went back to his office, signed the bills of lading, took my copy, gave him about 3 or 4 more of them all of the same tenor and date, took my clearance from the custom's house, went to the office of the American consul, cleared from him getting my crew list, register, articles, and bill of health, got some dinner, and when the boat came for me at about 4 PM I went on board. The mate had the hatches caulked, tarpaulins on, and by 5 o'clock everything was in shape to go to sea.

The next morning, July 6th, we sailed out with the land breeze. On Sunday, July 21st, after a passage of 15 days, we arrived safely in New York. And sorry to say I had to accept sugar rate for taking the locomotive to New York. But Mr. Vicini paid well for taking that locomotive to New York in the end. I now chartered to load on the Benner Line for Key West and Tampa, thence to Pascagoula to load lumber for New York. I did not make any money on this voyage and I will say very little about it. But the voyage was made safely.

At New York I chartered to load a cargo of cement in barrels at Rondout, New York, to Baltimore. Towed up to Rondout and took in 3,400 barrels cement. December 3rd, 1895, towed down the river and arrived and anchored close to the Statue of Liberty at 5:30 PM. The next morning I went on shore to ship a crew. Late in the afternoon I got on board. On Friday, with light westerly wind, clear and cold at 7 AM, got underway and sailed. At 11 AM passed out of the Hook. This was December 6th. Sunday, December 8th, weather threatening, I went in the Breakwater. Tuesday, the 10th, and Wednesday, the 11th, blowing a gale from northeast. Riding to both anchors with 45 fathoms chain out. This seems to be a week of bad weather. Thursday, the 12th of December, 1895, wind moderating. Got underway and went to sea. December 13th passed in the capes and at 8 PM came to anchor near New Point. Wind blowing a gale from the north. On Thursday, December 19th, anchored in Baltimore. Had bad weather all the way from New York. After getting out cargo of cement went to Wm. H. Skinner & Son's Railway. Hauled out and caulked her all over, bottom, topside, and deck.

X

1896–1898

I THEN chartered to load a cargo of kerosene oil in barrels and cases. I was then icebound and could not get away. On Wednesday, January 15th, 1896, got out and sailed for Jacksonville. Friday, January 17th, came to anchor under New Point, wind northeast and heavy rain. Saturday, January 18th, got underway at noon. Passed out of Cape Henry. January 20th, at 2 PM, passed Cape Hatteras. At 11:30 PM passed Cape Lookout. At 8 AM, January 21th, passed Frying Pan Lightship. Wednesday, January 22nd, arrived in Jacksonville and moored at the Standard Oil docks, seven days from Baltimore. After discharging cargo I chartered to Hodges & Godfrey to go to Satsuma Heights and load lumber for Philadelphia. Friday, February 10th, passed Cape Hatteras at 10:40 AM. Tuesday, the 11th February at 2 AM, passed the Winter Quarter Lightship. At 8 AM passed Fenwick Island Lightship. About this time wind shifted to the northwest blowing a gale. At 12 noon came to anchor under the beach near Hereford Lighthouse with 45 fathoms of chain and big anchor. Wednesday, the 12th of February at noon, got underway and sailed down toward the Breakwater. At 4 PM took a tow boat for Philadelphia. At 12 midnight came to anchor on the quarantine ground. Thursday, February 13th, at 7 AM, doctor came on board and gave us a pass to proceed. At 10:30 AM came to anchor off Kaines Point. At 2 PM took tow boat and docked at the lumber wharf, 6 days from Jacksonville. On this voyage we had gales all the way up from Jacksonville. After the cargo was out we got frozed up in Philadelphia for quite a while.

I then chartered to go to Nassau with a cargo of coal. The particulars of this voyage I have mentioned in the preceding. Then my mate, Fletcher Gantt, got arrested for shooting at one of the impudent laborers. I had to leave him there to be tried by the high court. I had to get along the best I could without a mate. Twenty six years later Captain Gantt died at this same place, Nassau. He was then master of the four-masted schooner *Purnell T. White*. I went to Nassau after the vessel and brought her home which so far has been my last activity in seafaring. From Nassau I went to Fernandina, entered, and went to Kings Ferry, Florida, and loaded lumber for Curacao, a Dutch island across the Caribbean Sea close to Venezuela.

Thence I went to Santo Domingo city; thence to Azua. I was consigned to Mr. Vicini, the Italian, again. There he undertook to make me loose a lot of time. Azua is about 6 miles up in the interior from the harbor. I telephoned up to the office of Mr. Vicini to send me a hack down to the harbor so that I could get up to the custom house and enter the ship. As you may understand I could not report the vessel ready for cargo until she had been entered at the custom house. This Mr. Vicini knew that and he wanted to hold me back as long as possible to give him time to get the cargo of sugar ready. I waited at the harbor until about one PM or perhaps later. I was determined that the vessel had to be entered that day so I pitched out to walk to the city of Azua which almost cost my life. Down to the beach the heat was not so bad but when I got up the road where the trees were thick and the sun shining on me I never suffered so much with heat in my life. At last I could stand it no longer. I got under a big lignum vitae tree, the most beautiful shady tree I ever saw or have ever seen since. I took my thin alpaca coat and began wiping the sweat off me. I was wiping the right side and then the left side of my face when I looked and there came the hack from around the turn in the road. I got in and rode but a short ways and I was in the city. I had walked nearly there. But I never suffered so with the heat in all my life. It seemed that my stomach yearned for something. I asked Mr. Vicini's clerk if he had any rum. I thought that might give me relief. He sent out and got a bottle of rum. I thought it was the prettiest bottle I ever saw. I have it in my home today as a memento of this trip or walk. I am sorry the rum is gone and has been for many years. When I drank the rum it gave me no relief. It was not the right thing for me.

I got my ship entered and gave them written notice I was ready for cargo. The next day he then ordered me to go to Ocoa to load, which was 20 or 25 miles from Azua. It was getting dark. I got my supper at the hotel and took the hack for the beach. Down here I got cooled off but I felt bad three or four days from the effects of my walk to Azua. The next day I sailed for Ocoa. This is the greatest place I ever went to in my life. The water is so deep close up to the beach. The wind blowed from the beach most all the time. I docked her as a man at Azua told me to do and that was to have my hawser and boat ready and to run her head on to the beach. The minute she struck to run this hawser ashore and tie to a tree before she got off the beach. This being done I let her drift off a certain distance and dropped my anchor in 21 fathoms of water. Then I runed a stern line from the port quarter and hauled her in along the side of the wharf. Then I runed my kedge and anchor from the starboard quarter with about 100 fathoms of line to it and hauled it tight to keep her from laying too hard on the shackly wharf. After she was moored safely I began to take in sugar. When I was loaded I had to go back to Azua to clear. Then I sailed for New York. I did all this labor and changing ports with no mate and some people will tell me I have had a good time in life.

From Azua I sailed for New York. On Tuesday, 7th day of July, 1896, arrived in New York making the passage in 14 days which was good for a sailing vessel and no mate. We went up to Yonkers to discharge. While lying here my old mate came on board to see me. I was glad to see him. He had been tried by the high court at Nassau and acquitted. He seemed to have friends there. He told me that many of the ladies gave him bouquets of flowers. The American consul then took him in charge, sent him to the hotel there, and paid his fare to New York.

After the cargo of sugar was out I chartered to go to Jacksonville to load lumber for New York. I had gone through so much in the past four months and needed a little rest and recreation. I put Mr. Gantt in charge of the vessel to make this voyage for me. He made it in good time and when he got back to New York I went on to meet the ship. While here I chartered to go to Kings Ferry, Florida, to load lumber for Curacao. About two days before sailing from New York I got a letter from Gray, Irelan & Company of Baltimore, saying they needed a captain to take charge of their vessel, the *Edward G. Hight*. While I did not like to give him up I could not do otherwise than to recommend him as he was worthy and well qualified. I spoke to him about it. He seemed to be proud of the job and I sent him to Baltimore with a letter of introduction. And thus we parted and were never shipmates again. I then shipped a German for mate and he was no comparison to Mr. Gantt and my voyage was not as pleasant as it would have been with Mr. Gantt.

On Saturday, September 12th, crew came on board. Took a tow boat and went in the river and came to anchor. On

Sunday, the 13th of September, got underway and proceeded. At Sandy Hook the wind came in from the east thick and rainey. We came to anchor under the Hook to wait for settled weather. On Wednesday, the 16th, got underway with wind north northeast blowing fresh and went to sea. Had a good run to Fernandina. Made it in 8 days. At 10 AM went ashore at Fernandina. Entered at the custom house. Got a towboat and was back to the ship at 11:30 and towed to Kings Ferry and tied up there at 6:15 PM. While there we had a dreadful hurrycane. It tore me from my mooring and carried me across the river. The *Harold B. Cousens,* a Boston schooner, broke from her moorings and came across the river. He hit my vessel and broke a plank in her stern. When I had crossed the river my first duty was to secure the ship before the next shift of wind. That would have blown us down the river or across from whence we came and would probably do lots of damage. As quickly as we could we got a new five-inch hawser on shore and began tieing it to the trees. And as fast as my men would get it tied to these large pines they would blow down. But we got the lines out to the bodies of the dozen trees and to some of the few that stood. Three or four of the young colored stevedores stayed by and helped me all they could. They got ringing wet from the downpour of rain and when they went home to change their clothes they found they had no home. Their homes were flat on the ground. I wish I were able to describe the damage this hurrycane did around Kings Ferry. Two or three days before the gale I was in a small apothecary shop, to me it appeared. The doctor had about $50 worth of goods or drugs in his place of business. When I got back across the river from the Georgia side I went to the place where this drug store once stood. I could smell spirits of nitre strong. The old doctor was surveying his wreckage. I said to him, "Doctor, you have met a loss." In a whine he said, "Yes, and $3,000 would not make my loss good."

Just shortly after I got the vessel secured to the trees on the
Georgia side and the wind began to moderate, there came a
young man down to the river and hollered across the river
to the Florida side for help, that a house had blown and a sick
boy was in the wreckage. The vessel now laying safely I went
up to this house. I do not think I ever beheld such wreckage.
The house had been blown about sixty or seventy feet. I could
not believe there was so much in a house, crockery, tinware,
cooking utensils, lamps, and straw mattresses all strewed along
on the ground from where the house started to where it stopped
and fell to pieces. There three or four men were standing
idle and said that the boy was in the house. "Well," I said,
"let us get him out." I got an ax and began cutting through the
roof which was now flat on the ground. In a short time I found
him and he was dead. He had a bruised place on his back
and he smelt so much like fever. They said his fever had
broken that day and he was getting better. He was eighteen
years old. But the most miraculous thing that could possibly
happen did happen here. They had a pony in a stable under
some live oaks. We went to look for him. It seems he had
gotton safely out of his stable when it blew down and he was
penned in between the limbs of these large live oaks for they
had all blown down. He did not have room to turn around
and he was not hurt. To those who have seen live oaks they
know how thick their foliage is. And on account of this thick
foliage lying on the ground we had quite a job to find
him. I must add in respect to Messrs. Mozelle & Brother, the
people who operated the saw mill at Kings Ferry, that he gave
all the negroes living at Kings Ferry the lumber free to build
their homes again.

The next day we got our ship over on the Florida side, the
storm having abated, and we began loading again. Messrs.
Mozelle & Brother told me they lost $12,000 worth of timber.
They had certain acreage in fine timber that no ax had ever

been in which they were holding in reserve and they were all broken down and would be lost. I asked him why he could not put men in there and get the timber out. He said that the timber would all be full of bug holes and become unsalable before he could get it out. After I finished loading and was towing down the St. Marys River my eyes never beheld such wreckage. Trees were blown down in piles, some with their tops blown off and so on.

I got down to Fernandina and cleared from the custom house for Curacao. *Keraso* is the way the natives pronounce the name of this city. I bought what stores I needed from the ship chandler and put to sea which was Thursday, the 8th day of October, 1896. On Saturday, the 10th, we got in another hurrycane which lasted until Sunday afternoon. After worrying with the different kinds weather, good, bad, and indifferent for 22 days, we arrived safely in Curacao Saturday, October 31st. We discharged our cargo of lumber and went to Bonaire and loaded salt for Baltimore. I must add here that I had a difficult time to buy a bill of exchange on New York or London. My consignee, Captain Leonard B. Smith, tried his best to buy me a bill of exchange but it seemed no merchants had an account in New York. But Captain Smith did get a bill of exchange from Bolton, Bliss & Dallet, New York steam agents, for $700. Then he went from place to place and got $800 in American gold and settled up with him. I will assure you that I never let anyone on board know that I had this gold on board or I may have never arrived back to the U. S. A. even if the ship did.

Bonaire has three salt pans, or three places, where they load salt. It is about the only industry there except some fishing. And the most beautiful coral I ever saw anywhere. It is cream color and represents leaves. The water is deep to the shore. In runing in I had to drop an anchor in 40 fathoms and the next one in 20 fathoms and lay between the two anchors. After

Captain Leonard S. Tawes, at right, and his brother, Captain John H. Tawes, who sailed with him on occasions. Photo taken June 14, 1920.

Steam yacht MARGARET, *in command of Captain L. S. Tawes, at Cornwall, Ontario, June, 1920, enroute from New York to Detroit where the vessel was to enter the service of the U. S. Army Engineers Corps.*

I was loaded I had a bad job getting my anchors. Captain Fowler, of the Baltimore schooner *Blanche Hopkins,* came on board with all of his crew at about 7 o'clock in the morning and we had drifted from the sight of land before we got her anchors and on the bow. Then I got her underway and sailed back to the island. It was 3 o'clock in the afternoon before his crew left my ship to go on board of his vessel. He certainly gave me a nice service and I regret to say just a few more years he and his wife and child were all lost at sea.

We sailed from Bonaire Wednesday, the 25th day of November, 1896, and after pulling, hauling, reefing, taking in sail, and setting again with difficulties too numerous to mention we arrived in Baltimore on Thursday, the 25th day of December, 29 days from Bonaire. I had a crew of New York sailors on board and they were crazy to get home for Christmas. It was now just about dark. They were grieving to think they had to stay in Baltimore two or three days, there being no possible way to get money to pay them off until Saturday the 26th. I said, "Boys, do not worry. I think I have a friend up the street that I can borrow enough money from to pay you off. I will go up and see. You eat your supper and by the time you are through I will be back." I went up town somewhere around Bond Street for I was laying at James Bondy's Salt Wharf. He was my consignee. In a little while I came back. One of the crew said, "What luck did you have?" I said, "Good luck. I can pay you off and you can go to New York tonight if you like." I went to my secret place in the cabbin, took out enough gold money to pay them off, made up their account, and called them in the cabbin. They said, "Captain, you certainly have got a friend here. And he let you have it in gold too." I settled with them and the next morning they all went to New York happy enough. I am writing this from the log books of the *City of Baltimore* that I found among the rubbage up the garret. At first I started to write from memory. I wish I had went up the garret and wrote from these books before for I have omitted many interesting stories.

After getting out the cargo of salt I went to the dry dock, hauled out, painted, put her in order and loaded a cargo of coal and went out to Curacao again consigned to my friend Leonard B. Smith. I must take the time to tell about him. He used to be a sea captain and he runed to Curacao quite a good lot. Across the river from the city of Curacao is another large town. There was no way to get from one of these towns or cities except by small ferry boats propelled by oars. Captain Smith, a keen observer from Bangor, Maine, saw that he could construct a bridge across that river. The water is so deep between these two towns, it being 30 or 40 fathoms deep, it was impossible to use piling to make a bridge. He got a concession from the government to build a bridge across the river. He constructed a lot of pontoons and linked them together and builded his bridge on them. At the west end he hung them something like a hinge on a door. And he had a steam engine also on the west side of the river by which, in 6 minutes, he could swing all of the bridge open the whole width of the river. When I first went to Curacao the pilot frightened me terribly. We had a smart breeze and we were coming in the harbor quite fast. I suggested to the pilot to shorten sail or we would nock the bridge down. He did not heed me but just let her go. When we got in a certain distance to my surprise the bridge opened the whole width of the river. Captain Smith and the government divided the tolls from the bridge and he became very wealthy. He made the island his home and became an importer of ice from Bangor, lumber from the southern states, and coal. He was also the American consul for a while. He died there some few years ago a very wealthy man. I want to say that he had a fine method of helping the poor. If anyone walked across the bridge barefooted they went over for half price. It was right amusing to see some of the colored people stop at the end of the bridge, pull off their shoes, buy a bare-footed ticket, and walk over barefooted and put their shoes on after they had crossed.

There was an old ship chandler there. He had four boys; one of them was named Henry Laba. Henry had been educated in New York and spoke good English. I carried a bycicle out with me on this voyage. I bought it in Baltimore from a man name Kline who kept a bycicle place on Baltimore Street. This bycicle was second-handed but had new tires on it. Bycicles were high in those days; I gave him $30 for it. Now Mr. Laba kept his ship chandlery across the street from where I lay. When I put my bycicle out to ride Henry came to me and said, "Captain, how would you like to ride out to my father's planta-tion tomorrow, Sunday morning?" I told him it would be fine. "Well," he said, "we will start early in the morning while it is cool." Just as soon as I finished breakfast the next morning we started on our bycicles. He had one, of course. We rode along quite some miles. The road we went on was quite shady and it was pleasant indeed. About 9 o'clock we rode up to his father's plantation. The old gentleman had the table piled up with silver money from which he was paying his laborers. We stayed there a while about an hour, got all the diferent kind of fruits we could, then we proceeded back to the city. Just as the sun was getting real hot we got back to the city. The old gentleman, through his son as the interpreter, asked a favor of me which I never had the opportunity to grant though I promised him I would. He asked me to bring him out a large Plymouth Rock rooster and hen when I came out there again. But I never went there again.

When I was there the voyage before this one I saw he was repairing his store and putting it in tip-top order. And when I was there this time I learned his reason. One day Henry came to me and said, "I want you to be at the store at 10 o'clock today. We are going to have a house warming." The old man was the Norwegian consul and there was a Norwegian bark in port from Newcastle with a load of coal. Henry asked him up to my ship and the bark up the river a little ways at the coal yard. We went together down to the ship chandlery. Here were the elites of the city to honor Mr. Laba. At 10 o'clock we formed an oblong square on the floor leaving one end open so that the waiters could come in and serve and pass out. I saw lots of cases of champaign laying on the floor. The Norwegian and myself stood close together in the ranks and when all was in order the champaign corks began to fly. Now all the champaign parties I ever got into previous to this one the glass was filled once and you just sip a little at the time and talk and listen. Not so in this party. I began to just sip a little but here would come a waiter and fill your glass. And they kept doing this. I thought to myself here is the time to fill up and I began to let it go down. The Dutch army and navy officials, and first one and then the other, were giving toasts and speeches. I could not understand Dutch but I knew how to drink champaign as well as they did. The party broke up at exactly 12 noon. There was a hotel upstairs over Mr. Laba's store. I was then feeling good. I said to the Norwegian, "Let us go upstairs and get dinner." When I got up there I was seated by the side of the American consul from Baltimore by name Stephens. I just felt rich and like loosening up so I said, "Mr. Stephens, have a bottle of champaign with your dinner." I said, "Waiter, bring 3 bottles of champaign." This he did. And it was the first and last time I ever treated to champaign. Mr. Laba had this store put in first class condition and turned it over to his four sons and retired to his plantation in his country home. I visited on Sunday with his son Henry and he gave this party as his farewell to doing business at the city.

About a week before this I sold my bycicle to a fellow named Santacruz for $50. I had known Santacruz for a long time. He was a minister's son there and like many other people he had the habit of making bills which went unpaid. I went to a dentist to get a tooth filled. He had been educated in New York and spoke good English. He was recommended to me by Captain Smith, my consignee. I found he knew his business as a dentist too. While filling my tooth he said to me, "Did not Santacruz buy a bycicle from you?" I said, "Yes." He said, "Did he pay you for it?" I said, "No, why?" "Well," he said, "you ought to get your money. Santacruz is a good fellow but he so often gets broke. There was a lot of Cubans came over here not so long ago. They brought over some splendid cigars and unfortunately for them they had to leave without their money." After this I went down to the English consul to get a suit of clothes made. He kept a very nice store. While he was measuring me he said, "Did not Santacruz buy a bycicle of you?" I said, "Yes." He said, "Did you get your money?" "No," I said. He just groaned. I knew what it meant and I asked no further questions about it. When my cargo was out and I had cleared I went to Santacruz and told him I was going to sail the next day and wanted my money for the wheel. He said to me in his mild and smooth way, "Now, Captain, you can help me out on this deal. You can take some cigars which I have and they are good ones. And you can take some gin. Curacao is headquarters for good Holland gin." I said, "Santacruz, I'd rather have my money. I do not know what to do with gin and cigars." "But," he said, "you can double your money on them." I saw there was nothing else to do. He had no money to settle with me. I told him to put the gin in barrels packed well and send them down to the ship as flour. And he did. I had the barrels of supposed flour put in the lazarette a certain head up and there they staid until I sold them for $75. I sold the 1,300 cigars for $52. I did well on this bycicle.

The next day after the party at Mr. Laba's, and getting settlement with Santacruz, I sailed for Macoris, Santo Domingo, to load sugar for New York. All the way across the Caribbean

Sea, 400 miles, I knew just as well how to handle my ship and navigate her as if I had never touched a drop of champaign. I was three days crossing dead on the wind and bucking into a high, head sea. I made the port of Macoris and went in like an old trader there though I had never been there before. Here I loaded sugar for my Italian friend, Mr. Vicini. In loading the sugar I just merely said to the steward, "Now sometimes the sacks get torn and it might be dificult to get all the sugar back in the sacks. You get enough out to fill your sugar box and give the crew all the sweet cake they want every night for supper."

We finished loading March 8. Took in 3,277 sacks of sugar. Got the ship ready and sailed March 10, 1897, for New York direct. After experiencing the storms, calms, fogs, and variable winds we arrived at Red Hook and anchored on Friday March 26, a passage of 16 days which was good for the month of March. I remember suffering a great deal with the cold on this run in. I remember I was about off the Delaware. I had not seen any land since I left Santo Domingo. It was thick of fog. A pilot spoke me. He wanted to know if I wanted a pilot. I told him I would not pay offshore pilotage. He said, "You will get a pilot when you get further north." I do not think he wanted to come on board anyhow for he knew what was coming and he would be far more comfortable on the pilot boat. When the wind came about 12 midnight it came out from the northwest and blew a gale. The sailors were all frozed to stiffness and we were all of three hours getting her reefed down. I was at the wheel all the time and I lost feeling in my feet to my knees, I was so cold. And when I got her on the starboard tack and headed in for the land I had been at the wheel 3 hours. I went below to warm myself and all the fire had gone out in the cabbin. It was as cold in there as in an ice house and I suffered with the cold intensely. After getting her reefed down I put her on the starboard tack and fetched in at Absecon at 12 o'clock noon the next day. I then put her on the port tack, turned the reefs out, and went to Sandy Hook in 8 hours. It was blowing heavy. I anchored under the Hook and layed there 3 days before it moderated sufficient to sail in the Hook.

After I got the cargo of sugar out I chartered to take a cargo of railroad iron to Wilmington. Then I loaded a cargo of lumber for Macoris, Santo Domingo. I had met a baker there by name Reis who chartered me. I dictated the terms and conditions of the charter party. In it I had specified my outward freight to be payable in American gold in Macoris of proper discharge of cargo at $6.50 per thousand feet, back on sugar at $2.75 per ton to New York. While I was discharging my cargo of lumber I would at times go to his office. He did a big business in the bakery. He would open his safe doors and call my attention to the big pile of Mexican dollars he had in there and say to me, "Este flete dinero por usted"—"this freight money for you." He could not speak English but could talk Spanish real fast. I said to myself, "When the day of settlement comes you will not get your Mexican dollars off on me." One day we were riding together, or in company, on our bycicles and in turning a corner we past the house Thorman and Beiderman. Mr. Thorman I had been knowing for years. We went out to the caves one Sunday in Santo Domingo in 1882 which was then my first voyage to the island. In turning the corner of the street I hissed at Mr. Reis to stop and I suggested we go in and see Mr. Thorman. When we got in Mr. Thorman's office I told him about how my charter party was made out and on proper delivery of cargo I was to be paid in American gold. And that Mr. Reis had about ½ bushel of Mexican dollars in his safe which he suggested would be my freight money. Mr. Thorman said to me, "Captain, stand by your charter party." Then he and Mr. Reis went into a long conversation in Spanish which I could not understand. When they got through Mr.

Thorman said to me, "Captain, when you have finished discharging your cargo bring me your charter party and bill of lading and I will settle your freight in American gold as per your charter party. I will use the Mexican dollars here to pay labor on the sugar plantation." And so he did.

Mr. Reis turned me over to the Porto Rico sugar estate to load me with sugar for New York. After being loaded I took 3 passengers for New York. We sailed Thursday, the 24th of June, 1897. We had considerable moderate weather on the run until I got into the southern edge of the Gulf Stream when the wind began to breeze up from the southwest. Very early in the morning it was blowing fresh and my old ship was moving swiftly. I was glad to see this breeze. She was shipping some water on the deck and the spray was flying over her abundantly. One of the Spanish passengers came on deck about 4 o'clock in the morning. He got frightened and ran back in the cabin and woke up his other Spanish friend, a Mr. Bueno, and told him the seas were angry. He came on deck terribly frightened, grabed me and huged me, and wanted to know if there was not danger. I told him not a bit, that it was just what I wanted. I had a hard time to assure him there was no danger, that he was safe. He got calm after a while. The *Baltimore* had in about 500 tons of sugar and she was as stiff as a brick house. The spars and rigging were strong and in good condition and I was determined she must get out of her lazy spell and go to New York. And she did. When I made Sandy Hook Mr. Bueno said to me, "Captain, you have a beautiful country and well governed but it takes a brave man to do what you do to run this vessel on the high seas. If I ever hear another Cuban say that he had been engaged in battle with the Spaniards and what narrow escapes he had I shall tell them that they had experienced nothing to what I had. I had made a passage on the schooner *City of Baltimore* from Santo Domingo to New

York which would surpass any daring bravery they had ever experienced."

Both of these Cubans had sight drafts on some sugar firm in New York. I went with them to get their drafts cashed. It was Saturday afternoon and the offices of the sugar firms had closed. They had no American money and I did not want to keep them on board until Monday morning. So I took them with me to the office of A. H. Bull and Company. They had not closed their office. I introduced them to my old friend the bookkeeper, C. Alex Cook. I told him of the circumstances, that I brought them from Santo Domingo with me as passengers, and that they were without money but had sight drafts on a sugar firm here in New York. I wished to know if he could cash their drafts for them. And this he did. They left Mr. Bull's office happy and I never saw or heard from them again. They were both from the Cuban army.

It was on Friday, July 9th, we arrived in New York. Discharged our cargo at the American Sugar Refinery, Jersey City. After the cargo was out we went to Gokey's Dry Dock, Erie Basin, hauled her out, painted bottom, put the vessel in good order, and chartered to go to Basse Terre, Guadeloupe, and Pointe-à-Pitre to finish discharging our cargo. From there we went to Ragged Island and loaded salt for Baltimore. We arrived safely about November 22, 1897, having to contend with calms and threatening hurrycanes. We were rather long on making this round, having to go to 3 ports.

I chartered this time to load a cargo of coal for San Juan, Porto Rico, December 12. Sailed on December 13 at noon. Went out by Cape Henry and after experiencing various kinds of weather for 17 days we arrived in San Juan safely on Wednesday, December 29, 1897. I well remember that we had an American consul by the name of Reid. He could not hear good. He was from Iowa. I spent a greater part of a day helping to dress up the consulate with flags, our flag, our Jack, and other bunting. All of this was to give honor to a new governer who was to arrive on this particular day from Spain to govern the island. He was met at the dock with pomp and splendor. The soldiers, marines, and police lined on each side of the street where he had to pass on his way up to the capitol where he was to take the oath as governor. They had small cannon lashed on the backs of mules, plenty of marshal music, and many other things I am unable to discribe. Unfortunately, about ten o'clock that night, he droped dead and Porto Rico was without a governor.

I must mention one more little incident that occured. I happened to be home off from one of my voyages when my daughter, then a little girl, had some candy. This candy was wraped in facsimile Confederate money. She happened to have two of these wrappers in her hand one day and I asked her to give them to me. I had no intention of doing anything with them. I put them in my vest pocket and never thought any more about them. When I got to Baltimore, and in Gray, Irelan and Company's office, there came in a pedler selling cheap jewelry. I bought ½ dozen watches for $2.62½ each. I carried them to Porto Rico with me. After getting my cargo of coal out, and laying in the stream waiting for the wind to cant around to the eastward so that I could sail out, there was a fellow out fishing close to me and he hailed and asked me what I had on board to sell. I told him I had 3 handsome gold watches and that I would guarantee that they looked as well now as they ever would. I had already sold the other three while I was laying there discharging cargo. This fisherman came on board to look at the watches. I think I sold them for $5.00 each, making $15. He paid me and said, "When you come out again bring me some Confederate money." Then I thought of these candy wrappers. I went back in the after cabbin and brought them out. He fell in love with them and could not take his eyes off them. He said, "How much you want for them?" His English was not plain; it was very poor. I said to him in Spanish, "Este dinero no bueno." Then I would say in English, "This money is no good." I said, "What will you give me for them?" He said, "I will give you 400 good cigars." I said, "Alright, you may have them but you cannot have them until I am ready to leave the harbor." I did not want to get mixed up with the Spanish authorities. I said, "When you see me getting underway and getting the sails on her you bring them out to me and you may have this no account money." In about 2 more days the wind hauled around to the eastward. I began to get underway. Here he came out and brought 4 boxes nice cigars. I gave him these candy wrappers. I then sailed out of the harbor of San Juan and in 3 hours San Juan was below the horison. At Pascagoula I sold them for $20. Some might think this not an honest deal. But I told the fellow both in Spanish and English they were no good and I accepted his first offer. I went to San Juan 3 or 4 times after this but never saw him again. This was in the early part of 1898 and it was the last time I was ever there under the Spanish regime as we had a war with Spain that year and drove the Spaniards out of the island.

At Pascagoula I loaded lumber for New York. Got in an awful gale of wind in lattitude 36° 52′ on the third day of March. The wind was from east northeast with heavy downpour of rain. At 5 PM, in wearing ship, the sea was high and a big one of them ran over us and ran up under the topgallant forecastle and took out every movable thing from under there. Even the grindstone and a barrel of kerosene oil, a thing which we mostly needed for lights. It is the most essential thing on ship board. Just before I wore ship to head her offshore, and seeing what we had to contend with that night, I remember saying to an old sailor named Jim, a very competant seaman, "Jim, I am going to put her in Hampton Roads tonight." It was snowing and raining very hard and thick. The night was coming on and old Jim looked at me with astonishment when I told him this. He knew it was impossible to do such a thing but as darkness set in I set my storm trysail in the mizzin, tied my foresail up, and took in my jib. She was now hove to under storm trysail, double reefed mainsail, and fore staysail. This was her favorite sail to ride to in a gale of wind. Now she was laying easy and rolling easy and taking care of herself in fine shape. I said, "She is now in Hampton Roads." He said, "Captain, I did not know what you meant when you said you were going to put her in Hampton Roads." I said, "Jim, I am going to do something I never done before. Instead of having the full watch on deck I am going to let one man stand the watch 2 hours each and that will releive you of a great deal of suffering this cold bitter night. But you must promise me you will get up on the fore gaff where you can keep a good lookout and let me know when you see a light. I will lay on my sofa ready to jump with the flare light to warn him not to run over us. But if I come up on deck and catch the man on the watch off duty I will make the full watch stand their watch." They all promised me they would not leave their post. And they never did as I was out 3 or 4 times and found them on duty. The next day they were all feeling fresh and good having about 8 hours below in a comfortable forecastle. When the gale moderated they could get her underway easily. Now having no oil on board I put her in Hampton Roads. After getting in the Roads I, for the first time, heard the *Maine* was blown up in Havana and the people seemed to be very much excited over it. After laying here until the weather became favorable I got underway and went to New York. It seems by the log book I was 27 days making this passage including the time I lay in Hampton Roads, arriving in New York Sunday, March the 13th, 1898.

I now chartered to take a cargo of cement to Fort Caswell, entrance to Cape Fear River, or at Southport. And then I was to load a full cargo of lumber for Santo Domingo city, West Indies. When I got to Fort Caswell I could see by the newspapers that our nation was getting warlike with Spain. And when I got the cement out I was in no hurry to get to Wilmington as I did not want to go to Santo Domingo if war was declared. So I would not take a tow boat to tow me up to Wilmington. The pilots at Southport was anxious that I should. They told me nobody ever sailed up the river. I told them about 16 years before this I used to sail up with a loaded vessel and that I was going to sail this one up. They gave me a river pilot by name of Burrows. It was Sunday. We had a fair wind and sailed up in about 4 hours. On the way up I looked at the pilot and he reminded me so much of a pilot that sailed me up the river 16 years before this that I said to him, "Was your father a pilot on this river?" I think he said, "No, why?" I said, "You look so much like a pilot that sailed me up this river 16 years ago when I sailed a schooner called the *William H. Knight*. We were 3 days beating up the river. It was January and icicles were freezing in the rigging." He said, "That was me." I was much surprized. He did not look a day older.

After getting up to Wilmington in the *City of Baltimore,* the next day being Monday, I hauled into the wharf of Northrup and Cadwell's mill where my lumber was laying ready to load. I nocked the ports out, cleaned up the hold ready for cargo, and on that day we declared war against Spain. I then refused to load the cargo. Mr. Northrup was anxious that I should do so because he could get his bill of lading signed, put it in the bank, draw his money, and leave me to do the best I could. I could not think of runing down through the Mona Passage close to Porto Rico, be captured by the Spaniards, and be made a prisoner and stay there until the war ended. Or probably be captured by one of Cervera's fleet as they passed by to the north of Porto Rico on their way to Havana to chalenge the American fleet laying off the port there blockadeing the city. And I may be left a prisoner down in the hold of the Spanish man-of-war when our ships would fill her as full of holes as a beehive and I and my crew would go down to David Jones' locker with the Spanish ship. After considering this all over I told Mr. Northrup not a stick of his lumber would I take, that I intended to get out of this charter if possible. Mr. Northrup appeared to be sorry that I was in this scrape. I wired Mr. Delgardo in New York, who had me chartered, if he would not release me from the charter. He wired me back he would if Messrs. Northrup and Cadwell would release him from the purchase of the lumber. I showed this to Mr. Northrup and he would not release Mr. Delgardo from the purchase of the lumber, as sorry as he was for me. I then got the schedule of the size and length of the lumber and came to Baltimore and got a lumber broker to try to sell it anywhere he could along our northern coast. Had he sold it I was going back to Wilmington, buy the cargo from Messrs. Northrup and Cadwell, then load it and deliver it wherever it was sold. But, unfortunately, the cargo was so cut that it could not be sold anywhere in the U.S.A. Then the last resort was to see Mr. Delgardo in New York and make the best possible terms for a release from my charter. It cost $500 and $50 traveling expense. Now I was free to charter again.

I then put my vessel in the hands of Mr. George Norris, ship broker in Wilmington, a man I always liked. But it seems that the old gentleman could find no freight. I beleive I waited on him 5 or 6 days. When an Austrian steamship that had been ashore on the Frying Pan Shoals and salvaged by the Merritt Wrecking Company had to be sold to the highest bider, there came down from New York a Mr. M. K. Knowlton who then was a partner of Mr. A. H. Bull, then working under the name Miller, Bull and Knowlton. Both of these gentlemen have been deceased some years ago. As soon as Mr. Knowlton arrived in Wilmington he looked me up. I had to go to the Hotel Orton where he was stoping and take meals with him and go to the baseball with him. In fact, he made me his companion the two days he was in Wilmington. I was with him when the Austrian steamer was sold. He bid up on her considerable over $200,000 but the Clyde Line bider out-bid him and she went to the Clyde Line Steamship Company. I told Mr. Knowlton I had nothing to do. He said, "Captain, if you want a freight I will put the boys at work in New York right away." In about 4 or 5 hours I was chartered to load a cargo of dry boards for New York at $4 per thousand. And they were in such a hurry for me that I had to go at once up to Chadwick Mill and load at once. They made another vessel that was up there loading quit and get out of the way so that I could haul in. And in 12 days I was in New York with a $1,280 freight earned. I had my $550 earned that I lost on the Santo Domingo charter.

On my way up to New York, about somewhere off the Delaware, it was rainey and thick. I saw two warships painted in war color and I began to feel real uneasy fearing they were Spaniards. But when they got close to me and I saw that one of them was the *Columbia,* the other the *New York,* all of my fear and uneasiness turned to joy. They were doing patrol work off the Delaware.

When my cargo of lumber was discharged I chartered to Rondout and loaded cement for Charleston, South Carolina. On Friday, the 10th day of June, passed out of Sandy Hook. On Tuesday, June 21, went into Charleston harbor making the passage in 11 days. Discharged our cargo of cement and loaded lumber for Bridgeport, Connecticut, and sailed from Charleston on the 6th day of July, 1898. On account of the harbor of New York being so full of mines and torpedoes I did not go in by Sandy Hook but went up around Montauk Point and came down the Long Island Sound to Bridgeport. Arrived there on Monday, July the 18, making the passage in 12 days.

My bill of lading was to order and I was nearly ½ day finding my consignee. Finally, by the help of the harbor master I found him. But in the meantime, while I was trying to find him, an English schooner who had a strait bill of lading came into the harbor by me and went direct to the wharf. There was one other vessel to this wharf ½ out and the river was so narrow there was only room for two vessels to lay. I saw there was going to be detention in getting discharged. Finally, I came to a young, nice looking man by name Burrows. I said to him, "Are you my consignee? Have you the bill of lading of the schooner *City of Baltimore?*" He said, "I have." "Well," I said, "you will please indorse my charter party." He said, "What do you want me to put on it?" I said, "The day and the hour I reported to you." He pulled out his handsome gold watch which showed 10 o'clock. He noted it on the charter party and signed his name. My lay days started from that moment. I said, "Where do you want me to come in?" He said, "I have no room here for you. You will have to lay out in the lower harbor until I can make room for you." I telegraphed for my wife to meet me in New York. I took the steamer and went to New York to meet her. We stayed there a day or two and we went to Bridgeport. Finally, one of these vessels was discharged. There being only room for two vessels to lay at the lumber yard, one had to lay outside of the other and wait for the other to finish discharging. I had to lay alongside of the English vessel and wait for him to finish discharging before I could begin. Mr. Burrows never gave time any thought. He was not used to it. Most all the vessels that ran lumber to him were small coasters, generally from Norfolk and James River, and were not posted on real maritime usages.

Finally, the little English vessel was discharged and my turn came for discharging. Lucky for me Mr. Burrows was to discharge my vessel at 50 cents per thousand feet. When he began he only had two lay days left. After the third day of discharging he owed me one day of demurrage. I took my bill for $30 in his office and laid it on his desk. He looked at me surprisingly.

I suppose he never had anything like this to occur before and he got mad with me. But the next morning I walked in his office and laid down another bill for $30. He said, "Look here Captain, I never paid demurrage in my life and I never intend to." "Well," I said, "the other day you told me you were 37 years old and people have done a thing for the first time older than you." The next morning I came in the office with another bill for $30. I felt a little uneasy going in on the third; I did not think but that he might throw me out of his office. But to my surprise he treated me civally, even courteous. I thought why such a change. I guess he has consulted some legal advice. The next morning, now the 4th day, I came in with another bill for $30. He laid it on his desk politely. The first 2 bills he tore them up and threw them in the waste basket. But after the 2nd day of demurrage he began working all night each night and would not take time to put the lumber on the wharf. He just got it out of the ports and let go overboard. When I was through there was a great big pile of lumber laying in the water under my bow. Now settlement came. He gave me a check for my freight. I took it. Then I said, "Mr. Burrows, there is $120 due me for four days demurrage." He said, "Captain, I did not make that charter party. Booth Brothers in New York made that charter party. You must look to them for your demurrage." I said, "I wrote to Booth Brothers about this and they told me they had nothing to do with it." He said, "I have nothing to do with it." "Well," I said, "the devil is in the wood cord somewhere and I am going to find him. I am going to attach that lumber in the water under my bow." He said, "If you do I will give bond for it." I said, "Mr. Burrows, you are the man I am after."

I went to some building where there was a marine lawyer and asked him if he did Admiralty business. He said that he did. I have forgotton his name. I showed him my charter party and bill of lading and told him there was $120 due me for demurrage. He said, "Why did not you collect this daily?" I said, "I tried and rendered my bill daily but I could not get it." I said, "What show have I to collect this money?" He said, "About 99 chances out of a 100." I said, "What will you charge to collect it?" He said, "10%." I thought that was reasonable enough and I gave him the charter party and bill of lading. I said to him, "If you can collect $100 without me coming here to attend court, settle it." By the time I got to Wilmington, North Carolina, I received the $100 less his commission. I regret I never met Mr. Burrows again to tell him he did something for the first time after he was 37 years of age.

I had some cargo to go to New Haven. I went there, finished discharging, and sailed to New York. Here I docked and painted her bottom and chartered to load fertilizer, or tankage, from Barren Island for Wilmington, North Carolina. We sailed from Barren Island on Wednesday, the 17th day of August, 1898, little thinking what was before us before we should get back to New York again. After experiencing the many various winds, squalls, and rains we arrived in Wilmington in 13 days. I remember being in company in a very moderate breeze with several vessels, the *Douglass Gregory,* Captain Lou Stilwell, and the *Jerome B. Look,* Captain McKensie. I was close enough to him to speak to him. Here a fresh northeast wind struck us. In trying to run boomed out I would have to change my course as much as 2 points to keep her from jibing which would at that time be very dangerous in breaking a gaff or boom. I did not have a man that could steer her before the wind and I had to do it myself. But in about 4 hours the wind got steady and I put a man at the wheel and gave him the course to steer, southwest ¾ west.

The next afternoon I rounded the Frying Pan and steered in for the entrance to Cape Fear River. That afternoon I never saw the sky looking so redish, more especially around the sun in the west. I got into Southport safely and towed the river to

Wilmington. When I arrived and went on shore Willie Harris, a ship broker there, told me I had better get my vessel into some wharf and moor her safely as there was a dreadful hurrycane striking in on the coast a little south and would hit Wilmington at 12 midnight. I told him I had my big anchor overboard and that I would give her a good scope of chain when I went back on board. She would lay at that as safely as tied to a wharf. The hurrycane did not strike Wilmington as predicted but hit in on the coast near Charleston and all the vessels that were in company with me off Cape Hatteras were either sunk or driven on the beach. The *Douglass Gregory* was sunk and most of her crew were drowned. The *Jerome B. Look* turned over and every man drowned. Captain J. Cornelius Woodland, in the schooner *Deering,* was driven ashore on the beach and no one drowned. If I had not been going to Wilmington I would have been one of the victims.

Here we discharged our cargo of tankage and loaded lumber for Kingston, Jamaica, B. W. I. I sailed from Southport Saturday, September 24, 1898. I think we had a quick run out to Kingston, done in ten days. We had a hurrycane just to the westward of us. We had a heavy sea from it but it did not hit us. In Kingston it was very hot. One Saturday I went with a gentleman, a Mr. George Hart, up to Mandarin on the train and spent Sunday with him and came back on Monday. I certainly enjoyed the ride and the scenery was beautiful. I had not rode only a few miles out of the city on the train before I perceived my skin was getting dry. I am sure it was the first time it had been dry since I arrived in Kingston. I said, "Mr. Hart, my skin is getting dry. I feel like as if I was in America." He said, "Yes, we are going up higher and higher." Shortly, we ran in the clouds and then out of them again and so on. It was real interesting to look down the mountain sides and view the banana plantations away below us in the valleys. Just a little before dark we arrived at our destination. A colored man met us at the depot. He had a single horse and a two-wheel buggy and we started for the summer home of Mr. Hart. I thought I never saw such beautiful roads. They were so well kept though they were of a very hard, stony surface but very smooth. And at some little distance you could see an orange tree hanging full of oranges close to the side of the road.

We stoped at a little country grocery store. It was just getting dark. I was real thirsty, so thirsty that I beleive I would have given $5.00 for a bottle of Bordeau wine, St. Julian Brand. The acid of this particular table wine was just what my stomach was yearning for. I had no idea this little country store had this particular wine but I got off the buggy and went in the store. Mr. Hart was in there. I asked if he had the St. Julian wine. He said that he did. I bought a bottle and it did me lots of good. He would not charge me a cent for it. Finally, we arrived at the residence of Mr. Hart and had a splendid supper. His wife, a very congenial lady, knew how to make a stranger feel at home. After a pleasant chat that evening I was shown to my room. I turned in for a sleep. I did not close the window blinds and sometime that night I woke up nearly frozed. The next night I closed the blinds and slept warmer. Window blinds is about all the houses in the West Indies have. They do not have window glasses. The window blinds are made close and keep out the rain.

The next day Mr. Hart and I took the single horse and two wheel buggy and drove over to one of his neighbors, a Mr. Levy, and spent the afternoon. While over here I met a young bragdosia Englishman and we happened to get in conversation about our war with Spain and the battle of Santiago, Cuba. This young fellow told me we had no ship of war, that our ships were only on paper. "Well," I said, "we cleaned up the Spanish fleet." He said, "Yes, but the Spaniards only had wooden bombs." Conversation seemed to drift along in the usual way until this fellow told me all the officials in our country were not honest. I said, "Young man, now you are going to the extreme. You know our big officials are honest. I would not say that all our small officials are honest." He said, "None are, from the President down." I felt stung at this. I can stand to hear an American nock our country but I could not stand it from a citizin from another country. Finally, I heard Mr. Levy tell Mr. Hart that he was out to some little town close by there and the tax collector said to him, "How is this, Mr. Levy, you are driving a four wheel vehicle and only paying taxes for 2 wheels?" He said, "I had a time to convince him that my buggy was in a blacksmith shop for repairs and that this carriage I was now using was my neighbor's. I had borrowed it and that mine was at the blacksmith shop for repairs." This arroused my curiosity and I asked, "How is this? You pay taxes on wheels?" They said, "Yes." "Well," I asked, "how much are the taxes on a wheel?" They said, "One pound sterling." I said, "That is a big tax." They said, "And we pay ½ pound for the horse and ½ pound for the driver. Five pounds altogether." About $24.21 in our money. I said, "Young man, I know now where you get the idea that all our officials are theives, from the President down. If that was law in our country they would get on good boxes and make speeches to turn the rascals out, that they are robing us. Even if our taxes was more than $2.50 a year on such a rig they would speak the same. And you cannot make such public speeches in your country or you would be getting yourself in trouble. You read our papers and that is where you get the idea that our officials are theives." Now I want to say this, "I thank our grandfathers for shaking the English yoke." Mr. Hart told me he was glad that I gave this young man something to think about. We spent the afternoon pleasantly and drove back on our two wheel buggy, had a good supper, spent the night, and took the train back to Kingston the next morning and found the heat as usual.

[325]

After we finished discharging our cargo we went down the coast to Black River to load a cargo of fustic for Chester, Pennsylvania. Fustic is a dyewood, yellow like mustard, and quite heavy. It is so precious that every small limb of the tree is saved and even the roots are dug out of the ground and sold by the pound. We also took on some logwood. It is also a dyewood and makes a dark blue clor. It is also scarce and valuable. They also take the small limbs of the tree and dig the roots out of the ground. Both of these woods are gotton out in very ugly shapes and in order to carry a good cargo I had to hire two men from the shore to saw them in pieces so that they would stow closely in the hold of the ship as I was paid by the ton to carry them to Chester. While we were loading I met a very fine captain from Maine. He loaded with logwood and fustic, the same kind of cargo I was taking in. He was bound to Boston. He was much worried about his crew, whose time was about to expire, but he got away one day before their time was up. To get a new crew to go to Boston at this season of the year was impossible, or about so. I wish I could remember his name or the name of the vessel but he got caught in the great gale of wind I shall soon try to describe and he never again come into port.

When I had finished loading I tried to buy some Irish potatoes but there was none to be had in at this port. I said to my stevedore, "I cannot find any potatoes and they are something hard to get along without on shipboard." He said, "Captain, why don't you buy some yams? They will take the place of potatoes when you cannot do better." I always thought they were the poorest excuse for food I ever saw. I was before the mast in a barque once out to Rio de Janeiro, Brazil. There the captain bought a lot of these yams to eat on the passage home. I suffered very much with hunger before I got to Baltimore and we were 49 days coming home. To resume my story I went up to the market with this stevedore and I bought 150 lbs. of yams having no idea they would ever become precious to us.

We finished loading our cargo about the 11th of November and sailed on Saturday, the 12th day of November, 1898. I had no chart west of Jamaica and I knew that the Grand Cayman Islands lay right in my track. I went on board of an English vessel lying there and I asked him if he had a chart of the west end of Jamaica and leading to Cape Antone. He had one but I could not get it but he let me look at it as much as I wished. I got me some tissue paper and held his chart up to the light and took a lead pencil and traced out a chart from Jamaica including the Grand Cayman, Little Cayman, and Cayman all the way to Cape Antone, west end of Cuba. I runed the *Baltimore* on this chart. I made all three of these islands and sailed on to Cape Antone. I made everything I runed for just as well as if I had had the best chart that James Imray in London had ever made. I rounded Cape Antone, came up through the Straits of Florida, and when about in the lattitude of Charleston I began the terible experience, a tale on account of its length, that has never been told. Many of the incidents I have forgotton as it has been 32 years since this occurred and my memory does not serve me as well now as it used to when I was younger.

When off the lattitude of Charleston we experienced our first heavy gale of wind. The two chickens I had on board, I had alotted to have them on the Thanksgiving. This gale of wind caused their lives to be spared and we were glad to get a piece of salt beef, a cup of coffee, and hard tack. Then we alotted they should be killed for our Sunday dinner but on Saturday, the 28th day of November, there sprang up one of the heviest gales of wind that ever blew on the Atlantic Ocean. It was in the forenoon of this 26th day of November, 1898, with wind strong from south southeast. I was runing a course north by east for as near as I knew for Fenwick Island Light intending this to be my landfall. I was carrying all sail which was drawing and going along nicely. At noon the sun was obscured and I got no observation for lattitude. But by dead reckoning I was in lattitude 36° 26′ north. Immediately after dinner the wind breezed up rather strong. I took in my mizzin topsail and outer jib and furled them. This done I took in my fore and main topsails and furled them. The wind kept increasing and clouds looking bad. I lowered the spanker down and reefed and tied it up, the wind increasing from south southeast and looking bad and threatening. I then lowered my mainsail and reefed it and put it on her. The rain was now falling fast and the *Baltimore* was runing like a scared dog.

There was a vessel not far from me bearing southwest. She was loaded with the same kind of cargo that I was The captain must have been a young man for in handling my ship he would do the same as I would do. When I took in my mizzin topsail he would take in his. When I took in my jib topsail he took in his. When I took in my fore and main topsails he took in his. When I lowered my spanker, reefed it, and tied it up he did the some. I now steped below in the cabbin and looked at my barometer. I saw she was falling fast. I knew we were going to get a shift of wind from the west. It was now blowing a gale from the south southeast. I now settled down on my mainsail and jibed it over, also the foresail and jibs, and headed her in on a northwest course. It was now getting near night. I reefed the foresail and thought to set it but the gale was increasing so rapidly and with such fury I ordered it furled. I was now runing her northwest under reefed mainsail, fore staysail, and jib. Now my friend did all I did. He jibed over when I did and headed to the northwest. But he reefed his foresail and set it and if he kept that reefed foresail on her all night I would not be surprised if he did not go to the bottom before morning. When night set in I never saw him again.

At 8 PM took in the jib and tied it up. The wind had hauled to the northwest with increasing fury. I set the storm trysail in the mizzin and hove her to on the port tack heading north by east. The *Baltimore's* favorite sails for lying to was the storm trysail set in the mizzin, a double reefed mainsail, and the fore staysail. I always thought she would ride safely under this sail as long as the wind would blow. But this gale seemed too much for her. At 2 AM Sunday morning a mountainous sea boarded her which almost wrecked us. It broke the lashings of our deck load and washed overboard some of our cargo. It hit her so hard that I thought our masts were broken off and gone. But I am glad to say they did not go. But it smashed our hatch house in and several barrels of water went in the poop.

Now here was my hatch wide open ready to fill her up when the next big sea would come on board, which was liable at any moment. I, with the help of the crew, with all possible haste for there was no time to loose, gathered up the fragment of this hatch house that had been left by this merciless sea which came so near destroying us. With these pieces we began to make preparations to cover this hatch. I happened to have a new tarpaulin in the cabin which I had made in my spare time for I was always at work when at sea, and in port for that matter. I had made two of these tarpaulins. One was to cover a hatch 14 feet by 14 feet. The other was to cover my fore hatch which was 12 by 14 feet. And just think this bit of industry on my part saved the ship and the lives on board. I went in the cabbin and got one of these tarpaulins, nails, saw, and hamer. I laid some pieces of this hatch house, that we had saved, across this open hatch and nailed them. As I did so, I expected a sea to board her and sweep me overboard at any moment. When I had these pieces laid over the hatch I doubled the tarpaulin four double and laid it over these strips. I let the tarpaulin lap over the hatch combings and drop to the deck. Then I nailed a strip on the tarpaulin to the deck. Now

I had the hatch all covered securely and I do not think I was much longer doing this job than it has taken me to write it up. But I must admit the Lord favored me in two ways. He never let one of those large, heavy seas board her while I was doing the job and the moon shined as bright as I ever saw her shine, and I could see how to drive the nails as well as if it had been day time.

This job now completed we caught the pumps and we were 3 hours getting her pumped out. This now being Sunday, the 27th day of November, 1898, was a strenuous day for me. At 9:30 AM our fore staysail boom broke and we lost our fore staysail. We were now laying to under double reefed mainsail and storm trysail. The hurrycane increased in force all the time. Finally, our lanyards began giving away and to keep our masts in her we must reeve off new ones. I had bought a whole coil of lanyard stuff of Clarence Maffit, a ship chandler, in Wilmington, North Carolina, which afterwards proved to be very little good. I told my 2nd mate, a Norwegian by the name Carl, to go down the lazarette and cut me off six fathom of that hemp lanyard stuff. He was scared so bad I could not get him to go down there unless I would go with him. I thought if one is to be drowned what is the diference of being drowned in the lazarette or out in the open ocean. We took a lighted lantern and got ready to make a jump below as soon as there was a chance. Finally, the ship steadyed herself for a moment. We raized the hatch and we both jumped down. The mate and the other men stood by to put the hatch on as soon as we were below. Carl and I, by the aid of the lantern, soon found the new coil of hemp rigging. We cut the ties that bound it together, measured off six fathoms, and proceeded to the hatch and nocked. Now the mate had to watch for a chance to lift the hatch and let us up. And we had to jump quick for by the least delay she might ship a heavy sea and take a ton of water in the poop. Now we are on deck. We proceed to get up tackles and reeve off a new lanyard. Now, could we set up shrouds to the windward in such a gale? Yes , we could when she would take a heavy roll to the windward. We got this shroud set up. It was not long before another lanyard gave way. Now we had to go all over this same trouble again.

What was worrying me was the gale kept increasing. I took hold of my main sheet which had 5 parts of a sheet of 3¾ inch manilla rope. There was so much strain on them that they felt like iron bars. About this time my cook Sam came along. He was scared half to death. I said to him, "I hope this sheet won't break for I do not believe she would run in such a gale and sea as this." I turned and went on about my other business. When I came back to the break of the poop where the main sheet was I saw that someone had taken the whole 22 fathoms of the sheet and passed it over the boom and back through the traveler until he had used up the entire 22 fathom of sheet. This was enough rope to have pulled her out of the water.

One thing and then the other would part all the day long and we were kept busy all the day repairing and replacing to keep the masts in her. I now began to worry about when night came. I would not be able to see how to repair and re-place things in the dark. I could not see how to do it. It ocured to me that all the English ministers will be praying for me all this day as the sun never sets on English soil. As fast as the sun goes down at one place it rises on another. I used to go to the churches when I would be in an English port and I would invariably hear them pray for the seafaring man. And I got very much consolation out of the thoughts of these English praying ministers.

At about 2 PM the cringle in the head of the storm trysail parted. This sail had to be taken in quick or it would soon blow into ribbands and we could no longer lay to. I jumped quick to the downhaul and ordered all hands to follow me quick to haul it down. When it was about half down the ship fell off 3 or 4 points for the need of after sail to hold her up to the wind. I had observed she was going rather fast through the water. I was pulling on the down haul with my strength to get the storm trysail in before it was lost. But I just took a look aft and I saw a great big, mountainous sea coming for the port quarter. I knew this sea was going to strike us heavy and cover us from aft to forward. I yelled out with all my voice, "Let go the downhaul and all hands look out for yourselves." I jumped for the top of the cabbin with the idea of getting on top of the mizzin gaff. But this was too fast for me. I had just got on top of the cabbin when it struck. It washed me under the spanker boom and I went into the half-down storm trysail. I felt myself take up but I did not know if I was overboard or where I was. But as soon as the volume of water cleared away I saw that the storm trysail had caught me. Had it not been for this half-down storm trysail my trouble would have ceased there and then as far as this world is concerned. That spanker boom was only about 3½ feet higher than the top of the cabbin and how I passed under that boom without my head hitting it and bursting my brains out has alway been one of the wonders to me. After getting out of the belly of the storm trysail my first thought was how many of my crew are gone. I looked around and to my most pleasing surprise they were all there. They had gone up in the rigging and all were saved. I got some cringle stuff and got up on the main gaff and stuck another cringle in there, hooked the mizzin throat halyards in it, and hoisted it. I was afraid to set it up real tight. I was afraid it could not stand the force of the gale and would blow to pieces.

After this being done our next trouble was the deadeye on the head of the mizzin chainplate which broke just below the top of the rail, something I never saw happen before. I was now at a loss to know what to do. Our mizzin rigging only had 3 shrouds to the side. Now there were only two shrouds on the windward side to hold my mizzinmast in. My mind was now much put to the test as how long will it be before another of these two shrouds give away. If so, it would be clearly impossible for one shroud to hold this mizzinmast in. And every practical seaman knows when the mizzinmast went it would pull the mainmast out and the mainmast would pull the foremast out. Then we would be a rolling, helpless wreck and in a short time she would go to the bottom and there would be no one left to tell the story. In looking over at this broken chainplate I saw there was an inch and a half space between it and the bulwarks. From her upper plank to the rail, a length of about 3½ feet, her chain plates were square. It occured to me that I could put a chain strap around this chainplate and it might take a nip or hold fast to the chain. If so I could get a tackle up in the rigging and set that shroud up. I had the chain in the poop and plenty of rope and spare blocks. Now for another trip down the lazarette. We lit the lantern and stood by to raize the hatch when the opportunity came. She is now steady. We raize the hatch. The crew on deck stood by and put the hatch on immediately when we were down. I had my 2nd mate Carl with me. Scared as he was he was a good worker. We now looked around and found these pieces of chain which were once used as our topsail sheets but were now too short since the outer links had worn out in the sheet block at the end of the gaff. We got these together and two of our big cargo blocks and enough rope to reeve off a fall, a strap to go on the rigging, and such other things we needed and took them to the lazarette hatch and nocked. When the mate saw a favorable chance he lifted the hatch open and let us up. We rove the tackle as quickly as we could. I tied a line around my body and went over the side and put this chain around the chainplate and hooked the block on. To my agreeable surprise the chain took hold of the chainplate and did not slip and we set this shroud up.

I have neglected to tell the trouble I had in getting the strap on this shroud. It was swinging and switching so badly from the rolling of the ship with nothing to hold it but the loose ratlines on it that I could get none of my crew to go up in the rigging and put it on. Neither could I get them to go up and hang the tackle on the strap. I had it all to do myself. You may imagine the job of taking a double 12-inch block with a 3-inch fall rove in it. It seems to me I had more strength that day than I ever had before or since. But I got that tackle up, the chain strap on the chainplate, and set that shroud up. This was a terrible Sunday to me but I must say the Lord was with us.

The days of November is short but we put in a lot of work. But now another job was facing us which was worse than any yet. The tarpaulin on our fore hatch was washing to pieces and the water would soon be pouring down the hold. We must by all means try to get another tarpaulin on or she might sink before morning. I got this other new tarpaulin I had made in my leisure hours out of the cabbin. And no one in this world would believe the trouble that eight men of us had in getting this tarpaulin on. I can never discribe it rightly by words or pen but I will do the best I can. This tarpaulin made out of No. 1 canvas in size 12 feet by 14 feet. I had it rolled up in as small a roll as we could get. I laid the edge of it over the hatch combing to nail it to the combing under an inch board. And everytime I would get ready to nail it to the hatch combing there would come a heavy sea over and take the hatch cloth and the eight of us from the hatch. We would now roll the hatch cloth up in another roll and lay it on the weather side of the hatch and try again to nail it. But the sea would come over and wash us all away again. We would roll it up in a roll again and try to nail it and the sea would sweep us away again. Our lives depended on getting this hatch covered for if we failed she would go down before the break of another day.

All this time the outrigger aloft, which kept the fore-topmast backstay spread out at the crosstrees to support the foretopmast, a piece of oak 4 inches by 4 inches by ten feet long, had got broken loose. This was swinging by a small piece of ratline used as a lift to keep the outrigger up off the cross-trees to keep from chafing. Nothing was holding this out-rigger but this short piece of ratline and that was rolling so it must soon part or break this piece of ratline and fall to the deck. Some seaman might say, "Why did not some one go aloft, rig a small gantline, cut this ratline, and send it on deck?" I am here to say no man could go to the crosstrees, carry a gantline, rig it, and send this outrigger down, it was so heavy. In trying to cover this hatch we had to work directly under this outrigger. There was no time to loose. We must stay our post which in my opinion was more hazardous than going over top which our boys put so much stress on during the war. I expected to be killed at any moment or see 3 or 4 of my crew killed from the fall of this piece of oak timber. I do not know if any of my crew saw it or not. I never called their attention to it for fear they may leave their post of duty. Finally, this piece of oak timber came down. It fell in the midst of us and never hit a man. The Lord was with us.

After about a two and half hour struggle we got this hatch cloth on. It was a great job conquored. In a smooth harbor it would have been a ten minute job. Now night was coming on. The energy of my men as well as myself was pretty well exhausted. It seemed my strength all the day was almost a miracle. I have often wondered how I could take a 12-inch block and fall and carry it up the 30 feet, put the strap on the rigging, and hook this heavy double block in it. But I did it hastily to get this shroud set up before another one gave away or parted.

We now got a little supper which we so badly needed, a cup of hot tea, cold, salt beef, and hard bread which tasted good to me. I will now praise the Lord again for his goodness and mercy. The ship laid and rode safely all Sunday night through and not a thing parted or broke during the night. And when I went below just to rest on my lounge in the cabbin I would imagine if I were in a ball and a boy was throwing it up in the air and catching it. When it decended the sensation would be the same.

The next morning the gale was raging just the same and during the day our lanyards were giving away. We would have to go in the lazarette with a lantern and light it when we got below, cut off our usual six fathoms, and get to the hatch and nock for the mate. He would open it as soon as he thought safe to do so or else a heavy sea might come over and a ton of water go in the lazarette in two minutes. We now proceeded to get up strap and tackle, reeve off the lanyard, and set the shroud up. We kept at this until we had rove off 20 lanyards. After using up all of our hemp lanyard stuff we had to resort to using my manilla peak halyard stuff which was $3\frac{1}{4}$ inch in size. Three and one-quarter inch manilla is fully as strong as $3\frac{3}{4}$ inch hemp when it is new. It was a fortunate thing I had laid in such a supply of rope before leaving New York. It all went to save the ship and crew. I do not remember how many lanyards we rove of on this dreadful Monday but it kept us repairing all the day.

It has been 32 years since this terrible gale blowed and I have forgotton many interesting instances. If I could just think of them. One is when this heavy sea boarded on Sunday afternoon it carried over my wheel box cover. This cover was about 7 or 8 feet long and about 3 feet wide. It covered the screw in the wheel to keep the sea water and rain from it. It always took two men to lift it off and two men to put it on. It was made of inch and half white pine and was heavy for two

Captain Fletcher Gantt,
who served as mate with Captain Tawes, shown on board the
four-masted schooner PURNELL T. WHITE *of which he was master.*

*Captain Leonard S. Tawes as he appeared at the time he
completed his journals, about 1930.*

men to lift it and sit on top of the wheel box over a tongue
and groove. It had two hooks on each side. It broke these hooks
and took the cover overboard. When it struck the big yawl
hoisted high on the davits aft the davits went through the yawl
both forward and aft which rendered her useless for anything more.

Monday the 28th the gale raged all day without ceasing.
My crew were nearly dead from exhaustion and exposure,
excepting my mate Robert H. Sterling who was young and
strong. The crew was so exhausted that they did not have the
life to bail the water out of the forecastle. I happened forward
and there was so much water in the forecastle it would come
nearly up to their bunks when the vessel rolled. I got a scoop
shovel and bailed the water out. Then I made a slide about
2½ feet high and put across the forecastle door to keep the
water out of the forecastle. The crew at the same time were
laying in their berths from exhaustion. We rove the lanyards
from time to time today as they would wear out from rolling
and chafing. Some more of the lower deadeyes pulled off the
chainplates and between the pumping, for she was leaking
quite much, I had to go over the ship's side and put small
chain on the chainplates for straps as I had done the day before.
Now I must take the trip down the lazarette to get blocks of
which I was supplied with, cut off enough of my 3-inch throat
halyard manilla rope to reeve off the fall, and when I would be
ready to come on deck I would nock on the hatch. Mr. Sterling
would be on the lookout for me. As soon as the sea would give
us a chance he would lift the hatch and I would throw out the
blocks, rope, chains, and straps and cover the hatch as quickly
as possible to keep the sea from runing down in it should one
board. Fortunately, this lazarete hatch was on hinges that I
took a notion to put on some years before. It may have been a
little larger than four square feet and it being on hinges it would
fall precisely in its place which saved us time if it had to be

placed on. I cannot just remember just what did part and give away today but we had to work hard all day to keep the mast in her.

Monday afternoon I told the mate to set the lee main rigging up while I laid down to take a little rest for I now felt about as badly exhausted as the sailors were. I staid below until nearly 4 o'clock. When I came on deck I saw that Bob had not set the lee main rigging up. I asked him why he did not do it. He said that he was afraid of being washed overboard. This had to be done or the lanyards would be chafed in two before morning and the spars would go out of her. So I rigged up tackles with Bob's assistance. I set the main rigging up and had it done before dark. But I must say I was up to my neck in water several times before the job was completed.

It was Robert's watch on deck from 12 to 4 in the morning. Along about 2 AM he came to my stateroom door and told me the wind was falling. I was glad to hear it. Tuesday morning, the 29th of November, at 8 AM, began to shake out reefs and get her underway with a nice southwest wind. We set all light sails. We are now on our course going toward our destination. But I did not like the barometer. She was very low. I did not tell Robert to set the topsails. But he was an industrious fellow and I said nothing but let him go ahead, which increased his labor very much. The crew were on deck all day repairing and replacing what the gale had torn up. At 4 PM the weather was looking very bad. We took the topsails in and furled them. The barometer was falling fast. We reefed the spanker and furled it. We reefed the mainsail and set it. We lowered the foresail down and furled it, also the flying jib. We were now runing under reefed mainsail and jib. At 5 PM took in the jib. The wind was backing to southward and increasing. By 7 PM it backoned to the southeast and blowed the hardest I ever saw a southeaster blow for about 5 hours. It seemed to me we had to be lost in this southeaster after a hard 3-day fight with the northwest gale. At 11 PM the southeaster died out. At once I went below and looked at my barometer and I saw she was 5 points lower than she was at anytime in this past 3 day gale. Sam, my cook, was laying in his berth but not sleeping. I said, "Sam, the barometer is 5 points lower than she was in the last gale." Sam was a real black man but Sam turned white, or really he looked like somebody had thrown ashes in his face. I went back on deck. It was now eleven PM and dark as a dungeon. High sea runing but stark calm. Bob and his watch had put in a hard day's work all that day and they needed rest. In the morning they shook out reefs and got her fully under way and by night they had cleared up and furled all the light sails and reefed all the lower sails. Two they furled and one they set. It was a heavy day's work and I would not call him or his watch. So I and my man bent the storm trysail on the mizzin mast and we set it. The man at the wheel would run from the wheel for 2 or 3 minutes at the time and give us a pull. When this was set, and the sheet pulled aft, all we could do was to wait for the blast from the northwest.

Eight bells came and I called the port watch. When Bob came on deck he was surprised to see it calm and the storm trysail set in the mizzin. He said, "Captain, why did not you call me? I would certainly come up and helped you." I said, "I know that, Bob, but you have done so much pulling and hauling today you needed the rest and I wanted you to have it." It died out at 11 PM calm and me and my watch did not have any great deal of trouble setting it though it was quite heavy because it was so full of water. I forgot to mention, in this 5-hour gale from the southeast the rain fell in torrents. I said, "Bob, I will go below for awhile. There is nothing to do but wait for the blast. The barometer is 5 points lower than it was in the last gale. It will not be long before it hits. Just try to let it hit her on the port tack." In a short while it did and it made a football of us for another 3 days and nights without ceasing.

Now in this 3 nights and days we had a hard job to keep her masts in her. Occasionally, a lanyard would give away which meant another trip down in the lazarette to cut off another. We had to light a lantern, pick our chances to raize the lazarette hatch, and dive below before another heavy sea would come over and fill the lazarette with water. When we had got it cut and ready to come on deck we would nock. When an opportunity offered Bob would lift the hatch and let us come up. Then we would rig up tackle and set the rigging. I made it a purpose to repair immediately when anything broke or gave away. I did not want to let the mishaps get too far ahead of me for as fast as we got one thing repaired it seemed that something else would part.

These two long northwest gales and the one southeaster had just lasted one week. The barometer staid low all the time now and we had nothing but westerly gales for the next two weeks. We were now facing other dificulties. Our provisions were getting short and hunger was now before us. And no favorable winds could we get. We were away offshore in longitude 71° 45′ west which would place us about 300 miles from the coast. The sea kept high all the time and when we were not reefed or lying to we could not work to the windward. Our coal oil was gone. You may imagine how bad it was when we had a chance to go below for probably a couple hours, or perhaps four of them. Then to pull off an oil coat all ringing wet, for we had to wear oil clothing about all the time, and lay in the corner of the dark cabbin. When you are called you have to feel in the corner to find it and, oh, how cold these wet oil skins would feel when you got it on. It would just chill me all over. I do not know of anything worse than these long December nights and having no oil to light the cabbin. What little we had we had to use it in the binnacle to see how to steer by the compass.

Bob for the first time in his life, I believe, began to look into the future. He come to me one day and said, "The flour is getting mighty low in that barrel and we ought to put everybody on two biscuits to the meal." I knew if we did that we could not take care of the ship. You take in the pulling and hauling, and to keep her underway, and the pumping which was all done by hand, to keep men strong and able to do this work they must have bread. I said to Mr. Robert H. Sterling, "No, I won't do that but just let them eat what bread they want. When it is all gone we will all die together."

I must now bring in the yam story. I never did like them. They are so dry. I never bought but 150 lbs. of them when I was at Black River. But I just felt sorry I did not get a quarter of a ton of them. One of these yams, about 18 inches long, was in the shape of a man's foot. It had 5 toes begining with the big one and went around in proportion to the little toe. It had a a big, flat bottom to it, and a heel just like a natural foot. It was such a freak of nature I told Sam not to cook that yam. I wanted to show it to the reporters as they most always came on board on the ship's arrival. One cold day I was at the wheel steering. Sam come aft and raised the lazarette hatch. The sea was not runing over the poop deck at the time. He went below and brought up this famous yam. I never said a word to him. My instinct told me this was the last yam. As much as I disliked them I would have given a big price for 500 pounds of them.

Our water was getting low and what we had was getting quite brackish. So much salt spray had fell in the bung holes of the casks. But the want of oil and provisions was worrying me the most. It is awful to be sailing on the ocean dark nights. When we would see the lights of another ship we would have to do the manuevering to keep clear of him. And I was always freightened if he came near me. No human mind can imagine what I suffered in mind and body on this voyage. The days wore on. Finally, the wind backed to the west northwest. I laid my chart down on the table and I saw from my position that I could fetch Gay Head. I put on prudent sail and pushed her for Gay Head, Massachusetts, intending to go in Holmes' Hole, or Martha's Vineyard it is now called. Here I intended to restore, give the crew a couple of night's rest, and then get underway and proceed for the capes of the Delaware. I see by my log book I got as far north as 40° 00′ north lattitude when the wind hauled to north northwest which was now a head wind for Gay Head but a good slant for the Delaware capes. I put her about and headed for the Delaware. By the time I would run a hundred or so of miles the wind would backen to west by north, or west, which would be a head wind in the Delaware but a good slant for Gay Head. So I got her around on the port tack and stood her for Gay Head. I did this as much as 4 times but the sea was too high and the wind blowing so strong from the westward I could not make any headway. It was reef and shake out again, over, and again. Monday, December 5th, 1898, in lattitude 39° 09′, longitude 74°01′ it snowed and blowing heavily all day and night. On this day by the log book I see we are 23 days out.

Latter part of this day we carried away our jib stay. We lowered the foresail and the jib. Tied them up and proceeded to set the jib stay up by getting the end of the hawser through the hawse pipe and putting two half-hitches on the jib stay just above the end. That was turned in and took the hawser to the windlass and set it up again. This was a mean job as we had to drop a small rope overboard so that it might at times swing across the hawse pipe and let us catch it with a boat hook. It was impossible for a man to go down over the bow to her hawse pipe and put a rope through. The sea and wind was too bad. But we accomplished the job. While doing this there was only two stays holding the mast in her, the fore stay and the flying jib stay and I was expecting to see them part at any moment. Then we had to rig a Spanish windlass to heave these two stays together so that we could seise them close together above the bowsprit that we might set our jibs. I thought how lucky I was that these two stays, the forestay and the flying jib stay, held and kept the mast in her until I got the jib stay set up.

Not more than two or three days after this the fore stay parted in the nip where it came through a bullseye and set up on its end. It was late in the afternoon when this happened. I had to get a tackle on it above the turned-up end and lead the tackle to the windlass head on the starboard and set it up. It took all the crew to hold this heavy stay. The ship was rolling heavy as it was blowing a gale from the northwest and awfully cold. The crew could not stay on the gallant forecastle to hold this stay. They had to let it fall aft directly under the foremast head and stand in the forecastle door and hold it while the mate and I rove off a tackle and got ready for setting it up. No one not acquainted with the circumstances can imagine the trouble it is to hold a heavy 3½-inch wire stay dangling from the crosstree of an 80 foot mast. It is a simple job to hold a stay of this kind and set it up laying in a smooth harbor. I came near freezing while doing this job and I got through with it by dark. While this forestay was gone there was nothing to keep the mast from breaking and falling over the stern but the flying jib stay and jib stays and one of them set up on the end of a hawser leading out of the port hawsepipe. It is remarkable to think that every head stay had parted and had to be repaired and set since we had left Black River in order to keep the mast in her.

In looking over my log book many recolections have come to my mind. Now I wonder how we ever lived from the cold exposure and the hard labor we had to do to keep the masts in her. And the reefing and setting of sails, the pumping which was all done by hand and called for manual labor, food runing short, and many other hard dificulties too numerous to mention.

Finally, I conceived the idea to construct a lamp. Light was so badly needed in the cabbin. My table had a rack that went all around it to keep the dishes from rolling off in bad weather. It hung on a hinge and we could turn it up when there was danger of the dishes rolling off. When turned up they were an inch and half higher than the level of the table. I took a drinking glass and set it in the corner where these brackets were. Then I bored a hole in the table close to the glass and put a stick in this hole. This secured the glass on sides and this kept it from rolling off the table. Now I filled this glass nearly full of paint oil. Then I took the piece of a tin can, the top of a tomato can. I cut a hole in the middle of it about the size of a lead pencil. Then I cut three points to this piece of tin. It then looked like a three-pointed star. Then I took the cork from a bottle and cut it in three pieces. I stuck them on the 3 points of the tin. These would float the tin on top of the oil in the glass. Next I took a small piece of No. 1 canvas and pulled these threads out of it until I had enough to fill the round hole in the tin. This made my lamp wick. I wet the top of this wick with the oil. I lighted it and it burned. No one can imagine the comfort this little dingy light gave me for by it I could see how to put on my coat and boots in the night. But it smoked my cabbin up so badly that it cost me $56 to get my cabbin cleaned up and painted.

On Monday, December 12, 1898, I remember it was very moderate but a big, heavy swell runing for it appears to me that the ocean could not get back to normalcy. The vessel was rolling heavily and the sails were slatting. I lowered the spanker down, and the foresail and jib. I had nothing up but the mainsail. The foresail needed some repairing in the clew. I had it hauled up on the two 500 gallon water tanks that I had in the middle to keep it dry so that I could repair the clew. Mr. Sterling, the mate, was setting up the mizzin rigging for while it was calm it was the time to catch up with these kind of jobs. In those days I was mighty handy with a palm and needle and I could probably surprise thousands of the young mariners of today if I were put to the test. But I have not been to sea for 25 years.

About the time I got strait to put a new clew in the foresail at the single reef cringle, for this is where it had given away, the mate sang out, "Captain, there is a steamer in sight steering directly for us." I said to Bob, "Set the flag." He set the union down which meant dire distress. I would not let him set it union down had I seen him but I had so much to do, and such a little time to do it in, I could not pay any attention to what Bob was doing. The big boat was out of commission. The seas had runed up on her in these gales and pushed both davits through her hanging at the davits on the stern. The small boat had the stern of her badly damaged laying across the fore hatch on the main deck. I told the crew to unlash her and I runed down the cabbin and got me some yards of 10 oz. Army duck and some small copper tacks and began tacking this Army duck over the stern to be ready to put her overboard by the time this steamer got up to us. I had to work quick but I had her ready to put over by the time the steamer was in hailing distance. I ran down the cabbin and got the $40 in gold I had but I had no time to doll myself up any. I had to board her in my old working clothes. I put the boat over the ship's side. In doing so she got about one third full of water. I jumped in her and bailed her out while the crew on deck were doing their utmost to keep her from striking the ship's side and getting her stove to pieces. When I got her bailed out I had a time getting a man to go with me. They were scared. While it was true there was a large, high sea runing they were smooth on top. Finally, by scolding, I got my little Norwegian 2nd mate to get in the boat with me. He was scared to death but we pulled up alongside of the steamer which proved to be the English steamship

Vedamore from Baltimore for Liverpool. They droped a ladder on which I jumped and I went up over the side.

It seemed to me I was dazed and could hardly tell what I wanted. Here I was in my old working clothes wet up above the knees where I jumped in the boat more than third full of water. I know I was a nice looking object. The captain approached me and said, "Mate, what can I do for you? Do you want to be taken off?" "No, sir," said I. But when I looked at my little schooner *Baltimore* rolling off there 2 miles from me under her mainsail I thought of how much I had suffered. I certainly felt like going to Liverpool. I said, "Captain, I have gold in my pocket to pay my bills with and I want some kerosene oil badly." Then he says, "You are the captain are you?" I said, "Yes, sir, my name is L. S. Tawes." He said "My name is Bartlett. Come to my room." He was cordial and treated me like a gentleman. I said, "Captain Bartlett, could you let me have some provisions as well as oil?" He said, "We use electricity here for lighting purposes but do use some kerosene around the machinery and I rather expect it is of poor quality." It did afterwards prove to be. After we got into his room he says, "What stores do you require?" I said, "I want some flour." He sent for his cheif steward and told him to tell the mate to get me a sack of flour out of the cargo in the hold. This sack of flour was 196 pounds, the weight of a barrel. I said, "I want some potatoes." He ordered them to get a sack of potatoes out of the cargo. This sack of potatoes was a barrel of potatoes in weight quantity. I said, "This is a very small boat I am in. She is only a 14-foot dinghy and in bad order." He said, "I think she will bear up alright." But it was I who had to go in that boat, not him. Then I said, "I want some sugar but not a big quantity." He told the steward to weigh out 35 lbs. It was common brown sugar, and I was glad the steward weighed out no more. Then they weighed me out 70 lbs. salt beef and pork. I now had flour, beef, pork, and potatoes. And now having all of a mile and half to row back to my vessel in a small 14-foot boat looked anything but good to me.

I exchanged longitudes with him knowing his longitude was correct as he was so shortly from Cape Henry. And I was now 30 days at sea and had been knocked about so much it may have changed the rate on my chronometer. By comparison of longitudes I found my chronometer was very much in error. I had heard my seamen talking so much about their tobacco being nearly gone, something I never used in my life and of which I never gave thought. In going over the side of the ship to get in what looked as much like a coffin as a boat the kind old skipper said to me, "Captain, how are you off for tobacco?" "Oh," I said, "yes sir, we do need some tobacco. Please let me have five pounds." When the steward brought it up I saw in a glance it was what we used to call, when I was a boy in Virginia, common tobacco. I knew my crew was used to a much better quality. I gave the captain an order on Gray, Irelan and Company, in Baltimore, to pay for the stores. He said that he did not know what they amounted to. When I got my bill I found I was not over-charged. On the other hand, they were very reasonable. I bid the old gentleman "goodby" and I never saw him again. I read in the papers later he was employed carrying troops from England to the Boer War in South Africa. And shortly after the Boer War was closed I saw in the papers he had gave up the ghost and went home to his Father. I always had a soft spot in my heart for the steamship *Vedamore* and I was much concerned when I read in the papers that the Germans had torpedoed her and sent her to the bottom of the sea while on her way from the United States to England. When I was about 50 yards from the *Vedamore* Captain Bartlett hailed and asked me how I was for water. I told him I could make out. I had rather drink the brackish water we had than to go back again in this little boat.

We were now a mile and half from our ship. Just a little
breeze, a ripple on top of these big waves, and Carl and I
would be gone for when the *Vedamore* started her engines it
was a short time and she was out sight. Finally, we got safely
to side of our *City of Baltimore*. She was rolling heavy, often
rolling her rail under. We had to use the utmost care to keep
the small boat from the ship's side and not let her hit or all
our stores would be lost. And when the schooner would roll
down we would pass the things out one piece at the time.
When her sides would roll up high as much as six or eight feet
we would have to keep the small boat from her with the oars.
Finally, we got the stores all on board safely without anything
getting wet. Then we got the little 14-foot boat on board safely.
Then after lashing to her beds we began to take stock of our
stores. I certainly felt proud that we had got back safely and
the stores were dry. Now we had a barrel of flour, a barrel of
potatoes, meat, sugar, and 2 gallons of kerosene oil. I said,
"Men, I know you are delighted I have got you some tobacco."
I began to unwrap it and I suppose they did not like the looks
of it. I do not know but, anyhow, I said, "Archie, how much
do you want?" He said, "Captain, how much is it a pound?"
I guess he thought there would be a sea price on it. I said, "I do
not know what it cost me but it shall not cost you but 50¢ a
pound." He said, "I do not beleive I want any, Captain." I
was astonishingly surprised. It was now clouding up and I suppose he thought the wind was going to blow from the east. It
looked like it to me though it had been several days, yes weeks,
since I had seen an east wind. If we could get the wind from
the eastward we would be in the Delaware in two days. As
Archie did not want any tobacco I called Sam. I said, "Sam,
how much tobacco do you want?" "Captain," he said, "I do
not care for any." I went to all the crew and none wanted any.
I then went aft to the poop deck where the mate was and I said,
"Mr. Sterling, how much tobacco do you want?" He said,

"None." "Well," I said, "if nobody wants any tobacco I am damed if I do so I'll throw it overboard." Just before I got to the side to throw it one man from forward yelled to me, "Hey there, Captain, I will take a pound." And another cryed out, "I will take a pound." And they everyone wanted a pound and I had to divide the 5 pounds in seven parts. Had I been as soft in those days as I am now I would given them the tobacco. But I had just a big venture to go and get that tobacco and it vexed me to think they did not appreciate it.

Sam cooked potatoes and made hash, something I always loved. We had a nice full meal for supper, something we had been a long time without. I ate so much it made me real sick. I was much needed on deck for at eight o'clock that night the wind was blowing a gale from the northwest again. We had to heave her to under the storm trysail and reefed mainsail. The mate and 2nd mate set the trysail and hove her to without my assistance and well they might. They had had lots of experience at this in the last 3 weeks. But now we had provisions. We could stand it for 3 weeks more.

In about two days this northwester died out. It got calm. Thursday, December 15, comes in with fine moderate weather. Turned out all reefs and set topsails with southwest winds. We are now heading our course for the Delaware which was west by north. Saturday afternoon it hit in thick and rainy. At 5 PM made the Five Fathom Bank Lightship. The weather now clearing up with gentle westerly winds. At 12 midnight we came to anchor under Cape May.

Early on Sunday morning, December the 18th, we hove the anchor short and got her under way. Just as we filled off one of Jim McCauly's tow boats came up to us and hailed and wanted to know where we were from and where we were bound. I told him from Black River, Jamaica, and bound to Chester, Pennsylvania. He said, "How long have you been out?" "Fourteen days," said I. "You certainly had a quick run up," he remarked. I said, "I do not think so." He said, "You know nothing about the gale of wind we had not so long ago? There was a hundred and sixty vessels lost." "Oh, my," I said, "is that so?" I did not want him to know the condition I was in for I wanted to tow up to Chester and I did not want to pay a high price. This I would have had to pay if he had known that I was in distress. He said, "Don't you want to tow up?" I said, "How much do you charge to tow me to Chester?" He said, "$135." I said, "No, I will sail her to Reedy Island and get towed up for $35." He said, "No, you won't. The Delaware is full of ice." I did not believe it for the weather had softened up a good deal in the last 3 days and gave me the southerly winds that brought me in to the coast. I dickered with him to get the price down as long as I thought it safe to do. I was afraid the crew would buck on me if I did not take him or if I would try to sail her up to Reedy Island. At last I got him down to $90 with the understanding he was to tow through the Cape May Channel. I made the contract this way to avoid the pilot boat I saw over toward Cape Henlopen. To escape the pilot would be a saving of $40. He agreed to do it. I had been through Cape May Channel some when I was a boy sailing in coasting vessels and I knew the *Baltimore* would go through. He towed me through Cape May Channel. I escaped the pilot which saved me $40 which cut my tow bill down to $50. In towing up the Delaware I found some ice but not as much as he represented when I arrived at Chester about sunset Sunday.

While the captain of the tug boat was standing on the poop deck and his tow boat alongside, a man came down to take our lines. He looked at me as he read her name on the quarterboard and said, "Why, she is not lost after all." The captain of the tugboat looked at me and said, "What does he mean? How could he think you were lost and only out 14 days?" "But Captain," said I, "I did not use the word only just for a purpose."

I said, "But truthfully I was 36 days." "Well," he said, "you know something about the great gale of wind we had?" "If you will look at the diferent tackles I have in the rigging," said I, "and the chains I have on 7 chain plates where the lower dead-eyes are pulled off, you would think I had been in something very dreadful. And all this had to be done in winds so strong it was a job to stand up. This had to be done to keep the mast in her."

As soon as I had gotten a line on forward and aft I signed the captain's tow bill and I headed for a telegraph office and wired home. When I got to the door I was told that office opened at six o'clock for a short while. It was then getting dark but I crowded up close to the door so as to get the first turn. And, fortunately, I got my message in first. I heard that the message was phoned all over Crisfield hurridly. There were so many nice vessels lost in this gale, many of which I knew. And I was astonished at the loss of some of them that were more sea-worthy than my little *Baltimore* was. There was one in particular I will mention. It was the schooner *Myra B. Weaver*,* Captain Vanaman. He had an old vessel, I think her name was the *Bill Russell*. The government chartered him to carry water to the war ships from Mobile. I heard her sides got badly scared up in rough weather laying alongside of the war ships. This was during the Spanish-American War. As soon as the war was over the government repaired all his damages, putting new sides on his vessel, which about made her look new. He sold her for a handsome sum and bought the *Myra B. Weaver*. She was a vessel built on the lines of the *City of Baltimore* only larger and about 3 years newer. Captain Vanaman chartered her to go from Jacksonville to Boston. While loading in Jacksonville he went to Mobile and married a young lady

---

*Editor's Note: Captain Tawes must have the *Myra B. Weaver* mistaken for another schooner. The *Weaver,* built at Bath, Maine, in 1889, was renamed *Pendleton Satisfaction* in May 1901 and was not lost until February 3, 1913, at Cap Haitien, Haiti.

he courted while he was runing water from Mobile to the war ships. He took his bride and her sister for a companion to his wife and I am sorry to say they draged ashore on the Hedge Fence in the Vineyard Sound and they all frozed to death. And the vessel and cargo was all lost.

While I was entering my vessel at the custom house in Philadelphia I met the captain of the large schooner named the *Matilda D. Borda.* He was anchored under Nobska Head in the Vineyard Sound. His vessel began dragging over toward the Gay Head where she would been a total loss probably on the Devil's Bridge. He slipped both of his anchors and put to sea. He was 20 days before he got back to the land. He lost both anchors and chains but he saved the ship and crew.

When I got my vessel discharged of her cargo at Chester, Pennsylvania, I had her towed to Philadelphia. And when I got the opportunity I went by train to Baltimore. I went into the Chamber of Commerce building. Though it was 32 years ago it merely seems as yesterday. I put my hands into the hands of J. H. Serech. He said to me, "Tawes, I never expected to put my hand into yours again." Mr. Serech was a handsome, strong-looking man. He was the agent of the Boston Marine Insurance in which company my vessel was insured. Mr. Serech has passed away many years ago. Such is life.

XI

1899–1901

AFTER putting my vessel in order, getting a new jib-boom, some new rigging, a new fore staysail, and the other things necessary for another voyage, I chartered to take a load of coal to Mayaguez, Porto Rico. On Tuesday, 17th of January at 3:30 PM, I took a tow boat and towed down to Dan Baker's where I came to anchor at 10 PM. From adverse winds and unsettled weather we lay in the Delaware until Sunday, 22nd day of January, when the winds came from the southwest with fine weather. At 10 AM got under way. At 2 PM passed out of the Delaware. Tuesday, January 24, fresh breeze from south southeast. At one o'clock PM kept off for Cape Henry. At 7 PM passed in the capes. At 11 PM came to anchor under New Point, Virginia. Friday, January 27 at 6:30 AM with fresh breeze from west northwest, we got under way and proceeded. At 10 AM passed out of Cape Henry. 3:30 PM Currituck Lighthouse bearing southwest by west, distance 16 miles. 11:15 PM got in the western edge of the Gulf Stream. Fresh northeast winds Saturday, January 28th, beginning with strong gale from east by north and high sea. 6:30 PM wind shifted from the north northwest in a heavy squall and a gale it did blow. We runed her under a small piece of the mainsail and the seas boarded her dangerously. Going fast head on into the old southeast roll it punished us severely for 3 hours until the sea got regular. I thought everything would be washed overboard that we had on deck. At midnight sea more regular. We set up the reefed mainsail Sunday, January 29th. This day, morning part, strong winds from the northwest. 8 AM turned reef out of mainsail and set it full. At noon, lattitude 31° 48′ north, longitude 13° 31′. 8 PM set all the heavy and light sails. Sunday, February 5th, 1899, at 5 AM, sighted Point Brungins bearing south by west ½ west, 12 miles distant. 10 AM took a pilot and at 11 AM came to anchor in Mayaguez, Porto Rico.

Here our army officers and a few soldiers came on board and greeted us. I thought our old calvary horses looked very poor. I suppose they were not used to the climate. Tuesday, February 14th, finished discharging our cargo. On Friday, the 17th day of February, we sailed for San Pedro de Macoris, Santo Domingo. On Saturday, the 18th day of February, at 4 AM, sighted the light at Macoris bearing north northwest 9 miles. Hove to for a pilot. 3 PM came to anchor on quarantine ground and lay here for 9 days as the port of Mayaguez was reported to be infested with small pox. While at anchor the prevailing wind was from the east and fine weather. A heavy swell set in most of the time and caused the ship to roll very much. While at anchor here these nine days we got our rigging set up in good shape and we burned all the old paint off the house and bulwarks and painted her up nicely. She looked nice and very different to what she did when we went into Chester a couple months before. We anchored inside the harbor and took the sugar out of lighters.

We lay here in company with an English schooner called the *Earl of Aberdeen*. She was very much larger than my vessel and I thought one of the prettiest models I ever saw as a vessel. He was loading for New York and so was I. He had never been down on the south side of Santo Domingo before and as I had been there several times he inquired of me about the best

way to go-to the westward and come around Cape Tiburon
and go through the Windward Passage, or beat up to the Mona
Passage and go through it. I told him to work up to the windward and go through the Mona Passage. But he should not try
to go through to west of Mona Island as a strong current
runed through there and unless he got a favorable wind he
would not get through. But to keep working to the windward
until he got close up to Porto Rico. Then he would get through
easily. It happened we finished loading together on a Saturday
and cleared. The gentleman was a religious man and would
not sail on Sunday so I waited for Monday morning and we
sailed together. Now I was real anxious to beat this beautiful
vessel and when we got to sea I got all my sails set and sheets
trimed to suit me. I was very much delighted to see I could
beat him working to the windward which I always thought
was the prettiest sailing in the world when in company with
another vessel. This was Monday, the 20th day of March. At
noon on Wednesday, the 22nd day of March, Mona Island
bore northeast 12 miles. I was so anxious to beat this English
vessel to New York that I would not work any further to the
windward. I tried to get through to the west of Mona Island,
just the thing I told the English captain not to do. I had
tried this two or three times before and failed. However, I
was so anxious that I tackled this job again and after working
2 days and nights I had to give it up and beat up to Porto
Rico some 40 miles further to windward. After loosing all of
this time trying to get through to the west of Mona Island
I had made up my mind my English friend was so far ahead
of me that I would never see him again. So much for being in
too big a hurry.

After getting through the Mona Passage we cruised along
on our course which was north by west ½ west with gentle
breeses and fine weather until Tuesday, April the 4th, in
lattitude 31° 19′, longitude 72° 36′. Approaching the eastern

edge of the Gulf Stream, in about the lattitude of Bermuda, the clouds began to form. The old sailor's saying is, "If Bermuda you should pass lookout for Cape Hatteras." Now the storm began to come down on us. At 1 PM took in all our light sails and furled them. At 2 PM reefed the mainsail and set it. At 2:30 PM reefed the spanker and furled it. Glass 29:50 and falling fast. At 3 PM reefed the foresail and set it, wind canting from the southeast to south southeast and increasing to a gale. Sea runing high causing the vessel to labor and ship big quanties of water. At 5 PM weather looking extremely bad in the northwest. Much lightening, thunder, and heavy rain. We were now runing under double reef mainsail and fore staysail, having the foresail in and furled. The mate's watch was from 8 PM to 12 midnight. I was much in hopes I would see no ship this night. At midnight I came on deck. It was terrible. About 1 AM I was standing by the wheel to see that she was runing north northwest which was my course as Hatteras bore that course and I wanted that course steered correctly. To run to westward of this course might run us on the Diamond Shoals before morning and I did not want to jibe the mainsail over to the port side. I was runing directly before the winds. I had a mighty good man at the wheel whose name was Ned. He could steer her as strait as a bald eagle could fly to his nest, I am proud to say. I was standing by him. The rain was falling in torrents. I was expecting a shift of wind from the northwest at any time and these sudden shifts from the northwest in the vicinity of Cape Hatteras are dangerous and destructive and tear sails up if you have to jibe. And that is why I wanted to keep my mainsail on the starboard side so that when the wind shifted I would only have to haul the sheet in or aft.

I intended to say before this that when about two very heavy seas struck our big yawl hoisted high at the davits on the stern I got a little alarmed. And fearing one of those big waves at any moment might wash her over the davits and on our heads standing at the wheel, and thinking one man was enough to be killed in case she did come over, I said to Ned, "You keep her strait on her course. I will go forward to the break of the poop and look out." I am now going to tell an unbelievable story. When I got to the break of the poop I put my left hand on the port mizzin topmast backstay and I looked to the starboard side and to my surprise all of her starboard side was under water. My knee caps began to travel up and down so fast that they reminded me of a telegraph ticker. I thought she was sinking and the decks were as full as a cup. About this time I saw a great sheet of fire up forward. It was so intense that it lighted up the whole deck. I thought that lightening had struck the foremast. I pushed back the slide to the after cabin and I said to Mr. Bragg, "The lightening has struck our foremast." It was blowing so hard you could not hear it thunder. The wind and the waves would drown the noise of thunder. I took a peep at the compass and found Ned was keeping her directly on her course. I then went forward to the break of the poop and stood by the mizzin rigging with my left hand on the mizzin topmast backstay.

Presently, my little second mate Carl touched me for it was so dark I could not see him. And how he ever got from forward to aft through all that deck load of water I will never tell. He said to me by speaking loud into my ear, "Captain, the fore staysail has blowed away." I said to him, "I do not see how it could blow away. It was put on brand new in Philadelphia this time." I said, "The halyards must have parted." He said, "Maybe they did." I said, "It may wash there tonight out. I would not go forward for a fore staysail." I knew that in runing before the wind it would stay down. But the most ridiculous and unbeleivable story is that when that was coming down the fore-stay it caused this sheet of fire that I thought was lightening from the elements. There must have been a weight of ten tons of wind and rain in that fore staysail to cause all of that sheet of fire. And the rain was falling in torrents at the time. It is all unbeleiveable but nevertheless it was so.

I was now runing under nothing but the double reefed mainsail after the fore staysail had took itself in. And that was enough sail too. At about 5 AM we got the expected shift of wind from the northwest and it blew with terrible fury. We hauled our main sheet in by the wind and set our storm trysail in the mizzin and hove her to. All day Wednesday, the 5th of April, it blew a violent gale from the northwest and a high sea was runing. At noon wore ship and lay hove to on the starboard tack trying to head to the westward out of the Stream. Thursday, the 6th day of April, came in partly cloudy and moderating. At 4 AM turned reefs out of foresail and the mainsail and set them, also the jib. And at 8 AM set all sails with winds from north northeast. With this wind I headed my vessel in for Cape Hatteras. The glass being low I was expecting westerly winds. I just had an idea I might get ahead of my English friend for most all English shipmasters give Hatteras a good berth. They seem to fear the danger that lerks around these shoals. Most all English shipmasters that I talked with told me they never go closer than 50 or 60 miles of Cape Hatteras. I thought if I got close in our coast, and got the westerly winds that I expected to get, I would make up on him the time I lost in the Mona Passage. But my barometer fooled me this time. I stood in close to our coast and the winds kept blowing from the east and in this I lost more time. I knew he staid offshore and got a good slant to Sandy Hook and I made up my mind I would never see him again. He would get to New York, discharge his cargo of sugar, and be gone before I got there. I had never sighted him since the first day we sailed from Santo Domingo.

I beat along with these northeast winds and finally, after out 24 days from Macoris, I got to Sandy Hook. I got a pilot on board and the first thing I wanted to know was when the *Earl of Aberdeen* came in the Hook. He said that he did not know and did not remember seeing of her. I asked him how long he had been down on the station. He said, "8 days." I thought if he had passed in more than 8 days ago he had beat me bad. In about 2 hours from the time I took the pilot on board we arrived at the quarantine office at Staten Island. When the doctor boarded us, and examined all the crew to see none had yellow fever or any infectuos desease, he gave me a pass to proceed up to New York. I asked him when the *Earl of Aberdeen* passed the quarantine. He looked on his book back for quite a few days and said she had not come in at all. This made me feel good and to think the two advantages I had and threw them away and then beat him in. I sailed up to Red Hook and came to anchor and told the mate to put a harbor furl on the sails. I went below to shave and wash up to go on shore. While I was turning my clothes over in my trunk to get the winter clothes from the bottom I heard a vessel come to anchor. When I got dressed and came on deck to my surprise there lay the *Earl of Aberdeen*. I just beat him about three hours in our 24 days at sea. He towed up from Sandy Hook while I sailed all the way up which quickened his time all of three hours. This was Thursday, April the 13th, 1899.

Monday, the 17th day of April, we towed to the sugar house and began discharging cargo. Tuesday, the 18th at 4 PM, finished discharging cargo and towed to 27th Street, Brooklyn. While lying here and doing some little repairs I took a charter to go out to Cayenne, French Guiana. On Monday, the 24th day of April, took a tow boat and towed to Pier 9, East River, to load cargo. On Tuesday, the 26th of April, we began loading cargo. While here, Captain Charley Hodgkins came on board and spent 2 or 3 hours. He was an old trader to Cayenne and he advised me on approaching the coast of French Guiana to run for Cape Orange which I did for probably 7 or 8 days,

I do not just remember. I know it was good advice and I would have profited by it ever so much had I heeded to it strictly. But when I was in about 60 miles of Cayenne, and having a real fair wind, I could not see the use of runing for Cape Orange any longer. It looked to me like throwing away time and I kept the ship off and steered her directly for the city. It was a mistake which I regretted. When I was in about 20 miles of the coast the wind came off the land which was dead ahead for me and the strong equatorial current swept me to the westward of the city 28 miles. This worried me ever so much. It took me down to Devil's Island, a French penal colony. Here is where they had Dreyfus imprisioned, a French Army officer they said, for giving the plans of the French forts to the Germans. I think he was put here for life. On this I am not posted but the English and American papers wrote articles over and over defending Dreyfus. While I was here the French sent a man-of-war to this island and took Dreyfus off and carried him to Rennes in France, gave him another trial, cleared him, and reinstated him in the army again.

To resume my story, I feared I would have to go away back north to get in the variable winds to make easting enough to get in Cayenne. But I happened to have a crew of Sabians with me who used to trade a great deal from their little island to Cayenne and they told me there was sufficient water for my vessel between Devil's Island and the mainland and that the current was not as strong. I had to be very particular not to get too close to this island as they would fire a warning shot to keep you away. I got just a little to the west of the island. It was midnight. I had just tacked ship heading offshore when a big fish jumped on board. He freightened me awfully, he made so much noise. And it was very dark. I did not know what it was and I did not go to see until he got quiet. When I did go I found it to be one of the bigest Spanish mackeral I ever saw and from it we had some mighty nice eating. Being guided by

these Sabians I went in between the Devil's Island and the mainland and I was then 4 days making 28 miles. I was certainly
glad to make the port without having to go away to the north
and get probably out of the trade wind before I could make
sufficient easting to fetch the port.

Before leaving New York there came on board a likely looking young man who was a shoe-cutter from Lynn, Massachusetts, and he was surely anxious to go to sea. He knew nothing
about the sea and usually these green people are of very
little use on a vessel like mine. I knew I would have to carry my
same complement of seamen and I told him I could not carry
him. He said he was not afraid to work and this part I found
true. I tried to get him on board of a bark laying alongside of
me loading for Tasmania but the captain would not take him. I
had told him he could eat and sleep on board of me until he
found a ship. After he was on board 2 or 3 days the mate took
a liking to him and so much so that he said to me, "Captain, I
will pay for half the cost of his outfit if you will the other half
and let him go, to which I agreed.

After we got all of the miscelleanous cargo on board, or the
hold full at Pier 9, we had to go over to Newtown Creek and
take on part of a deck load of lumber. Now at Newtown Creek
there is a gang who will rob the ship if you do not employ
one of them to watch the ship. And if you do employ the head
one at $1.50 per night you'll not be robed though you never see
him again until you are ready to leave when he comes on board
to collect his money. When I got my vessel over to Newtown
Creek here came this head gangster on board to get the job
watching. I told him I did not need him, that I had a young
man that I was going to put on. He said to me, "Captain, you
will be robed sure unless you employ me." I did not employ
him which was the worst for me in the end. When night came
I put White on as watchman giving him a pistol. I gave him
every precaution possible. Now I said, "Don't let nobody come

on board. If you do they will sandbag you and we will all be to their mercy. Also watch our lines. They may come down, cut the lines, and turn her adrift." White said, "Captain, you may rest easy. I will take care of her." At about 2 o'clock in the morning he came to my window and knocked and said, "Come out." This I did. He seemed very much excited and said to me, "Captain, there came two men down and began cutting our lines and I shot at them and they run." I could see nobody and everything seemed quiet and I went below and turned in for I was real sleepy.

The next morning this theif watchman came on board before it was real light and said to me, "Captain, I am real sorry you were troubled last night for I am going to be blamed for the whole affair." I said, "How did you find it out so early?" He said, "It was all the talk up the street." "Well," I said, "I am glad nobody got hurt." The next morning I went over to New York to look after my business and when I got back in the afternoon a couple of detectives had come down and arrested my man White. It seems this fellow got hit and he crawled into a lumber pile to keep from being arrested. But at about 10 o'clock he got under so much pain he came out and went to the hospital. Here he had to make a report. Then the detectives came to the ship and took my man White and jailed him. When I came on board at about 4 in the afternoon the mate told me that White was arrested but to just leave the case with him and he would get White out. The next morning I went over to New York and when I got back in the afternoon I saw the mate had been drinking and White was still in jail. The deck load was nearly on and I had to do something. I did not want to leave a man in jail who protected me and my property while I was asleep in my cabin. So when I went over to New York the next day I related my troubles to Mr. Bull's bookkeeper, one of the best old men in the world as I always thought and have never had any cause to change my mind, though he has now gone home to his reward.

After relating my story he said, "Captain, there is a good lawyer here by the name of Maddox. He is alright and if you say so we will go and see him. We have not far to go." I think Mr. A. H. Bull's office was then on Pearl Street. I said, "Alright, Mr. Cook, we will go and see him." Which we did. I told Mr. Maddox about having to hire a crook to keep from being robed and he said, "I am well acquainted with the judge over there in Brooklyn and I think I can handle the case as well as anyone." I gave it to him and he gave the doctor at the hospital $5 to produce this fellow in court and he gave the judge $5 to hear the case at once. So the next morning the mate and myself appeared in court. I was not there long before the prisoner was brought in. I saw plainly where the bullet went through his coat in his back. Then I was called to the witness stand. The prisoner was real hoarse. I think the bullet must have gone in his lungs. The judge asked my man what time the affair happened. White told him it was 2 o'clock in the morning and this fellow was in the act of cutting our lines to turn us adrift. The judge asked my man White if he ever saw this man before. He said that he had never. After a few more questions he was dismissed from the witness chair and the prisoner steped in. The judge asked him about where it was he got shot, what time of night it was, and what he was doing there at that time of night. He told the judge or my lawyer, I forget which it was, that he had been out drinking and that he was looking for a tow boat to go on board and sleep. The judge asked him if he ever saw my man White before. He said that he had never. And the judge said, "The defendant is dismissed." The prisoner was scared I was going to bring a charge against him but I was only after my man White and when I got him I was satisfied. I want to say that Maddox treated me nicely. He only charged me $30. $5 went to the judge, $5 to the doctor, and $20 to himself. I paid one half and charged the other half to the vessel.

The next day I finished taking on my deck load of lumber. I got the crew on board and I took my wife to the train and sent her home. I went over to New York to clear. After clearing I went to the office of Flint, Eddy and Company to sign bills of lading. I saw I had about 127 bills of lading to sign and I saw it was going to take me about three hours to get through, which would be after dark. I did not want to lay at Newtown Creek another night so I called up the North American Towing Company and asked them what it cost to tow the vessel to Red Hook. They told me. And to go out at Sandy Hook I was subject to pay a pilot, which I was anxious to avoid. I then asked them what it would cost to tow through the Hell Gate. They told me the price would be the same. I was very little acquainted with Hell Gate though I had been through there right much when I was a boy. I asked them if there was a safe harbor they could put the vessel in. They said they could anchor me at College Point. Then I asked them if it was convenient for me to get to College Point and if it was convenient for me to get on board the ship there. They told me it was and they told me what line of street cars would take me to College Point. I told them to go to the ship and tow her to College Point and to tell the mate to listen for me when I hollered and send a boat ashore for me. The old Sandy Hook pilot had been waiting all the afternoon for me to take me out of the Hook but when he found I was going down through Long Island Sound he took his cane and went on shore. Compulsory pilotage through Hell Gate had been abolished a long time before and it should be in and out of all American ports.

It was all of 8 o'clock in the evening when I got through signing bills of lading. When I got my papers and got all through I crossed the East River to Brooklyn and took the street car lines that I was advised to take. I found it a long ride to

College Point. I think it was eleven o'clock at night when I got to College Point. Everything looked strange here to me but I managed somehow to find the water's edge of the harbor. It was very dark. I hailed for the schooner *City of Baltimore*. Finally, they answered and sent a boat on shore for me. When I got on board I was tired and wore out. The next morning when I turned out I began to take a survey of the harbor by looking all around to see how to get the ship out. Nothing seemed plain to me. I then asked the mate which way we came in this harbor. He said that it was dark when he came in and could give me no advice at all. I got out my chart and began to study the harbor. Finally, I concluded I could take her out. After we got breakfast I got her under way but I touched bottom on my way out into the proper channel. I then proceeded on my way through Long Island Sound. After getting through the Races the wind began blowing fresh from the east and the weather was not looking good. I went into Gardiner's Bay and anchored and staid there until the next day.

I had been in Gardiner's Bay just 13 years before this. It then had a long point of dry land, very narrow, extending from Long Island to the westward and a lighthouse out on the end of this point which made a land locked harbor. When I came in this time I found this point of land had washed away and what was dry land 13 years before was now all under water. After laying here one night and day I got underway and proceeded out to sea by Montauk Point on Wednesday, May the 10th, 1899.

On Wednesday, the 7th day of June, we brought the good ship to anchor in the harbor of Cayenne after 28 days at sea. Here I was detained much longer than I ought have been. There was so much rain and the consignee did not care how much I was detained. When I got my cargo out there was $190 demurrage due me which I never got. When he settled with me I did not like the settlement and I said to him, "I will never come here again." He said, "Good bye." As much as to say I do not care. Then I began to think, as the convicts serve their time on the Devil's Island they come up to Cayenne and went into business.

A little incident happened while I was here that I will relate. On a Sunday morning my mate, Mr. Bragg, wanted some money which I let him have and he went on shore. Just about dark a ferry boat brought him on board. He was loaded with Cayenne Fighting Boose. When the ferryman got him on board he wanted two francs. The mate only wanted to give him one franc. The mate cursed and swore at the ferryman. I do not know what the mate gave him, whether one or two francs, but the fellow pulled his boat away growling fiercely and the mate swearing fiercely. When the mate got up on the poop in front of the forward cabbin door my little cook Karl came to him in a very nice way and said, "Mr. Bragg, have you had your supper?" He swore and struck at Karl with all his power. He missed Karl and his knuckles hit the forward cabin door which made his bones rattle. I was sure it gave him pain and made his temper go up to the limit. I was back under the awning by the after gangway. I never opened my mouth to him. He began slaming at me. He did not call my name but he was hitting at me. It was one thing and the other thing that was going on that he did not like. He would walk from one side of the poop deck to the other and letting his tongue go trying to get me into an altercation with him, which I would not let him do. I just kept quiet and let him go on. Finally, he said, "I know what I will do. I will go to my room and get my gun and shoot every g.d. son of b. on board." Now is the time I had to act and act quick. While he was going down the forward cabbin I was going down the after cabbin. I went down there to knock him in the head with a chair or anything I could get a hold on. I jumped in front of his stateroom door ahead of him and defied him to come any further. And he did not come. A drunken man always has some sense. I then searched his trunk and his desk and I found his pistol and I took her. He said, "I have got another." I looked through his trunk, his bed clothes, and of his belongings. I found no other and concluded he had no other gun. I kept this gun until I got to New York and when I paid him off I gave his threatening weapon to him. My little Karl said, "Captain, I was so glad you went down the cabbin to his room ahead of him for I was surely afraid of him." I got him in his room and fastened the door and he went to sleep. The next morning, Monday, I expected to have trouble with him, probably to pay him off or something of the kind. But on the contrary. He turned to and went to work as though nothing had ever occured and I never mentioned the affair to him nor him to me. But I never let him get that pistol until I got to New York.

Now they had kept me so long at Cayenne that my vessel's bottom had gotten real foul. It is the greatest place for barnacles to grow on a ship's bottom I ever saw. My yawl was hoisted to the davits every night and overboard only in the day time and barnacles grew on her bottom plentifully. I had to go from here to Macoris, Santo Domingo, to load sugar for New York. And I had to be at Macoris on a certain day and date or my charter would be canceled. As luck would have it I got there the very last day of the time. I had a very interesting run down through the diferent West India islands. I sailed between St. Lucia and St. Vincent islands and down by St. Kitts. This used to be a great molasses exporter. I sailed along many more of these islands. Not having my chart before me I cannot think of their names. I left Cayenne the 27th day of June and arrived at Macoris the 9th day of July. The 10th of July was my cancelation day but I went on shore and reported on the 9th though it was Sunday. Here I loaded a cargo of sugar for New York.

Here I found the 2-masted schooner *Bianca*. She was either loading or was going to load a cargo of sugar for New York. The captain was a young man and a nice one. I got my man White to row me up on board of him. He would have me stay and take supper with him and I will never forget how nice his salt beef hash tasted to me. He was just from New York direct and had potatoes, something I nor my crew had not eaten for a long time. Irish potatoes do not grow in the tropics. After supper the captain and I went up town. After cruising around visiting 2 or 3 coffee houses we came on board. Here I found my man White stretched out on the *Bianca's* deck loaded to unconsciousness with Santo Domingo rum. It was the first time I had seen him under the influence of liquor but I supposed the *Bianca's* crew had led him astray. I tried my hardest to wake him up but all I could get out of him was a groan. So I got down in my boat and pulled on board and left White on the deck asleep. The next morning about 7 o'clock I see White walking around on the shore toward my vessel. I sent the boat ashore after him and I do not think he drank any more rum the whole time I was in Macoris.

The *Bianca* and I loaded sugar close to one another. I got my cargo in and was ready for sea 2 days ahead of him. He and his mate, a Mr. Thomas, said they were going to send a letter, each of them to their wives, by me. I said, "What is the use? You will be in New York and cargo all out before I get there. I laid in Cayenne so long that my vessel is real foul and cannot sail but just a little bit." "Well," they said, "we are going to send a letter home by you anyhow." "Well," I said, "I will certainly mail them when I get to New York."

Saturday, 22nd day of July, finished taking in 3,244 bags of sugar and cleared for New York. On Sunday, the 24th day of July, 1899, at 4 o'clock in the morning, we got underway and sailed. With the usual pulling, reefing, and setting sail, we passed the Winter Quarter Lightship at 11 o'clock PM Sun-

Home of Captain Leonard S. Tawes
on South Somerset Avenue, Crisfield, Maryland.
His granddaughter, Miss Elizabeth W. Hall, now resides there.

Photo by Robert H. Burgess

Schooner PURNELL T. WHITE at Baltimore, February 25, 1931.
This vessel was Captain Tawes' last command in sail, when he brought
the vessel from Nassau to Baltimore in 1922.

day night, August 13th, 1899. On Sunday morning at 6 AM
it began to storm heavily from east northeast and a pour down
of rain. At 10 AM it was blowing almost a hurrycane at which
time we were fortunate enough to see the Five Fathom Bank
Lightship bearing northwest 5 miles. I then kept off for the
Breakwater which was a westerly course. It was so thick with
rain and blowing so hard that I put the mate on the topgallant
forecastle to keep a lookout that we did not run into any vessel.
I was sure I could make the Delaware having such a good departure from the Five Fathom Bank Light, a distance of 27
miles. At 2 PM came to anchor in the Breakwater. Gave her
the big anchor and plenty of chain, 40 fathoms if I remember
right. This was a long gale of wind from the northeast. When
I got on shore I mailed these two letters from Lewes and I
am sure these two letters were the last one these two wives ever
received from their husbands as the *Bianca* perished in this
hurrycane. We lay in the Breakwater six days with strong
gales from the northeast. On Sunday, August 20th, we got underway with north northwest winds and proceeded toward New
York. On Tuesday, August 22 at 7:30 PM, passed in by Sandy
Hook. We sailed up the Hook channel and by so doing escaped
the pilots. The mate seemed so elated that when I paid him off
I gave him $5 of the money I would have to give the pilots had
they spoke me. I also gave him his gun that he was going to kill
us all with in Cayenne. At 8:30, one hour after passing in
Sandy Hook, we came to anchor in Gravesend Bay and got a
night's rest. The next morning, August 23rd at 7:30 AM, we
got underway and at 9 AM passed the quarantine at Staten Island. And at 10 AM came to anchor at Red Hook, 30 days
from Macoris.

And discharging my cargo of sugar at the Yonkers sugar
refinery I went to the dry dock at Brooklyn. Took her out and
cleaned and painted her bottom, put in a new mainmast, and
put the vessel all in good order. Then I chartered to go to the

Delaware Breakwater to load fish scrap for Charleston, South Carolina.

While at the dry dock I met Captain A. Anderson, a very capable and reliable man, and I got him to take charge for the voyage so that I might have a little vacation at home. It was Saturday, September the 9th, before the vessel was ready to sail. I wanted to take the 8 o'clock train for home but it was so that I missed the morning train. Then I would have to stay in New York until Monday the 11th before I could take a train. So I said to Captain Anderson, "If you do not mind I will go to the Delaware Breakwater with you." He said, "I will be glad to have you as I never was in the Delaware Breakwater and do not know the way in." So about Saturday noon we left New York, sailed down as far as Old Orchard Shoals, and came to anchor for the night. At 3 AM the wind breezed up from the north northeast and we got under way and had a good run down the beach. At 8 PM came to anchor in the Delaware Breakwater. I anchored as close to the fish factory that we were going from as I could.

The next morning after we had coffee one of the men put me ashore. I had my trunk with me. Some gentleman who kept a boarding house close to the beach, seeing me landing my things, came to me and said, "Are you going to the train?" I said, "Yes." "Well," he said, "there is a lady in the house who is going to the train. She has a wagon at the house now waiting and I think you can get in the wagon with her." This was real luck as the station is about 2 miles from the beach. Had not this conveyance been there ready I would have had to stay over in Lewes until the next day. He said to me, "Have you had breakfast?" I said, "No." And I went up to the house and got breakfast. Meals in those days were 50¢. I was not hungry and never eat more than 5¢ worth but the convenience of getting to the station was worth lots to me. As soon as we were through breakfast we got in this wagon and drove to the station. The lady and I divided the expence of the team, bought our tickets, and boarded the train for Harrington. And it seemed to me we were in Harrington quick. I am sure we were there at 10 o'clock. Now I had to wait until 1 PM before the train came along for Crisfield. I walked all over Harrington. I had so much time in my hand. Finally, I began to get real hungry for I ate nothing at the boarding house on the beach. I went in the hotel, bought me a glass of beer, and I said to the manager or proprietor, "What time does the train leave here going south?" He said, "One o'clock." I said, "What time do you have dinner?" He said, "12 o'clock." I said, "I certainly want my dinner but I do not beleive I will have time to eat it." He said, "You will have all the time you want." I thought you do not know how hungry I am. But at 12 noon the bell rang for dinner. I got a table to myself and the waiter said, "Ham and chicken?" I said, "Both, if you please." He gave me a good serving. I cleaned that up and asked for another. When I had eaten this and the things that went with it I am sure I had eaten 49¢ worth. While at the beach that morning I had only eaten 1¢ worth. He made 49¢ on me while the innkeeper at Harrington only made 1 on me. I was through all in good time, caught the one o'clock train, and was home at 4 o'clock PM.

Captain Anderson loaded the fish scrap at the Breakwater and went to Charleston all o.k., discharged, and loaded a cargo of lumber and was back in New York October 29th. I came on board November 1, took charge, attended the discharging of the cargo, and chartered to go up to Rondout and load cement for Baltimore. Arrived safely in Baltimore, discharged the cargo of cement, went to Skinner's Shipyard and did some repairs, then chartered to take a general cargo to Tampa, Florida. On Friday, the 15th day of December, 1899, we finished taking in cargo and sailed.

On this voyage I took my 2nd son, Samuel. He wanted to go

and I have causes to regret he went as he got in bad health and I was south seven months before I got back to New York. I wanted him to go home from Pascagoula, Mississippi, but he said he did not want to go home.

Resuming my story, we had a good run to Tampa. We crossed the Salt Key Bank on Christmas Day, then 10 days from Baltimore, and layed to anchor 2 of these days on the Bahama Banks. Arrived at Tampa, December 29th, 14 days from Baltimore. It was a good run. There was only about 9 feet of water up to Tampa at this time so we had to anchor down to Ballast Point. We had to lighter our cargo until we were drawing not more than 9 feet. We then towed up to Tampa and finished discharging at the dock. Phillips and Fuller were my consignees. They were wholesale grocerymen.

When the cargo was out I chartered to go to Mobile, Alabama, and load a cargo for Havana, Cuba. I made this voyage in 19 days and did well. But now I made a mistake. Just for one 50¢ more I went to Pascagoula, Mississippi, to load for Havana for $6.50 per thousand feet on lumber. I was offered $6 per thousand to go back to Mobile and load for Havana. I made a mistake not to take it as I was very much delayed in Pascagoula on account of shallow water. I beleive I could have made 2 voyages to Havana from Mobile while I was making this one from Pascagoula. While here in Pascagoula the mate quit on me and it was hard getting another here so I made the voyage without any. While here I chartered with the Dantzler Lumber Company to go back to Pascagoula and load lumber for San Juan, Porto Rico, at $9.50 per thousand.

On my way back from Havana I had to go to Ship Island and go in quarantine for a week. The doctors at Ship Island plastered all the cracks in the cabin windows and doors and they did the same over all the hatches. We took out provisions enough on deck to last two days. We slept on deck under awnings for two days and nights, cooked, and eat on deck. Before closing the hold and cabbin entirely they put sulphur pots down the hold, in the cabbin, and galley. When they were all ready they poured alcohol on these large sticks of sulphur, lighted each pot, and walked away and ceiled up the last place of exit. This sulphur smoke killed every roach, every rat, and every living thing in the hold, cabbin, or galley. They kept us ceiled up for 48 hours. Then they opened her up and give her air. When we come off the quarantine they gave us a permit to proceed to Pascagoula.

We went up to Moss Point to Dantzler's Mill and proceeded to load our cargo. I noticed here that son Samuel was getting unwell. I have many times wished I had taken him home to his mother but he did not want to go home. The mate I had with me thought it much better to let him go on the voyage. And this mistake was the cause of his death. The 4th day of May we sailed for San Juan, Porto Rico, and arrived June the first. Discharged and sailed for Macoris on June the 18th. Arrived June the 19th. Took in a cargo of sugar and sailed for New York July 7th, 1900. We arrived in New York July 24, 1900, 17 days from Macoris. The first thing I did was to take my son home and put him in the hands of a good physician. He passed away August 30th and we all miss him even unto this day.

Discharged our cargo and went to Baltimore. Here I had the ship rebuilt. Put in a lot of stern timbers and did lots of other work. I spent $6,000 on her. When I was nearly through repairing and was about ready for business I met Mr. Fuller, of Phillips and Fuller, wholesale grocers at Tampa. He told me to lay my vessel on the berth and he would give me two hundred tons of guano at $4 per ton to start with. And he was sure I would get a full cargo out to Tampa and that I would get a good freight out. I took his advice, advertised her in Tampa, and took in his 200 tons of guano. This gave me $800 to start with. There was another grocery firm in Tampa who had lots of canned goods to go out. They wanted to charter the vessel on a lump sum basis. Fuller knew this and had they succeeded in chartering me Fuller's goods would have been left in Baltimore. But in laying her on the berth I carried all of Fuller's goods and I. S. Giddens' also. When I got the last order on board the vessel's hold was full and I had about 75 or 80 barrels of Heinz pickles and other goods on deck. This gave me a $2,250 freight out. When I had finished discharging Mr. Bryan, the manager of I. S. Giddens and Company, said to me, "Captain, the next fall you get in touch with me and I will give you a lump sum to come out for us. By you laying at the berth in Baltimore some of my customers put goods on board of you and I lost their business." So after that, for 3 or 4 years, I chartered to Mr. Bryan for $1,850 from Baltimore to Tampa and this always put me in the Gulf for the winter where I could run lumber between Cuba and the Gulf states.

When I had got discharged at Tampa I chartered to go to Sabine Pass, Texas, and load a cargo of lumber for Porto Padre, north side of Cuba. This charter was made by Mr. A. H. Post of the American Sugar Refinery Company of New York. Mr. Post wanted to insert in the charter that I was to go to Gibara instead of Porto Padre. Gibara was a new port then and it had not been surveyed or charted and I told him I would only agree to go to Porto Padre which was a Port of Entrance. He then said, "If you can go to Gibara will you do so?" I said, "I certainly will." I went to Sabine Pass and loaded at $8.50 per thousand which was a good freight in those days. And to make things better for me the cargo was mostly dressed lumber. It was intended to build houses for the people to live in in this new port. I had to go to Gibara to enter the ship and then run down the coast 15 or 20 miles for Porto Padre. When I ran my distance up I could see no entry. I took an observation, worked it up, and it put me in the longitude of Porto Padre. I could see no entrance and fearing the first might be wrong I took 3 or 4 more observations. They all put me in the longitude of Porto Padre. I then strained my vision trying to see the entrance. The wind was setting on shore and I was afraid I might get on the beach if I got in too close. But finally I saw a flag staff and I kept off and ran in toward the land. When I got close to the beach a little boat put out toward us which proved to be the pilot. This releived my anxiety wonderfully.

The land here was very high, almost mountainous. We ran in under the pilot's guidance and as soon as we entered the mouth of the entrance I saw the reason I could not see the entrance for it turned sharply to the right and we went in behind high land. We ran 2 or 3 hundred yards or more. Then we turned suddenly to the left. We run along like this up a narrow stream for 2 or 3 miles and suddenly a nice wide, beautiful bay opened up. It was the blindest place I ever tried to make in my life. When this beautiful bay opened up I looked to the southwest and there was a town in sight. I said, "Pilot, what town is that?" He said, "Porto Padre." I looked to the southeast and there looked like some small town or a few houses. I said, "What place is that?" He said, "Gibara." I said, "There is where I want to go." He said, "No, no Cappe. Cost you much money. Big fine." I said, "I do not care. I want to go to Gibara." He shruged his shoulders much as to say, "You will be sorry." The prevailing wind here is northeast. If I had gone to Porto Padre it might have been a week before I got out of there as the winds are most always ahead. I knew our troops were then in charge of the island and that probably they would not be able to force the old Spanish law of fining the vessels for everything. In sailing in to Gibara the water was very shallow but lots of mud. So in order to make the rafting or lightering the lumber ashore it would make it easy to get the ship as close to the shore as possible. When she stoped I droped the anchor.

I rigged up my sailboat, took my crew and ship's papers, and started for Porto Padre to enter and to get a pass from the quarantine. I left the pilot in charge of the ship. When I got to Porto Padre the sun was getting low. I did not want to violate the quarantine regulations so I kept my boat from the wharf and had no communication with anyone on the shore. But I hollered to a man standing on the wharf and he told me the custom officials had gone up to the ship. I began then to expect trouble and if Spain had possession of the island at this time I would have had. So I turned my boat around and started back for the ship. There was a point put out between Porto Padre and Gibara which had very shoal water on it. I could cross this point of flats in my yawl which shortened 3 or 4 miles. It would have been about 10 miles to go by the ship or deep water channel. It is invariably for the wind to die out in the ports of Cuba at night. The wind had now about died out and we were rowing along with oars when of a sudden I saw one of these Cubans strike a match to light a cigar or a cigarette. It was dark but I had an idea it was them returning to Porto Padre. So I told my crew to pull strong on the oars. There were no gasoline engines in those days. We caught them and sure enough it was the custom house officials. They lighted a lantern, examined my papers and crew. Then I heard them say in Spanish that they were going make me pay a big fine. Then I spoke to them the best I knew how in Spanish, "Me no payo uno centavo"—"I would not pay a cent."

We got on board about 8 o'clock hungry and tired. The steward got supper and we all turned in and took a night's rest. The next morning I went on shore to report. Here I met General Menecal who was in charge of the sugar plantation and was afterward the President of Cuba. I had dinner with him and he gave me a horse to ride to the beach. The next day he sent a big gang of laborers on board to get the cargo off. We had plenty of men to work, that is, with his gang. They put that nice kiln dried building material in the water and made rafts. I did not know whether he was going to charge me with this labor or not so that night I went up to the plantation and I told him it was my place to put the lumber over the side to him and his place to make the rafts and get them ashore. He said that Mr. Post wrote him to get the lumber out quick or he would have to pay me $35 per day. He said that the men were hired steadily to work on the plantation and he wanted to keep a good gang and get it out quick. I ate a good supper and spent the night and got breakfast next morning. I do not think I ever saw such good living, plenty of deer meat on the table all the time.

After breakfast he gave me a horse and I rode to the beach. On this second day here came up a custom house official from Porto Padre and put a fine on me for $40. I gave him an order on General Menecal to pay the forty but I wrote to the General that I promised Mr. Post in New York to go to Gibara if I could and if he thought I ought to pay the fine pay it and take it out of my account. But I had much rather paid the fine than to have gone to the port of Porto Padre because I would have lost so much time. But I did not tell the General so. I think the General paid the fine and told the officials he was going to make it a port of entry and compel them to come there to visit every ship that came into Gibara. My cargo was discharged very quickly and I cleared for Mobile, such a clearance as it was. There was no custom house at Gibara and officials at Porto Padre took my crew list. I sailed for Mobile without any. On leaving Gibara, General Menecal presented me with two Spanish $5 gold pieces. I showed them to Captain John Sterling. As he took a liking to them he gave me $4.66 for each of them and I would not be a bit surprised if they are not in the hands of some of his family today.

I left Gibara without a bill of health and it taught me a lesson not to leave a foreighn port without my bill of health as our government fines every ship $5,000 coming from a foreighn port without a bill of health. On arriving at Mobile the boarding physician asked for my bill of health and I had none. He asked me a few questions, examined my crew, pronounced them healthy, gave me a pass, and then told the custom house inspector he could come on board. He said, "Let me see your crew list." And I had not it. He just went down over the side and left me. On leaving a home port for a foreighn country, in clearing, they take the name of all the crew, their home, next of kin, and etc. and have to give a bond, at the custom house I sail from, $400 to return all of the crew back to the United States unless they died naturally or run away. If either happens it has to be certified by the American consul in the foreighn port I sail from. On arrival back in the United States you have to produce this crew list and if all answer to their names the custom house officers take the crew list and has your bond canceled at the last American port you sail from. When I had no crew list to show this custom house officer, well, he said, "I can do nothing for you." He just walked down over the side and left me but told me to report at the custom house.

Fortunately, I consigned my vessel to John Decosta, a ship chandler there, a man of influence and one of the best men I ever saw. He said to me, "Captain Tawes, you are in trouble. Now we have got to go about this thing right. The best thing to do is to pay the $100 fine on the crew list as this is a small matter considering the $5,000 bill of health fine." So we got our plans worked out and we went to the custom house to enter. When the fine of $100 was sprung upon me John Decosta paid it freely. But when the $5,000 fine was produced John Decosta demured. The collector said, "You have got that $5,000 to pay before I will enter the ship." Decosta said, "You will be taking this man's ship from him. We know that it is the law to have this bill of health but the captain is from a place which is not a port of entry. There was no custom house there. There was no American consul there and I do not beleive the United States requires a man to run all over a foreighn country to find an American consul to get a bill of health and I know sincerely if you go to court in this case we will beat you." The collector said, "We do not want to go to court and get beat. I will enter the vessel." My I was glad. I do not think I could ever do enough for John Decosta though I heard he has past on. He said to me, "Just wait awhile until things get settled and I am going to work on that crew list fine. I expect to get $90 of that money back." Finally, I chartered to go to Sabine Pass, Texas, again to load for Progresso, Mexico, at $8.50 per thousand on lumber. They stipulated in charter that I was not to draw of over 12 feet of water. When loaded I thought I was going to some nice smooth port but I got badly disappointed. When I got to Sabine Pass I got a letter from John Decosta with his check for $100. He got all my fine returned. There is honest men in this world.

When I got to the entrance of Sabine Pass I set my flag forward for a pilot and none come out. The wind being from the southward they did not care to beat out of the harbor for a light draught vessel. So I kept off and ran in without a pilot. Having been there just a short time before I knew the way. The harbor master was standing on the dock, saw me coming, hailed me, and told me to come to the dock I loaded to. I anchored close to, furled my sails, ran a line ashore, and hauled in. This saved me the expense of getting a tow boat to dock me. I made the harbor master a little present for the interest he took in my behalf. I got stevedores and began loading as fast as possible. I did not have to wait for cargo. I bought my stores of a ship chandler, I think his name was Gilligan. He was a nice fellow. He was a pilot commissioner. He said to me, "Captain Tawes, you came into port without a pilot, did not you?" I said, "Yes." "In that case," he said "you are not compelled to take one out." I said, "You can rest assured I will not take one out."

I cleared from the custom house and made arrangement with a tow boat to take me to sea. But to get along smoothly and nicely I went to the head pilot and I said to him, a red-headed Norwegian, that I would give him half the pilotage which would be about $24. He could stay ashore and I would take a tow boat and tow out. He said, "No, sir, I have got to have the full pilotage, $44." "But," I said, "pilot, it will be easy money for you. Why can't you agree to it?" "Why, because," he said, "if I let you go out on half pilotage other ship captains will expect the same." This vexed me and I said to him, "If I understand you, you are not going to stay out on the coast to bring vessel in simply because they come here light. And the vessel coming in the pilotage is too small the captain can get in port the best way he can. But when the ship is loaded, drawing a good draught of water, you just step on board, collect a big pilotage, and in two hours you are back home. Now, I am going to tell you I brought her in here and I will take her out and not give you a d- cent." In a little while I went down to the ship. The tow boat was there waiting for me. So was the red-headed Norwegian. I said to the captain of tow boat, "I am ready to go, Captain." He said, "I cannot take you out without a pilot on board." I said, "A pilot will be no good to you or me." He said, "I cannot take you out if there is no pilot on board."

It was a fine, fair wind blowing and I wanted to get out. The tow boat backed out and left me. I looked up the river and I saw another tow boat coming down from Port Arthur. This Norwegian stayed on board my vessel or stayed on the dock by her. I went up to this tow that was coming down the river and when he docked I asked him what he would tow me out to anchor for, close to where a bark was laying at anchor. I would not tell him I was going to sea. What I wanted to do was to get out of the slip so that I could get sails on her. And the pilot might go to the lower regions for what I cared. The captain of the tow boat said he would take me out to anchor for $10. I said, "Come right on, I am ready." When he got alongside the red-headed pilot spoke him. I did not hear him. I began taking in the lines and the tow boat captain came in the cabin to collect his $10. He said to me, "Captain, I can't take you out unless you have a pilot on board." I saw I was beat and I had just as well cave in. I said, "Alright, Captain, we will take a pilot out. You take me out to the bark so I can get her underway." It was a nice fair wind out of the harbor.

Then these two pilots let me know it was dangerous to sail out and they could not be responsible if the vessel ran on shore. "Oh, hell," I said, "you have been doing all in your power for the last two hours to make me take you as a pilot. Now you say you cannot pilot me out." They said, "The vessel may steer bad." I said, "No fear, this vessel steers herself out." Then the captain of the tow boat jumped the price on me for towing. He said, "Captain, it is worth $25 to tow your vessel out to where that barque lays." I said, "Captain, you agreed to tow me out where the barque lays for $10 a short while ago. Why is it worth more now?" The pilots wanted him to tow me out to sea so that the tow boat would bring them, or tow them and their little pilot boat, back into the harbor. All I wanted was to get out of the slip I was laying up in. It was ebb tide and the tide runs real strong ebb when the wind is blowing from the north. "Well," I said, "Captain, give me $10 worth of towing." He said to the pilots, "How much is $10 worth?" They said, "Just outside the slip." I saw their game. They thought I would get scared and pay more. I had my mainsail all loosed and ready to hoist the moment I was out of the slip. And the tow boat captain let me go by the time I was clear of the slip without any considerations of what damage that I might incur before I could get sails on the ship and gather steerageway. My crew worked well and I soon had the sails on her and the way we went with strong ebb tide and a fair wind. Sabine Pass has stone jetties on each side about 300 feet apart. They are about 2 feet above the high water and put out to sea about 5 miles.

This causes the current to run strong so as to wash and keep the channel deep.

While the ship was runing down the channel through these jetties I went below to address or write a letter or two. And while I was in the cabbin writing I heard these two pilots discussing how they were going to get home that night. One said to the other, "It will be impossible for us to pull our boat up this channel against this tide and with this north wind. We will have no flood tide before morning, if then, and it will be dangerous for us to stay out at the mouth of this channel tonight." "Well," said the other, "we can pull ashore on the outside of the jetties, pull the boat up on the beach as high as we can, and walk up through the marsh which is about 3 miles." I then saw their idea of having me to tow out to sea. It was so as to have a tow boat to tow them home all at my expense. I was then wishing they had to wade through marsh mud up to their knees. It was just sunset when I got to the sea buoy. How they managed to get home I never heard as I have not been there since and have no desire to. This was Wednesday, the 13th day of February, 1901.

I forget the kind of weather we had it has been so long ago. But on Tuesday morning, the 19th of February at 3 AM, I made the light at Progresso. My sailing directions advised that seamen crossing the Banks of Campeche should have fishing lines and hooks ready for fishing. And this I did. I hove the ship to at 4 AM to wait for daylight to run in. And as soon I was hove to I got out my fish lines, put some cooked, salt beef on them for bate, and droped it over. The hooks had not got to the bottom before a nice red snapper took it. I laid him in on deck and in a short space of time I had another. I soon caught another. This time Bob Sterling and my cook heard these fish making such a noise on deck and came up. It was then their watch below but this noise took all the sleep out of their eyes. They came on deck. I gave one of them my line and the other one got a line. And soon there was so many fish on deck I had to ask them to stop. We had no way of keeping them and I knew when the sun came up they all would soon spoil. But I had a job to get them to quit. By 9 o'clock, when the sun got hot, we had to throw all of them overboard.

Progresso, I think, was the meanest and most dangerous port I was ever in. We had to lighter most of our deck load. Then we sailed into the pier which was built of iron and put out from the shore into the sea. The shoal water of the Banks of Campeche smoothens the sea very much in moderate weather which makes it much better than it would be along our Atlantic coast. To make the ship fast to this dock we got our big hawser, made it fast to our foremast, and runed it a long way up the dock. Then we took our 5-inch hawser, runed it a long way astern, and made it fast to our mizzin mast. These we had to leave quite slack so the vessel could run back and forth. To have them tight she would snap them quickly because the sea swell makes the ship run back and forth in the day time. When working, we would put small chains out and haul her close into the wharf. We had to use chain because rope would soon chafe in two. Whenever we were through working we would take these chains in and let the ship lay by the two rope hawsers. We had a 7-inch hawser out forward and a 5-inch hawser out aft for fenders to keep the ship's sides from getting all scarred up. We strung our lashing planks along over the sides. They were 4 inches by 10 inches by 33 feet long. Before we left the pier the ship had about mashed these lashing planks up. Now we had to put this lumber up out the hatches on the cars that were on the railroad tracks. Considering all this hard labor did not we earn $8.50 per thousand on this lumber?

Before we were through unloading there came a heavy norther and she came near breaking loose from the pier. Her lines began to part from the heavy sea rolling in. I had to run to town and buy $50 worth of rope. And I had trouble getting someone to cart it down to the ship as they do not deliver goods there. You buy the goods, pay for them, and get them home the best way you can like they used to in our grandfather's days here in America. However, I just did get this rope to the ship in time to save her from breaking loose and going on the beach. There was a steamer laying on the opposite side of the pier just to the windward of me. He broke a lot of the heavy sea or I am sure I should have lost my schooner *City of Baltimore* as it was on the low water she pounded heavily for about 5 hours, from 6 PM until 11 PM. That night I expected her to bilge but being a strong-built vessel she stood the punishment.

After this blow was over we had a few days of fine weather and we made the best use of them possible until the wind began to breeze up fresh from the eastward and veered around to the southeast and blowed strong. I knew another norther was coming after this southeaster. It usually does. And when the wind had hauled around so as to blow strait out from the pier I took in my lines and let the vessel go out to anchorage. I never intended she should ride out another norther alongside of this pier. Sure enough, the next day another norther came. But we were riding safely to our big anchor. When this was over I went on shore to get lighters to come out after the cargo and I had the remainder of the cargo lightered to the shore. We could only lighter in moderate weather.

One afternoon after we had loaded one lighter I went on shore to hurry off another lighter to come early the next morning. I had a sailor name Bill to row me on shore. After I left Bill at the boat tied to the pier I went up to see my consignee about lighters for the next day. When I came down to the boat Bill was there but I noticed his bosom was all swelled out. I said, "Bill, what have you got in your bosom?" He said, "Just a few oranges, Captain." But I saw the impression of a bottle a little below the oranges. I tapped it with my hand and saw it was a bottle. I said, "Bill, that bottle of rum cannot go on board of my vessel." He said, "Captain, if this bottle does not go on board I am not going." I said, "The bottle is not going." So I got down in my small boat and I took the two oars and rowed on board. The next morning the lighter came alongside early. This made me one man short. I took Bill's place and tossed railroad ties over the rail until the lighter was loaded, which was about 2 PM. I was glad when she was loaded too for I was real tired.

After the lighter was loaded I washed up and took an Irish sailor to row me on shore to see the consignee about a lighter for the next day. On my way ashore I said to Jack the Irishman, "Where do you think Bill staid last night?" "And begorah, Captain," he said, "I think he staid with Mother Green. He had not a cent of money and there was nothing else for him to do but sleep on the green grass. And no one gives you a bite to eat in Mexico. If you lodge in a house you must pay for it. If you eat you must pay for it." When I got to the pier I left the boat in custody of the Irishman. I jumped out of the boat and I went by Bill just as if I did not know him. I went up to see my consignee, got my business attended to, and I came down to the pier and passed by Bill as if I did not know him. I jumped into my boat and began to cast her loose to go on board. Then Bill says, "Captain, I want to go on board." I am sure he did because he had been 24 hours without anything to eat. I said, "Where is that bottle of rum?" He said, "I threw it away." I said, "If you have no rum you may go on board. Get in the boat." Which he did and I never had any more trouble with Bill. Just a couple more of days and my cargo was all out.

At this place, Progresso, I saw an opportunity to make plenty of money. Ice sold for 3¢ a pound and the people had to go to the ice house to get it. The ice is all made in Merida and comes down to Progresso on the train. In my opinion, if an ice house were built in Progresso and ice delivered to the people like we do it, and sell it for 1½ or 2 cents a pound, a profitable business could be had. To buy the fish that could be bought from fishermen and salt them, and put them on cold storage until the pickle had preserved them in keeping for a tropical climate, and ship them to the different sugar plantations in Cuba and Mexico, a million dollars could soon be rounded up from Progresso.

I went to Wilmington, North Carolina, to load a cargo of lumber for Santo Domingo city at $7 per thousand. The most of this cargo was dressed for building houses. It was very light and I carried a big cargo. I was 12 days from Progresso to Wilmington. When leaving Progresso I put my word down to never go there again and I never did. From Wilmington I took a run home on the train to see my family for a few days. I got back to Wilmington in time to see the deck load put on and to get stores, rigging, and other necessary articles prepatory for a sea voyage.

We left Wilmington April the 12, 1901, and towed to Southport. Came to anchor, weather unfit to go to sea. The next day, Saturday the 13th, winds easterly. Did not go to sea. The next day, being Sunday, one of the crew was taken sick. Had to carry him back to Wilmington and ship another man. Stayed all night at Wilmington and came back to Southport Monday, the 16th of April. We then got underway and put out to sea. After the various changes of winds, good and bad weather included, we arrived at Santo Domingo Roads on the 5th day of May, 19 days at sea. Here we discharged our cargo of lumber and took in a cargo of sugar. On Monday, the 10th day of June, sailed for New York. On Friday, the 28th day of June, came to anchor at the quarantine ground at Staten Island, 18 days from Santo Domingo city. We discharged our cargo of sugar at the Jersey City sugar house. Finished discharging July 3rd.

On July the 5th began taking in a cargo of cement for Wilmington, North Carolina. Sailed from New York July 18th.

Proceeded down the coast in the usual way and on Saturday, July 27th, we were at Cape Hatteras Lightship. John Tawes, my brother, was then in command of the lightship. He lowered his boat and came on board and spent a couple of hours with me while I layed to around the lightship. Finally, he left me and I kept off and proceeded on our course toward Wilmington. On Tuesday, July 30th, took a pilot and sailed into Southport and came to anchor. On Wednesday, July 31, took a river pilot and sailed to Wilmington. Discharged our cargo of cement and loaded a cargo of lumber.

When I wanted to tow down the tug would not tow me unless I paid the full towage up the river and down. Here I struck a snag. I did not want to pay the towage both ways when I had sailed one of them. I just paid the bar and river pilotages both ways and left the pilot office, and I must say, much vexed. I wish to make it plain the pilot association owned the tow boats and they did not intend to sail any vessels. After leaving the office I saw a small tow boat which towed saw logs and small lighters on the river. I asked the captain if he knew the river down to Southport. He said that he did. I asked him if he would tow me down to Southport. He said, "Captain, I can't tow you against a flood tide." I said, "Can you tow me on the ebb tide?" He said that he could. I made arrangements with him about the price and he said he would start me down on the first of the ebb tide. We started and about half way down the river he ran me ashore. It has been so long now I have forgotton if it was bad pilotage or for the want of power to handle the vessel.

The passenger boats runing up and down the river reported me on shore both at Wilmington and Southport. Of course, passengers and others who saw me on shore asked several questions about who was my river pilot. And it caused a great deal of talk by curious people who had nothing to do with it. This made the pilots real mad. I got off on the next flood

tide and the little tow boat took me to Southport in good shape.
I anchored. He came alongside and I paid him according
to our agreement. I then went ashore at Southport to see about
a bar pilot to take me over the bar to sea. I did not know they
were so furious until I got up in their office. Here they cussed
me and one, by the name of Adams, called me a damn cur.
"Well," I said, "I did not come in here to be insulted. I came
to make arrangements for a bar pilot." They said that they
were not going to give me any. I said, "Alright, I will take my
big yawl and go out over the bar and get the location of the
buoys and I will sail my ship out. And when I get to New
York I will be down here on the train and put this pilot association in the hands of the United States District Court for collecting pilot money and refusing to render the service. I have
the pilot receipts on board where I paid them in Wilmington." I left and went down to my yawl to go on board when
one or two of them came down and said, "We will take you out
tomorrow morning." They asked me if I would like to have
a tow boat. I told them I would. The next morning they came
with the tow boat. They were all in good humor the next
morning and everything went off smoothly. This was Sunday,
the 18th day of August, 1901.

On Sunday, the 25th day of August, came to anchor in
Princess Bay. Monday, the 26th, took a tow boat and towed
to Red Hook and anchored. We discharged our cargo of lum-
ber and chartered to load a cargo of cement for Baltimore. We
towed up the North River to Rondout and loaded. Thursday,
September the 12th, finished loading and towed down the river.
Friday, September 13th at 3 AM, came to anchor at Red Hook.
At 4 PM crew came on board. Saturday, September 14th at 5
AM, got underway and sailed down the river and out of Sandy
Hook. The weather was looking very bad. I turned the ship
back and came to anchor in Gravesend Bay which turned out

to be very fortunate for six people that I never had the pleasure of knowing.

Sunday, September the 15th, I thought I would go on shore and go up to Coney Island and spend the day. So after breakfast I had two of my crew to lower the dinghy and row me ashore. I landed on the wharf which belonged to the New York Yacht Club and I sent the boat back on board. An Irishman came up to me and said, "What are you doing on this wharf?" I said, "I am going up and take the street car to Coney Island." He said, "No you are not. Do you know who this wharf belongs to?" I said, "No." Says he, "This wharf belongs to the New York Yacht Club and no one is allowed to land on it." I thought I would ask him what kind of people the New York Yacht Club people were they were so diferent from others. But I did not. I just hailed my boat and told my two men to come back after me. I said, "This is a place sure a man cannot even go to the post office and buy a stamp and get a newspaper." He said, "You may go up to the post office if you wish to get stamps and a paper but don't you go up on Coney Island." I promised him I would not. I think the post office was in a hotel. When I got up there I fell in with some of the yachting people and was never treated better. I stayed up in the hotel and chatted with them a long time until I feared the Irish watchman might think I had broken my promise and gone up to Coney Island. So I bid them goodby and came to the boat and went on board. Thomas Lipton and the New York Yacht Club were preparing to have a race and it was nearly time for it to come off which probably made the Irishman so particular.

I went on board and it was not long before Lipton and some of the yacht club came down from New York and landed on this wharf. There was 3 or 4 yachts laying to anchor not far from where I was laying. One of these yachts in particular was painted white and was square-rigged forward or, what we called

in those days, barkentine riged. The forward mast was square
riged and the main and mizzin mast were fore-and-aft riged.
This yacht had 3 real pretty sailing boats and her people were
sailing these little boats the most of the day around the harbor
and well out in the Hudson River. I amused myself looking at
the ladies in these boats when they would sail around us and
very often close to us. These boats, most of the time, would have
3 gentlemen and 3 ladies in them, six in all. When night drew on
there came up a squall. It lightened and thundered and the
rain was coming down in torrents. I only had my small anchor
out with 30 fathoms chain and fearing my vessel might drag
this small anchor I put on my oil coat, rubber boots, and south-
wester hat, and kept anchor watch. I did not want to let my
big anchor go overboard if I could help it. It was so heavy
and hard to get up again. I had no steam on my vessel.

While I was standing on the starboard quarter I thought I
heard a voice. It was very dark. I could see nothing. Finally,
between the peals of thunder, I heard this voice again. I called
the mate up on deck and told him I heard a voice like someone
in trouble. He said, "I hear nothing, Captain." But the next
time it was very plain to me. They yelled to the top of their
voice, "Hey, on board the schooner." I knew they were people
in distress. I hollered to the top of my voice that I heard them
and to be of good cheer that I would soon be to their rescue. I
ran forward quickly. I threw the forecastle doors open and told
my four sailors to get on deck in haste, I wanted to save the
lives of some people that were in distress. I ran up and down
the deck half crazy to get these sailors on deck quick but they
stoped to put their oil clothing on before I could get them out.
Oh, if I had the strength of John L. Sullivan just to go in the
forecastle and throw them out on deck. I would not have had
them people to get drowned close to me for $5,000 as hard as I
had to work for money. I got them on deck and lowered the big
boat and went to their rescue. When we got to them the men

jumped in our boat ahead of the women, they were so scared. We got them all in our boat and carried them to their yacht. They were the most grateful people anyone ever beheld. The women huged my sailors with grattitude. One fellow said, "I only have $41 on me." I said, "No, I do not save lives for money." At that time I felt rewarded enough to save them. They took my name and the name of the vessel and our destination and promised us a big reward. They offered the mate this $41 and he took it.

We then went back to our ship, hoisted the boat to the davits, and went below. After we got into the cabbin the mate pulled out the wad of money and laid it on the table and said, "Here is this $41." I took it up and counted it as careful as possible for it was all water soaked. I found there was $46 in it instead of $41, nine $5 bills and a $1 bill. I had now recovered from the reward of saving lives and thought that money looked too good not to get a divi out of it as I was the whole instigator of it being on board. I now said to the mate, "We all had a hand in saving these people. Suppose we give the 4 sailors forward $5 each and divide the remaining $26 which will give us $13 each." The mate said, "Captain, that suits me alright." The next day the wind came out from the northwest and early Monday morning we got underway and went out of Sandy Hook and proceeded down the beach. When we got down as far as Absecon Lighthouse the mate, who was Ned Wharton now past and gone, said to me, "Captain, when we get to Baltimore we are going to get a nice pile." I said, "We will never hear from them again." He said, "With all those great promises they made I do not know how you can imagine such a thing." Reaction has set in on them now. We did not get their names and they do not want their accident to be known. And we never heard from them and do not know who they were.

On Wednesday, September 18, 1901, we took a heavy gale from the northeast. We reefed spanker and tied it up. We double-reefed the mainsail and set it. We saw Fenwick Island Lightship at about 9 PM. It was now blowing so heavy and thick with rain that I was afraid to run for the capes. When I judged I was about off Chincoteague I tied up the foresail, took in the flying jib, set the storm trysail in the mizzin, brought her up to the wind on the port tack, and hove her to head offshore. When I got her around on the wind we lost our jib. I ran forward as quickly as possible to help get it in and to save what canvas I could. When I got up on the forecastle she did the Virginia reel and turned me over and sprained the ligaments in my right knee from which I suffered intense agony for more than a year. Thursday, September 19th at 4 PM, wind began to moderate. Wore ship and got underway and stood in for Cape Charles. At 8 PM sighted Cape Charles Lightship. The breeze was yet strong from the northeast. At 11 PM passed in the capes and about 1:30 AM Friday, September 20th, came to anchor off Back River.

At 8 AM blowing fresh from the northeast and raining. Got underway and proceeded up the Chesapeake. At 9 PM came to anchor off Hooper Straits. Saturday, September 21, this day comes in with light north winds. At 6 AM got underway and proceeded up the bay. At 6 PM wind hauled to the eastward. Proceeded slowly up the bay. Sunday, September 22, comes in with light southerly winds and fine weather and ends the same. Monday, September 23, comes in with light north winds. At 8 PM took a tow boat, towed up the river, anchored at Canton, and paid off the crew. So ends this day one week from New York.*

In Baltimore we chartered to load general cargo for Tampa, Florida. Put the ship on the railway at Skinner's Shipyard, painted ship's bottom, and otherwise put her in order for sea.

---

* *Editor's Note:* Captain Tawes stays on shore on this next voyage and turns the *City of Baltimore* over to a Captain Woodland. This is evident since Captain Tawes refers to the log books and the text lacks his more colorful descriptions and relies solely on the entries of the log books.

On October 1, 1901, began loading cargo for Tampa. Wednesday, October 2, loading can goods part of the day. Other part, raining and could not work. October 3, 4, 5 and 6 taking in cargo. Monday, the 7th, took in cargo. The weather fine. In the afternoon finished loading. Tuesday, the 8th day of October, all through this day weather fine. At 10 AM took tow boat and towed out clear of Fort McHenry and anchored. Crew bending sails and otherwise getting ship ready for sea. At 8 PM set anchor watch. Day ends with strong southeast winds. Wednesday, 9th of October, comes in with fog. At 8 AM the fog lifted with light winds from the southeast. Winds middle and latter part of the same. Thursday, the 10th of October, all this day light airs from southeast and fog middle and latter part. The same Friday October 11. This day comes in with light airs from southeast and fog middle and latter part. The same Saturday, the 12th of October, comes in with light southeast winds middle and latter part the same. Sunday, 13th day of October, this day comes in blowing fresh from the southwards and raining. At 8 PM light southwest winds, anchor watch set, pumps attended to. So ends. Captain John Woodland in command on this voyage.

Monday, 14th day of October, comes in with light winds from the north. At 7 a.m. got underway and proceeded. At 8 p.m. fresh breeze from the northwest. At 8:30 p.m. Cedar Point bore west. The wind now blowing fresh. Stowed away all light sails, took in the spanker and furled it. The day ends runing down the bay. Tuesday, October 15th, comes in clear with fresh breeze from the north. At 8 a.m. Cape Henry bears northwest. Set all light sails and the reefed spanker. At noon turned reef out of spanker and set it in full. Also set mizzin topsail. So ends this day. Wednesday, October 16th, this day comes in with fresh northeast winds at — a.m. Diamond Shoal light abeam. At 4 a.m. wind increasing from the northeast and a heavy sea runing. At 6 p.m. handed light sails and reefed the spanker. So ends this day. Thursday, October 17th, this day comes in with fine weather. At 8 a.m. set main and fore topsails and outer jib. At noon turned reef out of spanker and set mizzin topsail. So ends this day. Crew variously employed doing ship duty. There is no use of me going further with the daily runs of this ship.

Monday, October 28th, at 12 midnight at Tampa Bay and hove to until day. At 6 a.m. took a pilot on board, set light sails, and sailed in over the bar and up to the quarantine ground and anchored, 14 days from Baltimore. At 5 p.m. took tow boat and towed to the dock. Tuesday, 29th October at 8 a.m. stevedores began discharging cargo. At noon, Thursday, 31st October, finished discharging cargo. Friday, November 1, at 6 a.m., took tow boat and towed down through the Cut Channel and made sail. Wednesday, 6th day of November, arrived at Pascagoula and towed up to Moss Point to load lumber, six days from Tampa. Tuesday, November 19th, finished loading cargo. Took 252 thousand feet. Vessel drawing 12 feet 6 inches water. Tide too low to tow down. Friday, then 22nd, took tow boat and towed down the river and in the bay. Ends squally and rainy.

Saturday, November 23rd, this day comes in with fresh northwest winds. At 11 a.m. pilot came on board. Got underway and sailed out over the bar. At 12 noon discharged pilot and proceeded on our journey toward Arroyo, Porto Rico. Friday, December 13th, comes in squally. At 4 a.m. jibed over and set light sails. At 10 a.m. let vessel come to an account of squalls. At 11 a.m. cleared away. We then kept off and ran for the pilot boat. At 2 p.m. took pilot on board. The pilot boat capsized and one man was drowned. We brought the ship to anchor and lowered our big boat and picked up the pilot boat with one man in her. At 4 p.m. hove up anchor and beat up in the harbor 20 days from Pascagoula, Mississippi, a very fair run. Monday, December 16, began discharging cargo. Satur-

day, 28th day of December, finished discharging cargo. Using
11 working days, discharged 252 thousand feet of lumber and
100,000 shingles. Sunday, December 29, all of the day fine
weather. Monday, December 30, in the forenoon crew getting
ship ready for sea. In the afternoon cleaned and washed the
hold. First, middle, and latter parts of this day fine weather.

XII

1902–1905

WEDNESDAY, January 1, 1902, this day comes in with light easterly winds. At 4 a.m. turned the crew out and got underway. At 8 a.m. runing boomed out under foresail, mainsail, and topsails set over them. At 10 a.m. squally. Mona Island Light bearing northwest. This day ends with light east winds. Friday January 3, at 3 p.m., came to anchor in the harbor of Azua, Santo Domingo, and furled all sails.

Saturday, January 4, all this day fine weather. Crew engaged painting ship on the outside and oiling the decks. Sunday —throughout this day east winds and fine weather. Monday, January 6, first, middle, and latter part of this day fine weather. Ship ready for cargo but got none. Tuesday, 7th day of January, all this day fine weather. Received no cargo. Crew engaged doing ship duty. Thursday, 9th of January, all this day cloudy. Received 590 sacks of sugar. Friday, January 10th, all through this fine weather received 705 sacks of sugar. Saturday, January 11, all through this day fine weather. Received 698 sacks of sugar. So ends this day. Pumps and lights looked after. Sunday, January 12, throughout this day fine weather. Pumps and lights attended to. Monday January 13, this day comes cloudy. In the afternoon it rained. Had to quit work. Took in 627 sacks sugar. Tuesday, January 14, all through this day fine weather. Crew to work scraping topmast and setting up forward gear. Received no cargo today. Wednesday, January 15, all through this day fine weather. Crew engaged scraping lower mast and setting up topmast rigging. Received no cargo today. Thursday, January 16, fine weather all day. Crew busy doing various jobs, painting mast heads. Received no cargo today. Friday, January 17, all this day fine weather. Crew to work part of the day hoisting in cargo. Received 385 bags of sugar. Saturday, January 18, all through this day fine weather. Received 256 sacks of sugar. Part of the day crew painting bulwarks. Sunday, January 19, all this day fine weather. Monday, January 20, fine weather all this day. Took in 269 sacks of sugar which completes the cargo. In all have on board 3,520 sacks of sugar. Tuesday, January 21, all this day fine weather. Crew getting ship ready for sea caulking hatches and so forth.

Wednesday, January 22, this day comes in with light westerly winds. At 2 a.m. turned crew out and got underway and sailed out with the land breeze. Calm at 8 a.m. At 2 p.m. fresh breeze from the eastward. This day ends with fine weather. Pumps and lights attended to. Friday, February 28, arrived in New York after a long passage of 37 days. Provisions gave out, lost the bulwarks, and ship very much damaged.

I could never understand why Captain John Woodland should run from Azua, Santo Domingo, down around Cape Antone, Cuba, a distance of at least 800 miles out his way, to go to New York. If I, L. S. Tawes, had been on board I would have come around Cape Tiburon and through the Windward Passage and Crooked Island Passage and saved all of 800 miles of sailing. It certainly looked like he wanted to prolong the voyage.

We discharged the cargo of sugar, took her over in Brooklyn to put new bulwarks on her, and did lots of other work. Then we chartered to go to Jacksonville. Took in 700 barrels kerosene oil, 250 cases kerosene oil, and 62 spruce spars on deck. Saturday, 29th day of March, laying at Red Hook to anchor. Weather stormy from southeast. Sunday, March 30th, laying at Red Hook. One man short. Monday, March 31st, at 10 AM, got another man. Got a tug and towed out. At 3 PM came to anchor at Sandy Hook, wind southwest, weather not favorable. Thursday, April 3rd at 8 AM, got underway and came out of the Hook.

Tuesday, April 15th, arrived in Jacksonville. Wednesday, April 16th, began discharging cargo. Tuesday, April 22nd at 2 AM, got a tow boat and towed up to Palatka. Arrived at 1:30 PM. At 4 PM got one lighter load of lumber. Wednesday, April 23rd, began loading. Wednesday, April 30th, finished loading at Palatka. Thursday, May 1st, took a tow boat to tow down below the shoal 10 miles to finish loading. Vessel drawing 11 feet. Vessel got aground Friday, May 2nd. At 4 AM vessel floated and towboat towed her down in good water and anchored. At 9 AM, Saturday, May 3rd, got all deck load on and began lashing deck load. At 2 PM got a tug and towed to Jacksonville. Have on board 305 thousand feet dry cypress. Monday, May 5th, towed down to Mayport. One man laid up sick. Came to anchor at 5:30 PM, calm all night. Tuesday, May 6th, 9 AM, got tug and towed out over the bar. After the usual pulling, hauling, shortening and making sail, arrived in New York on Monday the 12th, 6 days from Jacksonville. Took a tug and towed up to stake boat at Hoboken. Got in the tow and towed to Albany. Discharged the cargo of lumber at Albany and towed down the Hudson River to New York.

Loaded a cargo of salt for Charleston, South Carolina. Sunday, June 1st, at 5:30 AM, got underway and worked down with the ebb tide. The wind came up from southeast. We came to anchor under Sandy Hook. Monday, June 2nd, 7:30 AM, got underway. At 9 AM passed out Sandy Hook, light breeze from the north. At 12 noon fresh breeze south southwest.

We are working down the beach. Friday, June 6th, 9 AM, close to Hatteras Lightship, 4 days from Sandy Hook. Sunday, 8th day of June, finds us working down the North Carolina beach. At 6:30 PM fresh breeze from southwest. Let go our small anchor with 20 fathoms chain out to the hawse pipe. The lighthouse on Bald Head was bearing southwest ¾ west, distance 10 miles. At 3 AM wind increasing. Monday, June 9th, comes in with fair weather. At 8 PM squally. At 4 AM strong wind from northwest which quickly hauled to northeast. Got underway as quickly as possible and runed for the Frying Pan Lightship. A heavy sea runing from the northeast and vessel shipping heavy seas. At 6:30 AM rounded the Frying Pan Lightship and kept off southwest ½ west. Tuesday, June the 10th, runing free with fresh northeast wind. At 7 PM sighted Morris Island Light bearing west 15 miles. At 8:30 PM furled all light sails. Jibed spanker and head reached offshore. At 10.30 tacked ship and stood inshore. At 5 AM bore away for the Rattle Snake Lightship. At 6:30 AM took a pilot on board. At 9 AM took tug boat and towed to the dock. At 1 PM began discharging cargo, 8 days from Sandy Hook. Thursday, June 12th, at 5:30, finished discharging cargo of cement.

Friday, June 13th, tug *Protector* towed us to the lumber dock. At 1 PM knocked out the ports and reported ready for cargo. Saturday, June 14th, begins with breeze from northeast. Stevedores worked and took in about 60,000 feet of lumber. So ends. Port of Charleston, South Carolina, Sunday, 15th of June begins with northeast winds and rain all day. Monday, June 16th, southwest winds all day and fine weather. Crew painting ship outside and varnishing deck. No cargo today. Saturday, June 21st, got the hold full of lumber and caulked the ports. Monday, June 23rd, at 6:30 PM, finished loading cargo. At 11 AM pilot came on board. At 11:30 AM tug *Waban* took us in the stream. Then made preparations for sea. Tuesday, June 24th, begins with east to southeast winds. At 12 noon took tug *Waban* and towed to sea. After the various duties necessary to navigate and handle the ship passed in Sandy Hook 7 days from Charleston, Tuesday, July 1st. Thursday, July 3rd, docked at the lumber yard up Newtown Creek. Friday, July 4th, displayed all our bunting. Saturday, July 5th, stevedores began discharging cargo. Wednesday, July 16th, finished discharging cargo. Thursday, July 17th, took tug boat and towed to Pier "D", Jersey City, and began loading cement for Wilmington, North Carolina. Monday, July 22nd, finished loading cement and took stores on board.

I took with me on this voyage 2 little boys from Onley, Virginia, sons of Nathaniel F. Walter. These were nice boys. One of them is now Commonwealth Attorney for Accomack County, Virginia. All of the log books from this date July 22, 1902 to July 11, 1904 have been lost and I will have to finish this story from memory. My brother, John H. Tawes, kept the lightship *No. 71* at Cape Hatteras. When I got down to the lightship, about noon in the day, I hove the *City of Baltimore* to and laid around the light for two hours. John lowered his boat and came on board and the mate took John's boat and the two boys, Harry and Jeff Walter, and carried them on board the lightship. John stayed on board of me. After about two hours I hailed Mr. Ridgeway and told him to come back on board. I wanted to be going. John bid me goodbye and went on board and I pursued on my journey. Got to Wilmington in due time. Discharged our cargo of cement, loaded our cargo of lumber, and returned to New York. These little boys went home but I showed them around Coney Island first, even the loop-the-loop. I looped with them.

After discharging the cargo of lumber I went to Gokey's Shipyard in Brooklyn and docked, painted her bottom, and did all other necessary work to put the ship in first class condition. Then we chartered to go up the Raritan River and load chimney brick for Wilmington, North Carolina. There I chartered

Schooner PURNELL T. WHITE *at Baltimore lumber dock,*
September 23, 1932.

The trans-Atlantic liner LEVIATHAN in which Captain Tawes served as sailmaker for three voyages in 1923.

to load for Gill Kitter to go wherever he wanted me to go in the West Indies. All the time I was loading he would not tell me where he was going to send me. I asked him one day to tell me where I was going, that I wanted to advise my wife and friends so that I may have mail to meet me there, but he would not tell me. He said that if the lumber merchants in New York knew where I was going they would quote low prices where I was going and drop the prices on him. But on the day of clearing he cleared me for Port of Spain, Trinidad. I beleive if it had been like it was in old times he would have given me sealed orders, not to break the seal until I was fifty miles offshore. But that cannot be done in these days in conformity with the laws. You have to clear publically and take out bills of health from the consul of the country you are going to as well as one from our country.

It was sometime in November we sailed and had some mighty rough weather crossing the Gulf Stream. We got a strong northeaster and the sea got high and troublesome. We shiped one of them which smashed our cabin windows on the port side and wet all the beding in the staterooms. And it took us a long time to get them dry again. I kept the *Baltimore* reaching ahead on the port tack and sometimes when she would raise her stern up the wind was so strong it would seem to take up a couple tons of water and blow it away off to the leeward. I kept her on the port tack and only making east southeast and southeast courses. I was worrying because I could not head up more to the eastward. But I took a chance and kept her on the wind expecting I might get a better slant as I got further to the southward. I kept her close to the wind thinking I would tack when I had to. One day, as I was getting well to the southward, I got my observations and worked them up and I pricked her off on the chart. I saw heading as I was that I would fetch to the windward of Barbuda and all the Windward Islands by just a safe margin.

It was my watch on deck from 12 midnight until 4 in the morning. She was making about 6 or 7 knots per hour. I left the mate in charge of the watch from 4 AM and everything seemed to be all right. I was below about half an hour, or perhaps ¾ of an hour, when to my greatest surprise the mate hollered out, "Breakers right ahead." I jumped on deck as quick as a rabbit could jump from his lair and there to my surprise the great white breakers were flying high in the air. I tacked ship as quickly as possible expecting her to strike the rocks at any moment and I steered back north northwest, the opposite I was steering before we tacked. When day broke there was the island of Anguilla. I was heading in for Whale Rock, named this because there was a subteraneous passage for the waves to go up in. And there was a hole in the rock about 30 or 40 yards from the entrance. The water would become compressed as it ran up into the entrance and blow ever so high in the air just like a whale blows. Only it was larger and blew more water than a whale would. After getting the ship off in safe water I got my slate and ran over all my observations of the day before. I went over them two or three times and I could find no error in my work. I was puzzled to know the cause of getting so close to the island. I took my chart down and looked at it and I discovered that I pricked off my position wrong. I had pricked her off one degree further to northward than I really was. I calculated to fetch to the windward of Barbuda Island and all the others.

It now being all daylight I saw I would have considerable beating to do to get to the windward of Anguilla. And the trades were quite fresh to work against, say nothing about the current setting to the westward. To make time I kept off and ran to the leeward of Dog Island and through the Sombrero Passage. I kept her on the wind and sailed in sight and under the lee of St. Martin, to the windward of Saba sticking up high out of the sea in the shape of a biscuit, then to the leeward of the little island of St. Eustatius. I have been told this little island is under two governments. Admiral Rodney stored his loot, or prizes, when the French and English were at war and I beleive Portugal was mixed up in this war also. I sailed along under the lee of the island of St. Christopher, a high mountaneous island. We used to get good molasses from there. I also sailed under the lee of Nevis, very small but 359 feet high. I then sailed under the lee of Montserrat, governed by the English, 2,412 feet high. I then sailed under the lee of Guadeloupe, a French island. We do a big commercial business with them. I sailed under the lee of Dominica, an English island sticking up out of the sea 4,747 feet and famous for making and exporting lime juice.

Then I sailed under the lee of the island of Martinique, a high mountaneous island, with Mount Pelee, 4,428 feet high. This mountain, in May 1902, erupted and destroyed the most beautiful city of all the West Indies and every soul was killed excepting one girl found alive in a deep cellar. It was the city of St. Pierre. I came within an ace of being in this explosion. Had Flint, Eddy and Company, exporters out of New York, treated me fair on a voyage out to Cayenne about six months previous to this I would have gone to St. Pierre for them. When they offered me the business I refused. Their agent on the New York Maritime Exchange said to me that when I refused to go for them that I was very independant. They chartered a Captain Sparks or Parks to go. When he was going down to the wharf to leave I told him I was offered the business but I refused as I did not like the wording of their charter party but I said, "Captain Sparks, you will do well on the voyage. You have a fair price." He went and just got there in time to be destroyed, ship and crew.

I sailed along under the lee of St. Lucia, 4,000 feet high, an English island. It is quite a stopping place for steamers to coal up. Then under the lee of St. Vincent, another English possesion, 3,404 feet high. I smelt the brimstone plainly as I passed along under the lee of this island. Then I sailed along under the lee of a chain of very low islands called the Grenadines. I am sure there is lots of sport there for fishing in the leads between the little islands. These low islands run about southwest and northeast all the way from St. Vincent to Grenada, about fifty miles. Passing the Grenadines I sailed under the lee of Grenada, a beautiful island 2,749 feet above the sea and well inhabited. I kept her close to the wind and fetched the island of Trinidad about 20 miles to the leeward of the Boca Grande where I had to go in to get into the big mouth of the Gulf of Paria, thence into the harbor of Port of Spain. Off the Boca Grande I saw some of the ugliest looking fish or animals called the octopus. It is large and full of legs. It gave me a chill to look at. I am sure if one fell overboard and he got hold of you you would soon be devoured. I never saw these ugly looking fish anywhere but just outside of Boca Grande.

Arriving in the harbor of Port of Spain I got a pilot and sailed up hard and fast on the mud to get close inshore so that the lighters would not have so far to come out after the lumber. I was consigned to the house of Gordon, Grant and Company and I beleive they are doing business there today. I have been to Port of Spain twice in my life and I found the climate very hot each time. While I was here this time it seems that Germany, Italy, and England were having trouble with Venezuela. The harbor was full of men-of-war of each nation. It seemed that Venezuela was about to be captured and no doubt would have been had it not been that Uncle Sam might interfere. I was offered a big freight to go from Trinidad up the Orinoco River to Ciudad Bolivar but before closing someone said, "You had better see if Uncle Sam will give you a war ship to escort you up the river." It seemed they had blockaded the whole coast of Venezuela. Sometimes I would go up to the hotel and take supper. I could hear the guests saying, "I wonder what Uncle Sam is saying about this. Those Germans are going to get our country in trouble with the United States if we are not careful."

I had a large yawl built for carrying wood, water, and other necessary articles that we often need. I had her built according to my idea for a tender, not a sailer, but she turned out to be both. She was a very fast boat. She was not a pretty model and I was always puzzled to know where she got the sailing quality she had. The mate I had with me then took great pride in this boat. He was out sailing in her whenever he had the chance. One day I said to him that we had a commander in our navy by name of Oliver Hazard Perry who fleeced the British on the Lakes. He died here with the yellow fever many years ago. "Now that the harbor is quite full of British," I said, "let us get an American flag and go to the semetary Sunday and put the American flag and a boquet of flowers on it." He said, "Captain, that is a capital idea." I bought a small American flag, bargained for flowers for Sunday that was coming, and we went to the semetary and went all over it. We got the keeper to assist us in finding it but could not. We suffered intensly with the heat looking for his grave. We never found it. His body must have been carried back to the United States.

Now we had a flag on our hands and to utilize it we put it at the peak of the sail of our yawl. In order to keep it from fouling, the mate, Mr. S. P. Ridgeway by name, sewed it to the leach of the sail at the peak and it always stayed clear after that. One Sunday afternoon we went ashore. The mate always got aft when he could because he so loved to handle the boat and I humored him. It is customary in these English ports to land at the Queen's Dock. It our country we call it the public wharf. The mate rounded the boat up to the wharf. On it were standing about 20 English midshipmen. They saw our flag was not made of bunting. It was a cheap flag that cost about 1 shilling and six pence. One said to the mate in a very polite maner, "Mate, your flag will run." He merely cast his eye up to the midshipman and said in a loud tone, "I will be damed if the English ever runed it anywhere." And he went on tying up the sail just as though he had said nothing. He was a very rough kind of a fellow and I felt mortified that he should speak to these gentlemen like that so unneccesarily.

After discharging our cargo I went to Pascagoula, Mississippi, to load for Kingston, Jamaica. I chartered for four voyages. I wanted to keep south all winter and I did too. Having no log book of these voyages I cannot give the dates of sailings and arrivals but I remember passing between Jamaica and Cuba on a Christmas night. I got to Pascagoula, loaded, and went to Jamaica by the way of Cape Antone. I found it a long hard beat from Cape Antone up the Caribbean against the current to Kingston. I think I was about 25 days making the first passage. I would get close under the Cuban land at night and catch the land breeze early in the morning. I often saw the Isle of Pines working up the Cuban shore.

I got to Kingston all o.k. and went back to Pascagoula from Kingston. I took two very distinguished passengers. They were a Mrs. Lawton and daughter. The mother wanted to get to Florida and there was no way for her to do so unless she took a sailing vessel bound to the southern states or take a steamer to New York and face the rigors of cold, wintry weather, which she wanted to avoid. She chose to take passage with me. I forget what kind of run we had to Pascagoula but I think a good one. On arrival they took the train for Orlando.

They must have given us a good reputation for on my arrival to Kingston I had an application to take seven passengers and I took them. They said that they heard from the passengers I carried before and were much pleased. These seven passengers consisted of a minister, his wife and three children, and two of his church attendants. The minister's wife was in bad health and it seemed that the steamships would not bring her to the United States fearing they would be delayed in New York on quarantine. This is what the minister told me but he said she had no contagious desease. I had him to get certificates from 2 practicing physicians in the city of Kingston. Then to get the American consul to certify that these two doctors were practicing physicians in the city of Kingston. The consul certified to this and sealed the envelope up with the American seal and gave it to me. I put this letter in with my ship's papers. On a Sunday afternoon someone knocked at the cabbin door and said that there was a lady in a carriage at the wharf that wanted to come on board. I went on the dock and to the carriage. She said, "I am Mrs. Eastman, wife of the minister." I said, "Where is Mr. Eastman?" She said, "He is holding services at the church and will not be down until after night services." I said, "Get out of the carriage and I will escort you on board and show you your quarters." She said that she could not walk. I thought to myself that I had overdone it sure and that I would have trouble with this lady. She was so helpless I had to take her in my arms and carry her on board. In a short time I had so much company on board, her freinds and church people, that I thought I would hike off. I had some acquaintances I wanted to say goodbye to so I told old John to provide supper for this lady, that I had to go on shore. I never came back until the Mr. Eastman had got through with his church services and was on board with his children. He certainly had a host of friends for it seemed the cabbin and deck was full till way late at night.

The next morning, at four o'clock, I cast off the lines and sailed out of the harbor with the land breeze and went to sea sailing along down the south side of of Jamaica. The weather was unusally moderate and calm. The minister and the passengers enjoyed themselves in lowering my boat and pulling up the fish pots scatered along the south coast. He and they would take the fish out of the fish pots and tie a few English shillings in a rag, about the worth of the fish, and lower the pots back. In this they got a lot of fun and we got a lot of fish. The calm weather was beginning to worry me. I had to be at Pascagoula by or before April the 15th. Quarantine went on after the 15th and if I was not there I would have to go to Ship Island and lay at quarantine for 10 days and be fumigated. And I was real anxious after I got around Cape Antone. But I must mention, we were tacking in toward Cape Antone on a Sunday morning when I asked Mr. Eastman to preach for us. I got all my sailors aft in the forward cabbin, gave them hymn books, and the passengers and myself in the after cabbin all were below except the man at the wheel. Mr. Eastman stood in the door between the forward and after cabbin. The sailors could sing nicely and Mr. Eastman preached a real nice sermon and we passed off this Sunday morning in fine shape. After getting around Cape Antone and entering the Gulf of Mexico the wind began to breeze up from the northeast very fresh and I do not think I ever carried sail harder in my life trying to get to Pascagoula before the 16th of April.

On the 14th, when I got my lattitude and worked her up, I said to Mr. Lynn at ¼ past one, "We will make Mobile Lighthouse." And we did. This I was anxious to do and get a bearing to run for Horn Island. I made Horn Island about dark. It was too late to get in. The wind was blowing from the eastward and stormy looking. At any other time than this I would have put to sea and laid it out under sail. Then I thought when the weather cleared off, and I got observations to run her in, it would take two or three days. Then I would have to go to Ship Island for quarantine. So I decided to anchor outside of Horn Island. It was very rough. I got my new 5-inch hawser and tied it to the crown of my anchor, rounded the ship to the wind, and let my anchor go and paid out 45 fathom of chain. She rolled hevily that night but did not drag. The next morning early I intended to heave up to 15 fathom of the anchor, then take the hawser to the capstan, and trip the anchor out. But the mate I had was not much of a seaman. I had got in conversation with the minister aft and the first thing I knew the mate had hove short and being rough she snaped the chain. I ran forward and told them to be quick and take the hawser to the capstan. She had now gathered very much stern way and she parted the hawser and I lost my anchor. I hauled in the hawser and got her under way and sailed her in the harbor before the pilots got out. By saving the pilotage in and out I saved enough to pay half the cost of another anchor and the trip to Ship Island for this was the last day I had.

When the quarantine doctor boarded that morning he examined my bill of health, the crew, and passengers and he said to me, "Captain, I shall have to send you to Ship Island for quarantine for you have a sick woman on here." I said, "Just wait a minute." I ran down the cabbin and brought up the consul's letter all sealed with the American coat of arms on it. I handed it to him, he read it, and said, "I will keep this and let you land the crew and passengers. You saved yourself a lot of trouble by having this letter."

I took a tow boat and towed up the river to Moss Point and moored at the lumber mill. From here I had to go to Pascagoula to enter at the custom house. The passengers had to go too and spend the night in order to take the 4 o'clock train the next morning to New Orleans. We got carriages to take us all down, a ride of about 3 miles. I went to the custom house and entered and in a reasonable time Mr. Eastman came to me and said, "Captain, I do not know what we are going to do with Mr. Lynn. The hotel won't admit him in." I said, "Is that so? Leave it to me. I will get him a place to stay." It was getting along in the evening. The weather was looking like rain and I was anxious to get him a place to stay. I took him to a boarding house and asked the lady if she would put him up. She said that she had no room. I then took him to a French boarding house. I had stoped there a few times when my vessel was laying out in the sound. Their name was something like Courdet. I walked in the house and said, "Mrs. Courdet, this is Mr. Lynn, a gentleman I brought in from Jamaica. He wants to go to New Orleans on the 5 o'clock train in the morning and wishes to stay here tonight. Could you accomodate him?" She said, "My house is full." I then began to do some thinking. Mr. Lynn was a merchant in Kingston and he must have had some Indian or dark, Spanish blood in him. He was clean, reticent, and a gentleman and I saw instantly where the line was being drawn. It would have given me much trouble to have carried him back to the ship some 3 or 3½ miles and I might be troubled to get a team to come to the vessel in time the next morning to meet the train. I thought of one more boarding house that I sometimes stoped to when the ship was at anchor off in the bay. This boarding house was kept by a Miss Benson. This being the last place to go to, and not to be outdone, I went to see Miss Benson and asked her if she could let me have supper and a room. She answered in the affirmative. "Well," I said, "I have a gentleman here with me and I would like to take him in with me if you do not object." She replied, "I can give him a room too." "Oh, that is nice," said I. Then I went to the teamster that was waiting for me and told him that I would stay in Scranton and not go up to the ship until morning. Miss Benson gave us a nice room. The beds had canopys over them to the floor and not a musquito bit us that night. The next morning she called about 4 o'clock and gave us hot coffee, bread, butter, and cake. When through we walked to the train in time to catch her alright. We beat the minister badly. His beds had no canopys over them at the hotel. The musquitoes bit them badly all night. They got very little rest and no cake and coffee either. And double the fare we did. I was a little money out, maybe three dollars, counting the cost of getting back to Moss Point the next day. I think Mr. Lynn was not so particularly carried away with New Orleans as he took the first steamer sailing for New York. This he told me when I returned to Jamaica. He came on board to meet me.

I found it such hard work beating from Cape Antone up the Caribbean Sea that I concluded to try another route. I told an old sea captain, by name of Albert, that I intended to run for Dry Tortugas and go up the Gulf Stream to Salt Key Bank. Then over to the Bahama Bank and work this Bank up to Lobos Key and work up the Old Bahama Channel and go to the eastward of Cape Maysi, east end of Cuba, and see if I could not make better time. He said, "Captain, you had better not try it. I have known masters to try that and spend two or three weeks beating then turn back and go around Cape Antone." When I left Pascagoula I chose this route. I knew there was a strong current runing to the westward in the Old Bahama Channel. I also knew my old *Baltimore* was good on a wind. So I let her go for Dry Tortugas up the Gulf Stream to Salt Key Bank then over to the Bahama Bank. I skined along on the edge of this Bank to Lobos Key Lighthouse. Then I had to take the channel and beat against a strong east wind and current. There is no soundings in the Bahama Channel. It is so deep it had to done by good navigating. The channel is not more than six miles wide and at the Lobos only 4 miles wide and it is not lighted and rocks abound on each side. I would always get close under the Cuba shore just at night and get a good departure to work from. And often I would get the breeze more from the land at night. This was hard work and very little rest for me. I was always glad to see the breaking of day and to relocate the vessel. I got safely around Cape Maysi and then had a fair wind over to the east end of Jamaica. I made the run from Cape Maysi over to Jamaica in 48 hours and the run from Pascagoula to Jamaica in 14 days where as it used to take me 25. Captain Albert judged the ship and the man wrong when he said I would loose 3 weeks time then turn back and go around Cape Antone, Cuba. In the life of Lord Nelson he boasted strangely of the fete of bringing his fleet of warships down through the Old Bahama Channel with a fair wind and tide when he was on his way down on the north side of Cuba to take Havana. I wonder what he would think today, were he living, of a man working a merchant vessel up through it against a strong current and adverse winds. I did it 3 times.

I staid around the West Indies so long that the sun was turning me very dark. On my third voyage to Kingston a lady approached me and spoke thinking she knew me. After she spoke she realized her mistake but said, "Are not you a Cayman man?" I said, "No mam, I am an American." She belonged to the Grand Cayman Island. They are a very dark people. The next voyage to Kingston the same thing happened again. A lady came up to me and looked at me curiously and said, "Ain't you a Cayman man?" I said, "No mam, I am an American." Evidently I favored some man who belonged to the Grand Cayman Island. I thought, gee, I must be getting black and I am going to quit the West Indies.

I chartered to go to Black River and load fustic and logwood for New York. Just before leaving Black River I bought from an old colored man 37 large sugar loaf pineapples. They are the best pineapples in the world to my way of thinking. He only charged me 3 cents each for them. I wanted to get them home for my family. I stood them up on their stalk ends in a spare berth I had where the air could blow through a window on them. When one would begin to decay I would give it to the crew. I was 22 days on the passage and the sailors got most of my pineapples. At New York I filled my trunk with what was left of them and expressed them home. I was anxious to get them home before they all spoiled. The next day I left the mate in charge and started home. When I changed cars at Kings Creek, to my chagrin, I saw them take this trunk of pineapples off. I thought they were home. We did get a few home sound. My wife cooked up the rinds from which she made some of the nicest jelly.

I had then been around the West Indies about 10 months. After discharging cargo, docking, and painting I chartered to take a cargo to Wilmington, North Carolina, and a cargo of lumber to New York. Before I had finished discharging my cargo of lumber I had chartered to Snow and Bryan, wholesale grocers, to go to Baltimore and load a cargo of canned goods and other general merchandise to take to Tampa. It was, I think, early in November. I had a fair run from New York to the Chesapeake. I then got westerly winds up the bay. I beat her up the Patapsco River up into Canton Hollow. A tow boat spoke me as I was about to anchor and said, "Captain, you go to the terminal warehouse. Your cargo is ready and waiting and Mr. Snow is there waiting." I took this tow boat and towed into the dock and made fast before I got my sails tied up. This time I did not have to anchor and furthur this was the last time the schooner *City of Baltimore* was ever in the city of Baltimore, though little did I think it at the time.

We loaded very quickly. I got my stores on board for the voyage and sailed. Had it very moderate down the bay. When off New Point the weather was threatening. I went in under New Point for harbor. When I got in ready to anchor, jibs down, a breeze came out from the north. It was then 4 o'clock in morning and very dark. I hailed the mate and told him not to cast the anchor but hoist the jibs up again. And I went out to sea. The *Baltimore* never came in the capes again and I have never taken another ship down the Chesapeake Bay. The wind blew fresh from the north for awhile, then blew from the northeast. I kept this wind all the way to Tampa and made the run from the capes of the Chesapeake to Tampa in eleven days. It was a good run.

After discharging at Tampa I chartered to Mr. D. C. Gillett for $1,000 a month, he paying all expenses except the crew's wages and grub bill. Here I loaded a cargo of lumber and went to Caibarien, Cuba. Going out over the bar at Tampa the sea was high and rough. There had been a strong northwester that night which caused this high sea. When on the bar the pilot said to me, "How much do you think she falls when she goes down?" I said, "Four feet." I saw he was worried. I said, "Ain't there plenty of water?" He said, "16 feet." I was drawing 12 feet. That meant all. A sharp sea then hit her and filled the deck full fore and aft. I drew myself up in a knot thinking sure she would hit the bar. And I knew that hard sand would burst her open. But as luck would have it she did not hit but went over the bar clear. I was much releived when the pilot said, "You are over." After he left I dressed her up with all sail and I had a nice run. I was only four days getting to Caibarien, or Frances Cay, where we had to anchor and lighter part of the cargo until she was up to 9½ feet. I then sailed her up to the city anchorage and rafted the remainder of the cargo ashore, which was slow work. We were here on Christmas Day. The mate and I took a bus drawn by mules and rode up to Remedios and eat our Christmas dinner there. Remedios is said to be a very old city. We got back sometime that night.

After discharging our cargo I sailed up the coast to Nuevitas. There we loaded, in the hold, a cargo of resawed Spanish cedar logs sawed just the thickness of cigar box stuff. The log would not be sawed all the way to the end but in about six inches of it. The log was then tied in sections with strong rapping to hold them together. When the hold was full we then took on a deck load of Spanish cedar logs in the rough hewed square. I then took them to Tampa. Mr. Gillett did charter me for another voyage. I went from Tampa to Pascagoula, Mississippi, and loaded lumber for Havana. I forget who my consignee was in Havana. He spoke good English and treated me fair. When I went to his office to collect my freight, which was $1,500, he paid all to me in American gold and in $5 gold pieces. Two of them were coined in 1836. Not so long ago I gave each of my grandchildren, there being only two of them, these two pieces of gold.

Before leaving Pascagoula this time I met another mill man who chartered me to make three voyages to Havana at $6 per thousand feet. I was about 4 months making these 3 voyages. While I was doing this I got in touch with Mr. D. C. Gillett and he wanted to buy the vessel. I did not know what to do about selling of her. She was a nice vessel. I liked her and hated to give her up. I would roll over and over in my bunk trying to get the consent of my mind. If my family would come to Pascagoula and live, where I had business, I would keep her. But I knew they would not. I then thought, here I am more than fifty years old. I have been going to sea steadily since I was sixteen years old and the vessel is no longer a new one, but a good one. I will sell her and quit. I knew my day was over for making money. I considered all these things. Finally, Mr. Gillett and I came to terms. I was to bring her from Havana to Tampa, put her on the railway to inspect her bottom, paint the bottom, and deliver her to him on cash terms.

I was in Tampa on the fourth day of July and at the Tampa Bay Hotel I heard Captain Napoleon Broward make his campaign address. He had been nominated for governor and was elected. When he was through with his speech I went up and shook his hand and said, "You don't know me do you?" He said, "I do." He then told the people there how worried I was when he knocked a little paint off the *Baltimore's* side when he was docking me at Jacksonville one time.

I got the vessel all in order as agreed and docked her where Mr. Gillett wanted her put and signed the bills of sale before a lawyer. Then Ed Gunby collected the check and went to the American National Bank and deposited it. The next day I packed all my things of more than 20 years accumulation, which was a good lot. I had to get goods boxes to put them in. They consisted of charts, nautical instruments, books, bedding, and so on. I sent them over to the train for Baltimore. Then the next day, on the 11th of July, 1904, after being on board of her 20 years, 5 months, and 9 days, I bid my old and my best freind goodby.

There were people in Baltimore that would not consent to sell their interests. A lady, Mrs. Lambdin, said the vessel paid her more than anywhere she could place the money. Another, Mr. George Skinner, viewed it the same way. I knew when they saw me they would change their minds. Therefore, I deposited their money in the American National Bank to be held thirty days and, if a bill of sale did not come with draft attached, to call the sale off and give Mr. Gillett his money. When I got to Baltimore I called on Mr. Skinner and told him that I had sold the vessel and had the money for all but him and Mrs. Lambdin as I expected he would want to sell as soon as he knew I was no longer on board. He seemed at a loss to know what to do. I told him he had thirty days to make up his mind to sell. We went to the custom house, got a blank bill of sale, had it made out for his share, got it signed before a notary public, attached a draught, and mailed it to the American National Bank at Tampa. And in a short time he had his money. I advised Mrs. Susanna C. Lambdin and she did the same. I came home and in about two weeks I sent all of their checks. And that cleaned me up for always with the schooner *City of Baltimore*. The most of my owners wrote me very pleasant and praising letters. They are now in my possesion.

Baltimore, June 13th. 1902 490

Capt. L. J. Tawes, In acct. with and Owners

To GRAY, IRELAN & CO.,

SHIP BROKERS AND COMMISSION MERCHANTS.

G. R. HEFFNER. 296, NO. 36 SOUTH HOLLIDAY STREET.

1902				$	
June	13	By Schr. City of Baltimore's Divd		192	35
1902		Dr			
Apl.	25	To Assessment	$ 3	63	
May	26	" "	2	88	
June	13	" Schr. City of Baltimore,			
		Balance Sailing Interest	34	06	
	13	By Balance	$ 151	78	4
			192	35	192 35
1902					
June	13	By Balance		151	78

On this and the following seven pages are reproductions of receipts and statements relative to the schooner CITY OF BALTIMORE, which have been preserved by Miss Elizabeth W. Hall.

Rio Grande, 24 de Dezembro de 1894

LOJA DE CABOS

Lonas, Tintas, Ferragens, Oleo, etc., etc.

19 · RUA RIACHUELO · 19   Telegrammas: SOBRINHO

O Lugar Americano *City of Baltimore* Compr

a *SILVA SOBRINHO*

Liv. Rio-Grandense 4

2 K^{os} de arrebem linho	5 000
1 lata tinta preta	12 000
5 Kilos de zarcão	4 000
Rs	21 000

Recebi i paguei
Por Silva Sobrinho
Per Silva

English

2 Kilos Seizing stuff
1 can black paint
5 Kilos Red lead.

Cable Address, GONZALEZ, HAVANA.
P. O. Box 250
Telephone 710.

Use watkin's Code and Appendix

Havana, March 21st 1904

Schr City of Baltimore

Bought of J. G. GONZALEZ & CO.

CHANDLERS and PROVISION MERCHANTS

SAN PEDRO, BETWEEN OBISPO and ENNA STREETS.

US Cy

40 lb. Fresh beef	@ 15	6 00
Vegetables		1 75
1 Bot Brandy		1 50
5 lb. Spunyarn		1 10
35 " Sugar		1 40
5 Gall Molasses		1 50
5 lb. Rice	25	13 50

Red Paymt
J G Gonzalez & Co

BALTIMORE & JACKSONVILLE PACKET LINE
GOODS FORWARDED TO ALL RAILROAD AND RIVER POINTS IN FLORIDA.

Shipped, In good order and Condition, by _____ on board the Schooner
called the "City of Baltimore" whereof Towe
is Master of the present Voyage, now lying in the Port of Baltimore, and bound for Tampa Fla   To say:

Marks.

One Thousand and one (1001) Bags of Fertilizer

200.000 lb

Insured 3000—

being marked and numbered as in the margin, and are to be delivered in the like good order and
condition at the aforesaid Port of Tampa Fla , (the dangers
of the seas only excepted,) unto Phillips Fuller & Co or to
their Assigns, he or they paying Freight for said Goods at rate of
Four Doll pr ton 2000 lb and #5 Insurance

cash on delivery without discount, with _____ per cent. Primage and average accustomed.

In Witness Whereof the Master or Purser of the said vessel hath affirmed to
three Bill of Lading, all of this tenor and date, the one of which being

accomplished, the others to stand void.

Weight, contents, condition and value unknown and not accountable for breakage, leakage or rust.

Dated Baltimore, Octo 6th 1900

Gray Ireland & Co Agents,

Per _____

BALTIMORE & JACKSONVILLE PACKET LINE
GOODS FORWARDED TO ALL RAILROAD AND RIVER POINTS IN FLORIDA.

Shipped, In good order and Condition, by Standard Oil Co. on board the Schooner
called the City of Baltimore whereof
is Master of the present Voyage, now lying in the Port of Baltimore, and bound for Tampa Fla   To say:

Marks.

J. J. Giddens
Tampa Fla
100 Cases Axle Grease

5700 32½
2600
10400
10400
11.7000

One hundred cases axle grease

5200 lbs

being marked and numbered as in the margin, and are to be delivered in the like good order and
condition at the aforesaid Port of Tampa Fla (the dangers
of the seas only excepted,) unto J. J. Giddens & Co or to
_____ Assigns, he or they paying Freight for said Goods at rate of
74½ pr 100 lb

cash on delivery without discount, with _____ per cent. Primage and average accustomed.

In Witness Whereof the Master or Purser of the said vessel hath affirmed to
_____ Bill of Lading, all of this tenor and date, the one of which being

accomplished, the others to stand void.

Weight, contents, condition and value unknown and not accountable for breakage, leakage or rust.

Dated Baltimore, October 5th 1900

Gray Ireland & Co Agents,

Per _____

Folio 391

KIRWAN BROS.

(W. E. KIRWAN.)

SHIP STORES AND CHANDLERY,

116 S. GAY STREET, near Pratt.

Baltimore, JUL 8- 1901, 190

Sold to Capt. L. A. Dawes
Schr. City of Baltimore

12	Cans Milk		1.20
15 lbs.	Best Lard	11	1.65
1/2 "	Hops		70
8 "	Prunes	8	64
8 "	Raisins	10	80
1/2	Bbl asst Pork		10.50
3	sc. Breasts 21" 13		2.73
2	sc. Hams 20 " 13 1/2		2.70
1	Bacon Side 37" 10 1/2		3.84
1	Pk. White Beans		65
1	Bbl Supf Best flour		5.75
1	Pkg. allspice		10
1	lb. Pepper		30
1/2 "	Ginger		20
2	Boxs Mustard	10	20
5	Pkgs. Oatmeal	10	50
2 lbs.	Best Tea	50	1.00
12	Cans Clams		1.50
12	" Peaches		1.00
1	Case apples 2' 95		1.90
2	Pkgs. Tapioca	10	20
2	" Corn starch	10	20
6 lbs.	Rice	6 1/2	39
1	Bx Lemon		20
1	Vanilla		20
3	Bots. Chow Chow	15	45
1	Box Pilot Bread 26" 6		1.56
1	Bbl Philada Beef		12.50
30 lbs.	Codfish	6	1.80
12	Cans Corn		90
1	Case Peas	1.20	2.40
Schr	3 doz asst wicks 10/5/15		37
			58.03

freight prepaid
to New York

		62.10
At Wilmington		26.24
Fr'g't wayf 10		
Baker Carver		1360
market at N.Y.	9.44	952
lights		1137
marketing		1363
1 Peck Split Peas		75
16 lbs coffee		160
Sugar & Molasses		15.00
		112.50

Moss Point, Miss., *April 15' 190 4*

At *The City of Baltimore*

TO STEAM TUG BESSIE H. DANTZLER, Dr.
OF MOSS POINT.

S. H. BUGGE, Master.

FOR TOWING *To Sea* $20.00

Received Payment
S H Bugge

W. A. Switzer.   H. L. Johnson.   Jno. FitzGerald.   A. S. Smith.   H. Miner.   H. G. Warner.

Port Tampa, Fla., *Nov 25* 190 *3*

S. S. *Sch City of Bottinson*

To Tampa Bay Board of Pilots, Dr.,

For pilotage inward *11* feet,   *8 00*   *33 00*

For pilotage outward _____ feet.

Pilotage, 8 feet and under, $2.50 per foot.

Pilotage, 15 feet and under, $3.00 per foot.

Pilotage, over 15 feet, $3.50 per foot.

Docking Quarantine Station.

Docking Port Tampa,

Pk L S Tawes.
to Snow & Bryan

PILOT IN, *Johnson*

PILOT OUT,

Paid

THE UNITED STATES OF AMERICA.

CLEARANCE OF VESSEL TO A FOREIGN PORT.

District of _____ PEARL RIVER _____

Port of _____ PASCAGOULA _____

These are to certify all whom it doth concern:

That _L. S. Tawes_

Master or Commander of the _Am sch. "City of Baltimore"_

burden _297_ Tons, or thereabouts, mounted with _no_

Guns, navigated with _(7)_ Men, _Wood_

_____ built, and bound for _Havana Cuba_

having on board _Lumber_

hath here entered and cleared his said vessel, according to law.

Given under our hands and seals, at the Custom House of _____ PASCAGOULA _____

Miss., this _1st_ day of _June_

one thousand nine hundred _four_, and in the _128_

year of the Independence of the United States of America.

_no_   _W R Mosley_

Deputy Naval Officer.   Deputy Collector.

Statement Trip No. 51 Schr. City of Baltimore
From New York to Jacksonville Fla and back
to New York

	Freight on Piling &c	$422.50	
	" " 299,536 ft		
	Cypress @ $5.50 pro. M	1647.44	$2069.94

Port Charges

N.Y.	Loading Oil & Empty Cans	$24.53	
Jaxville.	Disctg Piling - Mayport	17.41	
	Hoisting 700 bbls. Oil	4.50	
	Loadg. 300 M. ft. Cypress &c	120.00	
	Inward & Outward Towage	74.40	
	" " Pilotage	59.75	
	Labor Disctg. Oil &c	1.68	
	Telegrams &c	1.30	
N.Y.	Towage to Salt whf	8.00	
	" from Sea	3.00	
	Loading Salt	57.07	
	Wharfage - Erie Basin	13.46	
	Com." frt. to Jacksonville	21.10	
	" " on Lumber	82.37	
	Towage out	10.00	
	Disctg. Lumber	119.81	654.38

Net Freight		$1415.56
1/2 Sailing		707.78
- Owners		$707.78

Vessels Bills

1 - 8 ft. Oar	80	
Putting Chandlery Aboard	1.50	
Shipsmith	4.00	
Sheaves	7.00	
Chandlery &c	78.95	92.25
Dividend		$615.53

Baltimore, Aug 22 1916

Gillett Lumber & Transportation Co. and Owners,
for Sch. City of Baltimore

To J. S. BEACHAM & BRO., Dr.

Ship Yard and Marine Railway,

MARYLAND STEAM BLOCK AND PUMP WORKS,
MARYLAND BOAT AND LAUNCH WORKS,

C. & P. South 387.

SOUTH SIDE OF BASIN.

1916

Aug 22	Spars in Rough to Make		
	For Foremast 80' x 22" oregon 8 Square	230	00
	" Main mast 80' x 21" " 8 "	200	00
	" Miz mast 80' x 21" " 8 "	200	00
	Spanker Boom 51' x 10" end		
	13" in sling - Spruce	50	00
	2 Topmast 47' x 13" spruce	90	00
	1 " 47' x 14" " "	50	00
	1 Jibboom 47' x 15 in cap - oregon spar 60' " 60' x	75	00
	2 Gaffs 35 ft x 11" spruce	60	00
		955	00
	Cost to Handle Spars		
	on Cars	15	00
		970	00

Aug 22/16
Settled by Draft
on Gillett Lumber & Transportation Co.
J S Beacham & Bro
per Tall

After I was home for a couple of weeks I began to worry. I would see people working, boxing, and shipping goods. And here I was out of harness, something I was never used to. Finally, Mr. Gillett's business was growing and he wanted another vessel. He employed me to go look him up one. I found her. She was small; I do not think she would carry over* three hundred tons. But she was light of draught and would be the very ship to run out to Caibarien. I put her on the railway at Staten Island and examined her bottom. Mr. Gillett came up from Florida and looked at her. He was satisfied with her and paid Mr. Samuel R. Beacham $6,600 for her. We painted her bottom with copper paint and went up to Hoboken and took on a load of white pine lumber for Caibarien. I took a colored cook from Crisfield by name of Joe Sterling. Joe took hold very good. He suited me and I was glad to have him. After I was nearly loaded I got all the stores on board for the voyage. Joe stowed them all away nicely and that night he ran away and left all of his clothes on board. He left after supper and, as I thought, went up town. The next morning no Joe, no one to cook breakfast. I thought he might got arrested or something might have happened. I telephoned to all of the police stations. He was in none of them. I telephoned the hospitals. He was not in any of them and I had to give him up.

After the cargo was on board I had to go over to New York to sign bills of lading and send a crew over by the tow boat and tow her down to Red Hook. I sent word to the mate I would not be on board this night. I never cleared until nearly four o'clock afternoon. In the custom house of large cities there are 2 desks to clear from. One is the coastwise desk, the other is the foreighn desk. Vessels under register and clearing for a foreighn desk are liable to compulsory pilotage.

Editor's note: This was the three-masted schooner *Samuel T. Beacham*, built by J. S. Beacham and Brother at Baltimore, Maryland, in 1898. On March 30, 1913, this schooner collided with the British steamer *Teodoro de Larrinaga* in the Florida Straits and was stricken from the register.

The pilots keep a man on the watch and as soon as a captain goes to the foreighn desk and clears his vessel this pilot will come up and offer his services to pilot him to sea and the master is compelled to accept of his services or pay the full pilotage. In this case it was so near 4 o'clock, or time to close, the pilot went out probably to get a drink of water. Anyhow, I cleared and got out of the custom house without him seeing me. After leaving the custom house I said to clerk that was with me, "You go to your office and I will be there as soon as I pay Baker, Carver and Company their bill. While I was at Baker, Carver and Company's store it dawned on me that the pilot went back to the custom house. After he got what he went after, and as soon as he found out that I had cleared, he would be at the office of A. H. Bull and Company to catch me. So I called up the office of A. H. Bull and Company and I said to the listener at the phone, "Shut the door of your booth. I want to talk privately." With the door shut I said, "Is there a pilot in there, a pilot in your office waiting for me?" He said, "Yes." I said "Let him wait. Do not tell him where I am. You tell Mr. Cook, the bookkeeper, to make up my account for what I owe there and send it to Baker, Carver and Morrell and I will give him a draught for it." After a little time here comes the clerk with my bill. I gave him a draught and told him to let the pilot stay there and wait but tell Mr. Bull, Mr. Cook, and the clerks I said goodbye. Usually, ship masters used to stay at the South Ferry Hotel in those days but I went over to Smith and McNeill's, got a room, my supper, and staid all night.

I have understood it finable if the watch pilot lets a vessel clear and get away without him knowing it. When the pilot was turned out of Mr. Bull's office at closing-up time he went over to Hoboken to look for the vessel. An unpleasant job it was going around those lumber wharfs in the dark. He found out by the watchman here that the vessel had gone to Red Hook to anchor. From Hoboken he went to Castle Garden, a distance of ten miles, hired a ferry boat to pull him out to the vessel at Red Hook which cost him $2. He came to the vessel and called for me. The mate turned out and said, "What do you want this time in the night?" He said, "I am the pilot. I have come to pilot you out." The mate said, "The captain is not on board." "Well," he said, "I will come on board and stay until he comes." The mate said, "No, you won't. I do not know you are a pilot and you get ashore." He had to pay the ferry boat $2 more to take him back to Castle Garden. I always thought a lot of the mate for doing this.

When he got ashore he went the South Ferry Hotel to look for me. I was not there then. He ran over the red light district. He judged me wrong. These places I did not frequent. It was now getting toward morning and he gave the chase up. The next morning I turned out at Smith and McNeill's, got my breakfast, and went to a shipping office over on the east side and shipped a cook which proved to be a better cook by far than Joe was. But Joe was good and I liked him. The wind was blowing fresh from the northwest. I went across the ferry and landed away along South Brooklyn and then hired a tow boat to put me and the cook on board. When I got there the pilot was on board. He knew I did not want him and said that if he could he would take part pilotage and let me go. But he said the pilot rules were so strict it might break him for awhile. So I let him go ahead to take me out. I told him to get her underway. I soon saw he knew nothing about getting her underway. The tide was runing ebb. He was going to heave her up and keep her off. I soon saw he would foul some vessels to the leeward of us so I told him I would take charge of the job. I broke out the anchor and stood her close up under Erie Basin and tacked again which put me far enough to the windward to clear all the vessels anchored below us. When I got out the Hook I paid him and proceeded on my course toward Caibarien.

As night drew on I saw a storm was brewing and I went in the Delaware Breakwater for harbor. And a storm sure came. I laid there from Saturday night until Tuesday when the weather cleared off and become fine and I put to sea. And I have never been in there since. This was September 1905. From the Breakwater to Caibarien I was seven days. I landed a cargo of white pine lumber, collected the freight of $1,000, took in some cedar logs for Tampa at freight of $135. I was in Tampa in 31 days from New York and freighted $1,135 and the vessel at her home. Gillett paid me nicely and gave me a Pullman ticket to Baltimore.

XIII

1906–1922

THE next year Gillett got me to look him up another vessel. I located a nice light-draft vessel called *Brazos,* built and owned by Samuel T. Beacham of Baltimore. She was a little too high for Gillett. He wanted a cheaper one. When at last he bought her he had dickered too long. She had been chartered to take a cargo of cement to Charleston, South Carolina, and a load of lumber back to New York. He wanted this vessel badly for his business in Florida, but no use. This voyage had to be performed. I made this voyage for him. When I got back to New York I chartered to take a load of chimney brick from South River, New Jersey, to Tampa. I had on deck a mast for one of his vessels then at Tampa. It was very troublesome to secure safely on deck. It was so long that we had to come up with the fore and main rigging on the port side to get it on board. It occupied the entire length of the deck from forward aft. I got three chains with a hook and screws to make it secure and I thought it was secured beyond all doubt. Then I took a tow boat and towed down to South River, New Jersey, where they make everything of clay. Here we loaded and I towed down the river to South Amboy. From there I sailed down Princess Bay and out of Sandy Hook.

In working down the beach a little below Cape Henry I fell in company with the schooner *Maggie A. Phillips*. We had gentle head winds and we worked in company to Cape Hatteras. There we separated and I never saw him again. He was bound to the Bahama Islands after a load of fruit. About 8 or 10 days afterward I had got down to Abaco. Here I met such a strong current setting up through the Northeast Providence Channel that I could not beat against it to get around the Hole in the Wall. This was something I had never witnessed before and I had been down through the Hole in the Wall several times before. I felt very vexed at this current. This was on Saturday. I worked hard against the wind and current all night but could only get a little below, or south of, Elbow Key Light which turned out to be a fortunate thing for me. When day broke on Sunday morning, which was the 17th day of June, 1906, the weather looked fierce. Even the land looked so diferent than at anytime I ever saw. I put her on the starboard tack and drove her off to the eastward out of the Northeast Providence Channel. The wind from the southeast got worse and worse and the sea got real high. At noon I reefed her down all round. By two o'clock I was under very short sail. By 3 o'clock I was hove to under double reefed mainsail and the peak of the spanker. At 5 PM a hurrycane was upon us. At 8 PM the worst had gone by but a heavy gale blew at night and the sea swept our decks. The next morning the mate was on the lee side, not a rag of clothing on, sometimes up to his neck in water trying to secure this spar. One of the chains had come unhooked and the second one was getting loose. But after a couple hours of hard work between us both we got it secured. If that spar had got loose just two knocks against our bulwarks would have opened her waterway seam and she would quickly fill with water and needless to say those bricks would have settled her to Davy Jones Locker. I thought the *Maggie A. Phillips* was laying safely in the harbor of the port she was bound but sorry to say she never made her port and I feel positive that she foundered between the hours of 4 and 8 PM, Sunday, the 17th day of June, 1906. It turned out most fortunate for me that I did not get around the Hole in the Wall on Saturday. If I had I would not had sea room to handle the vessel. I should have been blown ashore on some of those rocky islands and the ship, cargo, and crew would have perished.

On the following Wednesday, 4 days afterwards, I rounded the Hole in the Wall, sailed down the Northwest Providence Channel, crossed the Bahama Banks, sailed by the Dog Rocks and Double Headed Shot Keys, through the Northwest Channel at Key West, and up to Tampa. The chimney bricks I took out was for the Tampa Electric Company and when the chimney was up it did not seem possible the schooner *Brazos* carried all of that chimney. It looked so much larger than the vessel did. We then took in a cargo of lumber and went to Nipe Bay, Cuba. Discharged and loaded a cargo of Spanish cedar for Tampa. The tow boat figured of getting a big tow bill out of me as he thought it impossible to sail out of the harbor without him. But the day I finished loading cedar there came a fair wind to sail out of the harbor. I had not paid my bills but I got her underway immediately and sailed her out of this harbor. When I was out I told the mate to run her over to Point Tobacco and anchor her. I instructed him how to sail her over. I then took the yawl boat and went back to the harbor, settled all my bills, and after I got my supper I sailed this yawl all alone across this bay. It was three o'clock in the morning before I got on board. I did all of this to save Gillett a $50 tow bill. A fair wind out the harbor of Nipe does not happen but once a month. The next day we got everything cleared up and straitened up and ready. Cleared from the custom house and sailed for Tampa.

Shortly after arrival I gave the *Brazos* up, came home to Crisfield, and went in the oyster business. It was through John

W. Lewis, a sailmaker, that I got into this business. We made quite a nice winter's work at this. Much better than we ever did again although we did business eleven years. We made some money every year. We shucked two years. We sold them in the shell and made nothing those two years.

In the year of 1912 D. C. Gillett wanted me to buy him another vessel. I went to New York and looked at one that he had been writing about and she was in such bad condition I turned her down. I wired him from New York it would take $2,500 to put her in order. The vessel went east with a load of coal. When she got back to New York he got me to go there and dock her and look at her bottom. I saw she was wormed some and that three planks in her bottom would have to be cut out. I turned her down again and wired him he did not need her as it would cost all of $2,500 to put her in seagoing shape. I came home. He bought her anyhow and wanted me* to go to New York, take charge, and bring her out to Tampa for him where he would do her repairing. I did not care to be drowned and I refused to do it. We took in a load of coal and went to Rockland, Maine. Discharged and I took her to I. L. Snow and Company shipyard to be rebuilt. We fell in good hands here. These people were regular shipbuilders and knew their business and were fully prepared to do the work. I went to their shipyard about the 15th day of April, 1912, and began cutting her open. Her ceiling was very much rotton. Her centerboard well was rotton. This we had to put in new. Also new keelsons and I began to get very much worried. Gillett was the only man in this world I would have done this for because he would be satisfied and say whatever I done would be right. Here I was over 2,000 miles from him. I could not talk anything over with him. I saw the bills were going to far

---

Editor's note: This was the three-masted schooner *Thomas B. Garland,* built at Bath, Maine, in 1881, by Goss, Sawyer & Packard. Stranded at Tampa, Florida, October 27, 1921.

exceed my estimate to him so one day I wrote that I was awfully sorry that the cost of rebuilding this vessel was going to exceed my idea. He wrote back to me a real consoling letter in these words, "Captain, you are worrying more about this matter than I am. You put the vessel in good shape and when you want money draw on me." With all this privilege I spent his money like it was all mine. I put the vessel in splendid order, a new stern on her, new foremast, all three new trestle trees, a lot of new deck, had all of her rigging new served, and new ratlines. Her frame was real good, good as new. We got through with her about July 1st. I had given I. L. Snow and Company draughts amounting to $6,600. I took in some spruce spars of diferint sizes and an oak rudder post for one of the vessels in Tampa.

July 3, I took the steamer and went to Boston to ship a crew. I was there July 4. Went to Faneuil Hall and heard the patriotic speeches and witnessed other patriotic celebrations. I called on N. J. McKinnon that used to steward with me a great deal. I paid him off in Boston in 1886 and I had never seen since. When he quit me in Boston just 26 years ago he went to keeping a resteaurant and did well. I wanted to see my old friend and shipmate again so I went to his resteaurant to get my dinner. I looked around and did not see him. I asked my waiter where he was. He said, "He is back in the kitchen." I said, "Go tell him to come out here, a gentleman wants to see him." He came. I got up and shook hands with him. I was surprised he did not know me. I had to tell him who I was. He was glad to see me. My dinner cost me nothing and he wanted me to go home with him and spend the night. I told him I had to go back to Rockland that night. I had just shipped a crew and I had to go out on the evening boat. Mack was a good fellow and had a good disposition. We always got along nicely. I had not seen him since I came into Boston with a load of dry hides from South America in 1886, 26 years ago.

I got the crew to Rockland, put them on board, hoisted the boat to the davits so they could not get ashore, and I sailed July the 5th for Tampa. And I have never been to Rockland since. I had a long seige of head winds to Tampa and I was 27 or 28 days making the passage. I had a good, hard working mate by the name of Ally and on the passage we cleaned and painted the vessel beautifully. I sailed her right up to the Cut Channel and Gillett came out in a tow boat and took her up in the harbor and went to loading her right away. He paid me nicely and gave me a Pullman ticket home. This was very nearly my last command.

In 1914 I took a yacht from Salisbury to New York. While I was on my way there a war broke out in Europe. In 1916 two Porto Ricans built a small fishing boat or trawler at Salisbury, Maryland. She was 47 feet long, six feet depth, and 12 feet beam and they seemed to be in a bad way to get her out to Porto Rico. She was too large to carry on the ships out of New York and too small to get a man to take her out under her own power. They were telling the custom collector here, Thom Steveson, of their trouble. Thom told them that we have a man here in Crisfield that will take her out for you. So they got Thom to look me up. I went to Salisbury and looked at her. I liked her model and I told them I would take her out for them. I brought her to Crisfield, stored her, and cleared.

From Salisbury to Crisfield I saw that we had an engineer that was not going to fill the bill. One Harris Pruitt was anxious to go and was a very capable engineer. He used to run our engine dredging oysters for us and I would like to have him go. But the owner wanted the man he got in Salisbury to go. He had great faith in him. He put the engine in for him. But there is a big diference in engineering on sea and engineering at dock. I saw this man was very nervous and I had no faith in him. That night before leaving I made up my mind not to go with this engineer. As long as he was not going to employ

Harris I would not go. I told him that I could not go with the Salisbury engineer and as long as he did not want Harris I would not go. I told him I would carry his boat to Norfolk where he could get a man and that I would not charge him a cent for what I had done. He changed his mind very quick. He wanted me to take him to Harris' house so as to get him. It was the best thing he did for that boat would never got there with that engineer.

I went to Norfolk, did some little job to the engine, and stored her up. Mr. Vilimil was along with us. He told me to go up to the market and get the necessary stores to make the voyage. I bought 3 hams, about 40 pounds of corn beef, two boxes pilot bread, 44 pounds potatoes, canned goods, and all else I thought necessary to make the voyage. I went down through the Dismal Swamp Canal, stoped at Elizabeth City, got gassoline and did something more to the engine, and proceeded down through Albemarle Sound to Beaufort, North Carolina.

Here we got a two-day storm from the southeast. We had to store up again. I never saw such eating in my life. On the second day of the storm Vilimil wanted to know why I did not go to sea. It is a very unthankful job to sail a boat for people who know nothing about weather or conditions of the weather. He thought that little boat ought to go up against any weather that a big steamship could go up against. I tried to reason with him that the weather was not fit for her to go out in. He began to murmur a lot about it. It would have served him right if I had got ashore and left him there. If I had there is where his boat would have rotted for no one else would have taken her. But to humor him I said, "Harris, get the engine ready and we will go out." I began to single up the lines for going when the people of Beaufort asked me, "Captain, where are you going?" I said, "I am going out." They said, "Captain, the weather is not fit to go out in." I said, "I know it." They said, "Why do you go?" I said, "The owner, Mr. Vilimil, wants to go. I told him the weather was not fit but he does not be-leive it and wants to go." "But," they said, "you cannot head off against this wind." "But," I said, "I will go as far as I can to show this man." When so many experienced men got to talking to him he changed his mind and concluded to stay in the port until the storm had passed. The next evening the southeast storm was abating and the barometer was falling. I was sure the wind was coming from the west. I got the boat under-way and runed down to the fort and anchored ready to go out by six the next morning.

It is right funny for me to say but at 8 o'clock, when it was dark, I went up forward and there set Harris on the pawl bitt cutting right and left on beef and bread. I said, "Harris, ain't you eating?" He said, "Yes, Captain, that corn beef you bought in Norfolk is so good I cannot get enough." We had already stored up three times and now I began to get worried. I said, "There will be no more stopping places where we can store up and what is here has got to last us to Porto Rico." The next morning at 6 o'clock we went to sea. There was a big swell rolling in from eastward, the effects of this last storm, and she was doing some pitching and rolling. I thought every-thing was going on nicely. About the time we got out to the Cape Lookout Lightship Harris came to me. I saw he was looking pale. He said to me, "Captain, that corn beef turned against me this morning and if I had not thrown it up I should have died." I said, "You should be careful and not over-load your stomach." I never gave it thought that he was sea sick. He never eat over a quart of food from then until we arrived in Mayaguez, Porto Rico.

About the second day out we were crossing the Gulf Stream. The clouds began to frown. I saw a storm was coming on us. It was just coming dark. I went around and put the window boards in to keep the sea from smashing the windows in. I had a fellow with me by the name of Bird. He was from Morehead City. He was helping me to put these window shutters in. The ocean was now getting white and it looked bad to Bird. And it did not look good to me. I had the cabbin closed in secure. I did not go down there anymore for two days and I never saw Vilimil the whole time. What sleep I got I got it down in the engine room and the rain was falling in my face. It is easy to imagine how much sleep I got during this storm. She danced like a feather on the water. When I did get back in the cabbin I found she had thrown the two ink bottles off the table over in my berth. My bed was all wet with sea water where it had leaked in around the window which was not properly put in for a seagoing boat. I could not get this bed dry and I had to sleep on a wet bed all the way out. I worried considerable about this as I had a lung trouble for more than a year. I wanted to get on a trip of this kind for some time because the Gulf Stream had always cured me of my colds when I was going to sea regularly. And so it did this time in spite of sleeping on a wet bed. This trip cured me of my lung trouble and I have been well all the time since.

These little boats are the hardest things in the world to navigate. If I had not been an expert at taking observations I should never got one. By the time you are up on top of the billow, and you get ready to draw the sun down on the horrison, she goes down behind the billow and the horrison becomes invisable. But by working quick as a gunner shoots a partridge I soon overcame this obstacle. After taking a sight in the morning for to obtain longitude she would roll so that I could not get in the cabbin to take off the time. I had to teach Vilimil how to take the time off the chronometer when I would holler, "Time." After this I had no more trouble on this line. Now my next trouble, I found my dead reckoning difered too much from my observations. I had crossed the Gulf Stream several times in my life and I never had the Stream to carry me so far to eastward before. The crew did not know the chronometer is a very delacate timepiece and should never be disturbed or moved. She was moved from one place and then another and I began to think they had changed her rate. I was trying every way possible to find my trouble. One morning at sunrise I took an amplitude and found my compass had 17 degrees westerly variation. After this I allowed for this westerly variation. And after this my dead reckoning and observations agreed very closely.

Shortly after this, just before sunset, Harris Pruitt said, "I see a four-masted schooner on the starboard bow." He showed her to me. I found she was only about 1½ points on our starboard bow. I concluded I would speak her. The weather had moderated very much and the sea was not so bad so I kept off for him and after dark I got up to him. I hailed and told him I thought my chronometer was out of the way and if he would be kind enough to compare times with his. He then gave me the bigest surprise of my life. He said to me, "Ain't that Captain Len Tawes?" I said, "Yes. Who is that knows me?" He said, "Fletcher Gantt." Finding a needle in a hay stack is small to finding an old friend that sailed as mate with me for two years. He brought his chronometer out and I did the same and we compared time 3 or 4 times. I found mine was out 9 miles. He wanted me to come on board to see him but we had only a flat-bottom skiff and I did not want to take the chance. I said, "Do you think your chronometer is correct?" He said, "I left Bermuda 4 days ago and she was alright." I have now got my chronometer's error and the error on my compass. I am just sure of going to Porto Rico as a bald eagle goes to his nest. Captain Gantt asked where I was going in such a small boat. I told him to Mayaguez, Porto Rico. Captain Gantt was one of the best mates I ever had. I taught him navigation because I liked him. Besides, he was a good sailorman. He died in the West Indies with pnewmonia in 1922 and I went out there and brought the vessel home which was my last cruise in a sailing vessel.

I made the passage in this little boat in 9 days and 8 hours without any trouble. In the storm we had in the Gulf Stream she washed the copper mettal off her bottom. I expect if we had had a read powerful engine in her she would have washed the planks off for she hit the seas mighty hard. I got there 3 days before the steamship sailed for New York. Vilimil paid me for my service and gave me a first-class ticket to New York. We arrived in New York the 30th day of May, just 24 days since I left Crisfield.

The 30th of May, 1916, was Decoration Day and a holliday. This being a day of idleness on my hands I thought I would take a look around the city. So I went down in Water Street and to the mission where Jerry McCauly used to preach when I was going before the mast in a fruiter in 1874. We used to land our fruit close to Catherine Market on the East River and of night I used to go up to Jerry McCauly's mission. It was a mystery to me in those days. I used to wonder how anyone could undertake to run a church in such a place. It was just the roughest people in the world. I could sit in his mission and hear them calling off dances across the street, "Ladies will prominade to the bar." The vile women would run across the street and take hold of the door knobs of the mission and shake them with all their strength. After I made a few more voyages to the West Indies and when I visited the mission I found there was no more dancing across the street. I heard the Mayor ordered they should not make any noise to disturb Jerry's meeting. He then kept the church going until midnight. This broke these dens up as they could do no business after midnight. I could hear some of the most wonderful experiences given in these meetings. One fellow said he was always in trouble until he joined this mission. Sometimes he would crawl in a box car drunk and wake up in Chicago. He looked like someone had tried to cut his throat once. He had a big gash on his throat. But he said, "Since I joined this mission I have no trouble with anyone. I just slip around as easy as a boy on skates." Now on this 30th day of May I took a walk down in Water Street. I went to the place where the mission used to be. I knew the spot by just a little bow or crook in the street. The mission was gone and to my surprise the nicest stores and business places was where these bad places used to be. I was surprised to see such a beautiful change. Jerry had gone home to his Father's but he left his good works behind him.

I came home and never thought about the sea anymore for quite awhile. We were now about to go to war with Germany and young seamen were needed. I got a job teaching a navigation school. I taught this for a while but could not get enough schollars to satisfy the government. We have a lot of smart young watermen here too but they had never sailed in vessels over 300 tons and were ineligible to go to the school. As I could not get ten schollars the government closed the school. This was in 1916. In 1918 I got a job from the government as inspector of shipbuilding. I held this job one and a half years, until April 1920.

I then got a job from the government to take a yacht, or* survey boat, from New York to Detroit, Michigan, by the way of the Gulf of St. Lawrence. It was a very interesting and historical trip. I had to put in to quite a few places for coal and water. She had no condensers. After leaving New York I stoped at Newport, Rhode Island. I took in water. The next day I went up Buzzards Bay and went through the Cape Cod Canal. In Boston Bay the cheif told me she was leaking badly and I lined her for Boston. When I had got up to Minots Ledge he told me he had found the leak and stopped it. I then turned

---

Editor's note: This was the steam yacht *Margaret*, built in 1913 at Morris Heights, New York, and which served during World War I for the U. S. Navy. After delivery at Detroit by Captain Tawes she was converted into a survey vessel for the U. S. Army Engineer Corps.

back and started for Cape Ann as night was drawing on. It began to thicken up and I went into Gloucester. Laid there that night. Then next day I went out. It got real thick then but I steered for the whistling buoy and made it close on the starboard bow. I then lined her for Portland Lightship. It staid thick all day but sometime late in the afternoon I made the light all o.k. and went into Portland, Maine. Our water was nearly gone. Here we coaled, watered, and provisioned. On Sunday morning we left and cruised along up the Maine coast.

At night we went into Bar Harbor. I called up an old sea captain I knew well but had not seen him for many years. It was Captain Charley Hodgkins. He was in harness when I used to be. I said, "I have called you up because I wanted to hear your voice. I am sure I will never see you again." He said, "Who is this?" I told him it was Tawes. He said, "Where are you?" I said, "At Bar Harbor." He said, "What are you doing there?" I said, "I am taking a survey boat from New York to Detroit." He said, "You ought to be kicked. Why don't you stay home?" He said, "Are you going out tomorrow?" I said, "Yes." He said, "Tomorrow is a legal holliday. It is Decoration Day. Stay where you are and come up to the new bridge we are going to dedicate to the honor of our soldiers who served in the late war." He said that it was about 12 miles up from Bar Harbor. I told him I would come up. He said, "I will be on the south end of the bridge." At ten o'clock the next morning my brother John and I took an automobile and we had a nice ride up through the country. It certainly was beautiful. The grass was new and green and the leaves on the trees looked so fresh and green. We got there quite a while before 10 o'clock but people were begining to come pretty fast. I walked from one end of the bridge to the other. They were taking moving pictures of the people as they passed and I am in that picture. We then went down to the water close by and there they had piles of manonoses, what they call clams, and plenty of rock weed ready for a clam bake. They had seven wash boilers filled with water for making coffee. I watched them. They put seven pounds of coffee in each boiler. I said to John, my brother, "There is going to be a show to get coffee and some of Maine's famous baked clams here today."

A little before ten o'clock I stationed myself at the south end of the bridge so as to meet Captain Hodgkins. I had some fear that I would not know him. Twenty six years often make big changes in some people. Shortly after 10 o'clock he came and to my surprise he did not look a day older than he did 26 years before. I said, "I am the man you are looking for." He gave me a hardy hand shake and said, "Tawes, I am surprised at the way you carry your age. You do not look a day older than when I saw you in New York when you were laying at pier 14, East River, loading for Cayenne, French Guiana." I said, "Captain, I can return the compliment. You are carrying your age fully as well as I." He gave my brother and I all the attention he possibly could. We had dinner with him. He and his family brought dinner with them in their automobile. They spread a table cloth down on the green grass and I had a sumptuos dinner with them. The bridge builders furnished coffee and clams to everybody free. After dinner Captain Hodgkins devoted all of the time to John and I. I told him I was sure he had many friends there that he might want to see and not to devote any more of his time with us. He did not adhere to this but just staid with us and occasionally introduced us to some of his friends. John met a man he knew well. He sailed with his father on many trips to Europe in the oil trade when he was quite young. We certainly had a pleasant day. There was a big gathering of people, about 2,500. I saw that Captain Hodgkins intended to entertain us and I was sure he had friends there that he would wish to see. So at 2 PM I said to John, "Let us take an automobile and go down to the harbor." Which we did.

The wind blew fresh that day. I should say a half gale from the southwest and I was worried some about the time we were loosing. But we lost no time. I am sure we would not went out had I been on board. When I got down to the ship I told the cheif to get up steam and we would go out. I did go out but when I got out from behind those high cliffs where the wind would get at us with its full force I saw it was not fit to cross the Bay of Fundy. I went back and tied up for the night. The next morning it had moderated some. I went out and I found it bad enough. There was a big sea runing in the Bay of Fundy and we got the worst rolling I had seen for many a day. All the sailors got seasick and laid out on deck paralized like old drunks. Late that afternoon we went into Yarmouth, Nova Scotia. Here we watered, coaled, and provisioned. I believe the cooks destroyed or sold the provisions. I could not say but I know it took a lot to run us. I used to know a very nice sea captain name Sam Messenger. We met a few times in our life and our travels. The first time I met him was in Fernandina, Florida. Then Rio Grande do Sul; Barbados; Guantanamo, Cuba; Delaware Breakwater, and New York. He was a very accomodating man. While at Yarmouth I inquired for him. He was very ill. So much so I was not allowed to see him.

I sailed from Yarmouth on a Saturday morning. That evening late I went in to the port of Canso. I think Canso is the greatest fishing place I ever was in. I asked the manager of the fishing company there if I could lay at his dock. He said I could. His name was Roberts. He was very nice and accomodating. I asked him if we could get water there. He said there was no water in that city or town but if I would lay over until Monday I could get a team to haul it from somewhere near the town or neighborhood. Then I thought I was really stuck to lay there until Monday. And to hire team to haul water was hard to think of. I was at a loss to know what to do. Then and there I made up my mind never to go in any steamer that had no condensers. He asked me up to his office that night. It was about 9 o'clock. He said to me, "Captain, have you got water enough to run you 28 miles?" I asked Mr. Chase, the cheif engineer, and he said that we had. He said he had a friend living at, I forget the name of the place, but it is where the cars are carried across the Gut of Canso. He called up this friend of his and said to him, "I have a friend going through the Gut of Canso and he will be at your wharf tomorrow morning at 9 o'clock. Can't you put a man on the dock and give him water?" He said, "Yes." This certainly was a releif to me. I asked him his charges. He said, "Nothing." "Well," I said, "I want at least to pay the telephone bill." But there was no bill. He gave us all the fish we wanted and a variety of some that he canned. I must say I found accomodating people all along on my way but this man Roberts was especially so. The next morning at 6 o'clock we got under way and started. We got to this port at 9 o'clock. It was raining and cold. I found the man on the dock waiting as per agreement. We got all the water we wanted and, if I remember, there was no cost for the water. I just paid the man for his services.

We then proceeded on our way through the Gut of Canso. I thought it was pretty going through there. I would love to go through there again. We crossed George Bay into Norththumberland Strait and that night went into Charlottetown. A storm was threatening and I was glad to get in there too. It was real stormy until Wednesday. At Charlottetown I met another acquaintance that I knew at Demerara. He came out there in a brig loaded in the hold with grain or oats, horses, and fowls on deck. He used to take the governor out on a spin with these fine horses which he sold on a big margin. He got out hand bills and sent them to every house in Demerara discribing these beautiful fowl he had. It was near Christmas and he sold these all to a big advantage. When the cargo was out of the brig she took in a cargo of sugar to go to New York. She sailed about 3 days before the steamer sailed for New York. Mr. Dean, Will Dean was his name, put up with me for the 3 days. He told me he made well on the voyage and he wanted to know if I would not come down to Charlottetown the next year and load for him. He said that I had such a big deck that she would just suit his business. But somehow we never got together. When I told him who I was he remembered me mighty well. It was approaching noon and he said, "I would like to ask you home with me to dinner but I never married and I have not the home I would like to ask you to." I said, "If I had my way with a man like you I would make you support two old maids." That night he came to the ship and took me to the theater.

The next morning the weather moderated and I sailed. He cautioned me about the Tryon Shoal that lay off in the straits just out of the harbor as it took up a good many vessels. We now had a long run ahead of us before we could get to another stopping place. We run all that day, all night, and until nearly noon the next before we got to the port of Gaspé. Here we coaled, watered, and provisioned. And here is where I came near being hung up. There was only one coal merchant and he wanted to know if I had the cash to pay for his coal. I told him I did not but I could give him a draught on the United States Government. He said, "Your government is about as bad as ours. They both owe me and I can't get my money and I cannot let my coal go without the money." Now I had to have coal or stay there. I said, "If you will let me have the coal I will give you a sight draught." He said, "Can you do that?" "I can," I said. "Well, in that case," he said, "you may have the coal." He gave seven little wheelbarrows for a ton and it was interesting to see how that fellow would cheat in the measurement of those little wheelbarrows. But he had us and we could not help it. I would sometimes wink at Mr. Chase and point to the small measure. It was against the government rules to give sight draughts but I felt safe if I had to pay that draught myself. I felt sure United States Senators of this state at Washington would someday see me reimbursed. I got the coal in and water. My bill was in the neighborhood of $500.

I had to go across a small creek to the bank for settlement. Here I hit another snag. They made out my bill in American currency and at that time there was 12% diference in Canadian currency and ours. I told him and the bank clerk they would have to take 12% of the bill for exchange or make the draught out in Canadian currency. They said, "Look, how long we will have to wait for our money?" I said, "Gentlemen, I am an old sea captain and have had experience in buying bills of exchange in foreighn countrys, sight draughts, and 30, 60, and 90 day draughts. I know how to figure exchange and now I am a director in a bank. And do you know that I know that a sight draught is payable immediately it is banked?" They took off the 12% and I saved our government $60. Now there was no other place I could stop to water or coal until I got to Father Point. I left immediately when the coal and water was on board and ran as hard as I could drive all that night and until I got to Father Point, which was all of four o'clock in the afternoon. Here I took a pilot on board. Then I questioned the pilot about what time it would take us to reach fresh water. He told me the next day at ten o'clock. I then asked Mr. Chase if we had fresh water enough to run us all night and until ten o'clock the next day. He looked the water over and said, "We can run until ten o'clock tomorrow." I said, "Then we will not go in this harbor but keep her going." We run all night. The pilot kept up all night.

The next day at ten o'clock we were in fresh water. I was really glad. I could say now as the Irishman told me at Jacksonville, Florida, once, "Old lady you can have all the water you can drink." In Jacksonville, Florida, I was short of one man to make up my full crew. I went to the jail to see if they had a man in there. They told me they had an Irishman in. I went in the jail to see if he would go with me if I paid his fine. He said that he would. The vessel was laying about 2½ miles down the river at anchor. I took him on board. I was all loaded and ready for sea. That night, about 9 o'clock, the Irishman came aft, nocked at the cabin door. I said, "Hello, what is up?" He said, "Captain, have you anything to drink on board that you would let me have? I have been on a wild spree, a big spree, and I am sicker than the devil's own father." I said, "Jack, I have nothing for you." The next day he had come around alright and I towed down the river and out to sea. Jack was a good Irishman and a witty one. Coming up the Chesapeake Bay I had been on deck all night. I seldom had a mate that knew anything about the Chesapeake Bay. Chris Woodland was the best one I ever had. He did know the bay. I was tired and I told the Irishman I was going to lay down and not to call me for no tow boat captain for I never took a tow below Sandy Point but to steer along north ½ east. After I was below awhile here comes Captain Mullen in the tow boat *Easby*. He wanted Jack to call me. Jack told him he could not do it as I had given orders not to be called. Mullen insisted but Jack would not do it. I was laying in my berth and I could hear every word. I knew it was his voice. In a short while I came on deck. I said, "That fellow wanted you to call me. Did not he tell you who he was". "No, sir," he said, "but I would know him should I meet him. He had the map of the 32 counties of Ireland stamped on his face."

Resuming my story we arrived at Quebec at 12 noon, got coal, water, and stores. Here the sailors were bothering me for money. They wanted to tank up. It was Saturday afternoon. I had a good excuse not to let them have money. The banks were not open and I could not make a draw. They begged me to let them have the little loose change I had in my pocket. They could not get drunk on what they got from me. That night at 12 we left Quebec for Montreal. Got to Montreal in the afternoon Sunday. Monday we went into the locks and we went through some 12 locks. We then went at water level, I beleive, through the Thousand Islands which was the most beautiful scenery I ever saw. We stoped at Ogdensburg and coaled up. We had an Irish fireman that punched a hole in one of the boiler pipes and we had to put into Erie, Pennsylvania, to have it repaired. We were here two or three days. Then we went to Detroit. Got there safely on a Sunday afternoon. The Army Engineers chartered a car to take the whole crew to New York. I was to pay for the car and each man to pay for his meals and we were to turn our account in at the office in New York. It was fun to see the account this Irishman turned in for his meals on the road to New York. They did not beleive him and they paid in proportion to what the bills were for the other men on this trip. Taking out some trials and vexations I had a good time. I could have made the run in less than half the time and half the expense if the little steamer had had condensers and I will never go in another unless she has.

I came home and went to oyster planting again. I had me a watch house built on 49 oak piling, 4 feet apart, 2 miles from land. I watched the oysters mostly myself. I had a wharf or platform 20 feet by 20 feet, and a one room house 14 x 14. Here I was comfortable but lonesome. I had a 20-foot gasoline launch, a capable sea boat that I used to go and come in. Here I came the nearest being drowned than anywhere in my life. It was on the 4th of April. It was blowing hard from the eastward. There was quite a sea on and just before dark I thought I would haul up my launch and get another line to her. When I jumped on her bow she threw me overboard. I just thought I could get in her without any trouble but on my first attempt I did not make it and went back overboard. My clothes were too heavy with water. I tried it the second time and it was the same. I went back overboard. I then said in an audible tone, "I am a goner." My strength was failing me. I then put my feet and legs over the gunwales of the boat and struggled and in that way I got back in the boat. I was very cold and numbed when I got in the shantee and I was very unwell for two or three days.

I had one more command after making my trip from New York to Detroit, by the way of the St. Lawrence River. It was August, 1922, when the firm of C. C. Paul and Company, ship brokers and ship owners, called me up on the phone from Baltimore and told me Captain Fletcher Gantt was too ill with pnewmonia to bring his vessel, the four-masted schooner *Purnell T. White,* home and wished to know if I would go to the West Indies after her. I told them I would. Captain Gantt used to go mate with me and I thought so much of him. Thinking I might help him in his illness I could not refuse. I was advised to be sure to bring my license with me and come to Baltimore at once so as to get the credentials necessary to be endorsed on the papers by the American consul at Nassau and to catch the steamer sailing on Friday. Mrs. Gantt was going too and did go as far as New York. She had even boarded the steamer and was assigned to her room when she got a telegram that Captain Gantt had passed away. I felt awful sorry for the poor woman. She was so distressed she had to give up going. The steamship company officials were very nice to her. They got a taxi and sent one of their clerks with her to Union Station, bought her ticket, had her baggage checked, and saw her on the train for Baltimore.

The next Tuesday I was in Nassau and everything was at random on board. The mate was rum-dum and the sailors were not much better. I went to the American consul's and got endorsed on the ship's papers as master. Then I went to look for the consignee to settle up the ship's business. He was a very fine man and rendered me all the assistance possible. His name was George Murphy. I told him I would like to go to the grave of Captain Gantt. He took the American consul and myself in his automobile and drove us to the semetary. He was buried in a very respectable place and on his grave there were placed two wreaths of flowers donated by some kind hearts. The vessel was laying off at anchor all loaded and ready for sea. I had a job getting this drunken mate on board and one or two of the crew. Cleared on Wednesday. Wednesday night I succeeded in getting all on board. On Thursday I sailed. I felt good when Nassau was bearing over the stern and she was leaving that city behind for now I was in charge. She had a good steward on board which was a big help to me in getting out of the port.

The following Saturday a heavy storm arose from the southeast. The spanker looked very poor to me and I tied it up. I reefed the foresail, mainsail, and mizzinsail and runed her under these sails with fore staysail and jib. It was beautiful to me to see the ocean all white with heavy billows, something I had not seen for so long. And with an able vessel under me I surely enjoyed it. This wind worked as I had figured it out. It shifted to the south and southwest with much cold rain even if it was August. It then went to the northwest. I let her go on the port tack until the wind went around to the northeast as I had figured it would. I was then very much to the eastward of the longitude of Cape Hatteras. I then put her on the starboard tack and being well in the Gulf Stream I made good time to the north. I was thirty miles to the east of Cape Hatteras when I passed it. I then laid my course for Cape Henry. I saw Currituck Light about 8 PM. The wind died out and breezed up from the southwest and began to blow a smart breeze. I steered very close to Cape Henry Light to keep the pilots from seeing me as I always like to avoid them when I could. It was two o'clock in the morning and very dark. It had been 19 years since I brought a ship in the capes and thinking my eyes might not be as good as they used to I said to the mate, "How does that light on the cape look? Does it appear close to you?" He said, "I just cannot say. I can see the sand close to it." My heart jumped up in my throat. I yelled out, "Keep her northwest by north." I was then steering northwest by west and I expected she would stop on the cape at any moment. But she passed in all o.k. It was so dark I did not think anyone could see that sand unless we were fast on it.

We succeeded in getting in without a pilot. I steered my old course which carried me alright. But somehow the lower part of the bay did not look like it did 20 years before. I was not used to lighted buoys and they bothered me some. And New Point Light had changed from a fixed to a flashing light. When day broke I was up to the Wolf Trap and with daylight the bay looked as natural as ever. When darkness came on again I was above Sharps Island and the lighted buoys bothered me again. I took one of those flashing buoys to be Thomas Point but when I made Thomas Point I was not bothered any more. I sailed her to the quarantine ground and anchored at two o'clock in morning just 24 hours from Cape Henry and 8 days from Nassau. And this was my last command and I am sure it will be my last forever. Mr. Berne White wanted me to stay on board and sail her for him. I would have done so but I had between 8 and 10 thousand bushels of oysters planted which needed my attention. Mr. White treated me nicely and wished I was 25 years old. The theives in Baltimore robed me and stole a gold watch I had for 38 years. She was a real pet of mine but Mr. White in his kindness made my loss good.

I got home safely and began looking after my oysters I had planted. I stayed at my shantee all alone and I used to amuse myself in diferent ways. I used to take my launch and go fishing, sometimes digging mananoses, and look over my oysters I had planted. Then of nights I would observe the altitude of the planets and the diferent stars as they passed the meridian.

The altitude of Jupiter never worked well for me. All the fixed stars that I observed the altitude of gave me the same latitude that the sun did which was 37°52′ north, longitude 75°52′ west, which was the location of my shantee.

I have been five years writing this story. I may have told some things twice and many things have come to my mind since that I have not told and will never be now. I was much opposed by some of my family in writing. This is my excuse for being so long about it. And now in my declining years I shall soon hear the last eight bells struck which will call me from the last watch on this earth to where I hope to obtain a glorious immortality where it is one bright summer always and storms never come.

L. S. Tawes

APPENDIX

The three-masted schooner *City of Baltimore* was built by Goss, Sawyer & Packard, Bath, Maine, in 1884. She had one deck, elliptic stern, and a billethead. Her measurements were 138 feet in length, 33.4 feet in breadth, and 9.9 feet in depth. Her official number was 126190 and she was of 356 gross and 338 net tons.

A letter of inquiry to the National Archives and Records Service, Washington, D. C., in December 1966, relative to the schooner's owners while under the American flag, resulted in the following:

Owners (As shown on the documents):	Period of Ownership
Emerson Rokes, John H. Lambdin, David Wilson and E. B. Hunting of Baltimore, Maryland, Leonard S. Tawes of Crisfield, Maryland, and various other minor owners.	Feb. 4, 1884-July 11, 1888
Brooxxe B. Rokes, James Bond, John H. Lambdin, David Wilson and E. B. Hunting, all of Baltimore, Leonard S. Tawes of Crisfield, William H. Moody of Rockland, Maine, and various other minor owners.	July 11, 1888-Jan. 25, 1889
John G. Johnson, Brooxxe B. Rokes, Susanna C. Lambdin, William H. Skinner and George W. Skinner, all of Baltimore, Leonard S. Tawes of Crisfield, William H. Moody of Rockland, Maine, and various minor owners.	Jan. 5, 1889-Feb. 6, 1891
Same, except Brooxxe B. Williams replaced Brooxxe B. Rokes.	Feb. 6, 1891-Jan. 14, 1896
Same, except Edward P. Johnson replaced John G. Johnson.	Jan. 14, 1896-Dec. 4, 1899
Same, plus George R. Heffner and Robert S. McLaughlin as major shareholders.	Dec. 4, 1899-July 11, 1904
Cuban-American Veneer and Transportation Co., of Tampa, Florida, Susanna C. Lambdin and George B. Skinner, both of Baltimore.	July 11, 1904-May 29, 1906
Joseph Zimmerman of Tampa, Florida.	May 29, 1906-Sept. 21, 1912
D. C. Gillett and M. E. Gillett, both of Tampa, Florida.	Sept. 21, 1912-June 6, 1916
Charles H. MacDowell, of Chicago, Illinois.	June 6-Aug. 24, 1916
The Planters Transportation Company of Gary, Indiana.	Aug. 24, 1916-Nov. 17, 1917
Armour Fertilizer Works, of Chicago, Illinois.	Nov. 17, 1917-Nov. 14, 1921
F. F. Bingham, of Pensacola, Florida.	Nov. 14, 1921—(End—see p. 447)

Under the Act of March 2, 1895, the vessel's net tonnage was reduced to 297 tons.

After having been rebuilt, the vessel was described on May 29, 1906 as measuring 137.9 feet in length, 357 gross and 286 net tons. No other change in the vessel's description was noted.

After Captain Tawes sold the *City of Baltimore* in 1904 the schooner's activities were confined primarily to hauling lumber from Gulf ports to Cuba and other West Indian islands. Occasionaly, she would engage in trade between Gulf ports. It was on such a passage as the latter that she endured the most severe beating she had ever experienced at sea.

Following, from the 1917 issue of *United States Coast Guard Annual Report,* is a description of the dismasting of the *City of Baltimore.* By that time the schooner had been sold by Gillett and was registered as owned by Charles H. MacDowell of Chicago, an official of the Armour Fertilizer Works. Apparently, that firm actually owned the vessel as, indicated in the records of the National Archives, it did from November 17, 1917 to November 14, 1921.

The Coast Guard report reads, "On July 5, 1916, the *City of Baltimore,* bound from Tampa, Florida, to Houston, Texas, with a cargo of phosphate rock, was overtaken by a northeast gale of hurricane violence and entirely dismasted. At the mercy of wind and sea for a time, her crew finally rigged jury masts, and with such spread of sail as could be improvised, steered for a harbor at Mobile. On the afternoon of the 8th, badly leaking, she anchored off the entrance of the port named and hoisted a signal of distress. Still at anchor, she was found on the afternoon of the 9th by the cutter *Tallapoosa,* which was cruising along the coast on the lookout for storm-crippled vessels. The schooner rode to the tide in the trough, with the seas breaking heavily over her. From the heavy and incessant pounding she was receiving by the seas falling upon her decks, it was feared her hatches might give way at any moment and admit the water below deck, the added weight of which would have sent her to the bottom. However, the cutter soon had a line on board, and the vessel in tow for shelter, and in a short time she was across the bar and riding at a safe anchorage in Mobile Bay."

On November 14, 1921, the *City of Baltimore* was sold to F. F. Bingham, Pensacola, Florida, and once more entered the lumber trade. On September 6, 1922, while bound from Pensacola to San Juan, Puerto Rico, with a cargo of creosoted lumber and cross ties, the schooner was reported southwest of Bogue Inlet, North Carolina, waterlogged and with sails blown away. She was towed into Wilmington, North Carolina. At that time her owner reported that the schooner was damaged beyond repair and would be abandoned in the harbor at Wilmington. This was not to be her fate, however, for her final document as an American-flag vessel was surrendered at Pensacola on November 29, 1922, and was endorsed, "Sold to Alien" (British flag.)

In December 1935, Mrs. Naomi Tawes Hall, daughter of Captain Tawes, wrote to one of the later masters of the *City of Baltimore,* Captain Thomas P. Holmes of Tampa. She inquired if he knew if there existed any of the furniture or keepsakes from the schooner. He replied that he knew of no relics and added, "The *City of Baltimore* lies in the harbor of Nassau (Bahamas), abandoned years ago."

During World War II Miss Hall spoke to a captain who visited the Chesapeake Bay area to obtain a two-masted schooner to take to the Caribbean for the Peter Paul Candy Company. She asked him if he had any knowledge of the *City of Baltimore* and he advised her that the schooner's remains were on Cat Island, near Nassau. Miss Hall later visited Nassau and inquired about the schooner but discovered nothing. A letter to the Captain of the Port of Nassau in 1965 revealed no information. No record of this schooner appears in Lloyd's Register after she is recorded as having been sold to the British.

Index

Index

Index

Index